GERMAN CINEMA—TERROR AND TRAUMA

Cultural Memory Since 1945

Thomas Elsaesser

Routledge
Taylor & Francis Group
NEW YORK AND LONDON

First published 2014
by Routledge
711 Third Avenue, New York, NY 10017

and by Routledge
2 Park Square, Milton Park, Abingdon, Oxon OX14 4RN

Routledge is an imprint of the Taylor & Francis Group, an informa business

Library of Congress Cataloging in Publication Data
Elsaesser, Thomas.
German cinema : terror and trauma since 1945 / Thomas Elsaesser.
pages cm
Includes bibliographical references and index.
1. Terrorism in motion pictures. 2. Psychic trauma in motion pictures. 3. Motion pictures—Social aspects—Germany. I. Title.
PN1995.9.T46E54 2013
791.430943—dc23
2013012972

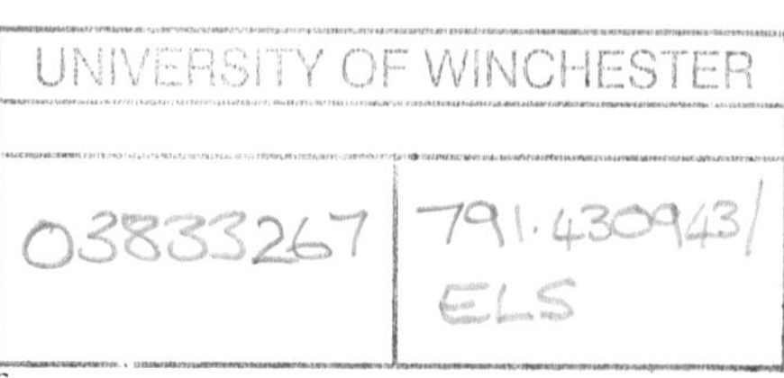

ISBN: 978-0-415-70926-2 (hbk)
ISBN: 978-0-415-70927-9 (pbk)
ISBN: 978-1-315-88564-3 (ebk)

Typeset in Bembo and Stone Sans
by EvS Communication Networx, Inc.

Printed and bound by CPI Group (UK) Ltd, Croydon, CR0 4YY

GERMAN CINEMA—TERROR AND TRAUMA

In *German Cinema—Terror and Trauma*, Thomas Elsaesser reevaluates the meaning of the Holocaust for post-war German films and culture, while offering a reconsideration of trauma theory today. Elsaesser argues that Germany's attempts at "mastering the past" can be seen as both a failure and an achievement, making it appropriate to speak of an ongoing "guilt management" that includes not only Germany, but Europe as a whole. In a series of case studies, which consider the work of Konrad Wolf, Alexander Kluge, Rainer Werner Fassbinder, Herbert Achternbusch and Harun Farocki, as well as films made in the new century, Elsaesser tracks the different ways the Holocaust is present in German cinema from the 1950s onwards, even when it is absent, or referenced in oblique and hyperbolic ways. Its most emphatically "absent presence" might turn out to be the compulsive afterlife of the Red Army Faction, whose acts of terror in the 1970s were a response to—as well as a reminder of—Nazism's hold on the national imaginary. Since the end of the Cold War and 9/11, the terms of the debate around terror and trauma have shifted also in Germany, where generational memory now distributes the roles of historical agency and accountability differently. Against the background of universalized victimhood, a cinema of commemoration has, if anything, confirmed the semantic and symbolic violence that the past continues to exert on the present, in the form of missed encounters, retroactive incidents, unintended slippages and uncanny parallels, which Elsaesser—reviving the full meaning of Freud's *Fehlleistung*—calls the parapractic performativity of cultural memory.

Thomas Elsaesser is Professor Emeritus of Film and Television Studies at the University of Amsterdam and since 2006 to 2012 was Visiting Professor at Yale University. His recent books include: *Weimar Cinema and After* (Routledge 2000); *Metropolis* (BFI 2000); *Studying Contemporary American Film* (Hodder 2002, with Warren Buckland); *European Cinema: Face to Face with Hollywood* (Amsterdam U[...] [...]ction Through the *Senses* (Routle[...] [...]tence of Hollywood* (Routledge 2[...]

CONTENTS

INTRODUCTION

Terror and Trauma

The Power of Nightmares

In 2005, the British television journalist Adam Curtis produced a three-part program for the BBC, called *The Power of Nightmares*, subtitled "The Rise of the Politics of Fear," in which he proposed the bold hypothesis that the Bush-Blair "war on terror" was not a response to 9/11, but the solution to an altogether different problem.[1] Instead of using the attack on one of the United States' most visible and best-known icons, the Twin Towers of the World Trade Center in New York, to restore a sense of rational order and national security to the country, or even to extract revenge on the perpetrators and their paymasters, the "war on terror" became an attempt to restore the authority of political leadership in Western democracies, by extracting a heavy price in civil liberties and individual freedom.

With the end of the Cold War and the disappearance of the Soviet threat, so the argument ran, the West no longer faced a foreign "enemy" powerful enough to detract from domestic problems, such as poverty, unemployment and lack of social injustice at home. Nor was there an enemy that justified American hegemony in large parts of the world, notably the oil-rich Middle East and other strategically vital regions. Traditional party politics had also suffered a dramatic decline in credibility in Europe because of the decline of the nation state as the primary social bond that would keep individuals loyal to their country and its government. Cynicism, voter apathy, anxiety and the end of any hope for radical social change had bred a crisis in the legitimacy of democratic governments, demoted to being managers of free market economies and bail-out bodies for bankers and multi-national corporations. Into this crisis, the 9/11 attacks and their aftermath came as an opportunity to change both the perception and the power politics of Western-style neoliberal governance.

Curtis, backed by a number of British and U.S. academics and policy makers, argued that politicians had used the traumatic impact of 9/11 and the climate of fear and uncertainty that it left, especially after further suicide bombings in Madrid (March 11, 2004) and London (July 7, 2005), in order to increase democratic governments' power over civil society and control over its citizen. Quoting a number of authorities who asserted that the idea of a conspiratorial worldwide network of Jihadists, out to destroy the West, is exaggerated and seriously misleading, *The Power of Nightmares* proposed an alternative scenario: "that politicians such as Bush and Blair have stumbled on a new force that can restore their power and authority—the fear of a hidden and organised web of evil from which they can protect their people."[2] The huge build-up of the security apparatus all over Europe and the United States, the Iraq war, the curtailment of civil liberties at home, the covert practice of torture and "rendition" of suspects, the outsourcing of military tasks and policing duties to private security firms, unaccountable and making enormous profits at the tax payers' expense, all fit into a picture of not letting a crisis go to waste, and acting on the famous adage by Milton Friedman, that "only a crisis—actual or perceived—produces real change."[3]

But Curtis complemented this by the then quite widely accepted view of a conservative and capitalist conspiracy—made famous a few years later in Naomi Klein's *The Shock Doctrine: The Rise of Disaster Capitalism*—with a possibly even more audacious hypothesis, based on a startling set of parallels. He pointed out that the "origins" of both the conservative "war on terror" and militant Islamist radicalism to which it claimed to be the response, were not only fundamentalist in inspiration (neo-con fundamentalism versus Jihadist fundamentalism), but had charismatic, if to the wider world little-known leaders, who developed their ideas at roughly the same time (1949), in roughly the same place (the American Midwest, i.e., Chicago and Colorado), and in response to the same perceived decadence of liberalism, materialism and individualism. If Chicago economist Leo Strauss inspired many of those who became the spokesmen of neo-conservatism during the Bush presidency (William Kristol, Paul Wolfowitz, Richard Perle, and Dick Cheney), it was Sayyid Qutb, an Egyptian exchange scholar spending time in Greeley, Colorado, between 1948 and 1950, who went on to found the Muslim Brotherhood that inspired Al Qaeda. The devout and learned Qutb was so traumatized by America's acquisitive consumerism and its loose sexual mores, that he resolved to protect his country and Islam from any and all of its blandishments and influences, not unlike the neo-cons who vowed to roll back the permissiveness and narcissism they saw as the legacy of the students' anti-Vietnam movement, the hippies and the sexual revolution: "Both [the Islamists and neo-conservatives] were idealists who were born out of the failure of the liberal dream to build a better world. And both had a very similar explanation for what caused that failure. These two groups have changed the world, but not in the way that either intended. Together, they created today's nightmare vision of a secret, organized evil that threatens the world. A fantasy that politicians then found restored their power and authority in a disillusioned age. And those with the darkest fears became the most powerful."[4]

The lessons that Curtis drew from his material are not always straightforward. When uncovering these unlikely parallels and dark cabals, he himself tends to subscribe to some version of a conspiracy theory or "grand design." The roots of *both* the libertine individualisms *and* of the conservative fundamentalisms that he claims arose against them in response can be traced back to the failures of Western Enlightenment, and its ideals of political liberties and individual freedoms. What, one wonders, did these essentially conservative and religious opponents of democracy have in common with left-wing critics of Enlightenment, such as Max Horkheimer and T.W. Adorno of the Frankfurt School? The latter were fierce critics of capitalism and, at least initially, advocates of socialism, while the former, at the least the neo-cons, were fervent believers in capitalist enterprise and self-reliance, coupling their moral critique of individualism with an economic and political critique of socialism, calling the European style social-democratic welfare state a "nanny state," fostering all kinds of dependencies. Whether the Muslim Brotherhood can be understood in such terms is equally debatable, given that it was opposed to Nasser's form of secular nationalism with a socialist agenda, as much as it now rails against Western capitalist policies, especially when espoused by their own autocratic leaders.

Perhaps Curtis' parallels make a different point: that power manifests itself in modern societies obliquely and indirectly, often via proxies and hidden agendas, with unforeseen and unintended consequences, across reactive moves rather than proactive strategies. Equally important, however, would be the insight that antagonists or rivals for power appear to achieve their goals not when they oppose each other, but when they consciously or inadvertently collude or cooperate with each other, as the "terrorists" and those waging "war on terror" seem to have been doing: each traumatizing civil society into accepting the consequences of the "politics of fear," and acquiescing in the resulting political paralysis or gridlock democracy. Terror and trauma, too, would then no longer stand in a relation of cause and effect, nor be in opposition to each other. Together they would make up an antagonistic mutuality, sustained by the complementarity that enlists trauma in a strategy for control, just as terror is always a strategy for intimidation. Terror and trauma would then be the two sides of a state of exception when governing the ungovernable: politics of fear from above and from below, with globalization and finance capitalism the twin dragons at the gates of hell.

Terror and Trauma: The Violence of the Past in the Present

In some ways, this book pursues a parallel project, even though it is conceived in a different context (Germany since World War II), has a narrower focus (the cultural history of German cinema), and is concerned with the consequences and afterlife of a different history (the Nazi regime and the Holocaust). But it is not unreasonable to think of "terror and trauma" as the alternative subtitle for "the power of nightmares" and vice versa. More specifically, this book came out of a slim volume published in Germany in 2007, to mark the thirtieth anniversary of the relatively short period of extreme violence and terrorism, at the origins of which was the Red Army Faction (RAF), a group of political activists who could be said to have practiced an earlier version of the politics of fear.[5] Known as the Hot Autumn (or *Deutsche Herbst*), the RAF's series of assassinations, bank robberies, hostage taking and counter attacks by the police and the government's security services shocked and traumatized the Federal Republic of Germany in the fall of 1977 into a virtual state-of-emergency.[6] The aftereffects of "Germany in Autumn" have been felt ever since, while its back-stories, prehistories and subsequent narratives are being periodically recycled, reevaluated, and reinterpreted, with no agreed version in sight about the motives of either the chief protagonists or the true significance of these events, half "past history" half "living memory."[7] 1997 and 2007 were particularly intense years of retrospectives and reassessments when, with varying degrees of cooperation, the perpetrators of the violence and the relatives of their victims, the representatives of the State and of the security forces had their say on television and in print, along with further "actors": eyewitnesses, participants, historians, sociologists, filmmakers, and trend analysts. A veritable RAF Industry has established itself around its afterlife, to which I have devoted chapter 4.[8]

What became evident was that the periodic returns of the RAF as a topic that just "would not go away" showed similarities with West Germany's other recurring trauma topic, namely the Nazi period and the premeditated genocide of the Jews. For this perpetually returning past, a special term was coined: *Vergangenheitsbewältigung* variously translated as either "coming to terms with the past" or "mastering the past," but quite odd in German, insofar as in the word *Bewältigung* resonates *Gewalt*, i.e., violence, and implies an obstacle to be overcome. It thus makes the past into something undead, a threat or at any rate, a force or agent that has to be wrestled down. The RAF and the Nazi past were also linked insofar as one of the justifications the group's members gave for their action was that the Federal Republic was still essentially a Nazi state, while those who condemned their politics as well as their actions referred to the RAF as "Hitler's children." How could the RAF be opposed to Nazism and emulate Nazism at the same time? What was behind this compulsion to repeat, to enact or act out, along with the inability to find closure? How did commemoration become such an important part of West Germany's public life, and why did the occasions for commemoration invariably produce scandals, missteps, misunderstandings and moments of intense embarrassment: for politicians, public figures and even for responsible and respected writers?

It was questions like these that prompted me to write the book. I wanted to listen more closely to this perpetual murmur of a country talking to itself about its repugnant past across generational, political and emotional divides—occasionally resulting in faltering dialogue, more often rising to a crescendo of mutual recrimination, and in one instance, the RAF episode, ending in deadly violence. What the interminable dialogue with the past and with each other also showed was evidence that the main antagonists often seemed inadvertently to complement each other, as if not only the RAF and the Nazi past might just be two sides of the same coin, but as if a trauma of unacknowledged or disavowed guilt and the terror unleashed by a small group of militants were also communicating vessels. As a film historian, I wanted to examine these delicate and troubling issues across their repercussions in the particular counter-public sphere of the New German Cinema, which during the 1970s and early 1980s had been an internationally recognized "new wave," creating a series of films that spoke critically about Germany, but also spoke on behalf of Germany: again a potential paradox, since the films were largely financed out of the public purse, but (with rare exceptions) ignored, shunned or even ridiculed by the general film-going public and television audiences in West Germany.

The first occasion for analyzing this intertwining of countervailing forces came in 1997, when for the twentieth anniversary of the Hot Autumn, German television screened a two-part docudrama, DEATH GAME (directed by Hans Breloer), seen by millions of German viewers. What caught my attention was that it echoed GERMANY IN AUTUMN (1978), an omnibus film directed by several of the iconic names of the New German Cinema, controversially received at home, but widely discussed abroad. DEATH GAME seemed to me best understood as a "remake," but one where repetition-with-difference called for an altogether more unusual interpretative strategy, one that required these multiple framings, retroactive causalities and shifting temporalities because the events had assumed the force of traumatic symptoms. Redolent of allegorical meaning, these symptoms had the power to act back on the events, as if the effects in retrospect altered the causes that had given rise to them. Breloer's docudrama retold the story of those months in 1977, but reversed many of the arguments of GERMANY IN AUTUMN as well as shifting the emphasis to a different cast of characters. It was like a mirror image of the earlier work, revealing not only the difference between an oppositional, avant-garde film, made for the cinema screen, and a more mainstream, compliant television production. DEATH GAME also marked the political shifts that had taken place between 1977 and 1997, with the end of the Cold War, the fall of the Wall and German unification being the main turning points. "*Antigone Agonistes: The Red Army Faction, Germany in Autumn* and *Death Game*" was first presented at a conference devoted to the figure of Antigone in literature, film and philosophy, organized by Joan Copjec at the State University of New York at Buffalo. As the text is available in book form and on-line, it has not been reprinted here.[9]

This rewriting of the RAF episode in DEATH GAME into something quite different from how it had appeared in the filmmakers' first-hand testimony that was GERMANY IN AUTUMN made me want to examine how the New German Cinema itself had dealt with the history of terror and violence it had inherited. Taking its intellectual figurehead, Alexander Kluge as my main example, I looked at the films not for a critique of Nazism, but for the more invisible traces of what in the 1960s and early 1970s was still referred to by the metonym "Auschwitz." The result, "Absence as Presence, Presence as Parapraxis," was given as a lecture at Tel Aviv University in May 2000. It was there that I first developed the concept of "parapraxis," the English translation of the Freudian term *Fehlleistung*, which was to become the major poetological, political and interpretative device, in a series of case studies of films and filmmakers that form the bulk of this volume. They are framed by essays of a more theoretical nature, on "Terror and Trauma: Siamese Twins of the Political Discourse," "The Poetics and Politics of Parapraxis," and a look back at "Trauma Theory," which an essay of mine called "Postmodernism as Mourning Work" had helped to extend to film and media, as a critique of "representation."[10] Other essays, notably "Memory Frames and Witnessing: Burden of Representation and Holocaust Films," "Generational Memory: The RAF Afterlife in the New Century," "From Holocaust Memory to Guilt Management," were expressly written for the present volume, and are meant to reflect on yet another intervening decade, taking us into the new century, where some of the issues still won't go away, and others resurface and return: turning "mastering the past" into the post-trauma of a perpetrator nation, either engaged in "guilt management" or reclaiming for itself, too, the status of history's victims.

Memory and Trauma—The New Markers of Identity

By way of a more general introduction to the chapters, I want to briefly consider Germany's persistent preoccupation with its recent past across several broader considerations that also point to present day Europe and beyond. Chief among them is the urge to invest so much of identity—personal, collective, national—in "memory," and to promote, as memory's most authentic manifestation, the search for and effects of "trauma." Much has been written in the last decades about "collective memory" and the late twentieth century European culture of commemoration, both for and against. Negative, as symptomatic for the penchant of this continent in geopolitical decline to cling to its past and to fetishize even horrific parts of its history, in waves of nostalgia, that act as a defense against an uncertain future. Positive voices, i.e., those in favor of more "memory studies" would argue that cultural memory is an ethical duty:

towards the many senseless deaths that the twentieth century has witnessed, but also as a salvage mission, to rescue from oblivion what "creative destruction" and relentless technical innovation are so rapidly discarding or rendering obsolete. This so-called memory boom,[11] with its nationally distinct memory discourses and periodically changing memory frames, is a theme throughout this study, partly implicit, because willy-nilly contributing to it, and partly critically reflected and challenged, as in chapter 4 on the RAF afterlife, chapter 10 on Holocaust memory, and chapter 11 on trauma theory.

What deserves special comment, however, is that memory has become one of the chief markers of identity, individually as well as collectively. Once upon a time, nations and communities tried to unite around a common project, directed towards the future (changing the world, fighting for a better life) that ensured a sense of personal identity and collective belonging. Now it is shared memories, or the retrospective construction of a group (manifest in the use of "generation" as a period marker) that defines self-worth and creates the (fraying) ties that bind. This in turn casts much of life under the signs of loss and disaster, making *survival* a generic term for being alive, if not the sole goal of life itself: a not altogether unproblematic development, as thinkers otherwise as different as Zygmund Baumann and Alain Badiou have argued.[12] It is in this context that one needs to see the emergence of trauma as such a central trope, outside any clinical application or context. Trauma has come to prominence not just within the various memory discourses, but in popular culture as well, where it tends to refer not only to victims of past and present disasters, but is extended to all "survivors," and can even include those that might once have been considered perpetrators. It is as if the catastrophes (of history, but also of life itself) are either of such enormity that individual or even collective agency cannot account for them, or that—in the case of violent events, such as a world war and unspeakably inhuman acts, such as the Holocaust—their afterlife in memory is what becomes the actual trauma, making all those exposed to this afterlife, regardless of their individual life story or role in the events, at once its survivors and victims.[13]

How did trauma become the new currency of identity *and* victimhood, indeed of identity *as* victimhood? How can it refer to an individual or a group that occupies positions of both victim and perpetrator? What is the role of the new public sphere of permanent media presence and twenty-four-hour news coverage in promoting such a broad array of potentially contradictory references? While an analysis of the term's current use is most certainly in order—my contribution was the essay on "Postmodernism as Mourning Work" and is the "Postscript on Trauma Theory," chapter 11 of this volume—I also found it necessary to look for an overarching concept that had a different pedigree, but shared similar properties, such as being inherently double-sided and self-divided, bracketing the tensions of active and passive, language and embodiment, intention and contingency, the past in the present, and the "other" bound into the self. For a number of reasons I hope will be clear in the chapters themselves, I did not want to resort to the vocabulary of modernism (ambiguity, aporia) or postmodernism (in-between-ness, hybridity, entanglement), or even deconstruction (undecidability, deferral, difference).

However, it would be disingenuous to claim that the idea of *parapraxis* that I eventually opted for, does not share many of the concerns expressed in these terms, and indeed their weaknesses, while possibly adding some more of its own. Crucial in my choice was the dual and reversible meaning of Freud's German original *Fehlleistung*, which gives this psychoanalytic term a broader reach as well as a more precise definition than that of the "Freudian slip." In particular, I wanted to demonstrate that it was especially illuminating when thinking about the cinema as a medium of conflict and of conflicted situations, establishing a dynamic field of active and passive, with its narratives generally tending towards closure, but in many cases capable of carrying apparently self-contradictory meanings that do not just delay or suspended resolution, but achieve an equilibrium all of their own.

The major gain of its double-sidedness, however, is that for my subject of terror and trauma, parapraxis can, in the encounter with moving images ("moving images" here understood in its widest sense, as visual and aural events) produce both a politics (in public life, the spheres of political action) and a poetics (manifest in literature, the cinema and other spheres of symbolic action). This claim of the centrality of parapraxis, especially when dealing with trauma, I try to make good with reference to the particular situation of Germany since World War II, in its politics and in its cinema. It leads to the hypothesis that Germany's particular ways of (not) mastering the past holds lessons for other nations, for other situations and perhaps for the West quite generally. Parapraxis, in other words, as a *pharmakon*: the poison as the cure.

Parapractic Politics: Failed Performance

The Freudian term *Fehlleistung*—which translates as "failed performance" as well as "performance of failure"—first suggested itself to me as the appropriate term by which to highlight a series of uncanny parallels and unexpected coincidences in the history and politics of West Germany since 1945. Some of these I detail in chapter 4, but their common denominator was that on certain public occasions, usually to do with anniversaries, commemorative events and official speeches, public figures often failed, in quite spectacular ways, to perform as they were expected and no doubt intended to. These *faux pas* or breakdowns of the symbolic mandates were more than missteps, because the truths they inadvertently let slip invariably referred back to *Vergangenheitsbewältigung* or some equally unresolved and deeply conflicted aspect of German national identity and self-image, indicative not only of divisions that could not be papered over, or of feelings that refused to be suppressed, but pointing to hidden connections and strange continuities across divided loyalties, divergent histories and deep ambivalences of affect and feeling. Such failed performances also occurred between the generations, where oedipal conflicts between fathers and sons were doubled by the son generation appearing to *act out* hidden or missing agendas of the father generations. In other words, such performances failed, but also succeeded, because it was only through their failure that their meaning could become manifest. Thus, *Fehlleistung* at first came to stand for a different way of making sense of the moments of collusion or sudden illumination, within the violent confrontations between the perpetrator-fathers and their rebellious sons (and daughters) around the RAF episode, but it eventually led me to a new understanding of why Germany's *Vergangenheitsbewältigung* could not (and perhaps should not) succeed: in its failure it was already succeeding, even if this insight was always a retrospective-retroactive one. These parapraxes, in the arena of politics and public life, highlighted the way that speech acts and body language, gesture and tone had become saturated and colored by the disavowals, the deferrals of responsibility, the compromises and sins of commission and omission accumulated since the Nazi period and pervading its afterlife. The stumbles of *Fehlleistung* signposted but also vindicated the difficult path to eventual accountability of official Germany and individual acknowledgement of the terrible wrongs done in the nation's name, across personal slips of the tongue, public gaffes and political scandals that nonetheless revealed their coherent historical frames and retroactive inevitability.

Parapractic Poetics: The Performance of Failure

As indicated, *Fehlleistung* is most useful for my purposes because the single word is a typically German compound that contains the potentially irritating but suggestive contradiction of "failure" and "performance," pitting intention against result, or maybe putting result before intention and thus appearing to mock the latter. Its reversibility and play with cause and effect are the main resources for its creative potential, which led me to identify a *poetics* of parapraxis. Here, the stress is on failure as something that needs to be *performed*: the more or less strategic deployments of failure (in different guises: mishap, bad timing, non-sequitur, absurdity, wordplay, bad puns, skewed metaphors) become textual effects or narrative strategies, a tactic observable above all, though not exclusively, in several key films of the New German Cinema.

It is in the various case studies, mostly of individual films that I track down some of the parapraxes and tease out the overt or hidden purposes they seem to serve. Of course, in a general way, these essays inscribe themselves in what by now is a vast literature, setting out to describe or analyze how West Germany and its cinema did or did not "master the past." As such, it may indeed seem that I am going over familiar terrain—over and over again—as if the very effort that the book represents is itself a symptom of its subject, i.e., of failed

Vergangenheitsbewältigung in the modus of repetition and parapraxis. This could well be true, and if the case, I accept at least one implication, namely that for a German of my generation, the generation born during or near the end of World War II, it is impossible to step outside a certain circularity, when talking about Germany and German cinema. Especially among those of us who have spent most of their professional lives abroad, any attempt to presume detachment and distance is to risk being in denial, just as too close a proximity can lead to a false sense of familiarity. Which is why, alongside parapraxis, related terms such as *witnessing* and *testifying*, *identification* and *overidentification*, *observation* and *self-implication* keep coming up throughout.

To be more specific, the aspect of repetition and return is relevant, insofar as the present volume is my third attempt to "come to terms" with the 1970s and 1980s. The intersection of cinema, national identity and the politics of representation during these two decades was unique in Germany's post-war history. This is why the period and some of its films are still my implicit reference point, now examined across a different conceptual lens from the way the prevailing *auteurist* perspectives tended to perceive the New German Cinema at the time (focused mostly on the singular vision and work of Wenders, Herzog, Syberberg, Fassbinder, Kluge, Reitz, Schloendorff, von Trotta, Sander, Farocki, Sanders-Brahms). But *Terror and Trauma* also differs from how I myself wrote about the New German Cinema in the 1980s and 1990s, which was from an institutional point of view, and had as one major focus the divergent reception of the films in Germany and the Anglo-American world.[14] At the same time, the book is a sort of sequel to my study on R.W. Fassbinder, in which I looked at the recasting of a nation's identity and its self-understanding across the cinematic oeuvre of an outsider who became—paradoxically and parapractically—a representative by the very force of his deviancy and unrepresentativeness.[15]

Fassbinder also seized on national trauma *in* his films (The BRD Trilogy, Lili Marleen, Berlin Alexanderplatz) as well as produced shock and scandal *with* his films ("I don't throw bombs, I make films"). Whereas in *Fassbinder's Germany*, the director's rewriting of German history in the form of doomed or impossible love stories was the central theme and guiding thread, in *Terror and Trauma* the key issue is *absence as presence*, i.e., what in the cinematic self-representations of Germany from the 1970s was also absent, or rather *what was present in its persistent absence*. It is in this sense that this is my third attempt to "read" the cinema of this most turbulent period of Germany's post-war history, principally to register the after-shocks of the non-representation of the "missing" (i.e., Germany's Jews, but in the twenty-first century also other victims), but then to pursue the consequences of this absence into their oddly overemphatic presence since the 1990s. If *Terror and Trauma* is the third volume of a trilogy of sorts around the New German Cinema, after *New German Cinema A History* (1989) and *Fassbinder's Germany* (1996), it is also a retrospective revision of the earlier books, with the benefit of a hindsight that nonetheless cannot afford to claim to be the view from outside, or of a detachment that comes with age.

Nor is my aim to make new discoveries of hitherto overlooked films and filmmakers. I return to some canonical figures (Alexander Kluge, Rainer Werner Fassbinder, Konrad Wolf), and include other, in this context less often cited, but by no means unknown names (Harun Farocki, Herbert Achternbusch). Of some of their films I offer readings that are not exactly counter-readings or symptomatic readings, but perhaps qualify as sympathetic interlinear readings—between the lines, across the gaps, with and against the grain—also in view of the aforementioned abundant literature on the subject.[16]

The Politics of Representation

Most studies of films dealing with the Nazi period and the Holocaust in German post-war cinema tend to operate within a classical concept of representation, which is to say, they either imply a realist epistemology, or take a constructivist position. Representations are judged as to their "accuracy" and veracity, or are evaluated in relation to the ideological assumptions they hide or disguise, and the rhetorical tropes deployed to this end. Specific films are praised for their realism and authenticity, or regarded as symptomatic, which is to say, ideological. This ideology tends to be indicative of "repression," "disavowal," "bad faith/bad conscience," and the films are generally judged to be incapable of speaking "the truth" about the Nazi crimes. To the more responsive (analytically troubled or theoretically versed) critics, other options have presented themselves: the "allegorical" hermeneutics of a Walter Benjamin, for instance, or Siegfried Kracauer's decoding of a filmic text's social hieroglyphics are frequently emulated models.[17]

The readings I am proposing differ from these approaches. They respond to the special challenges posed by the controversially debated "limits of representation" when addressing the overabundance of images of Nazi rule and the corresponding lack of images documenting the Holocaust. The latter's "unrepresentability" is not to be confused with the paucity of first-hand photographic evidence, but pertains to the enormity of the crimes to which no representational medium, mode or genre could be adequate or appropriate. Thus, rather than espousing either realist or constructivist perspectives, which might identify (positive or negative) "representations of …", I draw attention to the distribution of roles inherent in the images that have come down to us and through whose eyes do we see what we see, what role—witness, bystander, secret sharer—is assigned to us (chapter 2). Elsewhere I take another "limit of representation" as the specific dilemma of films made in (West) Germany about the recent past, summed up by varying Samuel Beckett's dictum: "it can't be represented, it must be represented."[18] Not that many filmmakers have risen to this challenge, but the ones who reflexively double this paradox of representation itself are singled out in the case studies of this book. There, I identify specific examples of how the Nazi period and especially the Holocaust are "present" in the films, even when and where they are "absent," implied or referred to in oblique and hyperbolic ways. I ask what different representational strategies are available, when it is not a matter of "truthfully" representing the historical disaster, but when aftereffects, deferred reactions, as well as unanticipated or unintended consequences (and thus other forms of "presence") emerge or manifest themselves, to which neither the term representation nor the usual meaning of "effect" (as in "cause-and-effect," or as "special effect") actually apply—although I am tempted to consider the evidence of parapraxis that I am highlighting as a sort of "special effect" in the semantics of representation.

In order to place this trope of "absence as presence" within the broader context of the politics of representation, chapter 2, "Memory Frames and Witnessing: The Burden of Representation and Holocaust Films" complements an earlier publication (not included here) "Subject Positions, Speaking Positions: From *Holocaust, Our Hitler* and *Heimat* to *Shoah* and *Schindler's List,*" in which I specifically address the issues of representation (and its limits) with respect to the Holocaust.[19] One aspect of the latter chapter had to do with melodrama as a genre of excess, but in "Memory Frames and Witnessing" I try to provide a perspective on remembering and representation by pointing to the successive transformations of the "politics of representation" in films that allude to Auschwitz in post-war German cinema from the late 1940s to the 1990s. The focus is less on what aspects (e.g., the lives of German Jews in Hitler's Germany, the camps, the post-war trials) or which protagonists (victims, perpetrators, survivors, returning exiles) are depicted and have their stories told, but on the possible spectatorial positions implied or solicited by the films. I have divided the variations of witnessing into categories: the forensic mode and the "witness," "the interview as testimony," and "the bystander as implicated observer." These categories suggest that there are distinct phases which overlap with but also diverge from other kinds of periodization: for instance, the one that sees German cinema and German society progress from the "repression" of the Holocaust (in the 1960s), to "trauma" (the 1970s) to "self-incrimination" (the 1980s), to "victim-culture" (1990s) and "normalization" (2003 and beyond). Common to both schemes, however, is a concern with identification which oscillates between identification through exclusion of the other, to identification with the victim; it also extends to overidentification and self-identification as victim. Within this broader perspective, the parapractic mode of spectatorship of the New German Cinema, analyzed in the different case studies, presents another possibility that sometimes amounts to a distinct counter-strategy.

To this one needs to add another feature that singles out the New German Cinema. Given its peculiar institutional nature as a largely state funded and thus "official" art form, the question that had already intrigued me in 1989, namely how did the filmmakers respond to this difficult and contradictory mandate? has returned in this book in a different guise. Instead of asking how did they represent (in the political sense) the new, that is, democratic Germany in the eyes of the world? *Terror and Trauma* examines how some of the films testify to the dilemma of representation itself (official representatives, answerable to the world/critical artists, responsible only to themselves) by staging a "post-traumatic" public subjectivity that shows itself "accountable" rather than "responsible," in a textual mode that is neither realist nor allegorical, neither constructivist nor postmodern, but parapractic. This parapractic mode, I argue, performs (in the mode of failure) the necessary but impossible, the desired but also demanded mandate imposed on both filmmakers and the films, always already answerable to the unspoken question of an imaginary other.

On this question of representative representation, then, the introduction of the idea of performed failure/failed performance (and the associated neologisms of parapractic politics and parapractic poetics) designates the way some of the films discussed respond to this (implied) demand, also by a gesture of resistance, while acknowledging the demand's existence and legitimacy. "Performed failure" thus establishes another dimension—hypothetical, counterfactual or virtual (an "as if" mode)—by which the films communicate with the spectator who is asked to recognize (in the "as if" and in the "not seen") the presence of something that is necessarily absent.

This is why parapraxis, in its expanded sense sketched above, holds the chapters together as a common thread. It best captures what, as just mentioned, made the period of the 1970s and 1980s so unique, i.e., the intersection of cinema, national identity and the politics of representation. Parapraxis figures the often contradictory and "thwarted" relations that the films entertain with the political sphere and official Germany (i.e., state-sponsored dissent, representative unrepresentativeness), as well as the no less self-divided relations the filmmakers had with their (often hostile) German audiences and critics, where a current of misunderstanding and distrust ran in parallel with a counter-current of understanding each other only all too well, but either disavowed or expressed in highly polemical language.

Since parapraxis is a term with, to my knowledge, no previous currency or pedigree in film studies or German studies, it is described and analyzed separately in chapter 3, hopefully strengthening the case made in some of the chapters merely en passant, for the notion's import and potential usefulness. Expanding on what has been said so far, chapter 3 on parapraxis gives a fuller account of its original Freudian use, as well as its special aptness as it relates to the body in discourse, and how it establishes a circuit of communication and feedback that gives rise to something as apparently paradoxical as "successfully failed communication." I also suggest how parapraxis differs from (but helps to refigure) latency, repression and disavowal, so often associated with memory and trauma.

Finally, chapter 3 also touches on the role of trauma in the general context of the conditions that allow a "working through" in so-called post-conflict situations that are inherently divisive and recriminatory, after a civil war, or to overcome ethnic rivalry and religious schisms. Such post-conflict situations are often paired automatically with trauma, in order to chart a therapeutic path towards truth and reconciliation. What a "politics of parapraxis" suggests is that such processes of healing, closure or of a national dialogue are possible and thus successful only when their parapractic elements, i.e., unintended consequences, unspoken resentments, slips, missteps and other blockages enter into the "speech situation" itself, rather than become excluded or remain repressed.[20]

Parapraxis and Trauma: Successfully Failed Communication

It is important to remember that Freud introduces *Fehlleistung* in his *Psychopathology of Everyday Life* (1901/English translation 1914) to demonstrate that we are connected to the world and each other across seemingly accidental occurrences and trivial errors. Parapraxis in the way deployed in this study may be a term imported from psychoanalysis, but Freud used it more broadly, as a particular inter- as well as trans-subjective form of communication. Building on this extended meaning, parapraxis can be considered a type of speech-act, where performativity and its failure are intertwined, implicating but also energizing each other. It becomes the porous and dynamic interface between public and private discourse, but it also maps out a terrain where actions and utterances are interpreted symptomatically, as speaking louder or ringing truer than intended or suspected. Parapraxis also makes room for contingency, error and coincidence in a manner that today will strike a much more familiar note than it would have done to Freud's contemporaries around 1900, although probably not in the 1920s when the Surrealists rediscovered the powers of chance.

However, the occasions for unintended consequences and successfully failed speech acts that interest me about German cinema and the media-sphere of public life are historically more specific, insofar as many of the parapraxes I am tracking derive from the pressure to attest to and commemorate recent history, the Nazi period and the Holocaust, become "traumata" precisely because of the parapraxes their persistent return gives rise to. Successfully failed communication is what ties this history to its violent rejection as reenactment in the events surrounding the RAF episode (the months of "terror"), as well as to its subsequent periodic visitations. In this situation, both "terror" and "trauma" have often been invoked rather loosely or metaphorically, trying to fit a volatile and combustible reality into categories not made for it. This, too, would be an effect of parapraxis (which thus becomes the category that encompasses both terror and trauma).

In chapter 1 "Terror and Trauma: Siamese Twins of the Political Discourse," I expand on the notion of terror in order to clarify these contexts, and to show

how terror, too, establishes a circuit of communication that both fails and succeeds, dependent on the perspective one takes. It is important to note that these perspectives do not divide between victims on one side and perpetrators on the other. The remarkable persistence of conspiracy theories concerning the RAF prisoners' deaths at the Stammheim high security detention facility in 1977, or even around cases as apparently clear-cut as the attack on the Twin Towers in New York and the Pentagon in Washington, DC, suggests not only deep suspicion of government and the authorities, but uncertainty over motive and result on both sides. Concerning 9/11, suspicion of conspiracy is also indicative of the sense that, apart from the thousands that lost their lives, the losers and winners of this terrorist act are not necessarily the ones the public is made to believe are so, especially when the attack is used as an excuse to wage a war justified as retaliation, but is in fact a preemptive strike against an entirely different enemy. Terror is parapractic precisely to the extent that its "success" and "failure," as propaganda by deed and as a war of images, cannot be measured by quantifiable criteria of intent and effect, but may be asymmetrical and counter-intuitive in its extended or unintended consequences.[21] The politics of fear as described above render almost any calculus of gain and loss jejune and invidious, especially when arch enemies converge in their tactics or even copy from another without being any less antagonistic in words or overt actions.[22]

Chapter 11 returns to trauma theory in order to examine its improbable appeal in the humanities, and to evaluate the criticism and reassessments that have been offered of its ever-growing use in the decade following the 1990s in which trauma theory first made its appearance. Here, my main argument is that I do see advantages in translating the clinical term trauma, as a definable psychiatric condition, into the realm of culture, as a many-sided metaphor: of an altered relationship to linear temporality, of a reversal or "disconnect" between cause and effect, and as a challenge to the demand for resolution and closure, when attending to symptoms and latency, to repetition and false memory might be the more honest as well as productive responses. Interpreting signs and symptoms—as well as their absence—are important challenges in the humanities, for which trauma theory can provide a counterintuitive, but conceptually rewarding focus that has the benefit of suggesting (historical) reasons why absent presences should preoccupy us today. Trauma also alerts us to the prevailing trend that seeks identity in an originary hurt or wound, as if it was special signs, symptoms and stigmas that make us human and confer the right to personhood, respect or compassion within our respective peer groups.

For the absent presences that preoccupy me, however, trauma would seem to be a misnomer, or even worse, a euphemism, since I examine the afterlife and memory left by the perpetrators. Yet parapraxis is not the opposite of trauma, as if the former was the symptom of the perpetrator and the latter that of the victim. As argued above, I locate parapraxis at another level of generality, where the opposition victims and perpetrators is not the one that defines or divides the nature of the affects or the actions involved: as the manifest effects of an afterlife, parapraxis might be the trauma of the perpetrators, in situations where everyone who has "survived" or merely "comes after" is prepared to embrace victim status. In other words, the conceptual lack of contour and definition that troubles the critics of trauma theory seems to enhance trauma's role as a cipher for refounding one's identity and self-worth in the paradoxically empowering narrative of psychic injury and possible recovery. By putting parapraxis alongside trauma I am thus signaling a shift away from this narrative of redemption, without thereby abandoning either the historical associations, or Freud's own evolving concept of trauma.

For Freud, trauma initially formed part of the dynamic of symptom formation due to repression. It manifested itself in repetition compulsion and somatic symptoms, which Freud, in *Studies in Hysteria*, still traced back to real events in the past, unavailable or unacceptable to consciousness. At a certain point in his clinical practice, he abandoned this theory, accepting that trauma might be the result of conflicting desires and fantasies, rather than of actual, life-endangering events. However, in *Beyond the Pleasure Principle* (1920), trauma was recast once more, as he came across or treated World War I combat soldiers who suffered from recurring nightmares or war-related phobias and anxieties. But here, too, he wondered whether such compulsive repetition was not ultimately a manifestation of the need of any organism to reduce tension and stimuli, what he came to call the death drive.

In *Totem and Taboo* (1918), aligned to universal as opposed to individual guilt feelings, engendered by the collective murder of the tribal father, a traumatic act both remembered and exorcised in the revered totem, trauma had already taken center stage, not as either a specific historical event or a balancing of conflicting desires and drives, but aligned to an Ur-trauma of guilt, engendered by the collective murder of the totemic father. But it is in *Moses and Monotheism* (1939) that one finds a theory of trauma closest to the one as now generally understood among psychoanalysts and literary or cultural theorist: thanks to the concept of latency, the lost memory of a traumatic event can return in the form of symptoms when recall is triggered by either witnessing or experiencing a (structurally) similar event. At the same time, Freud extends trauma to apply to a people or nation, where the trauma of a national calamity can shape an entire history, and bring forth narratives of identity and destiny.[23]

An important point is that Freud here associates trauma also with guilt, and thus trauma, together with its consequences of latency, screen memory and trigger event, can apply to perpetrators as well as to victims, indeed prioritizes perpetrators. I shall come back to this, but it is especially significant in the case I am dealing with—Germany's coming to terms with the Nazi past—that this past can have traumatic dimensions in a given present, even when its main victims are not represented, or indeed present at all, and when trauma, rather than tending towards a therapeutic "working through" for the victim, retains its ethical power for the perpetrator community primarily in the form of parapraxis.

Trauma Theory: Unrepresentability and Melodrama

An argument that envisages the possibility of perpetrator trauma evidently differs from the trauma theory as developed in the United States in the wake of Shoshana Felman and Dori Laub's seminal book *Testimony: Crises of Witnessing in Literature, Psychoanalysis and History* (1992). They, too, take up important aspects of Freud's theory, notably his change of mind around the reality of the traumatic event, and its subsequent significance. Freud's ambivalence on this point gives an opening to the philosophy of deconstruction, and it is the peculiar immaterial materiality of the traumatic event that led to one of the core tenets of subsequent trauma theory, most influentially in the writings of Cathy Caruth. The fact that Felman and Laub had done their research and writing at Yale, where Paul de Man, Harold Bloom and Jeffrey Hartman had been the intellectual figureheads within the humanities gave trauma theory its distinctive pedigree of psychoanalysis, Jewish studies and deconstruction. Caruth, a PhD student at Yale, added to this mix a critical reappraisal of feminism, its embroilment in the recovered memory, childhood abuse and "seduction thesis" debates, all of which "trauma theory" took to another level, just as her books were able to acknowledge, while also taking their distance from identity politics around victimhood and group victimization as powerful subject-effects and enablers of various forms of activism.

While these theoretical moves and their wider implications are discussed in more detail in chapter 11, I nonetheless want to briefly indicate which aspects of Caruth's trauma theory have been most relevant for my conception of parapraxis: trauma and (un)representability, trauma and temporality, trauma and therapy, and finally, trauma as a hermeneutic tool for interpreting cultural texts across genres and disciplines, i.e., her readings of novels, opera and movies in light of trauma theory as she had defined its most salient aspects.

In the field of cinema, trauma theory has intervened most strongly in the argument around representation and *unrepresentability*, one of the key theoretical problems raised by Holocaust memory (with reverberations in narrative theory, art history, modernism, postmodernism, deconstruction) and its cinematic/media representations. I have already commented on the issue of representation, which is discussed also in chapter 2. This chapter does not have parapraxis as its main concern, but engages with questions of genre and representation, touching on melodrama, which in chapter 10, "From Mastering the Past to Managing Guilt: Holocaust Memory in the New Century," returns as the recto to the verso of parapraxis, both involving excess, contradiction and incommensurability, but each figuring differently the task of achieving either some kind of narrative closure, or altogether eschewing symmetry and equivalence.

Melodrama was a major concern in my earlier essay "Subject Positions, Speaking Positions: From Holocaust, Our Hitler and Heimat to Shoah and Schindler's List" because in debating the unrepresentability of the Holocaust, those who challenged the prohibition against representation were either accused of resorting to a defense of melodrama, or they actively championed melodrama (and other popular modes of representation) as an adequate, if not predestined genre for a narrative-therapeutic "working through" of trauma.[24] Even though often counted among the defenders of melodrama, in the present study I take a slightly different, and hopefully more nuanced view, arguing that in the case studies I analyze the choice need not only be between (critical) realism and melodrama, but should include the parapractic poetics that I try to recover in certain key films as a third way.

Chapter 5 on Konrad Wolf's STERNE (1959) argues this possibility. Wolf, a communist filmmaker, is usually associated with a style identified as East Germany's version of neo-realism, somewhere between socialist realism and Brecht's critical realism, but in STERNE he was accused of having failed to give a convincing depiction of the Holocaust because he resorted to an overly melodramatic plotline. My reading emphatically argues against such a verdict, by showing how the melodramatic elements are embedded in a parapractic poetics that makes Wolf's film a unique intervention in the debate on the temporality of memory when considered in the context of representability. In the way that a future perfect informs and transforms the narrative present, STERNE becomes one of the touchstones of my argument, and therefore Wolf was included, even though he falls outside the general time frame of the study, and his is the only film not made in West Germany.

Caruth's trauma theory also provides a subtle and sophisticated vocabulary for thinking about cinema's temporal registers, since trauma signals temporalities that deviate, disrupt or reverse the linear flow of time. Trauma can induce a shattering or dissolution of chronology, but it also manifests itself in shock-like suddenness, impacting the subject with unexpectedness and immediacy. In particular, Caruth reaffirmed the importance of Freud's Nachträglichkeit, deferred action, now generally translated as "belatedness," both in the sense of the "too late" of a missed opportunity, and as a moment that reveals itself only through the insistence of its repeated appearance. Trauma is what takes hold of the subject, rather than the other way round, thus reversing agency: "The pathology [of trauma] consists [...] in the structure of its experience or reception: the event is not assimilated or experienced fully at the time, but only belatedly, in its repeated possession of the one who experiences it."[25] Time and timing are central also to the film experience, as are the deviation from the linear norm in certain genres, such as melodrama ("bad timing," "if only"), film noir (flashbacks as the symptom of belatedness) and what elsewhere I have termed "mind-game films."[26]

A poetics of parapraxis, too, highlights time in the forms of simultaneity and coincidence, as mistiming or by showing how separate events reveal an inner logic by a temporal convergence. Chapter 9, on Harun Farocki's RESPITE, details the several different dates and parallel time frames that give the Westerbork camp footage its almost unbearable poignancy.

With regard to trauma and therapy, and associated narratives of healing, one influential theory of trauma in relation to history is that proposed by Dominick LaCapra. He regards any inquiry into the past that involves contested memories as producing transference, defined by him as the affective investment and moral implication one has in this past, as well as a tendency to repeat—in the study of such events—the very elements associated with that event. Transference thus brings the past into the present, and vice versa, raising the question as to the proper distance to, one's self-implication with, as well as the degree "mastery" of the events. LaCapra suggests that there are two ways of dealing with transference—"acting out" and "working through"—terms taken from Freud's analysis of morning and melancholia. Sometimes, these two modes are juxtaposed by LaCapra, sometimes they are complementary phases of a single process. Each stage or mode is seen to have wider implications, and is reflected in theory as well as politics: "there has perhaps been too much of a tendency to become fixated on acting-out, on the repetition-compulsion, to see it as a way of preventing closure, harmonization, any facile notion of cure. But also, by the same token, to eliminate any other possibility of working-through, or simply to identify all working-through as closure, totalization, full cure, full mastery, so that there's a kind of all-or-nothing logic in which one is in a double bind: either the totalization or the closure you resist; or acting-out the repetition-compulsion, with almost no other possibilities. [...] And this very often links up with a kind of apocalyptic politics."[27]

Parapraxis has something in common with LaCapra's scheme, insofar as it, too, can be understood as transferential and to resist closure. It would evidently be more on the side of "acting out" than "working through," but ultimately offers another possibility. For the double bind identified by LaCapra points to the inadequacy of the model itself, even if we see "acting out" and "working through" as consecutive stages in a process of integration and narrativization, which is how trauma is generally treated in therapy. By starting with failure as the pre-given of a transferential situation, parapraxis (as a critical concept) overcomes the good/bad, either/or divide and leaves room for defining success within failure, rather than against it. Instead of the "acting out" of the traumatic event, or the transferential situation becoming indicative of the failure to acknowledge the emotional involvement and personal stakes, parapraxis as performed failure/failed performance would be the very manifestation of these conflicted investments and thus their acceptance would become part of the reality of the event and the authenticity of the response.

The difference between my position and that of LaCapra also reflects the respective shift in perspective. Throughout, my argument from parapraxis is envisaging the point of view of Germany, the perpetrator nation, or perhaps more accurately, the "perpetrator-legacy" nation, seeing that any discussion of cultural memory and collective trauma must include also the second or third generation after World War II, having to "master the past" as a trauma of guilt, half-assumed and half-disowned, half felt from the inside, half insisted upon from the outside. This implies a *necessary* dividedness for which parapraxis might be one of the appropriate *ethical* stances, rather than therapy, whether as "acting out" or "working through." Chapter 11, the "Postscript to Trauma Theory," elaborates this further with reference to the debates and critical points raised, following the positions taken by Caruth, LaCapra and others.

To briefly indicate just one of these points that recur, which also has a bearing on my understanding of parapraxis as a critical, if double-edged concept: first, the legitimacy (or lack of it) of transferring a psychoanalytic vocabulary (aimed at understanding the individual psyche), to trans-individual, historical and generally collective phenomena. This charge is by now addressed to a century of humanities scholars working with psychoanalysis, and is similar to the one that has dominated a considerable part of the trauma-as-cultural-metaphor debate, already alluded to above. My own position is that I continue to regard psychoanalysis as a sophisticated form of hermeneutics, especially valuable in the retrospective reconstruction of motive, intent and consequence, whether individual or collective. At the same time, I have deliberately opted for a term that is quite marginal, if not irrelevant, to psychoanalysis as a therapeutic practice, and has often been debunked as lacking any kind of verifiability. Precisely because of its proximity to other forms of "meaningless meaning," such as chance, coincidence and contingency (i.e., phenomena that appear meaningless at the moment they occur, but to which meaning is attributed retroactively), parapraxis seems to me especially suitable as a bridge between matters of high emotional charge, involving ethics and values, but also possesses formal attributes, such as reversibility, internal contradiction, asymmetry and nonsynchronicity, organized around the energized negativity that is "failure." Parapraxis is thus both a way of performing in the world, and a hermeneutics for analyzing this performance.

Parapraxis, Perpetrator Memory and Guilt Management

Ultimately, however, parparaxis makes most sense perhaps within a historical situation such as the one that Germans have confronted since the war. While there was discussion in the 1960s and 1970s about "acting out/working through" the symptoms of trauma or transference, notably thanks to the wide reception of Alexander and Margarethe Mitcherlich's *The Inability to Mourn* (which made so-called *Trauerarbeit* an integral part of *Vergangenheitsbewältigung*), the 1990s have seen a shift of paradigm, where "mastering the past" is being redefined (so I claim) as a matter of "managing (the symptoms of) guilt."

In 1997, the German public intellectual and political scientist Gesine Schwan published *Politics and Guilt*, in which she argues that "the question of guilt in politics plays an important role in public discourse all over the world, especially in the task of establishing and maintaining democracies following the collapse of dictatorships."[28] Schwan goes on to discuss the relation between guilt and democracy in some detail, citing South Africa's "truth & reconciliation" commissions, tribunals in The Hague, and the confessions of Argentine military officers and doctors who pushed people out of planes over the open sea. She also passes in review the "three-step approach" to guilt advocated by the Catholic Church of contritio cordis (contrition, repentance). confessio oris (public admission) and satisfactio operis (restitution through works), asking if any of these steps still apply, while wondering whether politicians' admissions of guilt, in the form of public apologies on behalf of their nations are merely calculated ploys, or actually serve to reaffirm basic democratic values of accountability, solidarity and trust, in order to right historical wrongs after periods of unchecked state power.

The major part of *Politics and Guilt*, not unexpectedly, deals with the legacy of guilt after National Socialism in West Germany, a dictatorship supported by the vast majority of the population, defeated by outside powers and not internal resistance or a civil war. The crux of the question for Schwan, however, is whether one can obligate someone to feel guilty: "What is the necessary condition before we can speak of guilt? Is it a subjective feeling or consciousness of guilt? Is it an objective factual situation? Are there rules that are timeless and valid in all cultures? If a person does not feel guilty, am I permitted to talk him or her into feeling guilt or to simply impose it? Would I not be violating that person's autonomy [...]? Most societies, following a change of political regimes, choose the path of keeping silent to themselves and others about guilt. Is this perhaps the right path to take because it is the most successful way of lifting a heavy burden and opening the future to something new?"[29]

Schwan concludes, as the subtitle of her book indicates, that silence in the end is a destructive force, by which she means it is detrimental to fostering democratic values and citizenship.

In chapter 10, "From Mastering the Past to Guilt Management," I propose a somewhat different analysis. As with LaCapra's "acting out" and "working through," Schwan's "keeping silent" and "speaking out" poses as stark alternatives what might be viewed as a relational equation, in which silence can be obdurate and resistant as well as a silence that speaks louder than words. What in chapter 3 I discussed as "absence as presence, presence as parapraxis" can also apply to the relation between silence and speaking out. On the other hand, I agree with Schwan that guilt is a political issue, and one not simply to be left to individual conscience. For guilt, shame, and accountability have public as well as private dimensions that touch the core of our democratic understanding of citizenship as well as patriotism. I may not feel personally guilty for something that my ancestors did, but I may feel (private) shame, as well as public accountability. But guilt can also be seen in formal or—dare I say—poetological categories: formal, as it is before a court of law, where a guilty verdict demands both proof (beyond a reasonable doubt) and punishment for the sake of justice, and poetically, when justice can be seen as a restitution of equilibrium and (mutual) exchange—"poetic justice." I try to consider the different facets in my discussion of German politics after the war, where *Schuld* (responsibility) was never publicly admitted, but converted into the quantifiable entity of *Schulden* (*guilt* into *Geld* [money], one might say) in a process of uneven, but politically stabilizing exchange. This corresponds, but also contrasts with the formal resources of balance and exchange in the cinematic genres I discuss, where melodrama tries to extract an equitable exchange out of excess, while the poetics of parapractic cinema balances failure and performance on a tightrope, stretched between the poles of paradox and mimicry, self-contradiction and self-effacement.

Conclusion and Summary

If this is a book about a small sample of films made in Germany from the 1970s to the present, on a common set of themes, and with related stylistic traits and strategies, then the analyses I offer are nevertheless embedded in several larger socio-historical and cultural contexts. One such context is the afterlife of two very different historical crises (Nazi rule and the Holocaust and the violent interventions of the Red Army Faction and 9/11), whose discursive identifications as "trauma" and "terror" are tracked in the cinema, politics and society across several decades.

Another context is the tendency, not confined to Germany, to understand (traumatic) history and cultural memory in terms of generations, regarded as distinct entities, with particular values and ambitions, and therefore possessing group coherence and a collective identity. From this follows a more personal context, in that the book is the third attempt to "come to terms" with the New German Cinema, and by extension, to reflect on the mentality of a generation: my generation. Born near or just after the end of the war, and bearing the brunt of the knowledge of the Nazi period, of Hitler and the Holocaust, this generation saw how such knowledge evolved (or metastasized) into guilt. The process took place during this generation's most active decades, the mid-1960s to the mid-1980s, and thus the same period when German cinema was a major ethical manifestation and creative expression of the state of mind, where many did ask themselves: "after such knowledge, what forgiveness."[30]

The most obvious and persistent context, therefore, besides that of Germany's "mastering the past" is that of the 1968 generation (referring to the student movement of that time) more generally. But the book also means to make a contribution to the "history and memory/history as memory," and the "memory-and-trauma/memory-as-trauma" debates all over Europe and beyond. The politics of the '68 generation had the overthrow of capitalism as its political goal, but as such aspirations faded or were seen to have failed, the 1980s saw (in almost every Western country) the Holocaust become the central reference point, as the universalized symbol of man-made historical catastrophe in the twentieth century, with Germany as the perpetrator nation, and the rest of Europe suffering the traumas of persecution and occupation. A connection offers itself: as capitalism has become the "untranscendable horizon" of our thinking and our experience, might it be that in recent years, the victim-perpetrator divide has also undergone a gradual recalibration? I mention this merely as a suggestion, since it is not what the present study is primarily about. It is focused more on the consequences closer to home; the shift from political activism to cultural memory in Europe, begun with the consolidation of the European Union and sustained since the end of the Soviet Union, when the formerly Communist countries, as condition of entry into the European Union, have also been enjoined to undertake their own "mastering the past," owning up to anti-Semitism, discrimination of minorities as well as undertaking to end past or persistent ethnic conflicts.

This implies that the memory-trauma debate around the Holocaust quite generally has a secondary source as a "trigger" moment, which appears to vary from country to country. In the United States, it was the Vietnam War and 9/11 that fuelled the "trauma" discourse; in France, it was the belated acknowledgement of widespread collaboration with the Nazi/Vichy regime, and second, the no longer silenced memories of the Algerian war; in Yugoslavia, it was the ethnic-religious wars that pitted the former parts of the federation against each other, which necessitated a new reckoning with older memories. In the countries of Eastern Europe (Hungary, Rumania, Slovenia, the Baltic States), the end of Soviet rule brought the revival of (neo-fascist) nationalisms, while the "trauma" of free-market capitalism defined the terms of the memory-trauma debate in Poland and the former GDR. And finally, in (West) Germany, it was the RAF episode in the mid-1970s, and the aftereffects of unification in the 1990s that gave the Holocaust and the memory debate a new urgency and direction.

The memory-trauma debate thus feeds on these sedimented historical layers and different genealogies, and it is in this sense highly symptomatic, or as some would say, a wholly ideological debate, asking all the wrong questions. In other words, it always stands for, covers up, disguises and displaces other elements that are also present and relevant to the contemporary moment. Therefore, it is not surprising that "memory-trauma" has polarized commentators and has proven quite divisive also within the academic community. The emergence of "memory" as a supposedly valid or authentic relation to knowledge of the past has incensed many historians; the idea of empathy and embodiment as the road to understanding and solidarity is also contested; the introduction of "trauma" into the debate has clinicians shaking their heads in disbelief, and cognitivists pity anyone who clings to the disproven and discredited concepts of Freudian psychoanalysis.

The "elephant in the room" in some of these polemics, I submit, is the cinema and the popular media, such as television. Although films are often cited alongside works of literature, theory and history, cinema and television are rarely discussed (as opposed to accused) concerning their role as root causes for the slippages between history, memory, trauma (and the proliferation of competing terminologies). The sound-and-image media have, over the last half-century, so thoroughly altered our relation to the past and to memory that it is still hard to get a conceptual grip on the full implications of this change, however much we may feel its effects or even know of its consequences.

What used to be called "historical knowledge" is, thanks to photography, the cinema and to factual and fictional television, a smorgasbord of heritage films and costume drama, of reenactments and docudrama, of combat film blockbusters and television series, of compilation films using archive material, often altering its documentary status by remixing (or adding) sound and even colorizing black and white footage.[31] Memory, which by many definitions is personal recall, and therefore discrete and unknowable to others, as well as subjective and therefore subject to the pressures of psychic life, now consists of the photographs we or previous generations have collected, and increasingly, is made up of the home videos that have come down to us from earlier parts of our lives, now substituting for personal recall. In both cases, it is visual material usually taken by others, with agendas of their own, and so already from the outset, a sort of *outsourced memory of ourselves*. Or memory is what we remember seeing on television, about the great events or calamitous moments that happened in the world during our lifetime. The movies we watched as children or young adults have also become our personal memory, but a memory we actually love to share with others. Groups now define themselves by their common memories of favorite television shows and their taste in music: a mark of adherence almost as important as belonging to a particular nation, or showing allegiance to an ethnicity or a religious affiliation.

Once it is evident that the visual media are to a large extent responsible for having made the boundaries between history and memory, as well as between memory and trauma so porous and permeable, then it is not difficult to comprehend why the Holocaust stands as a potent, but also problematic emblem for the confluence and overlap of these once (and for some, still strictly) separate categories. After all, the Holocaust is the very negation of the medium that lives by images and visual evidence. Yet the controversy over whether the true way to remember the Holocaust is to understand its multiple and complex causes, in order to ensure that genocide must never happen again, or whether one must "feel the horror" and get as close as possible to an "embodied memory" of the victims, remains an abstract debate, unless one factors in technologically assisted affect, empathy and emotional intensity, such as experienced in the cinema: the medium that has become the default value for all manner of experience, whether of love, sex or of the sublime, horror, fear or disgust.

If "images" and "Holocaust" borders on a contradiction in terms, then the very insistence on the unrepresentability—and incomprehensibility—of the reality of the camps, by one the part of prominent Holocaust survivors (the examples of Elie Wiesel and Claude Lanzmann are discussed in chapter 2) is part of the paradox. While it excludes any kind of witnessing, whether ocular or affective, the stance is itself highly emotional in its negativity. Conversely, there exists a school of trauma theory also relying on the argument from unrepresentability, that regards "proper" Holocaust memory (especially for those now distant in time from the events, but nonetheless moved to some form of witnessing) to require an affective and trauma-like understanding of the Holocaust through empathy, embodiment, reenactment and overidentification: forms of imaginative and bodily appropriation, for which the cinema (and television) has been the prime medium.

The case I am putting forward goes one step further with respect to the cinema and with regards to the Holocaust. My first presupposition is that this empathetic emulation must be (marked as) a failure, and I cite a number of examples of how it can and did go amiss both in German politics and German cinema. But rather than consider the case against such affective approximation proven and closed, I actually see the failure, under certain conditions, as an achievement, and even a necessary part of "mastering the past," at least as long as this past has the power to reach into the present, or when the present feels the need to actively recall and reclaim this past. As pointed out, the German term for mastering this past semantically contains the element of struggle and possible defeat (a *Bewältigung*), while the Freudian term for a lapse, a slip or a failure of intent acknowledges that it might be an achievement, a *Leistung*.

Furthermore, I argue that the cinema in general, and the particular films and filmmakers I take as my case studies, not only are aware of the degree of necessary failure in this collectively attempted mastery of a past that will not pass, but they appear to have developed narrative and stylistic strategies in order to emphasize achievement *and* failure, achievement *in* failure. The entire work, for instance, of Werner Herzog (to whom I only refer in passing) and of Alexander Kluge (to whom I devote a chapter) could be summed up in this last phrase. Thus, while the general term I settled on, for describing these achievements in failure, i.e., *parapraxis*, does not convey the subtle paradoxes encapsulated in the German word, it does give me the opportunity to identify both a politics and a poetics of parapraxis.

The additional step that I take concerning the Holocaust derives from the necessary perspective from which I write, namely Germany, the perpetrator nation. The whole memory-trauma debate in and about Germany has been skewed by the impossibility of speaking of perpetrator-memory or perpetrator-trauma without seeming to be provocative or insensitive. Mastering the past was therefore often foreshortened to mean "admitting guilt," or implied watching suspiciously for signs that Germans, too, considered themselves as victims. In either case, "failure" was once more written into the very terms of the proposition "coming to terms with the past." Hence my suggestion to think of parapraxis as referring to this implicit failure, while at the same time recognizing its performative side, which I call "guilt management." It follows from this that parapraxis serves as both strategy and metaphor for a situation in which "damned if you do, damned if you don't" not only prevails but persists, and thus parapraxis can be the name for a trauma—perpetrator-trauma—that I argue should be analyzed without provoking the charge of insensitivity.

Yet here, too, there are two sides to parapraxis: the failed performance and the performance of failure. It would be too easy to say that the first generation (the *Täter-Väter,* i.e., the perpetrator-fathers) are parapractic by enacting the former, while the second generation (the majority of the filmmakers I deal with) are parapractic in the sense of performing their (knowledge of) failure: the latter a typical trait of Wim Wenders' melancholy protagonists (a filmmaker I could have included, but didn't). Parsing parapraxis in this way, by assigning the more negative version to one generation and the more positive to the other, is too neat, not only because it merely repeats the (sometimes fatal) self-righteous superiority appropriated by the second, i.e., the '68 generation (with the RAF very much part of this generation, and ample proof of "failed performance"), but it also leaves out of consideration the next generation, who have inherited the same traumatic mandate of mastering the past, but now so removed from first-hand experience of the events, and the guilt they are expected to internalize, that their Holocaust memory, as civic duty and part of the national identity, has to reconstruct itself within an even more complex set of allegiances and sensitivities. On the one hand, they know what to think, the Holocaust being part of the school curriculum, on the other, they—like members of their generation elsewhere in the Western world—have to overcome their remoteness in time by seeking some form of affective engagement or empathetic investment, in order to "remember" the Holocaust in the proper way, which is to identify with the victims. Equipped with the same default values I mentioned above, they watch films, go to Holocaust museums or attend commemorative events and expect to be moved by the means and in the manner they are accustomed to, which are inevitably cinematic.

This brings me to my final two points: if the means of today's affective engagement are those of television and mainstream cinema, then my supplementary argument, which I make only in the margins of this study, because

I am not primarily concerned with either television or blockbusters, is that it is the media themselves that produce memory as trauma through "breaking news," the twenty-four-hour news cycle, the permanent repetition of images of disasters whenever and wherever these strike, and above all, when reporting on wars as well as of natural catastrophes, putting the focus solely on the victims *as victims*, who are then harvested for their expressions of shock, grief and trauma. Such a scenario—which also includes reporting on politics increasingly concerned with catching politicians catching each other out on gaffes and Freudian slips, i.e., parapraxes, failed performances—makes for a form of spectatorship/spectator-sport that can only navigate between trauma and disaster-fatigue, between overinvestment in the many kinds of wretchedness in this world, and underinvestment, that is, coldness and numbness to any sort of feeling other than cynical withdrawal. Spectatorship thus returns us to the pathological affectivity of trauma itself: between feeling too much and feeling nothing at all.

It is almost impossible, in these circumstances, not to see oneself as victim, by empathizing with victims "out there," but also because one cannot but experience one's own helplessness and disempowerment as a form of victimhood. Yet at the same time, who can avoid in such a situation to not also feel guilty: guilty in the face of the misery and pain of others, guilty by having it so (relatively) good; guilty even, because suspecting that we carry some of the responsibility for the persistence of suffering and injustice. In short, such a form of spectatorship may require its own kind of guilt management and may itself show symptoms of perpetrator trauma. To a *traumatogenic* television corresponds a *parapractic* cinema, as two sides of a crisis in agency, in the face of a generalized sense of guilt, with nowhere to go, not even the confessional, unless it's a television talk show.

Thus, if I feel obliged to devote a book to the cinematic and political consequences of Germany's cross-generational guilt management, negotiating between perpetrator-trauma and perpetrator-memory, across denial, disavowal, overidentification and victim-status, then the German example of (not) mastering the past by means of the many metamorphoses of parapraxis holds another lesson: a "coming to terms" and a reckoning with (our) guilt in the West is surely yet to come.

Notes

1. Adam Curtis, "The Power of Nightmares" (BBC, 2005). It was followed by "The Trap" (2007). See his BBC home page http://www.bbc.co.uk/blogs/adamcurtis/ and blog: http://adamcurtisfilms.blogspot.com/
2. Curtis cut the series to produce a feature-length documentary, which premiered at the Cannes Film Festival in 2005. See Stuart Jeffries, "The film US TV networks dare not show," *The Guardian*, May 12, 2005 (http://www.guardian.co.uk/film/2005/may/12/cannes2005.cannesfilmfestival4).
3. A similar, and possible more convincing argument, because it was more detailed, was

made by Naomi Klein in *The Shock Doctrine: The Rise of Disaster Capitalism* (New York: Metropolitan Books, 2007).

4. Introductory voice-over, *The Power of Nightmares*, Part I: "Baby It's Cold Outside."
5. Thomas Elsaesser, *Terror und Trauma: Zur Gewalt des Vergangenen in der BRD* (Berlin: Kadmos, 2007).
6. The longer period encompasses the history of the RAF (Red Army Faction), the hard-core terrorist organization made up of three (successive) generations, responsible for 34 violent deaths and whose de facto existence is usually dated from May 17, 1970 to April 20, 1998.
7. Books in German dealing with the RAF, the German Autumn and its consequences fill several shelves. Among the most cited: Stefan Aust: *Der Baader Meinhof Komplex* (Hamburg: Hoffmann & Campe Verlag, 2008); Gerd Koenen: *Das rote Jahrzehnt. Unsere kleine deutsche Kulturrevolution 1967–1977* (Köln: Kiepenheuer & Witsch Verlag, 2001); Wolfgang Kraushaar (Hrsg.): *Die RAF und der linke Terrorismus*, 2 vols. Edition (Hamburg, 2006); Butz Peters: *Tödlicher Irrtum. Die Geschichte der RAF* (Berlin: Argon-Verlag, 2004); Bernd Rabehl: *Linke Gewalt. Der kurze Weg zur RAF* (Albersroda: Edition Antaios, 2007); Ulf G. Stuberger: *Die Akte RAF — Taten und Motive. Täter und Opfer* (München: Herbig Verlag, 2008); Willi Winkler: *Die Geschichte der RAF* (Berlin: Rowohlt Verlag, 2005); Nicole Colin, Beatrice de Graaf, Jacco Pekelder, Joachim Umlauf (Hrsg.): *Der "Deutsche Herbst" und die RAF in Politik, Medien und Kunst. Nationale und internationale Perspektiven* (transcript, Bielefeld, 2008); as well as several bibliographical guides, such as Peter Hein: *Stadtguerilla und bewaffneter Kampf in der BRD und Westberlin. Eine Bibliographie.* Edition ID-Archiv im Internationalen Institut für Sozialgeschichte (IISG), Amsterdam 1989 (with supplement, 1993) and http://www.zeitgeschichte-online.de/site/40208488/default.aspx.
8. Wolfgang Kraushaar, for example, has published no fewer than six books on topics related to the RAF and its individual members.
9. See Joan Copjec and Mark Sorkin (eds.), *Giving Ground: The Politics of Propinquity* (London: Verso, 1999), 267–302 and http://www.rouge.com.au/4/antigone.html.
10. Thomas Elsaesser, "Postmodernism as Mourning Work," *Screen* 42(2), (2001): 193–201.
11. The term is used, following Pierre Nora, by Jay Winter, *Remembering War: The Great War between Memory and History in the Twentieth Century* (New Haven, CT: Yale University Press, 2006), 2.
12. Zygmunt Bauman, "Survival as a Social Construct," *Theory, Culture and Society*, 9 (1992), 1-36 and Alain Badiou, *Ethics—An Essay on the Understanding of Evil* (London: Verso, 2002).
13. Elie Wiesel had in the 1970s warned against identifying oneself as a survivor: "Suddenly everybody declares himself a 'Holocaust survivor,' reasoning that everybody could have become one [simply because Hitler] waged war on all Jews, all liberals, all non-Aryans." E. Wiesel, "A Plea for the Survivors," in *A Jew Today*, trans. Marion Wiesel (New York: Vintage Books, 1979), 238–39.
14. Thomas Elsaesser, *New German Cinema — A History* (New Brunswick, NJ: Rutgers University Press, 1989).
15. Thomas Elsaesser, *Fassbinder's Germany: History, Identity, Subject* (Amsterdam: Amsterdam University Press, 1996).
16. I want to single out two of the more recent titles dealing with "mastering the past" in post-war German cinema that posed similar questions to the ones that prompted me to write this book: Sabine Hake, *Screen Nazis: Cinema, History, and Democracy* (Madison: University of Wisconsin Press, 2012) and Tobias Ebbrecht, *Geschichtsbilder im medialen Gedächtnis: Filmische Narrationen des Holocaust* (Bielefeld: transcript, 2011). While neither engages with the RAF and its afterlife, each of the authors touches on one part of the issues I discuss, though reaching different conclusions.
17. Some of the best work, Eric Santner's for instance, can be characterized as inspired by

the former, while Anton Kaes has commendably extended Kracauer's critical practice by introducing the methodology of New Historicism to the study of key films.

18. According to Samuel Beckett, the situation of the writer is that "there is nothing to express, nothing with which to express, nothing from which to express, no power to express, no desire to express, together with the obligation to express." Samuel Beckett, *Proust and Three Dialogues with Georges Duthuit* (London: Calder and Boyars, 1965), 103. A similar and similarly self-contradictory but enabling paradox stands as the final words in *The Unnamable*: "I can't go on, I will go on." Samuel Beckett, *Three Novels: Molloy, Malone Dies, The Unnamable* (New York: Grove Press, 2009), 407.
19. See Vivian Sobchack (ed.), *The Persistence of History* (New York: Routledge, 1996), 145–83.
20. *Speech Situation* is a term introduced by J.L. Austin to indicate not only the context-dependence of an utterance but also how it comments upon itself: "to indicate the circumstances in which the statement is made or reservations to which it is subject or the way in which it is to be taken." J.L. Austin, *How to Do Things with Words* (Oxford: Clarendon Press, 1962), 3.
21. A forthcoming book of mine, *Melodrama Trauma Mindgames: Affect and Memory in Contemporary American Cinema* does engage with the issues of representation of history and memory, using some of the same conceptual tools. It is a companion volume to this one and focused on the films made in the United States, mostly prior to 9/11.
22. There is the often noted fact, for instance, that both Al Qaida and Hamas, two of the United States' most implacable political enemies engaged in acts of terror, are at least in part the creation of the U.S. government and its secret services.
23. Sigmund Freud, Studies in Hysteria, *The Standard Edition of the Complete Psychological Works of Sigmund Freud*, trans. James Strachey (London: Hogarth, 1955) 2: 1–306; Beyond the Pleasure Principle, *Standard Edition* 18: 7–64; Moses and Monotheism, *Standard Edition* 23: 1–138; Totem and Taboo, *Standard Edition* 13: 1–161.
24. For an early polemical intervention in this debate on the side of more popular forms of representation, see Andreas Huyssen, "The Politics of Identification: Holocaust and West Germany," *New German Critique* 19 (1980): 117–36. See also Huyssen's more recent statement: "When acknowledging the limits of representation becomes itself an ideology, we are locked into a last ditch defense of modernist purity against the onslaught of new and old forms of representation, and ethics is in danger of being turned into moralizing against any form of representation that does not meet the assumed standard." Andreas Huyssen, Lecture on 'Resistance to Memory: The Uses and Abuses of Public Oblivion' (Porto Alegre, 2004), quoted in Marcelo Brodsky (ed.), *Memory under Construction* (Buenos Aires: La Marca, 2005), 266.
25. Cathy Caruth, "Trauma and Experience: Introduction," in Cathy Caruth (ed.), *Trauma: Exploration in Memory* (Baltimore: John Hopkins University Press, 1995), 4.
26. Thomas Elsaesser, "The Mind-Game Film" in Warren Buckland (ed.), *Puzzle Films* (Oxford: Blackwell, 2009), 13–41.
27. Amos Goldberg, "An Interview with Professor Dominick LaCapra," June 1998, *Shoah Resource Center*, Yad Vashem, Jerusalem (www.yadvashem.org).
28. Gesine Schwan, *Politik und Schuld. Die zerstörerische Macht des Schweigens* (Fischer: Frankfurt am Main, 1997), 5; here cited from the English edition *Politics and Guilt. The Destructive Power of Silence* (University of Nebraska Press, 2001), 4.
29. Ibid., 7.
30. I am alluding to T.S. Eliot's lines in his poem *Gerontion*: "After such knowledge, what forgiveness? Think now/History has many cunning passages, contrived corridors/And issues, deceives with whispering ambitions,/Guides us by vanities." T.S Eliot, *The Waste Land and Other Poems* (Toronto: Broadview Press, 2011), 42.
31. http://www.faz.net/aktuell/feuilleton/medien/guido-knopps-zdf-abschied-es-ging-nur-noch-um-vernichtung-11893517.html

PART I

Terror, Trauma, Parapraxis

1

TERROR AND TRAUMA

Siamese Twins of the Political Discourse

The Changing Meanings of Terror and Trauma

Terror and trauma—two words already used up from overexposure before one knew what they came to mean. Since 9/11 they have become part of the political discourse without having necessarily been coined for political use; too often they serve to emotionalize violent incidents, and they bank on the rhetorical effects triggered by their opposition. Sometimes they are the words that make one speechless before horrific suffering, whether in the face of almost inconceivably cruelty, or by the sheer number of victims of hate and revenge, or of chance and arbitrariness. The Holocaust and 9/11, the Bali suicide bombings or the Breivik shootings in Norway are embedded in collective memory not least because of the scale of the lives senselessly sacrificed. On other occasions, the words stir up passion and generate heat, without the heat shedding much light. They can cut off debate or silence dissent, when distinctions should be made, when causes have to be addressed, and the reasons for violence or the cycles of retribution also need to be identified. However, these realities come to most of us in and through images, so that speaking in one breath of terror and trauma carries the risk of leaving physical violence indistinguishable from symbolic, somatic and semantic violence.[1]

Their everyday inseparability makes of terror and trauma the Siamese twins of a contemporary political and media discourse. They are in this chapter thought and brought together, precisely because of their by no means self-evident intimacy, as well as the duty to separate between them. For instance, are the two concepts transitive, implying causal agency, or do they behave intransitively, merely giving a name to an intangible nexus of situations and affects, without object, aim or origin? Together they evoke both the state of emergency so keenly felt in the Western world over the past decades, and the sense of paralysis—political, but also intellectual—that this state of emergency seems to have provoked. Often, it is not even clear who is inducing the panic and to what end the paralysis: is it the conspiratorial determination of the right, to use the politics of fear in order to retain or regain power, or the exhaustion and indecision of the liberal (United States) and social-democratic (Europe) left, secretly aware of being short of answers?

Second, terror and trauma are here brought together because they apply to Germany in a very specific context, where several generations of historical agents, and several frames of reference cross and intersect, having to do with the special kinds of remembering and forgetting, persistent returns, absence and presence I will in the following call the *afterlife*. The afterlife, or rather, the many different afterlives, I am referencing are the state terror of the Hitler regime, the traumatic destructiveness of WW II, the murder of the Jews, and the acts of terror committed by the Red Army Faction (RAF), one of whose declared aims it was to provoke into visibility what they saw as the hidden state terror of the West German government. These events, their sequence, and also their apparently cyclical return have implanted themselves in the collective mind, to the point of now being part of Germany's national identity. "Afterlife," "memory" and "identity" can in fact serve as key components of a preliminary definition of "trauma," as it is being used in this context.

Finally, the words *terror* and *trauma* suggest particular strategies of representation and communication, in which agency is highly symbolic and mediated, as well as utterly physical and direct. This applies to trauma's relation to memory, of which it is an exacerbated and peculiarly embodied manifestation, and it applies to terror, as above all the means for communicating a message in the language of extreme violence. "Terror," it will be recalled, comes from a Latin root, meaning "to cause to tremble," which is to say, it names not just an agent or cause (the "terrorist") but also the effect on the recipient: trembling being the physical sign of the state of mind we usually call fear, though it can also be the opposite, trembling with rage. Terrorism, as usually understood, is above all a method of per- and dis-suasion—"propaganda by the deed"[2] or "propaganda by violent means" as Ian Buruma described it[3] and even as a method of direct action, it has the structure of a complex communication: unlike another violent method of persuasion, torture, which involves a one-on-one situation, an act of terror does one thing (it kills people), in order to achieve something else (to strike fear into an adversary or a civilian population), but the fear is itself only a means to an end: to deliver a message of power, resolve, ubiquity, invincibility. Involving means and ends, methods and ideologies, messages and intermediaries, it is a form of communication between two antagonists, via a third; this third is not the victim (instrumentalized and degraded to the status of collateral damage), but the fear inculcated in the survivor or spectator. Meant to produce images, whose scale, traumatizing violence and shock is addressed to an audience, terrorism is a form of agency, but it is also parasitic on an entity already in place: a community, a public sphere, a ready mediascape and technologies able to record and disseminate the image-messages generated by acts of terror whose long-term effects (of repetition, iteration, replay) are also intended to be traumatic. Put in a nutshell: terrorism consists of material speech-acts, whose mode of performativity is trauma.

Terror and trauma inscribe themselves in cycles, but also in perversely self-renewing "dialogues" of blow and counterblow, where the means often stand in tragic discrepancy to the effects achieved, and a literally shocking asymmetry connects intentions and consequences. Their common support, platform or stage have been, since the 1970s, the mass media, at first television and then the Internet, but also the discourses, narratives and regimes, through which these messages are interpreted and given meaning.

Terror and trauma, however, should not be thought of together too automatically, as in several ways they do not belong together. Each term has a range of meanings, and each has gained topical currency under quite different historical and political constellations.[4] Terrorism means something different when referring to the Federal Republic of Germany in the 1970s, than it does in the Israel-Palestinian conflict, as it flared up in the late 1980s in the occupied territories, and then since 2000, when, after the dashed hopes of the Oslo Agreements, the second Intifada made resistance to occupation descend into the squalor and horror of the suicide bombings against civilian targets.

Terror once more changed scope and reference after September 2001, in the post-9/11 world, when the United States decreed a global "war on terror," introducing terms such as *axis of evil* and a language of confrontation and Manichean dualism that, for most Europeans, inadmissibly covered over these differences, by polarizing an already dangerously polarized world into those "with us" and those "with the terrorists," when, for instance, it would make just as much—if not more—sense to polarize between the "haves" and the "have-nots," or "the included" and "the excluded." If terror was the new prism through which we were asked to understand the contemporary world, and by which the priorities of the political scenario-agendas were set, then we needed to know what was the field of force into which it inscribed itself (the "clash of civilizations," "the fight for oil," "democracy"?) and which other modes of action (and response) it thereby stifled, blocked and obliterated. In all the interminable debates, was there still a discursive space to even begin to try and understand not only what terror's "causes" were, but also "historicize" the meaning of the term, without being accused of condoning the acts? What, for instance, happened to the term *resistance*—the key word of several generations of political actors in the twentieth century, and one with overwhelmingly positive connotations? To call all uses of violence not sanctioned by the state "terror" is already to assume the terrain as defined, when it is precisely this definition that is at issue: the use of the term has created an "outside," from which it is unassailable, and an "inside" that feels for most of us (not only in Europe) unacceptably self-defensive, emotionally claustrophobic and politically reactionary.[5]

Trauma, too, has come back into discussion under different signs and conditions: it referred first to the anguish of the victims of the Holocaust, haunted by what they had witnessed and were not allowed to forget; what they tried to work through or find relief from: initially, the indifference of the world at large about the reality of the camps; then the lack of justice and retribution handed out to the perpetrators; last and not least, it referred to the guilt feelings of those having survived. In a quite different context, trauma became a political issue in the United States, when in 1980 the American Psychiatric Association recognized post-traumatic stress disorder (PTSD) as a clinical symptom among Vietnam War veterans, creating a medical-legal basis for seeking redress: several other constituencies of victims (rape victims, child abuse victims, victims of other forms of domestic violence and social discrimination) began seeking attention for their suffering from the consequences of actual or imagined "traumas." Since the 1990s, trauma and its associated or emerging theories have become part of a cultural discourse, as opposed to a medical, legal or psychoanalytical one, hinting at larger shifts in the relation between consciousness, self-perception, the senses and the body, but also temporality, identity and subjectivity. Trauma with respect to history, memory, witnessing and evidence, has found an increasingly wide echo in the arts, theater, the cinema, in literature and philosophy.[6]

If separate and simultaneous, terror and trauma also belong together, however, because there exist a number of reciprocal relationships that have to be worked out if one is to make sense of some of the broader parameters just sketched. These reciprocities have at least two distinct dimensions: to begin with, there is the uncertain relation of cause and effect. At first sight, it seems that one (terror) is the cause, and the other (trauma) the effect: those subjected to terror are also the ones suffering from trauma. As indicated above, the purpose of terror is not so much to destroy lives or property, but to create—by an act of (self-) destruction—those survivors and witnesses whom the act traumatizes. But does trauma always follow terror, or is it conceivable that terror may be the consequence of trauma? Here, opinion is sharply divided, and the respective political options soon narrow and diverge. Can there be the "trauma of occupation" or the "trauma of daily humiliation" or the trauma of "absolute alienation" to which acts of terror become the desperate but, some would claim, also desperately effective responses? Is this line of reasoning permissible at all, or does it excuse the unpardonable—the sacrifice of innocent lives—by trying to rationalize it and dignify it with an explanation? Is there such a thing as state terrorism, which actually provokes terrorist acts? Who, conversely, benefits from the counter-terrorism legitimized by retaliatory cycles? Or is state terrorism by definition counter-terrorism, naming merely an obligation that invariably accrues to the state, whose prime task it is to protect its citizen? But what if there is no state, either because a people has to live in a "failed state," a state that harms its citizen, or, as in some cases, a people that has no state of their own, let alone one that could protect them?

Asymmetry, Auto-Immunity, Risk and Reflexivity

A second kind of reciprocal relation between terror and trauma can be established. It is not causal but names asymmetrical, intertwined power relations, when the mutual implication and possible reversibility of victim and perpetrator are at stake: intuitively repugnant to contemplate and yet difficult to repudiate in certain circumstances.[7] An example of such antagonistic reciprocity would be the assumption—paranoid from one perspective, the natural effect of networks from another—that the respective positions of victim and perpetrator are both masterminded, with those pulling the strings resolutely remaining off-stage.[8] In R.W. Fassbinder's Die Dritte Generation/The Third Generation (1979), an industrialist, played by Eddie Constantine, and a police inspector, in charge of providing him with protection (Hark Bohm), share a joke: namely that it was capitalism itself that had invented terrorism, in order to force the state to better safeguard capital's interests. Alternatively, the controlling instance may be inherent in the situation, rather than operating from outside. After 9/11 Jacques Derrida and Jürgen Habermas had a famous dialogue, resulting in a book called *Philosophy in a Time of Terror*. There, Derrida voiced the opinion that terrorism has now become an "autoimmunity disorder," with the seeds of 9/11 having been

> produced by the United States during the Cold War and after, a kind of "suicide of those who welcomed, armed and trained [the terrorists]." [The terrorists' act is] a product of that which it rejects, mirror image of its target. [...] The prognosis is sombre: product of the violence that seeks to suppress it, terrorism created a trauma that cannot be relieved by mourning because the heart of the trauma is not the past event but the fear for the future event whose catastrophic nature can only be guessed. Imagination is here fed by the media, without which there would have been no "world-historical event" in the first place. The circle is almost unbreakable: terrorism and that which it is against are locked in a reciprocal game of destruction where causes may no longer be distinguished from consequences.[9]

Derrida describes here, in so many words, the logic that made the Reverend Jeremiah Wright infamous in 2008, when he quoted Ambassador Peck quoting Malcolm X on *Fox News* in 2001: "America's chickens are coming home to roost." Fassbinder, Baudrillard, Derrida, the Reverend Wright: subversive jokers in dubious taste, or tellers of unpalatable, tabooed truths? The moves and counter-moves that for Derrida come together in the event of 9/11 and its aftermath—retrospectively rewriting for us the forty-five years of post-war history preceding it—have all contributed to joining terror and trauma in a hitherto unprecedented way. First, in order to combat the Soviet Union via proxy, the United States itself armed and trained the Islamist militants, helping to create the religious fundamentalists and post-ethnic local and tribal identities that then turned against the West.[10] What has made the situation worse than it was during the Cold War, more volatile and unpredictable was the Fall of the Wall in 1989, since "deterrence" and the single enemy no longer maintained a (symmetrical) balance of terror between two superpowers. Once power-relations became asymmetrical, and adversaries acted not out of self-preservation but staked their own lives (along with the lives of others), conflicts took on the logic of "pre-emptive" action, introducing incalculable consequences into any political situation, while suspending international law and the institutions that were formed to serve or preserve it. Yet as the past decade has also shown, preemption not only replicates and multiplies the enemy; its lack of legal basis and moral scruples undermined the very principles on behalf of which the interventions were supposed to be undertaken.[11] Hence Derrida (and Baudrillard) can call 9/11 "a double suicide": physically of the attackers, and morally, in the counter-response of the representative of the victims, the United States, based as it was on half-truths and falsehoods.

"Mastering the Past": On the Making of Media Memory

The narrative of action and reaction, response and counter-blow that I am mainly concerned with in this book is the German discourse of "mastering the past," which names the dual afterlife of Nazism and the Holocaust, in the way these now interdependent instances of terror and trauma have been worked-through, have been represented, are given a negotiated place in memory and thus have become part of the present, to the point of naming, in the new century, some of the most salient features of German national identity. For several decades after 1945, the processes of "coming to terms"—and the narrative(s) that resulted—were painful and disruptive ones. Sometimes the disruptions took the form of scholarly disagreements, such as the "Historians' Debate" in the early 1970s, at other moments they caused emotional outbursts and public scandals, and at times the difficulties with the past turned violent, which is why the "terrorism" of the RAF, in the two decades of its existence from 1967 to 1997, here stands as the most extreme emblem of the disruptive and contradictory aspects of *Vergangenheitsbewältigung*.[12]

The challenge I have set myself is to understand, within the framework of what I call "the politics and poetics of parapraxis," the various processes and logics that keep the memory of Nazism and the Holocaust active in the public sphere and the arts, notably in the cinema (and television). I see this "committing to memory" range from alleged repression and competing counter memories in the 1950s and early 1960s, via the protest movements and "direct action" of the late 1960s and 1970s, to the official embrace of commemoration since the 1980s. One of my starting points is the assumption that these inscriptions, transmissions and re-inscriptions of the past into the present have not only been accompanied, but have been significantly shaped by the audiovisual and electronic media, i.e., radio, the cinema, television, the popular press, but also the technology of surveillance and social control. Precisely because the forms which "mastering the past as collective memory" has taken in Germany also index the social and aesthetic histories of these media technologies, the question arises whether there is some form of reciprocity of influence, and what kinds of agency are involved in creating the *media memory* and *media presence* of Nazism and the Holocaust, of which—so my thesis goes—the physical, embodied and enacted manifestations, up to and beyond the bloody and violent actions of the RAF, are the "real-life extensions" and consequences, rather than the other way round, with the media merely recording or reflecting these actions. This fits the observation that the RAF members saw themselves as if in a film, as well as the just as frequent statements that the RAF were creatures of the mass media, whom they supplied, through their violent acts, with sensational stories, screaming headlines and special effects.[13]

This possibility of reverse agency is one of several special effects that the term *parapraxis* wants to signal. It follows that both the terrorist acts of the RAF and the traumas they revived or created must themselves be understood as media effect from the very beginning, directed at targets whose death and destruction would attract major media attention. Yet this is but one side of the issue, as it attributes agency to the RAF and its media coverage, but not to the past, as the phrase "the violence of the past in the present" implies. After all, the RAF always argued that their actions were reactions, necessary responses to unacknowledged, hidden or other invisible forms of violence, perpetrated by the state, capitalism and the undead legacy of Nazism. Gudrun Ensslin, following the death of Benno Ohnesorg, a student demonstrator shot and killed by a policeman, put it most notoriously: "They'll kill us all. This is the Auschwitz generation. You can't argue with people who made Auschwitz. They have weapons and we haven't. We must arm ourselves!"[14]

Ensslin's call is usually cited as the beginning of the RAF, with June 2, 1967, marked as the date when a group of activists turned to the armed struggle and began to go underground. Even if few then and still fewer now will see her analogy as a valid argument for killing bankers, judges and diplomats, the mention of Auschwitz is an indication that for a memory formation across terror and trauma, hyperbole and asymmetrical power relations play a decisive part. In the question that concerns me, namely what perceptions of agency are involved in the formation of a nation's media memory, not only the activists' pronouncements, but also the critical discourses and narratives (filmic and otherwise) point in the direction of escalation and asymmetry. A common notion, for instance, and not only on the extreme left, is the claim that the German government exaggerated the threat of the RAF in the crucial years 1975 to 1977, because it suited its security needs. The same is often said about the aftermath of 9/11: the disproportionate response of the U.S. government had much to do with the terrorist attack being seen as a golden opportunity for implementing all kinds of other ideological and military agendas.

In other words, what must be kept in mind, when joining the words *terror* and *trauma* is the transferential logic that connects individuals, groups or generations, to actions called terrorist and to events said to be traumatic, whose place in memory and recall is mediated through (sounds and) images, and whose causal nexus does not follow a single linear chronology. Instead, transfer and transmission occur erratically and recur in loops, but in the process they also release energies that can lead to a reassignment of agency, reverse cause and effect, implying that the antagonistic, but intertwined relations of terror and trauma have their own momentum. Indeed, this transferential logic even makes possible an ambiguity and reversal in the positions of victim and perpetrator, all of which is part of what I subsume under "parapraxis," my overarching bracketing concept already highlighted in the introduction and further examined in a separate chapter.

As with the refracted-replicated mirror-relationships, so widely discussed around the afterlife of 9/11, the different forms of retaliatory reciprocity and escalating tit-for-tat can now be seen more clearly also to apply to the RAF and its afterlife. In the latter case, one notes other patterns of asymmetry and wonders what are the dynamics that sustain the discursive and symbolic violence of the interminable debates and television talk shows? These have been staging encounters between victims and perpetrators, hoping for confessions or signs of shame and outrage, but failing that, they harvest other emotions: irritation, indignation or blank hostility. Equally relevant: who are in each case the players, the protagonists that in such instances assume posthumous as well as retrospective agency? I address the latter question, with regards to the first twenty years of the RAF, in the essay on *Germany in Autumn* and *Death Game*, published elsewhere,[15] but here follow it up with another chapter, mainly focused on the "third decade" (rather than the "third generation"), i.e., the films produced in the years since 1997. A repetition compulsion of return and replay now seems to be in place in Germany that has its own momentum, with familiar symptoms, but also rules. As seems likely, the same will happen with 9/11 commemorations, at least until our Western societies overcome their inability not so much of "defeating terror" but of "moving forward" in a political sense. Until then, the memory discourse, as well as "terror and trauma" are more like stand-ins, in a deferred or barred confrontation with perhaps quite different demons—a good many of our own making.

Derrida's insight about the shift in temporality is especially thought provoking: trauma would no longer be the attempt to recover and reconstitute a past, but a way of being detained in anticipatory waiting: "the spectre of terror and trauma lies not in a date in the past, but in an incomprehensible future intimated by that event." Derrida thus directs attention to the novel dimension that has entered (symmetrical) tit-for-tat situations, which goes beyond the usual calculus of "escalation" or (in more technical language) the "positive feedback loops" generated by the cycles of "retaliation" and "reprisals" that have hitherto characterized war-like situations of conflict. Terror and trauma, as temporally and causally reversible vectors, may now belong to one of the new epistemes of globalization, the one characterized by reflexivity, feedback and risk.[16]

The Federal Republic of Germany, whose history since 1945 was shaped by the aftermath, first of Nazi terror, then the political consequences of a nation ideologically divided and geographically partitioned for another forty-five years, has known more reversals and asymmetries, more retrospective revisions and temporalities of delay and deferral than most other countries. Perhaps nowhere else, then, is there a greater responsibility (as well as readiness) for understanding what is involved in the current conjuncture of terror and trauma. Yet, by the same token, there is hardly another place in Europe where acts of terrorism, wherever they occur, evoke such troubled memories and expose so many raw nerves and sensitivities as in Germany. The resulting dilemmas have become obvious in recent years. For instance, can German politicians and intellectuals speak with more authenticity and special authority when it comes to the "war on terror"? Or on the contrary, is Germany still so traumatized by its own role in the horrors of the twentieth century, that whatever is said (and even more, what is done) in the arena of the public sphere suffers from this slippage between physical or psycho-somatic violence and symbolic or semantic violence? Post-unification German foreign policy, aspiring as it does to playing a mediating role between the EU and Russia, undertaking humanitarian missions in Kosovo, supporting the NATO coalition in Afghanistan, but also refusing to be party to the invasion of Iraq in 2003 points to the first (i.e., using the authority of a country strenuously undertaking to master its past to become an "honest broker").[17] But domestically, the heated debates over the Dresden bombings, the minor and major scandals caused by politicians misspeaking or misbehaving at commemorative events, the controversies over the Berlin Holocaust Memorial in 2005,[18] the agonized discussions over the memory of the Germany's refugees from the East, or the abstention from supporting NATO's air strikes on Colonel Gaddafi's Libya in 2011, all suggest the latter, i.e., a jittery feeling of a nation still walking collectively on very thin political ice. The RAF and its afterlife definitely belongs in this category as well, feeding into peculiar kinds of irritation and agitation, with the aggravating circumstance of invariably producing a revolving door situation between victims and perpetrators, survivors and bystanders.

But what distinguishes the RAF episode, and links it to 9/11 while separating it from the Nazi terror against Jews, is that over practically the entire period in question, a permanent photo stream has been running alongside the events. The RAF actions were like "rushes," "takes" or "out-takes" of a movie-in-the-making, scripted not only by the terrorists, but seemingly by a Hegelian world spirit, inhabiting German history itself, which managed to enlist an impressive collective cast, while spectators and players supplied the live commentary as it unwound. In this new kind of co-production, where the RAF actions and responses seemed scripted and directed, "terror" and "trauma" came to be fatally associated with camera presence, movie spectacle and all manner of media events. It is an association that, inevitably, is now seen across a different magnitude of relevance and self-evidence with 9/11, so that it has become commonplace and clichéd.[19] But the underlying logic and genealogy is not quite so banal and merits further examination.

In Don DeLillo's 1985 novel *White Noise*, there occurs a conversation between Jack Gladney, a self-styled "Professor of Hitler Studies" and his wife, Babette: "He was on again last night," said Babette. "He's always on," answered Jack, "We couldn't have television without him."[20] In the intervening decades, De Lillo's insight—that "Hitler" is the name for the traumatizing agency that is television itself—has, if anything, become even truer, so much so that the ubiquitous History channel is routinely referred to as "the Hitler channel" by bloggers,[21] while in Germany, one would have to add that, besides Hitler, it is Baader, Meinhof and Ensslin who are "always on."

Just as the perpetual rerun of footage from Hitler's Germany has become an established reality in the international media, so the images and iconography of the RAF—tabooed and taboo breaking—is never for long out of sight in Germany. It suggests a complementary definition of what trauma is in the media age: at once omnipresent and latent, it attaches itself to historical names or incidents, but is not necessarily explained by them. Excess (of fascination and surplus meaning) lingers on, or is always ready to be summoned. It intimates that it is these images' ubiquitous, but also virtual presence, even more than what they reference, that is the trauma, and which rekindles the apparently inexhaustible fascination with Germany's Nazi past and the RAF's futile actions.

In the latter case, after an initial latency period from the mid-1980s to the mid-1990s (for which there have been a number of explanations),[22] the RAF has had a way of returning every ten years: 1997 and 2007 were conspicuous anniversary dates of commemorating the 1977 Hot Autumn, but the release in 2008 and 2009 of many of the RAF members sentenced in the late 1970s and having served their time in prison was also enough to set off the media flares and initiate another round of very public soul-searching.[23]

It seems, however, that the revivals also follow a different logic. If anniversaries used to be obvious moments of return, they are no longer needed; in the age of television and the Internet, the very idea of either a fixed site or fixed date for trauma's return has become obsolete, replaced by 24-hour news cycles, repeats and breaking news. The illusion of authenticity inherent in the moving image—capturing time itself and storing it forever—yields a powerful sense of presence, while repetition immerses this same presence in the timeless time of myth and melancholia. The RAF afterlife is yet another instance of the way moving images have a special relationship to history, loss and remembrance, and in one of their essential characteristics at least, namely, the unexpected suddenness and uncanny immediacy with which the past can return as present, they share a precise structural affinity with trauma.

After History Writes the Script, Homeland Security Does the Editing

While eminently plausible within both the German context and the post-9/11 world of disaster news, nonetheless, the idea that media images possess a particular kind of power and agency not only about the way we experience the present, but also over how we remember the past, covers perhaps too much difficult (political) terrain.[24] It does not pay sufficient attention to how this power has been acquired and ignores that the command of terror by the mass media may have left us with another trauma-in-the-making: the surveillance society.[25] What role, for instance, does the moving image play in having us acquiesce in the vast apparatus of social control, which monitors our movements in streets and public places, which reports and records, in the name of safety and security all our travelling, and which gathers, with our tacit agreement, data on everything else we do, think and say through our laptops and smart-phones? The RAF helped to put much of this apparatus (in Germany) in place, at the same time as it fought it through becoming clandestine and going underground. In the intervening years, and certainly since 9/11, these technologies of monitoring movement and mining data have incrementally increased in range, confirming Michel Foucault's (and Gilles Deleuze's) vision of the transition from mere surveillance to the fully-fledged control society.[26] They have also become immensely profitable not just in a political but commercial sense, if we think of Google or Facebook. And it is in this sense that the terror and trauma spiral has also been given another turn, suggesting a new definition for "direct action," militant activism and the question of agency generally. As will be argued in several chapters, there has been a concurrent shift in how we perceive ourselves in society as citizens, and in the historical process as human beings: from being able to determine the fate of our communities through the actions and decisions we take as individuals, the notion has taken hold that the disasters befalling the world—natural catastrophes, human error, environmental pollution, civil wars, climate change, greed and the opaque complexity of financial markets that hold our political systems to ransom—have disempowered the individual to such a degree that we now tend to see ourselves both in society and history above all as victims, and correspondingly, making victimhood a privileged subject-position.[27] In the chapter on trauma theory, I elaborate on this further, but here I simply want to flag the possibility that "terror and trauma" might have become merely the more extreme, because specially loaded, terminology that describes the condition of the "new normal" in the societies of control: traumatized not by this or that incident that has befallen us or our nation, but traumatized by history itself, or indeed traumatized by life.

The hitherto unstated thesis of the present book flows from the observation of this reciprocity of media and control, giving us "soft" versions of terror (the omnipresence and ubiquity of total surveillance) and of trauma (the resulting internalized paranoia that anything we say, do or think may become public knowledge). Here again, the concept of parapraxis seems helpful. First of all, insofar as the scandals and missteps, the gaffes, the slips and resulting resignations that I itemize in the history of post-war Germany have taken their toll: they have traumatized and paralyzed politicians into self-policing every utterance. The casualty is democracy as the space of public debate and decision-taking. Second, history, now that it has been taken in charge by media memory, has become parapractic, in that—due to its reversibility and undeadness in the media—the past is kept open for unexpected return visits and for permanent rewrites, as the special condition of its sounds and images enabling and empowering the present. This works both ways; it makes history even more an instrument of those in power, but it also opens new paths for a counter-memory, capable of maintaining a dialogue across ideological and generational divides. By keeping certain memories active, but also by acknowledging the almost bodily violence still inherent in this past, even single images from the archive or found footage can become the basis of a "poetics of parapraxis"—whose potential for recovering alternative futures or mobilizing unexpected agency goes well beyond either "working through" or "acting out"—the two therapeutic-performative models usually cited in response to the twinned conundrum of terror and trauma. This is, for instance, what the chapter on Harun Farocki's AUFSCHUB/RESPITE sets out to demonstrate.

Crises in Agency: Activism, Reactivism, Paralysis, Parapraxis

Not least thanks to 9/11, and its decade of commemoration and media reruns, one can see another connection in the conjunction between terror and trauma, which by way of conclusion to this chapter I want to touch upon in greater detail. In the aftermath of the planes, and the wave of suicide bombing since, much discussion has understandably focused on the idea, shocking to most, of using one's own body as a weapon, with which not only to take one's own life, but to destroy the lives of others. While in the 1970s the RAF was guilty of the most atrocious forms of "people's justice" and "hostage-execution," they, in the end, stopped short of becoming suicide bombers, although the Mogadishu incident might well have ended that way. Airplane hijackings, it will be remembered, were the first media-platforms and public stages for suicide bombers, from which a fairly direct line leads to the suicide bombers of the World Trade Center and the Pentagon; a form of activism which has as its zero-degree the use of one's own body as a peculiarly active-passive instrument.[28]

If one recalls how the RAF prisoners of Stammheim tried to disguise their suicide as murder, turning perpetrators into victims, another thematic strand becomes visible that in the subsequent decades emerged as one of the dominant themes of the German debate about "mastering the past": the gradual, if still tabooed self-transcription of a *Täter-Volk* (perpetrator-people) into a *Opfer-Nation* (victim-nation).[29] In a later chapter I examine this particular trope in contemporary Germany (and the discussions it gave rise to); here I simply want to highlight that the RAF suicides now seem like an excessive, because passive-aggressive pre-emption of the figure of the self-staged victim or martyr, especially as it has resurfaced in the wake of the Islamist attacks.

Put differently, a suicide performed as if it was a murder and a suicide performed as mass-murder mark the extremes in a spectrum of responses to a crisis of (political, but also personal) *agency*. It has often been discussed how the shift from the student protest movement to the RAF had to do with the turn from political activism to "direct action," i.e., armed violence. And it is this activism of the RAF—the desire and need to *do something*—that has become most alien to our public life, and has been most thoroughly pathologized since the late 1990s, as if any activity in the public realm must be regarded as either terrorism or vandalism. The context for action in the 1970s was different:

> How was it possible that a group of intelligent, politically alert and sensitive young people managed to escalate themselves, for a certain period, into an idea of the world, and into a form of activism, which had distinct traits of hallucination, of systematic denial of reality, indeed of madness?[30]

> The basic principle which finally turned the language of seriousness into an infernal time bomb was the surprisingly widespread, to us postmodernists barely comprehensible conviction, that it was cowardly to talk without acting. Theory without practice was treason.[31]

The manic activism that, according to these commentators, led to the RAF, stemmed at least initially, at the time of the extra-parliamentary opposition in the mid-1960s, from the perceived paralysis of Germany's political situation, and was furnished with frictional energy from frustration over the stagnant "alternative" in the "grand coalition" which had succeeded the West-orientation, the Nato-affiliation and unconditional Cold-War-support of the Adenauer governments from the late 1940s to the early 1960s. Hannah Arendt was not the only one, though perhaps one of the most pithy and forthright, to point out the connection. In her book *On Violence*, written partly as a rebuke to the student movement's easy embrace of violence, and partly as an act of solidarity, she conceded, somewhat ruefully: "I am inclined to think that much of the present glorification of violence is caused by severe frustration of the faculty of action in the modern world."[32]

That this potential for frustration turning into anger, and anger turning into action no longer seems to exist either in Germany or Europe, does not mean it has abated altogether. On the contrary, one of the most persuasive (though not exclusive) explanations of so-called Islamist fundamentalism of a decade ago can be found in this "frustration of the faculty of action." When one considers the paralysis that impedes the European Union, and compares it with the wave of activism, determined among Palestinian and Pakistani youth, and subsequently in the Arab Spring, then one can see the outlines of a general crisis of agency that is transforming the Arab nations, but throws into even sharper relief the agency dilemmas of the West. The unilateral, pre-emptive interference activism of the neo-con fundamentalists in the United States during the Bush War years has been followed by the near total paralysis of the Obama presidency, exacerbated by the economic crisis, but by now built into the U.S. government of whatever stripe. In Europe, too, the gap between the ever-narrowing field of action of liberal politicians in social-democratic countries, and the growing active-radicalism of the masterminds, the military and martyrs, ready for sacrifice, has if anything widened in the new century. It may have reached a plateau, as neo-liberalism is given another breather through governments taking out a mortgage on future generations, but it is still a paralysis endemic to large parts of the political spectrum, even beyond Europe and the United States.

In this respect it is necessary to connect terror and (post-)trauma with a more general and future-orientated question with regards to the status of human actions as such, namely the capacity to take command of one's own life or, conversely, to be at the mercy of chance, contingency and chaos. Caricaturing the case a little, one could say that *terror connotes too much agency, and trauma too little agency*, or one could argue that in contrast to an act of terror, planned meticulously, requiring perfect timing and with a specific target (and thus constituting a sort of ecstasy of agency), a post-traumatic situation implies an involuntary form of agency. Yet it, too, is both effective and catastrophic: effective in that it targets the "right" body (as proven by the reaction or response), and catastrophic, in that it returns unpredictably and always strikes at the wrong time.

This is another reason why the two terms, now looked at from the perspective of an agency in crisis—in their mutual insufficiency (which is the other side of panic and paralysis)—are inextricably interwoven with each other. We have seen how the suggestion of a permanent state of emergency, coupled with a culture of surveillance ("homeland security") charged up with libido/anxiety, has once more become a specific tool of politics ("the politics of fear," discussed in the introduction). Yet it fits itself quite smoothly around the body and the senses: like the new media technologies on which it to some extent depends, it is an immersive experience, and is able to turn paralysis, lack of agency, as well as the impossibility of managing distance and proximity, into a source of (unacknowledged) pleasure and of (embodied) subject-effects.

What would be the counter-strategies? If it is true that terror and trauma are two modalities of a damaged or blocked capacity for action, which mirror each other under the aspect of the excessively effective and destructive, the sacrificed and the mortified body, paralysis and hyperactivity, it is also true that they do *not* complement each other, pointing to the insufficiently differentiated polarization between active and passive, victims and perpetrators, transitive and intransitive. What is missing is a concept that transcends both the paranoia of conspiracy and the belief in "direct action," while remaining, nonetheless, on "this side" of the body and the senses, which is what an enabled agency implies. This concept would be, in a conjunction that will be argued in several of the following chapters, that of parapraxis (the "failure of performance" *and* the "performance of failure"), understood now as the necessary consequence or correlative of the disjunction of *movens* and *agens*, and which connects, subsumes and repositions both terror and trauma, when seen as pathologies not only of individual jeopardy, but also of contemporary political agency. By highlighting a communicative surplus in "negative" situations, this at first sight rather marginal concept in Freud of failed performativity/performed failure will, in the course of this study, be charged with considerable conceptual weight, for which it probably was not intended. But I hope that the examples given in the essays at least justify the experiment.[33]

This book is thus framed by a chapter on parapraxis, as a term with pertinence to Germany but also to intractable internal conflicts elsewhere, and others on trauma-theory and victimhood, each chapter addressing one side of the crisis in agency just outlined. The chapter on the politics and poetics of parapraxis elucidates the concept of a blocked and fractured agency, of activism inside out, both tragic and tragic-comic, under specific historical conditions, but also under specific technological conditions, namely those of the formation of media memory. Parapraxis is thus meant to give conceptual grounding to what I have been trying to argue so far, namely that the two terms *terror* and *trauma* are less easily kept apart than we might wish, but that they are also not altogether the Siamese twins they are sometimes held to be. To say, for instance, as two of my case studies do, that the films of Alexander Kluge and Herbert Achternbusch revolve around the disturbances of sensory-motor coordination, the pitfalls and pratfalls of human agency and intentionality, is perhaps to state the obvious. But by linking their protagonists' bodies to an emotional and ethical deadlock in German post-war history, I want to give the all-too ready language of national or generational trauma both specificity and a singularity, which I believe, only the cinema can provide.

Within the wider context of activism, unilateralism and decisionism, its frustrations, inhibitions and obstacles, as I have sketched them for Germany "mastering the past" and as it applies to the ongoing war on terror, the suggestion that Kluge's protagonists are "traumatized terrorists of their own lives" bears a message beyond the unique performativity of cinema. If, as briefly indicated, there is a tendency for us all to become traumatized by history, or "life" itself, as we lose control over its most basic or most intimate aspects (be this in the form of electronic surveillance or biogenetics), then parapraxis is not a handicap but a successful strategy of survival: "successfully failed performativity" being perhaps the best way of avoiding the two extremes of agency (traumatic paralysis and terrorist action), while still marking the place—autonomy, self-determination and sovereignty—that these extremes both imply and anticipate.

My general argument would then be that, against the failed terrorism of the RAF story and the various recurring "scandals" of its performative revivals, as well as against the equally incomplete but also interminable "coming to terms" with the Holocaust, one can map a possibly wider history of parapraxis, praxis and agency, whose contours have in the past emerged most clearly in Germany whenever one of the three topics—Nazism, the Holocaust and the RAF—are mentioned,[34] but which have since extended to the global situation. The politics of parapraxis seems a useful term, for instance, when considering the inner contradictions of the war on terror (Abu Ghraib might stand for such a parapraxis, as it revealed some of the inner truths of a war entered into under both fallacious and mendacious premises).[35] But the "moral hazards" now attributed to welfare state provisions and the social safety-net entitlements (arguing that these make recipients both irresponsible and depriving them of choice) also follow the logic of parapraxis (as clearly seen in the gaffes of the Republican candidate in the 2012 presidential election), while the global financial system seems parapractic almost by definition, when one considers that its spectacular "failures" (Enron, Madoff, the mortgage crisis; Iceland, Greece, the Euro crisis) are only the logical extensions (and not even the "reverse sides") of the much-vaunted performance of "the markets" in supposedly assuring our prosperity. In all these instances, parapraxis is both the evil twin and the benevolent double of "direct action"—whether direct action by "terrorists," or less extreme, but structurally related, by "can-do" populist politicians who "shoot first, and ask questions second," or as just mentioned, by high-performance financial analysts at the stock exchange who might overnight turn into "rogue traders," bringing venerable banks to the brink of collapse.

The films I analyze with respect to their "poetics of parapraxis" would be the ones that have found terms by which such logics can be made representable, and maybe even representative. Their protagonists bridge the gap between thought and action, between expectation and demand, between the overt system and the hidden code, not by praxis but by parapraxis: as a play of signs, slippages of meaning, rebus pictures and paradoxical situations, where intent and result not only have to battle it out, but where the result abruptly redefines intent. Between necessity and impossibility, they chart a path where self-defeating actions and involuntary gestures condense into a poetics of latency and stubbornness, which emerges as *the new language of resistance*, in the dual dynamic of failure and performance. Parapraxis can only deploy its poetic powers, when the missed remain present in their missing, and when every presence knows about the violence that its presence does to that which stays absent and unrepresented.

This suggests a final thought, namely that the interminable "coming to terms" with the Nazi period, the Holocaust and the RAF are also strategies of deferral and delay, with regards to an absence whose traumatic presence we have not yet fully registered: the lost belief in a changed, a "better" world, to which our agency—either individual or collective—might effectively contribute. That this lost belief is traumatic is evident, given the failure of bourgeois individualism and the sovereign subject, as well as the even greater failure of its intended solution: socialism and the associated ideas of collective agency, in the shape of the proletariat, the party or the revolutionary subject of history. So momentous are these failures and still so close to us in time, that even putting them up for discussion is for the most part tabooed, either by a shrug of indifference or a panicked demand to know what is the "alternative" to the state of affairs which is the status quo.

In this permanently "transitional" situation, I want to argue, the form of agency I call "parapractic" may be the most hopeful sign we have even in the political realm, because it is an indication that politicians, once they become entangled in the parapraxes that their media performances invariably produce, may not be able to give up altogether on shared concerns or purposive action, or conversely, that they will be brought up short, when they go right ahead, even if they do not know where it might lead them or indeed, where they lead the rest of the world. Not hesitancy or paralysis, but "successfully failed performativity" is what I detect as the underside of the debates regarding history and memory, Europe and democracy, the West and its Others: in short, regarding all those areas where coalition, co-operation, but also dissensus are demanded, but where the conditions for such mutually empowered or negotiated agency are not (yet) given. Parapraxis would be praxis at the limits of rational choice, at a time and under conditions that make agency (other than self-defeating, suicidal agency) all but impossible. It obliges us to continue to look for ways that the collective aggregate of human actions can shape the scope of what individuals can do and vice versa. In this sense, parapraxis would be the appropriate acknowledgement of both terror and trauma, turning their effects towards the future rather than the past. As a form of inner dialogue, parapraxis keeps open the obligation to overcome the deadlocks of agency, while remembering our historical—and present—failures to do so.

Notes

1. For a definition emphasizing the medial intentions and effects while offering further differentiations of the words *terror* and *terrorism*, see the contributions in Matteo Galli, and Heinz-Peter Preusser (eds.), *Mythos Terrorismus: Vom Deutschen Herbst zum 11. September* (Heidelberg: Universitätsverlag, Winter 2005), and Wolfgang Kraushaar (ed.), *Die RAF und der linke Terrorismus* (Hamburg: HIS, 2006), especially Kraushaar's introduction, "Zur Topologie des RAF Terrorismus," 13–63.
2. "Propaganda of/by the deed," after Paul Brousse's pamphlet "La propagande par le fait" (1877). See also for the German context, Andres Elter, *Propaganda der Tat: die RAF und die Medien* (Frankfurt: Suhrkamp, 2008).
3. Ian Buruma, "A Free-for-All on a Decade of War," *New York Times*, September 7, 2011 (http://www.nytimes.com/2011/09/11/us/sept-11-reckoning/roundtable.html).
4. "Before 9/11, before terrorism took on a foreign face, there was terror chic: the Weather Underground, the Symbionese Liberation Army, the Black Panthers, the Baader-Meinhof Gang. This was intellectualized, secular terror of the sort that college radicals could embrace as others of their generation found thrills in rock music or fast cars." Mark Fisher, "Baader-Meinhof," *The Washington Post*, April 12, 2009.
5. "A dominant power will always try to impose and, thus, to legitimate, indeed to legalize (for it is always a question of law) on a national or world stage, the terminology and thus the interpretation that best suits it in a given situation." Jacques Derrida, in Giovanna Borradori (ed.), *Philosophy in a Time of Terror.* Dialogues with Jürgen Habermas and Jacques Derrida (Chicago: University of Chicago Press, 2003), 105.
6. Among many others, see Mark Seltzer, *Serial Killers: Death and Life in America's Wound Culture* (London: Routledge, 1998), and Kirby Farrell, *Post-traumatic Culture: Injury and Interpretation in the Nineties* (Baltimore: Johns Hopkins University Press, 1998), but especially Hal Foster, "Obscene, Abject, Traumatic," *October* 78 (Fall 1996), 107–24.
7. "When in the three novels I devoted to the German Autumn I began to look more closely at the relation between Herold [head of West Germany's counter-terrorism unit] and Baader, starting with Herold's admission 'I loved him [i.e., Andreas Baader]' I realized that there existed a desire to make the RAF appear bigger than it was. There was a real desire for an enemy, on both sides." F.C. Delius, "Es war alles ganz anders," *Die Welt*: 20.01.2001.
8. This was a view put forward in several contributions to *Semiotexte: The German Issue,* 4, no. 2, 1982.
9. *Philosophy in a Time of Terror*, 95. Here quoted after the review and paraphrase of Martti Koskenniemi, *The German Law Journal,* no. 10 (October 1, 2003) (http://www.germanlawjournal.com/article.php?id=319).
10. A similar argument about the dynamics of re-ethnization under the sway of outside interference and internal destabilisation has been put forward by Klaus Theweleit, under the term *enforced loyalty*. See "Playstation Cordoba," *Cultural Critique,* nos. 54 & 55 (2003), 1–24 and 1–28.
11. Jean Baudrillard, *Power Inferno. Requiem pour les Twin Towers. Hypothèses sur le terrorisme. La violence du mondial* (Paris: Galilée, 2003).
12. What is worth noting is that West Germany has also known (and still suffers from) right-wing terrorism, but until recently, it has primarily occupied politicians and the courts; since the rise of xenophobia in Europe, it is beginning to acquire its own cultural imaginary. See Bernhard Rabert: *Links- und Rechtsterrorismus in der Bundesrepublik Deutschland von 1970 bis heute* (Bonn: Bernard & Graefe, 1995) and, on the more recent neo-Nazi terror-wave, Christian Fuchs, John Goetz: *Die Zelle. Rechter Terror in Deutschland* (Reinbeck: Rowohlt, 2012).
13. That the mass media were generally assigned agency was shown during the assassination attempt on Rudi Dutschke, which was squarely blamed on the hate campaign orchestrated by the Springer Press.

14. Quoted in "Die schiessen auf uns alle," *Der Spiegel*, 26/1997 (http://www.spiegel.de/spiegel/print/d-8732298.html).
15. Thomas Elsaesser, "Antigone Agonistes," in Joan Copjec and Mark Sorkin (eds.), *Giving Ground: The Politics of Propinquity* (London: Verso, 1999), 267–302 and http://www.rouge.com.au/4/antigone.html.
16. For one of the first formulations of this new episteme, see Ulrich Beck, Anthony Giddens, Scott Lash, *Reflexive Modernization: Politics, Tradition and Aesthetics in the Modern Social Order* (Stanford: Stanford University Press, 1994), 1–55.
17. Many commentators would disagree regarding any beneficial influence of Germany's foreign policy since unification. See, for instance, Klaus Theweleit, "Playstation Cordoba," *Cultural Critique*, no. 54 (2003), 1–25.
18. For a bibliography of essays in English covering the controversy of the Berlin Memorial to the Murdered Jews, see http://www.utexas.edu/courses/arens/301history/memorial.html
19. "Germany 1977 [...] was also the first image war in the history of media and terrorism. The underground scene mingled reality with media dreams. Some members of the Red Army Faction were indeed actors and filmmakers. The cinema seems to have been an important source of inspiration for the RAF. The feeling of experiencing yourself as in a movie, and seeing yourself doubled as active and as spectators keeps coming up in the RAF memoirs. And it is the movies that teach you how to stylize your own death as outlaw and folk hero." Markus Metz and Georg Seeßlen, "Das Todesspiel: Die RAF im Film" (WDR 5 Radio, April 27, 2007).
20. Don deLillo, *White Noise* (New York: Penguin, 1985), 68.
21. See http://www.sexstone.net/mettenarch28.html for several references to the History Channel as the "Hitler Channel."
22. It must not be forgotten that the "third generation" of the RAF was able to conduct a number of spectacular actions and assassinations between 1978 and 1993, including bombings of U.S. installations in Frankfurt, the storming a women's prison in Weiterstadt, as well as killing five prominent personalities: Zimmermann (armaments), Beckurts (Siemens), von Braunmühl (Foreign Office), Herrhausen (Deutsche Bank) and Rohwedder (Treuhand), indicating that the RAF during the 1980s was not yet a historical subject, but a clear and present threat. Another explanation was that the films made by the leading directors of the New German Cinema about the RAF, such as Margaretha von Trotta's DIE BLEIERNE ZEIT/MARIANNE AND JULIANE (1981) and Reinhard Hauff's STAMMHEIM (1986) did not appeal to a German public, and only found audiences at festivals and abroad. "[These films] tried to go deeper and make the human beings visible behind the hype, the hysterics and the apocalyptic atmosphere. Yet despite their cautiously distancing stance, the films were attacked in the press and even boycotted by the movie-going public. As a consequence, the RAF and the trauma of terrorism disappeared from [German] cinema and television screens." Stefan Aust, "Er was een generatie voor nodig om met deze geschiedenis onbevangen en nuchter om te gaan," Interview, *NRC-Handelsblad*, September 26, 2008.
23. See the various dossiers of *Der Spiegel*, e.g., "RAF Member out of Jail," December 19, 2008. (http://www.spiegel.de/international/germany/raf-member-out-of-jail-prison-releases-german-terrorist-christian-klar-a-597511.html) and "A Conviction without Clarity: Court Sentences RAF ex-terrorist Verena Becker," July 6, 2012 (http://www.spiegel.de/international/germany/court-sentences-former-raf-terrorist-becker-in-1977-buback-murder-a-843077.html).
24. See in this context Michael Ignatieff's harrowing essay on artrocity videos: "[I]magery has replaced argument; indeed, atrocity footage has become its own argument. One horrendous picture seems not just to follow the other but also to justify it. From Abu Ghraib to decapitation footage and back again, we the audience are caught in a loop: one atrocity begetting another in a darkening vortex, without end." Michael Ignatieff,

"The Terrorist as Auteur," *New York Times*, November 4, 2004 (http://www.nytimes.com/2004/11/14/movies/14TERROR.html?_r=0).

25. Before 9/11, the notion of "postmodern terrorism" gained some currency, to indicate that the old distinctions of left-wing and right-wing terrorism no longer held, nor the reference to the ideals of the Enlightenment. See Walter Laqueur, "Post-modern Terrorism: New Rules for an Old Game," in *Foreign Affairs*, 75, no. 1 (September/October 1996), 24-36.
26. See Gilles Deleuze, "Postscript on the Societies of Control," *October*, 59 (Winter, 1992), 3–7. At the same time, there is also a sense in which the very obsolescence of some of the communication technology used on both sides creates a nostalgia effect, as is the case with the RAF "Wanted" posters that went up at post-offices and town halls. These posters are now traded on e-bay as nostalgic objects, their primitive harmlessness evoking effects of memory and recognition, apparently no different from fashion items from the time (http://www.sparbillig.de/x/result.jsp?q=raf+fahndungsplakat http://preisvergleich.ebay.de/like/390553189860?clk_rvr_id=460708698717), and yet as media *dispositifs*, those structures which maintain control over society, they represent the archaeological traces of an entirely different control society, while inadvertently acknowledging the Wild West atmosphere of those frontier days of terrorism.
27. "An action is the more easily disqualified as "terrorist," the more (under the name of "trauma") a position of pure or innocent suffering can be juxtaposed as its complement." Drehli Robnik, "Bemerkungen zur Geschichtsaesthetik am Beispiel Quentin Tarantinos *Inglourious Basterds*," in Helmut Konrad, Siegfried Mattl (eds.), *Terror und Geschichte* (Vienna: Böhlau, 2012), 212.
28. The first suicide bombers were three members of the Japanese Red Army, who at Tel Aviv airport in 1972 used grenades and automatic rifles to kill 26 people and wound more than 100, before dying themselves. On plane hijacks as media events and indices of cultural change (including fashion), see the video film by Johan Grimonprez *DIAL History* (1995/97).
29. On the occasion of the sixtieth anniversary of the dropping of the atomic bomb, Peter Reichel wrote: "For the vanquished, too, the disaster proved to have a political use. The Japanese High-Command quickly recognized that the deployment of the atomic bomb was 'a gift sent from heaven' (according to the Minister of the Marine Mitsumasa Yonai). [...] By dropping the bomb the American literally overnight had turned a perpetrator country into a nation of victims." *Süddeutsche Zeitung*, 5, no. 8 (2005).
30. Karl Schlögel, "1968 — Eine künstliche Erregung," *Literaturen*, June 2001.
31. Stephan Wackwitz, "Es war was faul im Staate Deutschland," *Süddeutsche Zeitung*, 28 (May 2001).
32. Hannah Arendt, *On Violence*, quoted by Benjamin Kunkel, who added: "Hannah Arendt observed this tendency from her own sharp angle. A central article of her thought is the definition of 'action' (as opposed to mere private behavior and routine labor) as activity that introduces new meanings into the shared public world." Benjamin Kunkel, "Dangerous Characters," *New York Times*, September 11, 2005 (http://www.nytimes.com/2005/09/11/books/review/11kunkel.html?pagewanted=all).
33. Freud first mentioned parapraxis in a letter to Fliess on August 26, 1898, but the most sustained discussion is in *The Psychopathology of Everyday Life*, and the most succinct definition comes from the Introductory Lectures: "It is probably the case that every single parapraxis that occurs has a sense. Parapraxes are the product of mutual interference between 2 different intentions, of which one may be called the disturbing intention and the other the disturbed one. In a slip of the tongue the disturbing intention may be related in its content to the disturbed one, in which case it will contradict it or correct it or supplement it. Or, the content of the disturbing intention may have nothing to do with that of the disturbed one. Parapraxes are mental acts, in which we

can detect sense and intention. They come about through mutual interference between two different intentions. One of these intentions must have been in some way forced back from being put into effect before it can manifest itself as a disturbance of the other intention." Sigmund Freud, *Introductory Lectures on Psychoanalysis* (1916/17), Lecture IV (Parapraxis concluded).

34. This invariably follows the logic of the famous John Cleese *Fawlty Towers* sketch with the German tourists, "Don't Mention the War," in which the very injunction makes sure that it becomes irrepressibly present (http://en.wikipedia.org/wiki/The_Germans).
35. See, for instance, Errol Morris, "The Most Curious Thing," *New York Times*, May 19, 2008 (http://opinionator.blogs.nytimes.com/2008/05/19/the-most-curious-thing/), in which the filmmaker sets out his evidence for challenging some of the received wisdom about the Abu Ghraib photos, in particular, the role of the young women in posing with the detainees.

2

MEMORY FRAMES AND WITNESSING

Burdens of Representation and Holocaust Films

Remembering the Holocaust

When remembering the Holocaust—the name for the persecution and deportation of Europe's Jewish populations, their internment, forced labor, humiliation and extermination during the years of Nazi rule—what is it that we are trying to recall and are called upon to commemorate? Do we want to bring to mind the all-too-real, but in their innumerable acts of inhumanity still unimaginable crimes? Is remembering the necessary if inadequate attempt to bear witness to and document the millions of singular individual lives? Is it a warning addressed to the future ("never again"), or a retrospective admission that the most ambitious project of modernity—to live by reason and rational planning—has proved a license for barbarity (the "failure" of the Enlightenment)? Is remembering the Holocaust answering the demand to accept collective guilt and individual responsibility, as a way of restoring the moral universe we need to believe in, after being so grievously violated? Or is it part of fostering solidarity in defense of universal human rights, for everyone on this planet, in and for the future?

All of the above, and many similar questions, have been asked, both rhetorically and anxiously, by way of ritual repetition and out of a personal sense of accountability, every time we mark an anniversary that remembers the victims. The "we" here is not (only) rhetorical: it names Germany, its government and its people, to which I belong and am bound to by family and kinship. Over the past six decades—the succession of almost three generations[1]—public prosecutors and defense lawyers, historians and writers, filmmakers and television producers, museums and memorial sites, philosophers and politicians have all tried to respond: sometimes to great effect for the nation and its international standing, as when President Richard von Weizsäcker's addressed the Bundestag on May 8, 1985, in which he declared that "all of us, whether guilty or not, whether old or young, must accept the past. We are all affected by its consequences and liable for it."[2] At other times, remembering the Holocaust took forms in Germany that were considered neither pc ("proper coping")[3] nor appropriate, although as I argue in several chapters of this book, their very "failure" to do so may have a logic and a purpose of its own.

What remembering a particular past raises in exemplary manner around the Holocaust is not only how we know what we know, how this knowledge can be represented, transmitted, how it can be acted upon, but also how it can take hold of us and have its own agency, including that of forgetting, disavowal and misremembering: in short, the ambiguous agency of memory itself. Memory, in this instance, is a beguilingly broad and diverse category that over the past thirty years or so has had a remarkable career in the humanities.[4] When not confined to individuals, it can refer to the past of a nation, where it becomes a matter of forging from memory a "usable past." Usable for whom and for what? The present chapter (as well as others that follow) will explore some of these uses, by politicians, by writers and filmmakers, by citizens and audiences, by a country's self-understanding and by its image as perceived by others. Usable memory is prone to being instrumentalized, and is also purposive and directional. That is, we remember in relation to a prompt or an impetus, in response to something *in the present*, and in view of some use or project *for the present*. Not only is memory selective, it is *choosy*: it has to see the necessity or the benefit of recall (a calculus of *Nutzen und Nachteil*, as Friedrich Nietzsche already recognized and formulated it in respect of history).[5] In the case of remembering something painful or disagreeable, as remembering the Holocaust evidently must be, one would expect resistance, and a correspondingly complex affective economy of liabilities and benefits.

Hitler and the Holocaust: From the Historians' Debate to Memory Frames

The existence of *collective memory*, alongside and conditioning individual memory, was first proposed by Maurice Halbwachs, whose *magnum opus* on the subject was published posthumously in 1950. Halbwachs argued that groups situate themselves within the larger community such as the nation, by way of social "frames," within which group memory and individual memory "work" on past and present experience. These memory frames are made up of shared values, recollections and narratives, passed on but also constructed in order to secure identity and ensure the sense of belonging.[6] These notions counter Freudian ideas of memory, more strongly marked as Freudian memory is by negative associations: indelible traces, repression, trauma and loss, and thus, one might argue, more suitable in connection with something like the Holocaust and other traumatic events. Yet it was in the context of Germany's recent past that Jan and Aleida Assmann took up Halbwachs and developed the idea of "cultural memory," to which they opposed "communicative memory," with especially Aleida Assmann (though originally a scholar of English literature) devoting much of her writings on memory to post-war Germany.

The distinction cultural versus communicative memory becomes salient in two separate ways. Building on Halbwachs, the Assmanns' concept is more strongly focused on what they perceived was the growing tendency towards memorialization in the form of recurring dates, anniversaries, museum displays, exhibitions, festivals, i.e., soft "cultural" practices, and not just through stone monuments, military parades or political speeches, or stories that support the collective social frames. "Communicative memory," on the other hand, refers to the passing on of events or experiences that have been participated in or witnessed by an individual or group, and which therefore ceases with the bodies, life-worlds or physical persons communicating them. Both cultural and communicative memory, however, stand in contrast to "history," where subjective telling or reliving is put to one side, in favor of a more objective ordering of the material traces left behind *after* an event, which a historian will try to causally connect and fashion into a sequential narrative or reasoned argument.

Without further entering into the extensive debate around these distinctions and their genesis, it is worth retaining that collective or cultural memory as a separate category—and as a field of study—has had an extraordinary and no doubt symptomatic rise since the 1980s and 1990s. Often referred to as the "memory discourse" or "memory boom," its almost viral proliferation has made it a target for attack, notably from historians: their arguments and counter-arguments will be discussed in the concluding chapter. But why this resurgence of memory as a separate category? Does it reflect the impact of machine memory (i.e., digital storage media and internet servers), which both supports and competes with human memory? Or have cinema and television, by their very existence as the cultural forms that now preserve and transmit the past (but not as "history," i.e., written sources), necessitated a new category, for which "memory" is the provisional stand-in? Cinema is always "memory," even as it deals with history: each screening activates the presence of recall, so that a film is always more than the traces of an event located in the past.[7]

In Europe, however, the enormous interest in memory matters is also prompted by questions of national and supra-national identity in times of crisis or change. Such critical turning points have been the revolts of May 1968, the end of the Cold War in 1989/90, and the consolidation, expansion and subsequent crisis of the European Union since 2004 and 2008. For Germany, the memory discourse reaches further back: it is the "liability" of remembering the national disasters and human catastrophes of Nazi rule, for which the Holocaust stands both as the pre-eminent consequence and as a general symbol: reasons why this chapter refers to cultural memory as "Holocaust memory."

This requires a further clarification. For historians, the Holocaust has become a separate, highly specialized field, as has the study of Hitler's Germany and the Nazi regime. Broadly speaking, historians divide between "functionalists," who see diverse and even contradictory circumstances, initiatives, factions, motives and institutions of state and government involved in planning and executing the Holocaust, and intentionalists, who regard anti-Semitism and the so-called Final Solution as the single most important driving force behind the Nazi regime, with Hitler intending to eliminate Jews from German soil from the very beginning. Each camp of historians divides into different schools and sub-sets: for some anti-Semitism was a by-product of Nazi ideology (and a European phenomenon), for others it was foundational to Nazism and, in its genocidal forms, uniquely German; for some, the Holocaust was a war-time expediency, with major population resettlement policies on the part of the Soviet Union as well as the Nazis' running out of time and out of control, for others Nazi population policy was always targeted specifically at Jews, even if millions of other nationals and different religious or ethnic groups were also killed by the Nazis during the war; some see the Holocaust as the work of "ordinary Germans" acting as "willing executioners," others point to the monstrous logistics needed to implement it, and thus to the coldly efficient bureaucrats (such as Adolf Eichmann) and modernizing technocrats (such as Albert Speer), instructed by mystic ideologues (such as Heinrich Himmler) and skilled demagogues (such as Hitler).

The public discussions—notably the so-called Historians' Debate in the 1980s—sparked by these divergent analyses of the Holocaust, and their political implications, have been examined elsewhere.[8] What concerns me in this chapter are three interrelated issues: first, in the general discussion of cultural memory, I want to argue that by their very presence in the public sphere at least since WW II, cinema, radio and television were instrumental in bringing about the shift from history to memory, a fact which the notion of "cultural memory" does more to elide than to illuminate, with the result that the technical media are often the structuring absence in the debates over memory and history. My second argument is that within film and media studies, where a notion such as that of "prosthetic memory" wants to signal the affective power of moving images over our conceptions of the past, we also need a complementary idea, namely that of "parapractic memory." It stands for a more conflicted, but also unpredictable relation between remembering and forgetting, between past and present, but above all, between subjective remembrance and public commemoration. This insight, finally, I want to bring to bear on the habitual periodization of West Germany's ("failures" in) "mastering its past," across the formation and transformation over time of Holocaust memory as the key "regime of memory" within a number of competing "memory frames" of Germany since 1945.[9]

From these shifts in perspective I expect to derive criteria for evaluating the role of specific films in generating "Holocaust memory," arguing that certain films have not only been crucial in shaping and firming up, but also in destabilizing this memory. The latter is the case, where questions of resistance to images and the voicing of counter-memories arise, in what have increasingly also become struggles over memory's discursive authority. Here, films about the Holocaust have given body to several memory frames, with distinctive national and transnational imaginaries, i.e., different narratives of reception, ownership and appropriation. In this respect Holocaust films often have their own identity politics, enabling acts of testimony and exploring spaces of witnessing that can be credibly occupied by individuals or groups of spectators. This is the subject of the second half of the chapter.

Cultural Memory, Counter-Memory, Media-Memory

As indicated, proponents of collective memory tend to see it as the particular achievement of *culture*, rather than, say, of new technologies, whether of the interested parties that promote them, or the users that adopt them (hence "cultural memory").[10] This culture in turn is usually defined by high-culture practices: literary texts, individual works and artists, museum exhibits, debates by public intellectuals and opinion-leaders in the press and media, as well as —in the spirit of Maurice Halbwachs, known for advancement of the idea of collective memory and Pierre Nora, known for his work on French historical memory—preserved in everyday customs and established habits, or manifested in language, turns of phrase, icons and mementoes, meals or foodstuffs, as well as particular sites or places. By contrast, the technical or electronic mass media (i.e., photography, the cinema, television and the Internet) have for Aleida Assmann a relatively subordinate role in the formation of cultural memory. At times, they are even set up as its very opposite: ephemeral, enslaved to novelty and the new; or second-hand, prosthetic, distractive, but in either case, fostering a culture of forgetting and amnesia, rather than one of memory and remembrance. To the extent that the present study focuses on the cinema and memory, such a pejorative conception of the memory work of the popular media is contradicted both by my case studies and by the key concept—*parapractic memory*—which I see as uniquely enacted by the cinema.

The turn to cultural memory, however, has also run into criticism from another quarter. It tends to be viewed as an ensemble of coexisting narratives or practices, rather than as a site of contest and competing claims. Assmann's idea of cultural memory thus risks depoliticizing the very real struggles over who owns a particular history, or whose version of past experiences is adopted or finds itself delegitimized, which in turn would be symptomatic of the more general loss of faith in politics, and its replacement by culture.[11] Cultural memory, in its inclusive embrace, bypasses or ignores the bitter feuds over incompatible versions of the shared national past that, for instance, raged in France in the 1970s, when notions of "counter-memory" and "popular memory" were circulating. These types of memory were meant to combat the sentimental and nostalgic side of the memory discourse, and to retain the markers of class and class struggle as relevant to the meaning of the Resistance. In the case of West Germany, it was a whole generation that tore itself apart over the "everyday fascism" in the Federal Republic, the highly contentious memory frame within which both Nazism and the Holocaust tended to appear in the 1970s.[12]

In what way, then, is Holocaust memory political or depoliticizing, when held against the more contested versions of a given national past? One could argue that it is hegemonic, insofar as it insists both on the Holocaust's exceptional nature and its universality, while also reflecting and enacting the objectives of a particular group. In the context of the European Union, for instance, Holocaust memory is widely seen as an "elite project," promoted by national elites, and aimed at fostering cohesion through compassion, via a paradigmatic victim group, bringing together former enemies and national rivals.[13] Documenting the fate of their respective national Jewish communities became obligatory for new member states in Central and Eastern Europe, almost as categorically as were the changes to their legal systems or their property rights.[14] By contrast, Russia, as heir to the Soviet Union, has so far resolutely declined to adopt any of the memory regimes on offer in Europe or the United States, with regard to the World War II and the Holocaust. The combination of pride in having defeated fascism and liberated Central Europe under huge human sacrifices, along with residual anti-Semitism and especially a reluctance to see itself as the colonial oppressor from 1945 to 1990, have all contributed to Russia maintaining a very different "cultural memory," and in particular, refusing to accept the analogy, now often drawn in Western Europe, between Nazi concentration camps and Stalin's Gulag labor camps.

In the case of Germany, there are, within the broader memory regime of Nazism and the Holocaust, several memory frames which, as we shall see, succeeded each other, leading to the remarkable result that memory of the Holocaust is not only part of "making amends" and "mastering the past," but has become one of the cornerstones of Germany's national identity. This is the narrative the present book aims to tell, in the form of a parapractic narrative, that is, through its gaps and hiccups, disturbances and disruptions, through "failed performances" and "performed failures," more than across the landmarks, turning points, and public successes that might normally be considered the constituents of "cultural memory."

It is at this point that the parapractic narrative of post-war Germany's memory regimes and the parapractic poetics of a certain cinema intersect, rather than converge. For much of the past forty years or so, the plight of the Jews under National Socialism and the systematic, planned nature of their destruction have been known to a wider public mostly through the visual media, while the work of the professional historians has largely been ignored. Thus, speaking of Holocaust memory invariably conjures up films and television programs, visual narratives, photographs. Note the word "Holocaust," although Hebrew, is an American import which reached Germany in the company of a television series of the same name.[15] In light of what was said above, the revival of the term *collective memory* and its related coinage *cultural memory* is therefore a *rearguard action*, designed to carve out a space that is not mass media memory, to which, as indicated, a string of negative qualifiers—including "trivialization," "vulgarization" and "Disneyfication"—is often attached. Historians have always considered visual evidence and the technical media as the soft supports of their work, because they are selective, too specific, and unreliable. Films and photographs are distrusted as sources and contested as evidence because—even when purporting to "document" a given event or reality—they are often staged and constructed, they can be altered and tampered with. But the mass media are also distrusted by proponents of cultural memory, not least because photographs are said to supersede or usurp and contaminate personal memory, rendering it less "authentic." Since, however, what we remember most vividly from our own lives is often what has been preserved in moving images and photographs, it becomes difficult to regard Aleida Assmann's "communicative memory" as an autonomous category. Rather, it would be a special case of cultural memory, instead of its opposite.

Such arguments are another reason why it is impossible to posit a cultural memory that is not already mediated and saturated by (technical) images that circulate at large: belonging to everybody, anonymous in origin, and instantly recallable, if only thanks to a search engine, on a computer screen or an image-bank, rather than on one's own memory screen. Better then, perhaps, to conceive of cultural memory as media memory from the start, where the distinction between high art and the technical media becomes not only moot, but inappropriate. British dramatist David Hare put it even more dramatically. Asked whether he thought that documented reality, i.e., photographs can be superior to works of the imagination, Hare used the example of Yad Vashem, the Israel national memorial to the Shoah: "Visiting Yad Vashem in Jerusalem did make me question exactly what it was I did for a living. The museum commemorates the murders in the camps with black and white photographs which have extraordinary power. And then there are also some awful sculptures and paintings. You want to say to the artist, "For God's sake, get out of the way. It's impertinent for you to interpose yourself between what we want to look at and our reaction to it."[16]

Hare reminds us of the powerfully evidentiary effect of photographs, and by extension, also of moving images. But visual evidence of the Holocaust, however, poses special challenges that the appeal to a more "authentic" eyewitness testimony can neither overcome, nor invalidate. Photographs of the ghettos, the camps, round-ups and executions have given rise to bitter disputes: should they, for instance, exist at all, and if so, need they be sealed and locked away?

Even without the various ethical objections and religious prohibitions as to their use, are they not inherently unreliable and untrustworthy as evidence, given that they are invariably also the ammunition in a "propaganda war of images"? Any answer must reckon with another stark fact, namely that the eye behind the camera, and thus the agency to which this evidence "belongs," was in the majority of cases that of the perpetrators: the SS, a German soldier out for a souvenir, a camp commandant taking trophy shots or documenting his zeal for his superiors, or the war photographers employed by the *Wehrmacht* whose task it was to glorify Nazi exploits and victories.[17] This, then, would be one particular "burden of representation" confronting filmmakers who use such visual evidence, as well as anyone reflecting on what it means to remember the Holocaust not out of a personal stake, or because of any bonds of family, nation and religion, but as a public duty and part of one's citizenship.

The challenge is to see that the Holocaust, unique event and rupture in the fabric of civilized life that it is, has also been institutionalized as paradigmatic for cultural memory. And as a paradigm, it serves political and didactic uses, it is a moral rallying point, and it has become a means of renegotiating national identities, after the demise of the political ideologies and social utopias at the end of the twentieth century. The making of a human disaster and monstrous crimes that happened in the past carry the weight of hopes for the future and are also a burden of representation: "never again" as a pledge and a promise, which has proven exceptionally hard to keep or to enforce.

That this memory was in large part fashioned from unreliable, objectionable but indispensable visual evidence, and has been sustained by the genres, narratives and visual tropes of television and mainstream cinema, motivated as these media no doubt also are by commercial considerations, adds another challenge or burden. Yet once these filmic representations are seen not under the aspect of the historians' standards of truth based on verifiable fact, nor as travesties and betrayals of the Holocaust's singularity and essential unrepresentability, but viewed as part of an ongoing and open process, as a framing and reframing of memory, then the divide discussed above between verbal, written, public discourse ("cultural memory") and "images" as discourse ("media memory," "historical imaginaries") does indeed all but disappear, or at the very least, presents itself within a different overall perspective. Hence my proposal to speak of Holocaust memory as already a form of media memory, including the oral testimony of survivors.[18]

Such a media memory, no less than individual or collective memory, is neither stable nor fixed; it is contested, and inflected by the respective present, subject to revision and rewriting, embedded in forgetting and distracted attention, and layered by patterns and narrative prototypes originating from elsewhere. In addition, Holocaust memory in the "perpetrator nation" is held in place—and at times displaced—by micro-resistances and counter-memories, by images but also gestures and forms of embodied speech that exceed and disturb narrative, intervening in its temporal flow and obstructing the protagonists' self-presence. My argument is therefore that remembering the Holocaust in Germany across the cinema and through the moving image has not only posed major epistemic and ethical dilemmas regarding cultural memory as a concept and the legacy of communicative memories, but it has also implied another special burden of representation, now concerning the "point of view" (or speaking position) taken by the filmmaker, and the "point of reception" (or subject position) adopted or inhabited by the spectator.

From Representation to Memory: Discursive Struggles over Ownership

As indicated, already the word "Holocaust" confronts one with an epistemic dilemma, since the very term implies a point of view and opts for one of several interpretative frames under which the events thus named can be represented. I recall that in my school days in the 1950s, if referred to at all, teachers would speak of *Das Dritte Reich* (the "Third Reich") and *Die Endlösung* (the "final solution"), by no means with audible scare quotes, thus perpetuating the Nazi's own terminology. Since the 1960s, the preferred term has been *Auschwitz*, emphasizing the very geographical and topological reality of the unimaginable as a *pars pro toto*. "Auschwitz" was replaced in Germany by "Holocaust" in the late 1970s, which in turn was (partly) ousted in the 1980s by "Shoah" (the last two changes occasioned by film titles). Each locution carries its own historical burden, each refers to a distinct semantic (and religious) perspective, and each figures a set of representations that are taken in charge by discourses, kept in trust by national and international institutions, or fought over and jealously guarded by different (interest) groups, and to this extent, too, all of them are multiply mediated. This raises the paradox that something whose uniqueness and utter singularity needs to be reaffirmed and insisted upon, exists by now above all as a second-order reality of semantic pluralism: the terms *Auschwitz, Holocaust, Shoah* say more about the speakers' positions than about the singularity of the referent. Furthermore, while some regret the degree to which the mediatized Holocaust has numbed us to the terror (and to atrocities committed elsewhere since), others have complained that this human catastrophe, as well as its victims, have been "instrumentalized," by serving all manner of ends and purposes, unseemly even when not outright commercial in intent.[19] All of which suggests that memory does indeed rarely occupy neutral ground, and especially in this case, comes with (often unacknowledged) claims of ownership, or it is accompanied by (often unconscious) gestures of appropriation.

How to comprehend the unevenly distributed dynamics of power at the level of word, act or image? Cultural memory, like representation, involves both mediation and delegation: an image stands for a situation or a moment in time, a narrative stands for an action or a state of affairs, an individual stands for a community or a group, and a place and a name stand for a history, while a single event has to stand for a concatenation of actions and their consequences. But if representation is thus always a form of substitution, always a "this for that," then the question is not only who "owns" the representation, memory, meaning of the Holocaust, but who has the authority (moral, political, didactic-educational) to determine the terms of a specific "this for that" which remembering the Holocaust through its memory and representations imposes; in short, who or what assumes, presumes or disavows these various burdens of representation? Remembering the Holocaust thus means remembering also how intense the struggle over this authority and legitimacy has been during the past sixty-odd years, and how it is reignited, often in almost identical terms, decade after decade across quite disparate or unpredictable occasions: triggered by books, films, trials, television programs, and—as I argue throughout this book—"failed performances" by politicians.

In (West) Germany, some of the major landmarks in defining the popular narratives of the Nazi regime and creating Holocaust memory were the Nuremburg Trial in 1945-46, the publication (and film) of *Anne Frank's Diary* in the late 1950s/early 1960s, the Auschwitz Trial in Frankfurt of 1963-65,[20] the television broadcast of the NBC mini-series *Holocaust* in 1979, the showing of Claude Lanzmann's SHOAH in 1985, the Historians' Debate of 1986, the release of Steven Spielberg's SCHINDLER'S LIST in 1993-94, the exhibition of *Wehrmacht* photographs in 1997, the publication of the German edition of Daniel Goldhagen's *Hitler's Willing Executioners* in 2001, and the opening of the Holocaust Memorial in Berlin in May 2005. There are other occasions, more incidental and more local, but no less symptomatic, which I refer to as the *parapractic* logic of Holocaust memory.

These struggles over interpretative power, labeled "controversies" or "scandals" by the press and public opinion, have been preceded or paralleled by similar debates especially in France and the United States, and more recently in Central and Eastern Europe. Sometimes individual survivors lay claims to this history, but mostly it is countries that have fashioned the narratives of the Holocaust in the image of their national agendas. This is why one can look at Holocaust films as a genre that has a transnational and a national component, as well as time lags, delays and other forms of belatedness. Auschwitz films from Poland preceded those of France, and French preceded German ones, while Czech ones preceded Italian ones, and British ones are altogether missing. Sometimes the reception and response were more important than where or when a film was made. Hollywood has made films about concentration camps since the 1940s and 50s (including comedies), but Holocaust films became an issue only after the publicity surrounding the television series *Holocaust* in 1978. It was the charge of trivializing the Holocaust, leveled against the series by Elie Wiesel, a survivor living in the United States, that sparked a major debate.[21] The accusation was subsequently taken up in Germany, when the series was broadcast there in 1979, where it marked a watershed in public awareness of the Holocaust, sent shock waves through the filmmaking community, and was the single most important factor inaugurating Holocaust memory as a public fact.[22]

Fifteen years later in France, Claude Lanzmann polemicized against SCHINDLER'S LIST in much the same way, and again, the arguments were picked up and also reverberated in Germany.[23] In 2000, in the United States, the claim of "instrumentalization" was aggravated into an accusation of "exploiting" the dead and their suffering for personal gain by those who came after. Norman Finkelstein's highly polemical *The Holocaust Industry* (2000), was itself prompted by Peter Novick's *The Holocaust in American Life* (1999), to both of which in turn David Levy and Natan Sznaider would respond (in *The Holocaust and Memory in the Global Age,* 2005). The latter argued that "instrumentalization" need not be a bad thing, and in the case of the Holocaust, the various forms of "nationalizing" and then "transnationalizing" the Holocaust had actually done considerable good. A similar case was made about what Pierre Nora had disparagingly called "prosthetic memory": historic theme parks, popular museum exhibits, simulations and reconstructed historical habitats, blockbuster movies. These Alison Landsberg, taking the term and turning into a badge of honor, saw not only as democratizing the past, but fostering empathy through embodiment and sensory stimulation, for what was alien, foreign, or remote in time and place.[24]

Yet there are differences: it matters whether an Auschwitz survivor or a German film director, an American Jew, a French intellectual or an Israeli historian voices such arguments of trivialization or makes the case for or against the charge of instrumentalization. Not only are their respective speaking positions and moral vantage points distinct. Their political agendas also differ, as individuals as well as on behalf of the community they represent or address, while in the case of the cinema, French and German critics may find themselves perhaps too readily agreeing in their anti-American sentiment, easily mobilized around supposed cultural vulgarization and commercial speculation.

The charge of trivializing the suffering of the victims by casting their fate into standardized story formats is further complicated by the different understanding in the United States and in Europe about the place and agency of the individual in historical events: especially when this fate is the manifestation of a system so utterly contemptuous of individual worth and dignity as was that of the Nazi government. Whereas Americans understand a disaster through the eyes and actions of a specific person or group of human beings, Europeans tend to see such personifications of historical forces as the very hallmark of Hollywood soap operas.[25]

The positions that in 1979 (the year the series *Holocaust* was shown on German television) and in 1994 (the year of SCHINDLER'S LIST) confronted each other are well known in their seemingly irreconcilable opposition: on one side were those who felt that any audio-visual depiction of the death camps was an egregious falsification of the historical record (since few such authentic images existed);[26] they argued that fictional narratives desecrated the victims twice over, by suggesting that the experience of persecution, torture, humiliation and murder could be "represented" and by putting the camera metaphorically (once more) in the hands of the perpetrators and executioners, while these had done everything either to destroy the very traces of their crimes, or had exulted in documenting their deeds as personal trophy or for entertainment. Elie Wiesel summed up this position by saying: "a film about Sobibor is either not a film, or it is not about Sobibor."[27] And Claude Lanzmann, when challenged, said: "*If I had found an existing film—a secret film because filming was highly forbidden—shot by an SS-man, that shows how 3000 Jews, men, women, children die together, choking, in a gas chamber or crematorium, then not only would I not have shown it, I would have destroyed it.*"[28]

For both Wiesel and Lanzmann, any truth of representing the Holocaust can only be grounded in acts of witnessing, in all their ontological impossibility, considering the victims' ultimate testimony is their death. What remains is bearing witness through the almost complete absence of traces, and in all the self-silencing or self-incriminating guilt of the survivors, whether on the side of the victims or the perpetrators. By insisting even on its unfeasibility, Wiesel and others confirm the need, in addition to any historical documents, to give testimony, however incomplete, lacunary or unreliable, on behalf of those millions whose bodies perished, whose voices were never heard, whose cries stifled and agonies muffled. For, if as Jean François Lyotard argued, Auschwitz represented a seismic moral catastrophe of such proportions that it destroyed even the measuring instruments that might have recorded its impact, how then could a medium of banal everyday reality such as television, or an industry as commercially oriented as Hollywood, presume to render the "reality" of the camps?[29] But as Wiesel had also asked: "How to tell a story that cannot be told and that nonetheless should be and has to be told?"[30]

On the other side, sometimes in direct answer to Wiesel, stood those who thought that in the face of the inevitable disappearance of the survivors and eyewitnesses, the mass media did have an important task to fulfill in the shaping and transmission of memory. Unlike other historical events, where the historian takes over from the witness and from living memory, the representational issues and moral dilemmas of remembering the Holocaust—that is, the epistemic and ethical challenges referred to above—were such that a wider public must be reached, informed, and educated, and to this end, the imaginative resources of fiction and historical reconstruction were permissible, indeed required.[31] They pointed to the fact that all the personal accounts, testimonies, authentic diaries, novels, historical monographs, sober documentaries had not been able to break through the wall of silence and indifference that had surrounded, especially in Germany, the fate of European Jews and the question of individual responsibility or collective accountability. The millions watching *Holocaust* on television or who saw SCHINDLER'S LIST were taken as proof that an emotional barrier had been breached. Researchers from the Fritz Bauer Institute in Frankfurt, notably Ronny and Hanno Loewy, together with others compiled a filmography, which lists over two hundred titles of films made in Germany between 1945 and 1990s that feature Jews. Yet awareness and response to this material by the public has been negligible, not only compared to the impact made by *Holocaust* or SCHINDLER'S LIST, but also as material used or requested by schools, in order to teach the next generation.[32]

The over one hundred—mostly documentary—titles even from before the 1970s therefore do not disprove as much as they confirm the impression, widely held, that throughout the 1950s and 1960s, West German society, refused to take note of or discuss anti-Semitism, nor to probe too closely the post-war careers of former Nazi elites in business, the judiciary, education and politics. It should not be forgotten, for instance, that virtually all the media occasions that shook consciences, caused controversy and brought forth a public debate actually came from outside Germany, mostly from the United States.[33] To counter this by saying, as the filmmaker Edgar Reitz had done in 1979, when he protested against the showing of *Holocaust* on German television, that "the Americans have taken away our history" indicates just how deep a chasm the belated and reluctant confrontation of Germany with its Nazi past had revealed—a chasm finally not even bridged by Reitz's own reclamation of German history through popular memory, the sixteen-hour television mini-series *Heimat*.[34] Impressive though it is by many standards, *Heimat* confines itself to the microcosmic world of a single family in a peasant village of the Hunsrück, and can thus plausibly treat as marginal the persecution of Jews in the nearby town and hint only indirectly at the existence of labor or concentration camps. His reply, when challenged, was that "Auschwitz" and the deportation of the Jews were so well known that he would have felt embarrassed to insult his audience. This highlights the other dilemma already hinted at: what kind of "knowledge" is called upon, when referencing the Holocaust? The historical "facts," the moral knowledge of its epochal and world-historical consequences, or the "knowledge of the heart": that in the face of so much injustice we need to know every name and preserve the personal details of every man, woman and child who had to perish only because they were "Jews," and who died under such barbaric circumstances?

Silence can be respect before the dead; silence can be a cover for not wishing to speak. Harald Welzer once remarked that in German families in the 1950s and 60s, there was "a way of not speaking whose silences made audible a content that couldn't possibly bode any good."[35] Speaking, however—talking, debating, discussing, having your say—is just as ambiguous: it can be an effort to give voice to grief, shame or guilt, but it can also be a way of silencing through too much talk. It can even be a more convenient form of silence, when commemoration merely pays "lip-service" to memory.[36] These positions, for or against *Holocaust* and SCHINDLER'S LIST, and the "limits of representation"[37] they entail with regard to the unimaginable reality of the camps, I have discussed more fully elsewhere.[38] At issue here is the extent to which "Holocaust representation"[39] differs from the working of, the function and use of "Holocaust memory" in contemporary Germany.

Periodization across Different Narratives and Memory Frames

For students of "The Holocaust in cinema," one of the problems with the issue of representation has been how to put some order into the long list of films that over the decades have purported to deal with the topic of the Holocaust. Since the mid-1990s, the German and English-language online database *Cinematographie des Holocaust* has provided the essential conditions for such taxonomies, allowing one to search chronologically, by country, topic, name or other keywords.[40] It complements and expands on, but does not supersede the earlier, evaluative studies, grouping films by genre or cycle, assessing them by their respective impact on the general discussion, or by authorial voice and aesthetic value. Nor can one dispense with the studies that read these films symptomatically, as to their ideologies, their stereotyping, hidden agendas and covert biases. Annette Insdorf's *Indelible Shadows: Film and the Holocaust* from 1983 and Ilan Avisar's *Screening the Holocaust* from 1988 were early examples, and they set the template for others that followed, such as Yosefa Loshitzky's and Omer Bartov's books, looking at specific films or representational stereotypes. Similarly, the second edition of another early study, Judith E. Doneson's *The Holocaust in American Film* (2002), focuses on an issue that has become topical, namely the "nationalizing" of the Holocaust. Her book explicitly examines "how specific films influenced the Americanization of the Holocaust and how the medium per se helped seed that event into the public consciousness,"[41] thus reflexively shifting the emphasis from the "representation" of the Holocaust to the impact of the "memory of the Holocaust" as "seeded" by the cinema.

In a similarly reflexive turn, one can identify a number of German memory frames regarding the way both the Nazi period and the Holocaust were "remembered" in German society, as represented/reflected in cinema. I start from the conventional division of German film history since 1945 into *post-war cinema* (of the late 1940s, 1950s and early 1960s), the *New German Cinema* (of the late 1960s to mid-1980s), and the *post-unification cinema* (from 1990 onwards). This periodization is useful because of its looseness, mixing film-historical dates (1962: the Oberhausen manifesto) and film-political criteria (the change in film financing in the mid-1980s) with external political breaks (Hitler's defeat in 1945, German unification in 1990). Conventional wisdom has it that during the first period, memory of the Jews was entirely repressed, and the films, insofar as they dealt with the recent past, did so in an apologetic or self-pitying manner, showing ordinary Germans either at war (where they fought bravely and behaved decently) or where they were themselves victims of Nazi terror. Frequently cited examples are DIE MÖRDER SIND UNTER UNS (Wolfgang Staudte, 1946), EHE IM SCHATTEN, (Kurt Maetzig, 1947)[42] as well as the 08/15 trilogy of war films (Paul May, 1954/55).[43] During the second period, one sees an intense preoccupation with the Nazi time, usually in the context of the nuclear family, as the younger generation challenges the parent generation at home and in public life. It is in the late 1980s and the 1990s that German films take up the Holocaust explicitly or feature Jewish characters as main protagonists.

Obviously, this scheme could be (and has been) further elaborated on, but it can also be set off against another period scheme, which I take from Eric Langenbacher's sociological study of German collective memory that makes no explicit reference to the cinema per se. It distinguishes a number of "memory narratives," which it divides between "German-centered," "Plural" and "Holocaust-centered." Thus, it identifies as "German-centered" the period between 1945 to late 1960s, when the focus is "on inner-directed working through of German suffering; Germans-as-perpetrators downplayed." This is followed (or paralleled) from the late 1950s onwards by a new memory narrative, competing with the German-centered, and "allowing for plural memories, working through to Nazi victims." By the mid-1970s, this plural phase combines "generational interventions" (what I called "the younger generation challenging the parent generation") with "greater though still limited diffusion of memory processes through society" (this is the period of the so-called Hitler wave with books and television series about Hitler and the war, but without much mention of the expulsion and extermination of the Jews). It is in the late 1970s that one can see a "battle for dominance/rise of Holocaust-centered memory," with the "Holocaust conception of the German past almost becoming dominant, though resisted," the latter reflected in "public-political debates, mediatization, extensive diffusion and internationalization" (i.e., the impact of the television series *Holocaust*, obliging the media to take the topic of Jewish suffering, deportation and mass murder out of the specialist historians' hands and into the public sphere, but eventually igniting the already mentioned Historians' Debate). From 1990 to 2002, according to Langenbacher, there is a clear "dominance of Holocaust-centered memory, where the German past is equated with the Holocaust, rather than the "Third Reich," where the "older conception of the past withers," and the (Holocaust-centered) "memory discourse experiences a wide diffusion in society, with a continuous public debate." Finally, from 2002 onwards, the study finds "renewed competition and a return of German-centered memories." This return is "notable for the empathy" now extended to the Nazi generation, to Germans as victims (of the Allied bombings of German cities, of the mass-expulsions from the East) and surprises because of "the resonance [this finds even] amongst leftists."[44] In other words, Langenbacher's memory scheme describes a circle, from 1945 to 2005: German-centered—Plural—Battle for Dominance between the Hitler wave and Holocaust—Holocaust-centered—German-centered.

While the period breaks are drawn around the known turning points (such as the first Auschwitz Trial, the *Holocaust* television broadcast, SCHINDLER'S LIST, the publication of Jörg Friedrich's *The Blaze*), and thus identify a war crime trial, a television series, a blockbuster film, a work of non-fiction literature (and the public debates they generated) as the triggers or catalysts of changes in the nation's memory frame, the main interest of Langenbacher's analysis are the findings which identify particular "narratives" and further differentiate according to demographics, i.e., age, class, educational attainment and political affiliation.[45]

As the Nazi period recedes in time, subsequent periods take on greater significance, in line with the respondents' life-worlds, childhood experiences, and peer-groups. It is therefore remarkable that distinctive views about Nazism and the Holocaust persist among two-thirds of Langenbacher's respondents, which suggests that to the impact of the mass media one must add the role of the education system in trying to foster such an awareness, where, however, it meets a different kind of resistance than that which popular movies encounter.[46]

Langenbacher's other findings concentrate on demographic variables, such as age, educational background and class. They confirm that the succession and overlap of German memory frames over the past sixty years are marked by class ("elite versus mass") and follow a generational model. By contrast, party-political affiliation or region (even East versus West) played only a minor role.[47] The study also confirms that it required major media events and an impulse from outside Germany to redirect the memory frame towards the Holocaust. However, once in place, the "Holocaust memory" frame seems to have proven remarkably consistent and resilient (supported by the schools' history curriculum), even in the face of the next generation once more showing an empathetic interest in the lives (and possible suffering) of their grandparents, while nonetheless remaining committed to the Holocaust memory narrative as the validation and moral justification for their support of human rights and other, more abstract ethical principles:

> Here the evidence is unequivocal: these factors greatly influence the political thinking of contemporary generations of Germans especially in the realms of foreign policy and general political worldviews. Many of the historical and memory questions, especially the "final line" questions [i.e. Holocaust memory is important because the genocide was a violation of basic civilizational or ethical norms against murder. Holocaust memory helps universalizing of Human Rights] were consistently statistically significant and exhibited substantial effects [...] often as strong if not stronger than the most important demographic predictors.[48]

These findings are paralleled by other sources and indicate the success of the "elite" version of German cultural memory, which puts awareness of the Holocaust as a universal moral lesson at the center of a national as well as a European world-view. As such it does indeed represent a "hegemonic" discourse, although one must not exaggerate the effect Holocaust memory has had on European identity formation: "Even in the European context, where elites have aggressively fostered the development of transnational identities, there is no indication that these efforts have produced anything approaching a European identity among significant parts of the population."[49] Nonetheless, if the Holocaust memory discourse has indeed shored up the spirit of civic solidarity, in the manner advocated by von Weizsäcker, and if it has, in Germany at least, become a core reference point of national identity and is even providing moral guidance in the way that church or party once did, this would be itself be a remarkable achievement.

Periodization Across Subject Positions of Testimony and Witnessing

Yet the achievement may well have come at a price, i.e., "institutionalizing" Holocaust memory, as well as making of it a metaphor. Institutionalizing Holocaust memory (made symbolic and visible in the Monument to the Murdered Jews of Europe in the middle of Berlin), predictably perhaps, led to a relaxation of one of the most closely observed taboos, namely expressing loss, grief or sympathy for the suffering of Germans during and after the war. The official version, namely that the mass expulsions from the East and the bombing raids on civilian targets in major German cities were to be accepted as just punishment for having supported or followed Hitler's murderous and megalomaniac designs, began to seem less self-evident, once Holocaust memory was part of the nation's identity. In one sense, it was a "return" to the first response in the late 1940s and 50s when Germans did indeed see themselves as Hitler's first victims, rather than as perpetrators, and resentment against the reparation and retribution demanded by the Allies was keen and vivid.[50]

Yet the feelings and sentiments emerging around 2000 may not only have been a reactionary relapse: there is evidence that this "return" is of a different kind, as I shall argue in a second chapter on "Holocaust memory" since 2000, which I call "guilt management." Rather than being a direct reference to the "German plight," the return to a victim's discourse partakes in what I see as part of the price to be paid for the success of Germany's official memory policy, namely that Holocaust memory has become a metaphor—for ultimate evil, but also for extremes of suffering—which universalizes it, but also allows it to be attached to other instances or forms of suffering and victimhood. Whereas in the 1950s—and again, briefly during the Historians' Debate in the late 1980s—speaking of German suffering was indeed an attempt to relativize or minimize the crimes committed against Jews, by trying to draw up a balance sheet of "their" victims against "our" victims, speaking of German suffering after unification and in the new century, does not compete with the Holocaust, but ennobles this (German) suffering by its comparison with the Holocaust. One may wish to argue if this is any less reprehensible or problematic, but it is important to note the difference.

I shall leave the other implications of the universalizing tendencies for my second chapter on Holocaust memory, and now want to compare the overview of German memory frames from Langenbacher's sociological perspective, with one that focuses more specifically on the films made in or seen in Germany on the topic of the Holocaust (also before it became the Holocaust)[51] during the first phases of "mastering the past" and the establishment of a memory discourse, i.e., from the late 1940s to the mid-1970s, stressing the dynamic and fluid nature of this process of memory formation. This time I focus on specifically cinematic genres and modes of address, in order to test the shifting memory frames against particular films and television programs that are known to have shaped the debate and contributed to the appropriation of the Holocaust for a national memory regime. I also want to consider the inverse possibility, namely that the cinema has different resources and strategies by which to contribute to or constitute "memory": in view not so much of fostering a "national identity" in the sense discussed, but rather, a media memory that reflexively enables particular "subject positions" to emerge, including those that destabilize the hegemonic version of memory. I propose distinct modes (of address, of presence and of witnessing), which appear to follow each other: the forensic mode, the testimony mode and the involved bystander mode, and contrast it to a participatory mode of "being there," not easily available to a film made in Germany, but attempted in DER UNTERGANG/THE DOWNFALL, a film discussed in chapter 10.

These modes are distinct from the "representation of ..." perspective, as it tends to prevail in film studies when examining cultural themes and their ideological or political meanings. Rather than chart and map the films that have Nazism as an explicit theme, that reference the camps or feature protagonists explicitly depicted or named as Jewish, I want to concentrate on the role assigned to the spectator. For example, during the immediate post-war years, one finds quite a few Jewish characters in the films produced both in the Western and Eastern Zones, sometimes starring returning émigrés like Peter Lorre (DER VERLORENE, 1951, dir. Peter Lorre) or Fritz Kortner (DER RUF/THE LAST ILLUSION, 1949, dir. Josef von Báky). But the protagonists identified as Jewish are usually not central to the narrative, which attends more to ex-Nazis or "ordinary Germans" forced to face up to a guilty past. The general consensus has been that these films not so much "repress" the fate of the Jews as they fail to acknowledge the scale or enormity, and show little awareness of the consequences of these crimes for generations to come.[52] Few such films were either popular successes at the time or registered in public discussions, although most of them have retrospectively come in for extensive critical reevaluation: proof, I would argue, that we now see these films from our own Holocaust memory frame, and thus not as representations as much as indices, evidence (of an absence or lack), in the forensic even more than the hermeneutic sense, because this lack of awareness that now strikes us so forcibly would not have been perceived as such at the time. A closer reading should therefore be less concerned to highlight what the films did not show or displaced by way of symptom formation, but try to reconstruct what the not-shown or not-said tells one about the contract the film has or wants to have with its spectators.[53]

This is why I devote a separate chapter (and several individual case studies) to the films of the New German cinema, because there are—with perhaps one or two exceptions that prove the rule—virtually no explicitly Jewish characters in the films of the prominent directors. Here the non-appearance of the Holocaust is the salient feature. It is especially striking in light of the fact that since unification hardly a film on a historical topic seems to be made that does *not* feature a character with Jewish roots or a Jewish theme. My argument is that one needs a different hermeneutic frame to read these respective absences and presences in the successive periods.[54] Just as no-one in the 1950s—not even the Jews in Israel—could have known that by the second half of the twentieth century, the Holocaust would have become the single most important event of the entire century, so the absence of Jewish figures in the films of the New German Cinema, as well as their presence in the post-unification films, tells us less than we might think about the "representation of the Holocaust" and more about memory formation and subject positions.[55] In other chapters I argue in more detail why this presence followed by absence followed by presence deserves special attention, not least because the matter of Holocaust memory is, as argued above, invariably caught up in questions of ownership and gestures of appropriation. Absence and presence in representation are thus indicative of several contending memory frames, superimposed, and not merely a "return" to an earlier one, or the "repression" of a painful or disagreeable one.

Witnessing: The Forensic Mode

The first phase or period, from 1945 to the late 1960s, is marked by two much publicized trials (the Nuremberg Trials, 1945/46, the Frankfurt Auschwitz Trials, 1963/65, to which one should add a third: the Eichmann trial in Jerusalem, 1961/62, widely reported in the German press). In each case the media played a significant role, both in transmitting the trials and shaping their meaning. The basic mode was that of forensic witnessing: perpetrators and victims or survivors confronted each other before a judge or tribunal, actual or imaginary. In the Nuremburg Trials, film was used extensively: NAZI CONCENTRATION

CAMPS, a sixty-minute compilation film, from material shot mostly by U.S. war photographers when the U.S. Army entered the camps of Bergen-Belsen, Buchenwald, Dachau, as well as footage from Mauthausen and Ohrdruf, was shown to judges, lawyers and defendants. The editing was under the general supervision of the film director George C. Stevens, assisted by E.R. Kellog.[56] From this compilation is taken most of the footage we are now so familiar with: the piles of dead bodies, the emaciated faces, the decomposing corpses, the men with hollow eyes clinging to barbed wire fences. The material was presented as incontrovertible evidence; it was to speak for itself and to this day furnishes a powerful, devastating, unbearable document. But the camps filmed were concentration camps, not the extermination camps in Poland. The crimes the accused were indicted for were classed as "war crimes," and the film did not specifically refer to Jews at all. A further twenty-two-minute compilation film, drawn from much the same source material, was directed by Hanus Burger, with the editing supervised by Billy Wilder. It was shown under the title DIE TODESMÜHLEN (The Death Mills) to Germans in some of the Allied zones (Bavaria, Hesse and West-Berlin) for reeducation purposes between January and May 1946. It included footage of inhabitants of Weimar being taken to Buchenwald, to see with their own eyes the horrors perpetrated just outside their town.

The general consensus is that these so-called atrocity films were a failure, if their purpose was to open hearts and minds for signs of remorse or contrition.[57] The obligatory viewing appears to have only hardened German resistance, self-pity and obduracy. Given that many of the inmates of the labor camps were political prisoners, or forced laborers from France and other occupied countries, the genocide and systematic extermination of the Jews was neither mentioned in the films, nor a matter of public debate. The reeducation screenings in the occupied zones were soon abandoned by the U.S. authorities, not least because after 1947 and the division of Germany through the Iron Curtain, the priorities of the Cold War took precedence over any thorough attempt to bring to justice former Nazis.[58] Nor was there the political will to examine in public the complicity of ordinary Germans in the deportation and expropriation of German Jews, or to delve deeper into the industrial system of the forced labor and death camps. The fact that at Nuremberg, genocide (a term whose juridical definition by the United Nations dates from 1948) was not part of the many war crimes committed by the Nazis during the previous six years, allowed Germans to believe that with the end of the war and the completion of the trials, the matter of the camps, too, was closed.

Not so in films coming from Eastern Europe, notably from Poland. Most remarkable was Wanda Jakubowska's THE LAST STOP (OSTATNI ETAP, sometimes also translated as THE LAST STAGE), made in 1947 and partly shot on location at Auschwitz. Although rarely shown in the West, and "rediscovered" for film historiography in the early 1990s, THE LAST STOP turned out to have been a widely influential prototype for the Holocaust film, as already Béla Balázs had predicted in his original review.[59] It depicted the fate of a group of female prisoners as they try to survive the rigors, deprivations and humiliations of their internment. Jakubowska used lay actors, some of whom were former inmates, who thus returned, so soon after the end of the war, to the very site of their ordeal, asked to reenact scenes they had lived through, within the very same barbed wire fences. Almost all the key situations and many of the typical iconography one now associates with camp films are present: denunciation by fellow prisoners, sadistic punishment for trivial offences, the arrival of the trains by the ramp at night, the unloading of the wagons under the glare of searchlights, with rain or sleet turning the ground into a sea of clinging mud.[60] Notable, however, is the extent to which THE LAST STOP avoids mentioning the Jewish identity of the prisoners—a reticence attributable both to the director's own experience as a non-Jewish prisoner, and to the prevailing ideology of Poland immediately after the war, where "coming to terms with the past" had to be in the service of several competing and conflicting agendas around national identity, of which the easiest was to reinforce the master narrative of Polish suffering.[61]

The "arrival at the ramp at night" from THE LAST STOP is perhaps the most often copied of these scenes,[62] from KAPO (Gillo Pontecorvo, 1959)[63] and THE PAWNBROKER (Sidney Lumet, 1964) to SOPHIE'S CHOICE (1982) and SCHINDLER'S LIST (1994). It is also cited in Alain Resnais' NIGHT AND FOG (1955), which was the only film widely screened in West Germany and discussed by the press. I shall return to the status and reception of NIGHT AND FOG in later chapters; here it suffices to point out that its rhetorically powerful voice-over commentary (written by Jean Cayrol) frequently hints at how the visible evidence of the sites, and the (media) memory of the images destabilizes any strict separation of past and present. Made as a documentary essay, NIGHT AND FOG has influenced also subsequent feature films, in that images from the camps came to be shown as reflexively doubled by a troubled memory: either that of a guilty participant (STERNE, 1958) or that of a traumatized survivor (THE PAWNBROKER, 1964). Flashbacks therefore constitute the dominant trope in the fiction films—as if the scenes were to be recalled in order to provide evidence in a RASHOMON-like dispute of memory and counter-memory, and presented to an invisible but implied judge: the spectator.[64]

An especially important example of the "troubled memory" mode was Andrzej Munk's THE PASSENGER (Pasazerka, 1961/1963). Only fragments exist of the original project, because the director suffered a fatal car accident during the shooting of the film. Originally a radio play, the story tells of a sea cruise where a German passenger, returning to Europe, thinks she recognizes another woman passenger as a former concentration camp prisoner. She confesses to her husband that during the war, she worked as an overseer (a Kapo) in Auschwitz, but that she once saved a woman's life. When Witold Lesiewicz, a friend of Munk's, took it upon himself to try and complete the film, he and his collaborators realized that it had to remain in some crucial sense "unfinished business." The sequences set in the camp and already shot were combined with production stills (of the encounters on the ocean liner) and a voice-over commentary, which ruminates both on the film project, Munk's tragic accident and the motivation of the (fictional) characters.

These Polish-produced films, along with several others made by East Germany's DEFA film company dealing with deportation and labor camps, were either not distributed in West Germany or had little public resonance. Coming from the countries of communist rule, they could be dismissed as propaganda. Even Konrad Wolf's STERNE (discussed in chapter 6), which won a prize in Cannes, failed to stir a sustained debate in West Germany. As a GDR-Bulgarian co-production, it could not even be shown at Cannes as a "German" entry, since West Germany did not recognize the GDR as a legitimate state entity.

The defensive, but more often merely indifferent response to Jewish persecution on the part of German public opinion changed briefly with the Auschwitz Trial in Frankfurt from 1963/1965, conducted by the Federal State Prosecutor of Hesse, Fritz Bauer. Once again, the forensic juridical framework also had a major influence on the modes of representation, especially among West German writers, notably Martin Walser, Rolf Hochhuth and above all Peter Weiss' *Die Ermittlung/The Investigation* (1965). Based on the Frankfurt trial and its transcripts, Weiss shaped a dramatic text, which he called "Oratorio in 11 cantos," arguing that it should *not* be staged as a courtroom drama: "No attempt should be made to reconstruct the courtroom before which the proceedings of the camp trial took place. Any such reconstruction would, in the opinion of the author, be as impossible as trying to present the camp itself on the stage."[65] Similarly, no actual names are used to identify the protagonists other than by their functions: "Defendant," "Witness," "Prosecutor," "Judge." Weiss, too, begins with the arrival of the trains (Canto "Platform"). Such an emphasis on anonymity and depersonalization, with all its metaphoric significance, is rarely found in the cinema, where psychology, affect and a melodramatic plot tend to interlace a complicated timeline of uncertain recall with moments of (failed) recognition.

A configuration typical of both melodrama and the courtroom did become the center of affect and key narrative trope in the only German feature film directly inspired by the trial, even though it makes only oblique reference to it. Featuring a witness who testifies against the defendant, doubling also as the victim confronting the perpetrator, ZEUGIN AUS DER HÖLLE (Gorke Trave/Bitter Herb, 1967) was a co-production undertaken by the commercial producer Arthur Brauner, himself a survivor from the Jewish quarter of Lodz in Poland, with a Yugoslav company, Avala Film. Directed by Zivodad Mitrovich, it is the story of a trial judge who learns about a possible witness against one of the doctors on trial for barbaric experiments in the camps. The female witness, Lea

Weiss, however, refuses to testify, claiming that her testimony, given immediately after the war to the Allied Forces, was fabricated. The investigating judge distrusts her disclaimer and travels to Yugoslavia, to contact a writer who knew Lea after the war, and who might persuade her to testify. He succeeds, and she reluctantly consents. Realizing that neither the prosecutor nor the judge have any understanding of her feelings of guilt and shame (she had survived by allowing the doctor to have sex with her), but are merely interested in using her evidence to indict the doctor, whose defense lawyer put more and more pressure on her credibility as a witness, she has a nervous breakdown and once released from the hospital, commits suicide.

The fact that the film was a German-Yugoslav co-production gives some indication of how delicate and difficult it was to mount such a project in Germany. For the main role of the witness, Brauner had engaged Irena Papas, famous from her role in ZORBA THE GREEK, with Daniel Gélin, a well-known French actor, as the writer. The judge was played by Heinz Drache, popular for his roles as commissar in the EDGAR WALLACE crime films. Despite these box-office oriented casting decisions, the film was not a success at the time, although it has since been screened widely at themed events and retrospectives for its historical importance and symptomatic value in focusing on the dilemmas of witnessing, and the trauma of survivors' guilt.[66]

ZEUGIN AUS DER HÖLLE may be a melodrama and a commercial production, but it persuasively thematizes the emotional and psychological stress that survivors were under, when called as witnesses against their tormentors, and it is the first West German film that features a Jew from the camps as the central character. The fact that the film left no mark on public consciousness and gave rise to no public debate, once again indicates that in this respect, too, the mode of witnessing was not a successful way of opening up a space for critical reflection, for soul-searching or awakening what might be called empathetic memory, however much the female character was conceived of as a tragic figure, offered to the spectator for compassion and identification.[67]

Most other films made or shown in Germany during these twenty years from 1945 to 1965 that deal with Nazi crimes are centered on Germans who, often through a chance encounter, are suddenly confronted with their guilty past, which they have been hiding successfully from their families or colleagues. This is the case with the already mentioned DER VERLORENE (Peter Lorre, 1951) and several others (including, incidentally, THE PASSENGER, 1961/63). The best-known films of this genre or cycle were DIE MÖRDER SIND UNTER UNS (Wolfgang Staudte, 1946), ZWISCHEN GESTERN UND MORGEN (Harald Braun, 1947) and DAS ZWEITE GLEIS (Joachim Kunert, 1962). Although the films do not feature courtrooms, their encounters with the hidden or repressed past lead to confrontations, themselves occasions for flashbacks. Stylistically, they are reminiscent of pre-war Ufa productions (even featuring Nazi-era stars and directors), filled with allusions to Expressionist lighting and a *film noir* atmosphere of anguish and duplicity, as they present the point of view of the Germans, for whom the Jews remain "the other."[68]

An exception is LANG IST DER WEG/LONG IS THE ROAD, an independent film made in Germany in 1948.[69] It is a semi-documentary feature film depicting the fate of a Jewish family from Warsaw, deported, dispersed—the son manages to escape from the train taking him to Auschwitz—and interned. After the war and liberation, the mother as sole survivor is eventually reunited with her son in a U.S. Army-run Displaced Persons Camp, from where they plan to emigrate to Palestine. The film was hardly shown in Germany at all.[70]

Testimony, Archive, Counter-Memory

If during the first phase the trope of witnessing in the forensic or judicial sense predominates, the second phase stands under the sign of more intimate testimony and personal memory, contributing to and eventually constituting the ongoing "archive" of documentary images, in contrast to the settings, props, costumes and color schemes that would eventually take over as the screen memory of the Holocaust in the 1970s. Begun as "bottom-up" rather than "top down" history, it initially functioned as a televisual oral history project and as counter-argument to the more spectacle-driven films. Framed by the historians' debate and its "revision" of narratives of rescue and resistance, these films of the counter-memory were also initiated from outside Germany. The debate began in France, with Michel Foucault one of the leading thinkers of popular memory as counter-memory,[71] and Marcel Ophuls as counter-memory's outstanding pioneer film director. Interviewing survivors and victims, Ophuls encourages them to go on record, or in the case of perpetrators, lures them into betraying themselves to the camera and the interviewer. Paradigmatic for this offensive are Ophuls' investigative documentaries (THE SORROW AND THE PITY, 1969; THE MEMORY OF JUSTICE, 1976; HOTEL TERMINUS, 1988) and the films of Claude Lanzmann (SHOAH, 1985; SOBIBOR, 2001). Passionately concerned with the difficulty of remembering and testifying, as well as their absolute necessity, Ophuls' and Lanzmann's films dispense with so-called archive footage, precisely in order to create a different kind of archive, where the struggle over memory, its resistances or tergiversations, its breakdowns or overpowering emotions, its disavowals and violent self-betrayals are as much part of what we need to know and keep in mind as "evidence" as are photographic images and printed documents. Both Ophuls and Lanzmann made their films in France: Ophuls wanted to foreground proof of collaboration among the French elite, their often covert and overt sympathies with Nazi ideology and anti-Semitism. Also highlighted in his films are the cover-ups effected by the Catholic Church, thus revising the dominant post-war Gaullist historical compromise between French conservatives and communists, of a nation united in opposition to the Occupation and heroically serving in the Resistance.[72] By contrast, Lanzmann traveled to Germany, Poland and Israel, and his films put a relentless emphasis on the many ordinary human beings that were involved in making the death camps possible, mostly engaged in routine and mundane tasks. He shows in painstaking detail how many wheels within wheels, how many chains of command it took to keep the Nazi machinery of death going, as well as the fact that it did keep going under the most extreme conditions, extreme even for the perpetrators, and would have continued to do so, had not the Russians and the Americans put an end to it.[73] These films of witting and unwitting testimony have been of crucial significance in filling the gaps in the record of how Europeans experienced the war, and of how the Nazi occupation and extermination policy functioned day-to-day, over the excruciatingly long and absurdly short period it took to destroy centuries of Jewish life in Europe.

Yet the years 1969 (THE SORROW AND THE PITY) to 1985 (SHOAH) were also the period when a veritable flood of personal reminiscences, memoirs and biographies was being published and consumed by an avid readership, while Nazi memorabilia, photographs, family albums and home-movies resurfaced on television, or became coveted collectors' items. Perceived by some to be a backward-looking, nostalgic turning away from the present (and thus in France called *la mode retro*, i.e., retro-fashion), by others as a belated act of mourning for their lost ego ideals invested in the *Führer* (i.e., leader, and known in Germany as the "Hitler wave"), the persistent popular interest in this period of European history remains ambiguous. At first, a profound unease attached itself among historians and intellectuals to this groundswell of absorption into personal narratives, this hunger for human-interest stories, at the margins of momentous events. Was the Third Reich once more reverberating with the thrill of the forbidden: transgressing taboos, touching on hidden secrets or vicariously experiencing evil at close quarters? Or was such dwelling in reminiscences of adolescence or young adulthood merely an index of a generational shift, the paradoxical discovery of sensations of joy and happiness, even innocence, before the bombs rained down, bringing ruin and devastation to the millions of civilians?

Either way, the general lack of curiosity about the fate of all those ("Jews," "gypsies," and other "undesirables") removed so efficiently from their midst by the Nazis was indeed a troubling aspect of the new popular memory discourse of the early 1970s, as typified in the success of Joachim Fest's *Hitler — eine Biographie* (1973), which in a book of 1,280 pages devotes just three pages to the persecution of the Jews. Made into an even more successful feature-length documentary, HITLER — EINE KARRIERE (Joachim Fest, Christian Herrendoerfer, 1977), Fest's biography had at least the effect of polarizing the discussion in Germany about the nature of the Germans' attraction to a figure such as Hitler, who, according to Fest, lent his charismatic personality to deep longings as well as deep resentments, fatally shaping their destiny both prospectively (after 1945) and retrospectively (in the way even nineteenth- and twentieth-century

German history came to be read as foreshadowing Nazism), and thus far beyond the years he was in power. While Fest's emphasis on Hitler's (and Albert Speer's) gift for political theater and mass-media spectacle could be said to have influenced R.W. Fassbinder's view of the Nazi-period in LILI MARLEEN (1981), it also set the template for two decades of German television documentaries on the period (many signed by the journalist and author Guido Knopp).[74] However, Fest's notion of the German people finding a voice through Hitler, who was thus as much their projection and puppet as he was their demonic seducer, becomes the very premise of H.J. Syberberg's HITLER — EIN FILM AUS DEUTSCHLAND (1977). Even Ingmar Bergman had been influenced by Fest's biography when writing the script of THE SERPENT'S EGG (also 1977).[75]

At the opposite end would be Edgar Reitz' HEIMAT (1984), a chronicle "from the bottom up," where, as with Fest, the deportation of German Jews and the camps are, as pointed out, hardly mentioned, but where Hitler, too, is a very remote figure to the good folk of Schabbach: only when two of them make a visit to Berlin do they witness a scene from their hotel window which picturesquely reflects the very real flames of fanaticism and racial hatred.[76]

In a sense, the HEIMAT family chronicle of Reitz and the investigative testimony films of Ophuls and Lanzmann—despite their aesthetic and ideological differences—are already aware of their *belatedness*: engaged in making up for lost time, as if gathering up a testimony that should have been collected if not transmitted years before. Insofar as they are concerned with participants and witnesses, many of whom by then were in their seventies and beyond, the films put on record the bodies, voices, words and gestures of a generation about to disappear. Even where the form is fictional, as in Reitz, or where the situations (as in Lanzmann) are deliberately restaged and recreated, an archival impulse prevails. However, while Lanzmann's SHOAH insistently shows the past as it is present in and to the present, using reenactments—of conducting trains, shaving heads, singing a song—to solicit the body's corporeal memory more than the protagonists' visual memory, Reitz relies on the power of fiction, of staging and acting. Yet he, too, uses material objects, gestures and body language to evoke a world made dense and heavy through lived time, which transmits itself to the spectator over the more than fifteen-hour duration of the series' first part, covering the years 1919 to 1982.

What Reitz and Lanzmann have in common with Syberberg is their films' inordinate length: fifteen, nine and seven hours respectively. While "epic" is the word that comes to mind, the effect is also that of slow motion, as if these terrible years between 1933 and 1945 were at the same time so compressed, so multi-layered, and such an insane acceleration of German history, that it would take all of the second half of the twentieth century to process, to reexamine, and to comprehend these twelve years under the magnifying glass of the *slow motion action replay*. Parapractic memory is also the name for this delaying, reversing and deferring effect, as laid out in more detail in chapter 9, on Harun

Farocki's AUFSCHUB (RESPITE, 2007), which already in its German title literalizes deferral. Alexander Kluge's films, too, often literalize the metaphor of an *anamorphosis in time* by using slow motion or its opposite, time-lapse photography, most strikingly in THE BLIND DIRECTOR (*Der Angriff der Gegenwart auf die übrige Zeit*, 1985). According to Kluge, only the cinema can show how a single moment can consume everything that went before and came after ("wie ein einziger Augenblick alles Vorher und Nachher verschlingen kann"),[77] a notion that would find its echo in Alain Badiou's philosophy of the event, and which will also be discussed in chapter 8, around the significance of the year 1979. As to the belatedness or "latency" between 1945 and 1975, before the memory discourse and the archival impulse gained their hold over the popular imagination, it was as if after the three decades of silence and disavowal, an inverse, and perhaps no less disturbing pathology made itself felt: a repetition compulsion, for which television became the predestined medium.[78]

The Bystander or (Implicated) Observer

During the same period of the 1970s and 80s, another strand of cinematic restaging of the Nazi past was emerging, interwoven with the Hitler wave, but which, in the periodization I am proposing, inaugurated also another trope: neither that of the witness, nor of giving witting or unwitting testimony, but of the bystander and (implicated) observer. Like other media events that jolted Germans into "working on their memories" (Reitz), this phase begins with an American film, Bob Fosse's CABARET (1972), a huge success all over Europe and also in Germany. Based loosely on Christopher Isherwood's Berlin story *Goodbye to Berlin*,[79] CABARET depicts the life of a group of American and British expatriate thrill seekers in the nightclub, bar-fly, gay and lesbian milieus of Berlin in the early 1930s, just prior to Hitler's accession to power. CABARET set the stage for many of the thematic motifs as well as defining a whole iconography of decadence, blending show business and Nazi-insignia that would return in the films concurrently made as part of the Hitler wave.

Usually named alongside films filed under the label *retro-fashion*, such as Visconti's THE DAMNED (1969), Bertolucci's THE CONFORMIST (1970), Louis Malle's LACOMBE LUCIEN (1974) and Truffaut's THE LAST METRO (1980), CABARET broke dangerous new ground within the German context in that it violated the previously held taboo against a fictional representation of the (pre-)Nazi period as sexy and glamorous. But by acknowledging the ambiguity of "fascinating fascism" (Susan Sontag) in the way it used spectacle, show business and the erotics of perversion, CABARET's cheerful use of color—including the red, black and brown now associated with Nazism—also broke with both neo-realism and *film noir* as the dominant filmic idioms for films set in Germany's dark period of the recent past.

Yet what also strikes one about CABARET—besides an often hallucinatory sense of suspended or dilated temporality, of waiting and anticipation, of energy in a void—is a new form of spectatorship, or rather—thanks to the permanent charade of performative presence, sexual ambiguity and make-believe—the possibility that the spectator, too, is becoming confused as to his or her role. Not only do we see the expats, pleasure seekers and sexual outsiders being—reluctantly or inescapably—drawn into an increasingly violent and polarized scene, but we come to realize that instead of being detached and above the fray, the show manipulates us, plays with us, teases us, making us complicit, only half against our will.

Although inaugurated by Hollywood and sustained by several films from Italy and France, this new stance of the morally torn, because fascinated observer is, I would argue, also typical of what was to be the next phase of Germany's cinematic memory work. In this mode, the witness stand and the participant's testimony have given way to the perspective of the spectator and the bystander.[80] Although retrospectively traceable to examples from the mid-1970s, it is much more typical and pervasive in and for the 1990s, which is to say, it corresponds to the (life-experience of the) third generation since 1945, too young to have personal memories, not driven by the need to build either evidence against their parents or an archive against forgetting, but saturated with the media-representations that began to dominate the television screens from the mid-1980s onwards. Again, a non-German film can stand as paradigmatic: SCHINDLER'S LIST is in some respect the fully worked out example of this mode, both in its conception of Schindler, as a marginal (who is being drawn in, at first reluctantly, and with dubious motives), and in the way the film accommodates not the voyeurism of the peephole perspective, but the somatic, traumatizing, embodied sense of "being there," standing in the middle, confused, dazed, overwhelmed, but also carried along.

The differences, with respect to the films from the 1970s and 80s are that the scenes into which these forms of spectatorship are now inscribed, include the depiction of the life of Jews in Germany and elsewhere, in German cities among "ordinary Germans," in the ghetto and even the camps—sites that (since the *Holocaust* television series) are no longer off-limits to either fiction or reenactments. The second difference is that the role assigned to the spectator is not that of the voyeur of classical Hollywood film, but as imaginary participant. This participant has a presence both inside and outside the event, as if "looking at him/herself looking" had been added as a further dimension, not as a critical act of distanciation, but as a reinforcement of presence, a doubling in space and a displacement in time, as it is also typical of nostalgic longing. By giving the illusion of knowing what it feels like "being there," as well as feeling safe in the knowledge of surviving the experience, this stance induces a mixture of nostalgia and sentimentality, but grounded in the mode of heroic survival. It was one of the aspects that most offended and shocked Lanzmann about SCHINDLER'S LIST. To him, the film presumed to make the almost accidental rescue of a handful of Jewish prisoners "stand for" and "represent" the millions that had perished, and in the process, take even the sting out of slave labor. Spielberg's specific mode of generating this form of participatory spectatorship, locating the spectator inside and outside the action, is one that he first developed around the Hollywood blockbuster, where the resources of suspense and anticipation are mustered to engage the viewer in a bodily, visceral fashion. Applied to a historical subject, its reference is memory and trauma, no longer based on actual memories, but built around moments of intense tactility and physical presence, which complement the visual illusion of "being there" with appropriate bodily sensations.

"Being there" would characterize the fourth mode of spectatorship in the cinematic representation of past events, after the forensic, the testimony, and the involved bystander mode. In Hollywood, "being there" is associated with historical reenactment films, such as PEARL HARBOR (Michael Bay, 2001), LETTERS FROM IOWA JIMA (Clint Eastwood, 2006) or LINCOLN (Steven Spielberg, 2012). The mode extends into traumatic historical territory the hybrid blend of theme park rides and computer games from action cinema, but "being there" is also present in the trend towards participatory exhibition displays in museums and at memorial sites, increasingly conceived to provide the immediacy that comes from spatial proximity and bodily sensations. A theoretical elaboration of such an aesthetics of "being there," also with respect to the Holocaust, is offered by Alison Landsberg's idea of "prosthetic memory," briefly mentioned above. She characterizes it as an active, affective and even empathetic form of memory, experienced by the body, and replacing an absence, like a missing limb, rather than intuiting a presence in and through this absence. The virtues of prosthetic memory, according to Landsberg, are that it is "portable, interchangeable and non-essentialist": virtues directly owed to its commodification and spectacle mode of representation, both of which she defends against the common critique of inauthenticity and emotional exploitation.[81] Landsberg's deliberately polemical argument thus fully embraces one side of the divide (between modernism and realism, minimalist restraint and melodrama, absence and void versus spectacle and sensory immersion) that has accompanied the limits, burdens and challenges of representing the Holocaust in the visual media since the 1950s.

An especially interesting example of confronting head on some of these thorny issues of representation, as well as of spectatorship is Roman Polanski's THE PIANIST (2002), a Holocaust narrative that stays within mainstream cinematic conventions, but knows of its belatedness, i.e., that it comes after the *Holocaust* television series and after SCHINDLER'S LIST as well as the heated debates these two commercially successful works occasioned. Polanski, himself a first-hand witness and survivor of persecution and deportation, takes a historically documented case as his plot premise, but transforms his protagonist into a different kind of "involved bystander," muting any sense of heroism in his survival. Based on the memoirs of Warsaw pianist Wladyslaw Szpilman, it chronicles the invasion of his native city by the German *Wehrmacht*, the gradual segregation and deportation of its Jewish population, including the members of Szpilman's fully integrated, bourgeois family, and Szpilman's several escapes, sometimes protected by benefactors, more often surviving by mere chance. Destitute and emaciated, he witnesses the destruction of the Warsaw ghetto, and survives, thanks to the clandestine help of a German officer, until the Soviet army liberates the city.

Polanski's mise en scène manages to sustain an intriguing tension between physical proximity and inner distance (a "being there" in the mode of not being there), to which corresponds a look at unspeakable cruelty. It dares the spectator to practice a form of observation and attention that discovers even in scenes of horror a space of witnessing, past fascination and revulsion, and thus probes the very conditions (and limits) of empathy.[82] On the one hand, Polanski tests the urge to put oneself in the place of the other (for instance, in the place of the old man who has to wait to be shot, while the officer reloads his handgun), and to experience in an absence the presence that once was there (as in the scene of the square littered with left-behind possessions). On the other hand, Polanski keeps Szpilman at arm's length, mainly because at first he seems so detached and self-enclosed. As a consequence, the spectator as bystander is implicated not so much because we are made to witness situations where the unseemliness of our voyeurism no longer protects us from the knowledge of our inability to intervene. The central protagonist himself, in several scenes, faces the dilemma of the spectator-bystander, avoiding the fate of his family and other fellow-Jews in Warsaw, because of luck and accident as much as his usefulness as a pianist. Neither hero nor anti-hero, Szpilman is an *impotent witness*, somehow beyond either resistance or survivor's guilt, and towards the end, more in the position of the abject, the Musulmann, seemingly indifferent to his fate.[83] As we watch some of the most horrific scenes of destruction through his apathetic eyes, we cannot but be aware that he also stands in for us, a sharp reminder of our own ambivalent position. Slipping from one side (the ghetto) to the other (the "Polish" side) and back again, often not sure where he is and why, he has a privileged view of the ghetto, but at the price of its destruction. A victim, whose position is that of an observer, he limits our sympathy but also blocks our empathy, since his situation forecloses our putting ourselves in the place of the other: we *are* already in the place of this other by our very position as spectators. By depicting Warsaw under German occupation as the site of an intricate spatial geometry—fractured and divided so as to box in the Jews, disorienting to Szpilman, but also providing him with hideouts—Polanski obliges us to reconsider what it means to be a spectator and a witness in the first place.

We are also made aware of what it means to record and document (and thus what is involved in a representation): while the Germans are putting in place an elaborate architecture of confinement and control for all points of contact or transit, THE PIANIST shows them filming their own actions, notably the construction of the ghetto, its divisions and its demarcations. In such scenes Polanski reflexively doubles his own film, ascribing to the occupiers the same mise en scène of complex spaces he has constructed for his film, while also inscribing into it the memory of many of the images by which we "remember" ghetto life. Yet these scenes are not the restaging of well-known photographs; rather, they explicitly implicate the viewer in what I earlier noted was one of the particular burdens of representing the Holocaust: the knowledge that much if not all of the visual evidence we have of the terrible conditions of Jews in Polish ghettos (as well as of other sites of persecution and execution) would have been recorded by the camera eye of the perpetrators.

Witnessing as the Privileged (and Precarious) Proximity to Events

Polanski's THE PIANIST—coming late in the cycle of Holocaust films—is thus a kind of summary of the debates around the representation of the Holocaust from the perspective of witnessing and testimony. It serves as a conclusion of sorts to the taxonomy of spectatorial positions presented here, and it invites some final remarks about witnessing. Through the writings of Emmanuel Levinas, Giorgio Agamben, and especially Shoshona Felman and Dori Laub's book *Testimony: Crises of Witnessing in Literature, Psychoanalysis and History*, which focused on the oral testimony of Holocaust survivors, the conjuncture of trauma, witnessing, testimony and language has become part of a much broader debate about memory in the humanities, to which I return in the final chapter. In the present context, where spectatorship and cinematic representation are at issue, the cinema of the Holocaust challenges such categories of identification, empathy, voyeurism and critical detachment as they are traditionally invoked when discussing the spectator's relation to the screen. Concentrating on witnessing, it is clear that the witness is a privileged observer, in that she or he is deemed to have access to a more direct experience of an event, through his or her own eyes and senses. But a witness is also in a precarious position, because of his/her added authenticity. Being the "surrogate sense organ of the absent,"[84] his or her evidence potentially conflicts with the added fallibility of memory and recall when testifying to extreme situations or traumatic experiences. The position of an observer is precarious in another sense: a witness carries the burden of a certain complicity, which in turn demands a form of accountability that makes bearing witness an ethical act. That the stakes can be very high is indicated by the fact that witnessing plays a central role in religion, legal proceedings and when it comes to surviving and attesting to acts of mass violence such as genocide, or extreme physical pain or mental anguish as in torture and systematic humiliation. As John Durham Peters puts it: "These three domains [law, theology and atrocity] endow 'witnessing' with its extraordinary moral and cultural force today, since each ties the act of witnessing, in some deep way, to life and death. The procedures of the courtroom, the pain of the martyr, and the cry of the survivor cast light on basic questions such as what it means to watch, to narrate, or to be present at an event. Witnessing, as an amazingly subtle array of practices for securing truth from the facts of our sensitivity to pain and our inevitable death, increases the stakes of our thinking about media events."[85]

Peters' final sentence alerts us to the fact that what I have called the aesthetics of "being there" and Landsberg's "prosthetic memory" may well raise, in the domain of spectatorship, some of the same issues attendant upon witnessing in the domains listed above. In other words, watching a film about suffering, cruelty and the putting to death of human beings, whether in a fictional mode or by way of a documentary using archival material, can entail these dilemmas of proximity and precariousness, of complicity and accountability. In the case of Holocaust films, we may well wish to avert our eyes from sights that sear our conscience, and yet, we may feel the ethical impulse to look, and to look closely, in order to bear witness and assume the task of testimony, as part of our humanity, our recognition of the other, and our willingness to acknowledge complicity and accountability. This, at any rate, would be my reading of Polanski's filmic strategies highlighted above, and of Landsberg's claims that even prosthetic, i.e., artificial, grafted memory can have consequences of an ethical kind, such as empathy and solidarity with victims. This said, I also maintain in several of the subsequent chapters that being a victim should not be one's only or even chief claim to humanity and empathy. Especially in respect of THE PIANIST, Polanski is at pains to show that the members of the Szpilman family are "real life characters who happen to be victims rather than victims who just happen to be characters."[86] This is an important point to bear in mind quite generally, since the dominant memory frame, namely that of the victim, can also be a trap, and is, in the case of Germany, only one side of the dilemma.

For the problem of empathy and complicity poses itself most acutely when one is obliged to recognize at least part of oneself in the perpetrators, rather than the victims. This would be the invariably precarious situation of German spectators when watching a Holocaust film: their heightened awareness of complicity may well conflict with their sense of empathy, each blocking the other, or at any rate interfering with each other. It might explain why my examples of both the position of the spectator as implicated bystander and that of "being there" are drawn either from non-German films or are hyphenated productions, as in the case of THE PIANIST, shot mostly in the Potsdam-Babelsberg studios, but financed by no less than fifteen different (French, German, Polish) companies. In chapter 10, I shall examine more recent, German-made films, such as AIMEE AND JAGUAR and ROSENSTRASSE, trying to negotiate the fraught positions of being bystanders and witnesses—usually by casting the narrative into a retrospective time-frame of mourning, reminiscence or traumatic recollection in order to mitigate or avoid the dilemmas around the participatory forms of spectatorship that I summarized under "being there." These films also tend to treat their *protagonists as victims first, and characters second—even where they are depicted heroically.* In this respect, the 1990s indicate quite clearly the extent to which the Holocaust as Germany's cultural memory had become in some sense official, and its appropriate modes of representation increasingly molded by television and its genres of docudrama: types of remembering and testimony that relied on an ambiguous blend of historical footage, reenactment and talking head witnesses.

This chapter has restricted itself to the cinema, a limitation I readily concede is both tenuous and increasingly obsolete—not least because, since the mid-1970s, films in Germany have invariably been made with television funds. At the same time, scholarship on the various (sub-)genres that have emerged from television's appropriation of Holocaust memory is abundant and thriving.[87] My restriction has nonetheless its justification, in that it wants to provide a context for the following chapter, which focuses on German filmmaking between the 1960s and the 1990s, i.e., the period of the New German Cinema. There, as already indicated, the burden of representation takes a different turn, insofar as the mode of agency and spectatorship that I define as "parapractic" both highlights and bridges the paradox of empathy and accountability. Parapraxis would be the form that embodiment takes, when "being there" is not an option, and when accountability demands distance, *even where the spectator is unaware of the meaning of this distance,* caught up as she or he is in the proximity of victims, bystanders *and* perpetrators.

Notes

1. Aleida Assmann speaks of the "40-year rule" when marking the memory span of a generation. As to the discourse on generations in Germany, see Sigrid Weigel, "Generation as a Symbolic Form: On the Genealogical Discourse of Memory since 1945," *The Germanic Review*, 77 (2002), 264–77.
2. Richard von Weizsäcker, "Speech in the Bundestag on May 8, 1985, during the Ceremony Commemorating the 40th Anniversary of the End of War in Europe and of National-Socialist Tyranny" (http://www.mediaculture-online.de/.../weizsaecker_speech.../)
3. "Pc" in the sense not of political correctness, but "proper coping" was first suggested to me by Eric Santner.
4. To name some of the best-known examples, relevant to the present study
   Aleida Assmann, *Erinnerungsräume. Formen und Wandlungen des kulturellen Gedächtnisses* (München: C. H. Beck, 1999).
   Jan Assmann, "Collective memory and cultural identity," *New German Critique*, 65 (1995), 125–133.
   John Brockmeier, "After the archive: remapping memory," *Culture and Psychology*, 16/1 (2010), 5–35.
   Paul Connerton, *How societies remember* (Cambridge: Cambridge University Press, 1992).
   Jeffrey Herf, *Divided Memory: The Nazi past in the Two Germanies* (Cambridge, MA: 1997).

Andreas Huyssen, *Twilight Memories: Marking Time in a Culture of Amnesia* (New York: Routledge, 1995).

Reinhard Koselleck, *Zeitschichten* (Frankfurt/Main: Suhrkamp, 2000).

D. Levy, and N. Sznaider, *The Holocaust and Memory in the Global Age* (Philadelphia: Temple University Press, 2006).

J. K. Olick, *The Politics of Regret. On Collective Memory and Historical Responsibility* (New York: Routledge, 2008).

5. Friedrich Nietzsche, "Vom Nutzen und Nachteil der Historie fürs Leben," first published in his *Unzeitgemäße Betrachtungen* (Leipzig: Fritsch, 1874).
6. "When people think they are alone, face to face with themselves, other people appear and with them the groups of which they are members." Maurice Halbwachs, *On Collective Memory*, ed. and trans. L. A. Coser (Chicago: University of Chicago Press, 1992), 49.
7. Thomas Elsaesser, "Subject Positions, Speaking Positions: From Holocaust, Our Hitler, and Heimat to Shoah and Schindler's list," in Vivian Sobchack (ed.), *The Persistence of History: Cinema, Television, and the Modern Event* (New York: Routledge, 1995), 145–83. Thomas Elsaesser, "One Train May be Hiding Another: Private History, Public Memory and National Identity" (http://www.latrobe.edu.au/screeningthepast/classics/rr0499/terr6b.htm) and Thomas Elsaesser, "Migration und Motiv: Die parapraktische Erinnerung an ein Bild," in P. Geimer and M. Hagner (eds.), *Nachleben und Rekonstruktion. Vergangenheit im Bild* (Munich: Wilhelm Fink, 2012), 159–76.
8. See Elsaesser, "Subject Positions, Speaking Positions."
9. On "regimes of memory," see Susannah Radstone and Katherine Hodgkin (eds.), *Regimes of Memory* (London: Routledge, 2003), 1–2. The term *memory frame* I take from Eric Langenbacher (see Note 44).
10. See Aleida Assmann, *Der lange Schatten der Vergangenheit. Erinnerungskultur und Geschichtspolitik* (Munich: C. H. Beck, 2006). In English, see Aleida Assmann, "Four Formats of Memory: From Individual to Collective Constructions of the Past," in C. Emden and D. Midgley (eds.), *Cultural Memory and Historical Consciousness in the German Speaking World Since 1500* (Bern: Peter Lang, 2004), 19–37.
11. This shift, polemically argued by Slavoj Žižek and Jacques Ranciere, among others, is the subject of another essay: Thomas Elsaesser, "Politics, Multiculturalism and the Ethical Turn: The Cinema of Fatih Akin," in Boaz Hagen, Sandra Meiri, Raz Yosef, and Anat Zanger (eds.), *Just Images: Ethics and the Cinematic* (Newcastle: Cambridge Scholars, 2011), 1–19.
12. For France, see Jean Baudrillard, "Simulacra and Simulations: History: A Retro-Scenario," http://www.egs.edu/faculty/jean-baudrillard/articles/simulacra-and-simulations-ii-history-a-retro-scenario/ and Michel Foucault "Film and Popular Memory," reprinted in *Foucault Live* (Interviews, 1961–1984), edited by Sylvère Lotringer (New York: Semoitext(e), 1996), 122–32; for Germany, see Thomas Elsaesser, "Antigone Agonistes: Urban Guerrilla or Guerrilla Urbanism?" (http://www.rouge.com.au/4/antigone.html).
13. On Holocaust narratives as part of an elite advocacy of transnational identities, see Wulf Kansteiner, "Sold Globally—Remembered Locally: Holocaust Cinema and the Construction of Collective Identities," in Stefan Berger, Linas Eriksonas, and Andrew Mycock (eds.), *Narrating the Nation* (Oxford: Berghahn Books, 2008), 154.
14. The best-known example would be Poland, obliged to "come to terms with" past anti-Semitism, notably within the Polish Catholic Church.
15. This is ironic, since it is Elie Wiesel who claims to have introduced the word into English, through his book *Night* (1960), and who became one of the fiercest critics of the television series that bore this name. The German translation of Holocaust, meaning "sacrifice by fire" occurs in one of the first stories about the extermination camps, Alfred Goes' *Das Brandopfer* (1954). See chapter on "Guilt Management."

16. David Hare, interviewed by Michael Billington, *The Guardian*, January 19, 2009.
17. Photographs taken by German soldiers on the Eastern front became the explosive material of the Wehrmacht-Ausstellung.
18. See, for instance, the debates over the Fortunoff Video Archive for Holocaust Testimonies at Yale University. Caroline Wake, "Regarding the Recording: The Viewer of Video Testimony, the Complexity of Copresence and the Possibility of Tertiary Witnessing," *History & Memory*, 25, no. 1 (Spring/Summer 2013), 111–44.
19. Martin Walser's controversial Peace Prize acceptance speech ("Wege in die Gegenwart") where he voiced his fear that "Auschwitz [might have become] the moral stick to beat us with" can be found at http://www.hdg.de/lemo/html/dokumente/WegeInDieGegenwart_redeWalserZumFriedenspreis/
20. One may want to add to this list the reception in Germany of Stanley Kramer's JUDGMENT AT NUREMBERG (1961) and Sidney Lumet's THE PAWNBROKER (1965). These two films were customarily dismissed on aesthetic grounds, thus sparing the critics the trouble of examining their considerable audience appeal.
21. Elie Wiesel, "Trivializing the Holocaust: Semi-Fact and Semi-Fiction," *New York Times*, April 16, 1978. See also Elie Wiesel, "Art and the Holocaust: Trivializing Memory," *New York Times*, June 11, 1989.
22. Friedrich Knilli and Siegfried Zielinski (eds.), *Holocaust zur Unterhaltung. Anatomie eines internationalen Bestsellers* (Berlin: Elefanten Press, 1982).
23. Martina Thiele, *Publizistische Kontroversen über den Holocaust im Film* (Münster: LIT Verlag, 2001).
24. Alison Landsberg, *Prosthetic Memory: The Transformation of American Remembrance in the Age of Mass Culture* (New York: Columbia University Press, 2004).
25. "In the U.S., a story can be told only across an individual, conveyed by the actions of the protagonist. The totality of the destruction [signalled by the Holocaust] is thus its complete opposite, as Elie Wiesel pointed out. Extermination renders any attempt to tell it as a story futile, but the belief that it might be possible points once more to the likeable American persistence in the illusion that an individual can make his happiness, if only he puts his mind to it. Dealing with the Holocaust in the U.S. is marked by this contradiction; seen as the most extreme confrontation between the individual and social totality, [the struggle against Evil] takes on almost mythical character, embodied in the perfect individualization of the confrontation. [...] In Germany, such a pretention to individual sovereignty in dealing with this subject is deemed unserious. Here, Wiesel's objections were not seen as a call to debate the means of representation, but as the assertion of unrepresentability as such. It was not the fear of the survivors that trivialization might denigrate the memory of the victims, which shaped the debate, but the opposite concern: that trivialization might indeed generate empathy." Tjark Kunstreich, Die Wundreiztherapie: Wie die Westdeutschen lernten, *Holocaust* zu lieben. *Jungle World*, no. 5 (January 21, 2004; http://jungle-world.com/artikel/2004/04/12210.html).
26. Claude Lanzmann picked another fight with the art historian Georges Didi-Huberman over the legitimacy of showing images taken from within Auschwitz in 2003. See Karoline Feyertag, "The Art of Vision and th Ethics of the Gaze" (http://eipcp.net/transversal/0408/feyertag/en) and Sally Shafto, "Just Images," *Framework: The Journal of Cinema and Media*, 45, no. 2, Article 15 (2004).
27. "Art and Theresienstadt were perhaps compatible in Theresienstadt, but not here—not in a television studio. The same is true of prayer and Buchenwald, faith and Treblinka. A film about Sobibor is either not a picture or not about Sobibor." Elie Wiesel, *And the Sea is Never Full: Memoirs 1969* (New York: Schocken, 2000), 121.
28. Claude Lanzmann, "*Schindler's List* is an impossible story." *Le Monde*, March 3, 1994, translated by Rob van Gerwen, from *NRC Handelsblad*, March 26, 1994, 11 (http://www.phil.uu.nl/staff/rob/2007/hum291/lanzmannschindler.shtml).

29. The broadcast of and concurrent debate over *Holocaust* in West Germany has spawned a sizeable literature. Among the best-known are Peter Märthesheimer and Ivo Frenzel (eds.), *Im Kreuzfeuer: Der Fernsehfilm Ho-locaust. Eine Nation ist betroffen* (Frankfurt/M: Fischer, 1979) and Joachim Siedler, *"Holocaust" — Die Fernsehserie in der deutschen Presse* (Münster 1984). For a retrospective on the impact twenty-five years later, see Jürgen Wilke, Die Fernsehserie "Holocaust" als Medienereignis, *Historical Social Research*, 30, no. 4 (2005), 9–17.
30. Elie Wiesel, *Conversations* (Jackson: University Press of Mississippi, 2002), 125.
31. As Gerald Green, the screenwriter of *Holocaust*, wrote in reply to Wiesel's article: "Mr Wiesel will discover to his delight that our 'imagined, improbable' film will have provided him with a larger audience than he ever had before." Gerald Green, "In Defense of '*Holocaust*,'" *New York Times*, April 23, 1978, D1, 34.
32. See the website of the Fritz Bauer Institute's Cinematograghie des Holocaust (http://www.cine-holocaust.de/).
33. Günter Rohrbach, controller at WDR, vigorously defended his acquisition of the series, and its diffusion on public television: "It would be curious indeed, if of all people the Germans, forthright protagonists in the destruction of the Jews, were to show special scruples when it comes to the treatment of the topic by others" (*Die Zeit*, June 15, 1978).
34. There were to be two sequels: *Leaving Home* (*Die Zweite Heimat*) and *Heimat 3* (*Chronik einer Zeitenwende*), which brought the story up to the new millennium, but their impact, both in Germany as well as abroad, was negligible, compared with the first *Heimat*, dealing with the years from 1919 to 1982.
35. Harald Welzer, "Schön unscharf: Ueber die Konjunktur der Familien- und Generationsromanen," *Literatur* Nr 1 (Beilange zum *Mittelweg 36,* Hamburg, January/February 2004), 53–64.
36. "Holocaust was a milestone, not least because Germans learnt that endless talk can be just as effective as obdurate silence." Kunstreich, *Jungle World.*
37. Saul Friedlander (ed.), *Probing the Limits of Representation: Nazism and the Final Solution* (Cambridge: Harvard University Press, 1992).
38. See note 7.
39. Among the best-known studies of the representation of the Holocaust in cinema are Annette Insdorf, *Indelible Shadows. Film and the Holocaust* (New York: Cambridge University Press, 1983); Ilan Avisar, *Screening the Holocaust* (Bloomington: Indiana University Press, 1988) and Omer Bartov, *The "Jew" in Cinema* (Bloomington: Indiana University Press, 2005).
40. The Cinematograghie des Holocaust now lists information on more than 1,730 individual films.
41. Judith E. Doneson, *The Holocaust in American Film* (Ithaca: Syracuse University Press, 2002), back matter.
42. David Bathrick, "Holocaust Film before the Holocaust: DEFA, Antifascism and the Camps," *Cinemas* (Montreal), 18, no. 1 (Autumn 2007), 109–34.
43. Jennifer M Kapczynski, "Armchair Warriors: Heroic Postures in the West German War Film." In Paul Cooke and Marc Silberman (eds.), *Screening War: Perspectives on German Suffering* (Rochester, NY: Camden House, 2010), 23–34.
44. Eric Langenbacher, "Memory Regimes in Contemporary Germany," conference paper ECPR Edinburgh, 2003 (www.essex.ac.uk/ecpr/events/jointsessions/.../Langenbacher.pdf).
45. To quote from Langenbacher's conclusion: "The Nazi period is the most salient period for [only] about 35% of Germans today. Almost two-thirds chose more recent periods, which, however, included the current period (the unified country from 1990). There is also evidence for the existence of competing memories. A quarter to a third of respondents chose the German-centred memory in the two formulations (that Germans were

also victims of Nazism and that the suffering of Germans was comparable to other groups). Nevertheless, there is also support for the Holocaust-centred memory, with two-thirds of the sample believing that there was a basic difference between the experiences of Germans and Jews during the Third Reich. These memories, especially the Holocaust-centred one, are not superficially but rather intensely held, as the questions ascribing importance to the past for the present country attest."

46. The problematic nature of this awareness is documented in a transnational study by the Israeli historian Yair Auron, translated into German as *Der Schmerz des Wissens — Die Holocaust- und Genozid Problematik im Unterricht* (Lich/Hessen: Edition AV, 2005), and widely discussed in Germany. See also "Holocaust im Schul-Unterricht: Keine Zeit für Gefühle" *Süddeutsche Zeitung*, May 17, 2010, and Peter Steinbach, "Holocaust und Schulunterricht" (http://www.tribuene-verlag.de/TRI_Steinbach.pdf).
47. "As for demographic variables, the more leftist, better-educated respondents with higher incomes and higher status occupations were closer to elite-validated or 'progressive' views and vice versa. Indeed, age/generation, income and education turned out to be the most important background factors in the various statistical analyses. This is clear evidence that the mass-elite difference is salient regarding acceptance of the current memory regime and that 'generation' is still a powerful differentiating force. It bears repeating that the [party political] variable was a surprisingly weak explanatory factor. Any real differences are on the extremes—with Green and PDS sympathizers closer to the 'progressive' views. Although CDU voters do not fully accept the [Holocaust] memory regime, the distance is slight, as is that with the other catchall party, the SPD. It appears that the effects of partisanship have weakened and are washed out by elite-mass and generational differences. Other factors like East-West residence, gender and religion played similarly weak roles." Langenbacher, "Memory Regimes in Contemporary Germany."
48. Ibid.
49. Kansteiner, "Sold Globally — Remembered Locally," 171–72.
50. The literature on this first phase of Germans claiming victimhood is now substantial. For a guide through some of it in the 1990s, see Omer Bartov, "Designating Enemies, Making Victims: Germans, Jews and the Holocaust," *The American Historical Review*, 103, no. 3 (June 1998), 771–816; Y. Michal Bodemann, "Eclipse of Memory: German Representations of Auschwitz in the Early Postwar Period," *New German Critique*, no. 75 (Autumn, 1998), 57–89; and the essays in Paul Cooke and Marc Silberman (eds.), *Screening War: Perspectives on German Suffering* (Rochester: Camden House, 2010). For arguments that see the victim discourse since 2000 as an ominous return, see Helmut Schmitz (ed.), *A Nation of Victims? Representations of German Wartime Suffering from 1945 to the Present* (Amsterdam: Rodopi, 2007).
51. David Bathrick, in his essay with the programmatic title "Holocaust Film before the Holocaust," focuses on the representation of Jewish suffering and the camps in DEFA (i.e., East German) films between 1946–47 and 1978, when the television series by that name universalized the term *Holocaust*.
52. Notably Die Mörder sind unter uns (Wolfgang Staudte, 1946).
53. See chapter 10 for a detailed discussion of genre films from the 1950s in the parapractic mode as analyzed by Drehli Robnik.
54. For a historian's way of reading absence, see "Germans as Jews: Representations of Absence in Postwar Germany" in Omer Bartov, *Germany's War and the Holocaust: Disputed Histories* (Ithaca, NY: Cornell University Press, 2003), 221–35.
55. In the revised edition of her *Indelible Shadows*, Annette Insdorf remarks that "it never occurred to me that, by the year 2001, films about the Nazi era and its Jewish victims would be so numerous as to constitute a genre—including consistent Oscar winners—nor did I foresee how this genre would be part of a wider cultural embracing of the

Shoah." Annette Insdorf, *Indelible Shadows: Film and the Holocaust* (Cambridge: Cambridge University Press, 2002), 245.

56. This film is not to be confused with *The Memory of the Camps*, a title given by the Imperial War Museum Film and Video Archive to edited unreleased footage shot in 1944-1945 by service newsreel cameramen with the British, American, and Russian armies liberating various Nazi concentration camps. It was edited by Stewart McAllister and Peter Tanner with Alfred Hitchcock acting as "treatment advisor." Commentary by Colin Wills. Produced by Sidney Bernstein and Sergei Nolbandov.
57. See Brewster S. Chamberlin, "Todesmühlen: Ein früher Versuch zur Massen-'Umerziehung' im besetzten Deutschland 1945–1946," *Vierteljahrshefte für Zeitgeschichte*, Heft 3 (1981), 420–36, and Jeanpaul Goergen, "Aufnahmen beglaubigter Kameraleute: Die Todesmühlen," (D/USA, 1945) in Filmblatt (Berlin), Jg. 7, Nr. 19/20 (Sommer/Herbst 2002).
58. "Ich meine wir sollten jetzt mit der Naziriecherei Schluß machen (I think it's time to stop sniffing out Nazis)." (Chencellor Konrad Adenauer, 1952), quoted in Norbert Frei, *Vergangenheitspolitik. Die Anfänge der Bundesrepublik und die NS-Vergangenheit* (Munich: C.H. Beck-Verlag, München 1996), 4.
59. See Béla Balázs, "Ostatni Etap/The Last Stop," *Slavic and East European Performance* 16, no. 3 (Fall 1996), 66–68. Hanno Loewy and Stuart Liebman have been crucial in bringing both Jakubowska's film and Balázs commentary back to attention. See Stuart Liebman and Leonard Quart, "Lost and Found: Wanda Jakubowska's The Last Stop," *Cineaste*, 22, no. 4 (1997), 43–45.
60. On The Last Stop and other Polish films on the topic, see Marek Haltof, *Polish Film and the Holocaust: Politics and Memory* (New York: Berghahn Books, 2012).
61. Discussing Alexandr Ford's Border Street, Wulf Kansteiner contextualizes the ambiguities: "While acknowledging or even emphasising the difficult ethnic relations in pre-war Poland, Polish filmmakers unequivocally represented Jews as part of the national collective. In the case of Ford, that strategy was a conscious critique of the virulent anti-Semitism of the war and post-war years. Yet despite his best intentions, he thus reduced the suffering of Jews to yet another example of the long-term suffering of the Polish people that was already one of the overriding themes of Polish culture prior to the war." Kansteiner, "Sold Globally — Remembered Locally," 156.
62. See on this Hanno Loewy "Fiktion und Mimesis," who argues that because the film was made so soon after the events, and used former inmates as part of the cast, The Last Stop was treated almost as a documentary. See Margrit Frölich and Hanno Loewy (eds.), *Lachen über Hitler-Auschwitzgelächter?* (Munich: text + kritik, 2003), 37.
63. Kapo was well regarded at the time, but when the film was released in France, Jacques Rivette, in an article called "De l'abjection" and printed in *Les Cahiers du cinéma*, no. 120, 1961, wrote a blistering attack, centering on a single camera movement, just after Emmanuella Riva throws herself against a live electric wire: "l'homme qui décide, à ce moment, de faire un travelling avant pour recadrer le cadavre en contre-plongée, [...] cet homme n'a droit qu'au plus profond mépris." ("The person who decides, at this point, to use a forward tracking shot, in order to reframe the dead body in reverse angle [...] this person only deserves the most profound contempt.") This infamous scene, or rather, Rivette's comments then served Serge Daney thirty years later as a manifesto to reformulate his ethics of cinema: "Le travelling de Kapo," *Trafic*, no. 4, 1992, 5–19.
64. Night and Fog returns as "screen memory" in two films connected to the RAF. In Margarethe von Trotta's Die Bleierne Zeit (The German Sisters, 1981), the young Gudrun Ensslin is made to watch the film at school, becomes nauseous and has to go to the bathroom to throw up. The heroine in Christian Petzold's Die Innere Sicherheit (The State I Am In, 2000) is also shown watching a scene from Night and Fog. In contrast to Ensslin, this young woman—the action is set in the 1990s, rather than the 1950s—shows no outward emotion.

65. Peter Weiss: *The Investigation* (New York: Macmillan, 1996), 1.
66. For a detailed description, see Ronny Loewy, "*Zeugin aus der Hölle* und die Wirklichkeit des Auschwitz-Prozesses," in Claudia Dillmann, Ronny Loewy (eds.), *Die Vergangenheit in der Gegenwart. Konfrontationen mit dem Holocaust in den Filmen der deutschen Nachkriegsgesellschaften* (Frankfurt am Main: Deutsches Filminstitut – DIF, 2001).
67. ZEUGIN AUS DER HÖLLE, or at least the dilemma of the witness might have been the implicit but attenuated reference point for one of the opening scenes in Alexander Kluge's ABSCHIED VON GESTERN (1966), when the heroine is on trial for petty theft and the judge derisively asks whether the fact that her parents were persecuted by the Nazis as Jewish had anything do with her transgression.
68. For a detailed discussion of these films, see in addition to the essay by Bathrick already mentioned, Robert R. Shandley, *Rubble Films: German Cinema in the Shadow of the Third Reich* (Philadelphia: Temple University Press, 2001) and Anke Pinkert, *Film and Memory in East Germany* (Bloomington: Indiana University Press, 2008).
69. Directed by Herbert Fredersdorf, Marek Goldstein and produced by Abraham Weinstein, *Lang ist der Weg* rarely turns up in German film histories, but is a foundational film for Israeli cinema.
70. "Written by Israel Becker, this is the first feature film to represent the Holocaust from a Jewish perspective. Shot on location at Landsberg, the largest DP camp in U.S.-occupied Germany, and mixing neorealist and expressionist styles, the film follows a Polish Jew and his family from pre-war Warsaw through Auschwitz and the DP camps" (http://www.imdb.com/title/tt0040527/).
71. Michel Foucault, "Film and Popular Memory" reprinted in *Foucault Live* (Interviews, 1961–1984), edited by Sylvère Lotringer (New York: Semoitext(e), 1996), 122–32.
72. The script of *The Sorrow and the Pity* with an introduction by Stanley Hoffmann and translated by Mireille Johnston was published by Berkeley Publishing Corporation, New York, 1975. For a broader context of "negationism in France," see Susan Rubin Suleiman, *Crises of Memory and the Second World War* (Cambridge: Harvard University Press, 2006), especially 77–105.
73. On SHOAH, see Stuart Liebman (ed.), *Claude Lanzmann's Shoah: Key Essays* (New York: Oxford University Press, 2007).
74. Wulf Kahnsteiner, *In Pursuit of German Memory: History, Television and Politics after Auschwitz* (Athens: University of Ohio Press, 2006) and Judith Keilbach, *Geschichtsbilder und Zeitzeugen: zur Darstellung des Nationalsozialismus im Bundesdeutschen Fernsehen* (Münster: LIT Verlag, 2010).
75. Chapters on these films and relevant to the present argument are: Thomas Elsaesser, "Our Hitler — Film by Hans Jürgen Syberberg," in Karolien Machtans and Martin A. Ruehl (eds.), *Hitler — Films from Germany* (Palgrave MacMillan, 2012), 72–98, and Thomas Elsaesser, "Ingmar Bergman's The Serpent's Egg: Reflection on Reflections on Retro-Fashion," in Maaret Koskinen (ed.), *Ingmar Bergman Revisited* (London: Wallflower Press, 2008), 161–79.
76. See, among others, "Dossier on Heimat," *New German Critique*, no. 36 (Autumn, 1985), 3–24 and Christopher J. Wickham, "Representation and Mediation in Edgar Reitz's Heimat," *The German Quarterly*, 64, no. 1 (Winter, 1991), 35–45.
77. http://www.kluge-alexander.de/filmemacher/der-angriff-der-gegenwart-auf-die-uebrige-zeit.html
78. Whether television can ever fulfil this role has been a matter of intense debate. See, for instance, Michael Ignatieff, on the ethics of television: "Television images cannot assert anything; they can only instantiate something. Images of human suffering do not assert their own meaning; they can only instantiate a moral claim if those who watch understand themselves to be potentially under obligation to those they see." Michael Ignatieff, *The Warrior's Honour: Ethnic War and the Modern Conscience* (Toronto: Penguin Books, 1999), 11–12.

79. Christopher Isherwood, *The Berlin Stories* (New York: New Directions, 1963).
80. An intriguing example from East German cinema in this mode is JAKOB DER LÜGNER (JACOB THE LIAR, Frank Beyer, 1975, after the novel by Jurek Becker), where ghetto life is presented in such a way that the Jewish victim reverses his role not into that of a heroic resister, but a bystander. See Daniela Berghahn, *Hollywood Behind the Wall: The Cinema of East Germany* (Manchester: Manchester University Press, 2005), 92–94.
81. Landsberg, *Prosthetic Memory*, 20–21.
82. Landsberg has nuanced her "prosthetic memory" thesis in response to criticism, arguing that a complex ethical form of empathy is indeed compatible with what I am calling the aesthetics of "being there." Interestingly enough, she uses Polanski's THE PIANIST to make her case. See Alison Landsberg "Memory, Empathy, and the Politics of Identification," *International Journal of Politics, Culture, and Society* 22.2 (June 2009), 221–29.
83. On the figure of the "Musulmann" in the camps, see Giorgio Agamben, *Remnants of Auschwitz: The Witness and the Archive* (New York: Zone Books, 2002), 82–85, who borrowed the term from Primo Levi.
84. John Durham Peters, "Witnessing," *Media Culture Society* 23, no. 6 (November 2001), 709.
85. Ibid., 708–09.
86. "Szpilman's family have just learned that they will soon be deported; rather than just simply feel sorry for themselves however, their response is wide ranging; one family member wants to leave for the country, the other wants to fight, another is just baffled. These are natural human responses, which bring the victims to life and highlight the absurdity of the situation. [... The family members] are portrayed as real life characters who happen to be victims rather than victims who just happen to be characters." Laurent Kelly, "Anatomy of a Masterpiece," (http://whatculture.com/film/anatomy-of-a-masterpiece-roman-polanskis-the-pianist.php).
87. See, for instance, Judith Keilbach, *Geschichtsbilder und Zeitzeugen: Zur Darstellung des Nationalsozialismus im bundesdeutschen Fernsehen* (Münster, 2008); Wulf Kansteiner, "Entertaining Catastrophe: The Reinvention of the Holocaust in the Television of the Federal Republic of Germany," *New German Critique*, no. 90, Taboo, Trauma, Holocaust (Special issue, Autumn, 2003), 135–62; and Mark A Wolfgram, "The Holocaust through the Prism of East German Television: Collective Memory and Audience Perceptions," *Journal of Holocaust and Genocide Studies*, 20, no. 1 (Spring 2006), 57–79.

3

THE POLITICS AND POETICS OF PARAPRAXIS

On Some Problems of Representation in the New German Cinema

Preface: Germany's History as Memory Syndrome

At a certain point in the late 1970s, it will be recalled, the New German Cinema, which nominally dates back to 1962, began to show a marked concern with the recent German past, and more generally, with the questions of traumatic memory. In one sense, this turn to history as latency and trauma in cinema merely followed a similar turn in West German literature that came to be known as Vergangenheitsbewältigung: *"mastering the past," by confronting the legacy of the Hitler years, acknowledging the enormity of its crimes, but effectively reliving it as (post-)trauma. The biographies, autobiographies and memoirs that began to be published were themselves "belated," in that they were catching up with the divisive and emotional debates conducted among German historians. While this difficult, but so insistently explored topic of "coming to terms" has received extensive commentary—also in this volume—there remain nonetheless, when speaking of the filmic legacy of the 1960s and 1970s, some unanswered questions. These have to do with the different temporalities that this particular period in history has engendered, and the sense that the past is not being revisited by the present, so much as that it is always already visiting the present: in other words, the unbidden returns would be the traumatic aspect of this cultural memory. Especially notable is a particular paradox: no matter how many books are written, how many drama series and documentaries, compilation films or fiction films, oral histories and eyewitness testimonies are made and collected, or how much public debate and media attention is devoted to these topics, the notion persists that—in regard to Nazism and the Holocaust—something stays hidden, repressed, buried, unexplained, and therefore unexpiated. It is as if this particular past was meant to remain an eternal present, not making the transition from personal, embodied memory, to public, documented history. Why should this be so? The obvious answer is that the enormity of the atrocities committed, the irretrievable loss of so many innocent human lives, but also the loss of all moral standards and human values makes it imperative that these acts and their perpetrators should stand exposed forever in their infamy, and above all, that the victims should never be forgotten.*

Another answer, however, is that it is the cinema itself, which is the historical reason and epistemic condition that has made (not only this) history a permanent action-replay, in the sense that it revives the past as a perpetually relived presence, either consoling and life-affirming, or ghost-like and haunting. If the latter, it can become part of a repetition compulsion whose most visible symptom, and thus most plausible materialization in the last century is the trauma of the Holocaust. It would then be an open question whether it was the Holocaust that obliged the cinema to confront these different temporalities, or whether something inherent in the cinema is responsible—namely that it stages a presence where there is absence—which found in the Holocaust its most pertinent historical and ethical reference point.

Rather than decide right away which is which, I want to keep both possibilities in play on the assumption that at some level they may indeed imply or necessitate each other, as Gilles Deleuze famously suggested, when he tried to explain the transition from the "movement image" to the "time image." While I do touch briefly on the "time image" in a later chapter, the manner in which cinema and Holocaust memory implicate each other is in my general argument more grounded in the relation between absence and presence within the filmic images and narratives themselves. From these I extract or hope to discover another logic of representation, one that attributes a special value to absence, rather than to presence (in representation). I see here a distinct, and so far perhaps not fully appreciated, contribution of certain directors and films: some closely identified with the New German Cinema, others not.

As a film historian I tend to see the ongoing and seemingly interminable history-memory debate in Germany framed somewhat differently from the way it usually is presented by literary scholars and cultural historians.[1] *For instance, rather than asking what (positive-therapeutic or negative-trivializing) part the cinema—and television—played in West Germany's "mastering the past" (both at home and with its image in the world), I concentrate on the repetitions and returns per se, i.e., what role moving images themselves might have had in making this "coming to terms" such an apparently indefinitely drawn out process. What began in Germany in the 1970s and 1980s then spread throughout Western Europe, and since the 1990s has also includes the countries of Central and Eastern Europe: the reexamination and self-examination of WW II, in light of the persecution of ethnic or religious minorities, and the part played by the civilian population. If at first only Germany sought to refashion its identity as a nation through this "working through its history as (traumatic) memory," now it seems that the European Union as a whole is seeking to forge a supra-national identity by constantly remembering and commemorating the same period of Europe's twentieth-century history, and especially the (image-saturated) history of Nazism and the (image-less) memory of the Holocaust.*

Thus, the question of representation became central to the extent that I wanted to know how films and filmmakers enter the public sphere (and give rise to debate), not by giving accurate or authentic depictions of history, but by deploying the cinema's peculiar performativity in the service of staging this permanent present tense of the past. The ability of the cinema to produce presence I also see as a gain, albeit one that comes with an ethical mandate. By performativity in this context I understand first of all the fact that cinema is not a series of static images, but a procession of images and of image processing; that it is an ongoing exchange between spectator and screen; that it has to work positively with (deceptive) appearances, projection, repetition, doubling and make-believe.

At a more complex level, and in a different sense, the cinema's particular performativity is the subject of this chapter. By analyzing the various meanings of this term more closely, I hope to clarify my initial question, whether it is the cinema that makes the Holocaust a permanent present or the Holocaust that reveals the cinema's deferred, reversible, non-linear and non-synchronous temporalities.

Absence as Presence[2]

If the common assumption has been that looking for traces of the Holocaust in post-war West German films of the 1950s and 1960s is a vain endeavor,[3] it would seem that the same is no less true of the so-called New German Cinema of the 1970s. While in the films of some of the well-known names—Edgar Reitz, Alexander Kluge, Hans Jürgen Syberberg, Rainer Werner Fassbinder, Volker Schlöndorff—Nazi Germany, Hitler and especially the German family under National Socialism eventually became major topics, the Jewish experience of persecution and annihilation, however, rarely figured. Nor did the post-war Jewish diaspora and the difficult Jewish-German dialogue, already discussed as the "negative symbiosis" after Auschwitz, play a role in the films.[4] In the case of Wim Wenders and Werner Herzog, neither National Socialism nor the Holocaust are mentioned before the 1990s. The few occasions where Jewish characters do appear, their representations have invariably given offence. Elsewhere I discussed Fassbinder disastrously controversial play "The City, Garbage and Death," made into the film SCHATTEN DER ENGEL (Daniel Schmid, Germany/Switzerland, 1976), Syberberg's resentful remarks about West Germany after the war having too readily accepted the Jewish emigré version of "German" culture, or Edgar Reitz' *Heimat*, where the brief mention of deportations and the camps was seen to have alibi function at best.[5] What more plausible than to note a pervasive disavowal, and to conclude that in the face of these unimaginable horrors at such close proximity and the guilt-feelings they gave rise to, repression and invisibility had been the easier options? One could be forgiven for fearing that the most gifted generation of filmmakers in Germany since the 1920s had been guilty, not of the crimes against the Jews, of course, but of complicity with their disavowal. Or at the very least, they had sinned by omission, not breaking the silence, made deafening by the very clamor and violence with which the "sons" accused the "fathers" of their Nazi past.[6]

Such a judgment is, of course, retrospective and afflicted with the wisdom of hindsight, for it speaks from a doubly distanced vantage point: one that postdates 1979, the year the television series *Holocaust* (U.S., 1978) was first screened on German television (with momentous consequences for West Germany's media-memory), and postdates 1989, the year prior to German unification, after which the Holocaust became the abiding topic of Germany's public life, taking over—or being taken over by—television, as well as dominating literary and historical research for at least a decade. There are thus several points that this ubiquity of the Holocaust since the 1990s raises about its "absence" in the films from the 1960s and 1970s. First, one could not help noticing how this absence was not just a gap or an omission, but was always read across the tropes of "repression," "denial" and "disavowal." In other words, how perfectly legible this absence had become from the vantage point of a Freudian discourse of unconscious motives, and from the seeming security of one's own position of knowledge or mastery of this motivation.

An example of the performance of such a denial—barely commented on by critics at the time, but now almost jumping at the viewer—can be found in Alexander Kluge's first film ABSCHIED VON GESTERN/YESTERDAY'S GIRL (1966) where the heroine Anita G. appears before a judge for shoplifting. After going through her personal data and noting that her parents had been deported to Theresienstadt and their property confiscated, the judge provocatively asks whether Anita claims that what happened to her parents in 1938 had any bearings on the case for which she was being tried. "No" replies Anita, "none whatsoever." This scene, one could argue, makes denial visible, aggressively on the part of the judge, auto-aggressively on the part of Anita, and thus drawing the spectator's attention to the fact that "Theresienstadt" and what it stands for may indeed be a crucial fact in Anita's life and thus a motive for her actions. If today, the scene reverberates around this taboo-breaking mention of a concentration camp, at the time of the film's first release in 1966, it was read quite differently: the knowledge position of superior irony was entirely directed at the judge. Framed from the back with a thickset neck and a rasping voice, he stands as the epitome of the arrogant ex-Nazi, sitting in judgment over others when it should be he who probably deserves to be tried (given that most senior judges of the BRD well into the 1960s had served under Hitler). But the exchange also makes clear that the identification of Anita G. as Jewish does not thematize "the Holocaust" (or its absence) in German post-war society in the way that we now cannot but read the scene. After all, the very term (or its counter-term *Shoah*) would not have been in use in 1966, and before the 1967 Six-Day War, even in Israel, the fate of European Jews during WW II was rarely considered the crucial part of the nation's self-image as a courageous, combative, and self-confident.

This issue of framing and reframing is crucial in at least two respects. First, it suggests that the discourse from hindsight often implicitly relies on a fairly naïve notion of realism: the assumption that one could "accurately" or "fully" represent on film what it meant to be a Jew under the Nazi regime. It is as if, once the name had become a common designation, the Holocaust had not given rise to a major debate about the very limits of representation, indeed about the impossibility of representation, alongside the need for representation. Did this not oblige one to query the way "presence" and "representation" is equated, and to challenge any argument or work of fiction, where these terms are given a positive, normative value, in a binary opposition that made absence the purely negative term?

This very question posed itself when German films with Jewish protagonists did in fact appear, as happened in the 1990s, with films like AIMÉ UND JAGUAR, ABRAHAMS GOLD, MESCHUGGE, VIEHJUD LEVI, ROSENSTRASSE. Irrespective of the historical basis of the stories, a problematic appropriation of Jewish lives and Jewish suffering was taking place, proving that "the pain of others," in Susan Sontag's phrase, may require more than empathy.[7] The result is that the Jewish characters' newly acquired presence and visibility on German screens did not fill a void, it merely made the void more apparent.

Perhaps out of a sense of loyalty for the filmmakers of my generation, perhaps out of the realization that I, too, had not noticed that there might be a problem not only about there being virtually no Jewish characters in the films, but also that too easily, one tended to think about German Jews in terms of "us" and "them" rather than "us" and "us," I began to rethink my own critical premises, as well as the premises of those now expecting—and apparently getting—due representation. I came to believe that the debate about positive figures and negative stereotyping, of sympathetic Jews or unsympathetic Jews, in short, the typical identity politics of minority representation had in this instance missed a crucial point and that an altogether different conceptual focus would be needed to come to grips with the issue.

In other words, by the same Freudian logic that spoke of repression or denial, regarding the films from the 1950s to the 1970s, one would want to ask: what is it that in turn is now barely seen, what is being overlooked in the intensive probing and looking that took place during the 1990s and beyond?[8] For instance, to demand, in the interest of the politics of representation, that Jewish characters assume significant roles in West German films arguably falsifies an even more important reality. Given that the aim of the Nazis had been to eliminate the Jews from Germany, and that they largely succeeded in doing so, the Jews' significance after 1945 was above all, precisely, their absence: a human absence (from public life and the body politic), a material absence (the physical destruction of the signs and evidence of centuries of German-Jewish presence), but also an absence in the minds—the thoughts and emotions—of the Germans themselves, and thus absent also in the minds of the New German Cinema's protagonists, even if their *Weltschmerz*, longing and seemingly incurable melancholia (in the films of Wenders and Herzog, for example) can be—and perhaps should be—construed as hinting at something that was missing.

In other words, the absence of Jews in the films of the New German Cinema in the first instance confirms, mirrors and in this sense, truthfully records (the enormity of) the fact that *their absence* in the public and private life of West Germany in the 1960s and 1970s *was not missed*. The issue becomes one of representation itself. We now "see" the nonrepresentation of the Jews, the absence of positive Jewish protagonists, the failure of "German" protagonists to show signs of regret or repentance, and see it as evidence of bad faith, bad conscience and cover-up. But what exactly was it that we think was not "seen" or not "represented" in the 1960s and 1970s? What would the presence of say, credible, positive or sympathetic Jewish characters in these films have signified? The depiction by a German filmmaker of the Holocaust from the perspective of the victims, or a credible version of the Jewish experience in Germany after the war would be both too much and too little. Too much, in that it would have presumed an act of empathy, as well as an understanding of the "other" that clearly was not present at the time. Too little, in that it might easily have given the illusion of normality, i.e., that Jews in Germany after 1945 could simply be Germans among Germans, or "people like you and me." Furthermore, the good Jew, the positive identification figure in a fiction film easily becomes a screen of projection that compensates either latent aggression or unacknowledged guilt-feelings. It was a trap that Fassbinder consistently wanted to expose in his films (also with respect to other minorities: foreign workers, homosexuals) and that Henryk M. Broder once satirized in his (imaginary) West German citizen who says: "If I take the trouble to be a philo-Semite, the least I can expect is that the Jews know to behave themselves."[9]

Broder's quip suggests that, if the Jews were missing from the films of the New German Cinema, their obligatory presence in so many films from the 1990s became so problematic, because the identity-politics of positive representation disguise another particular burden of representation. In any film made by a German director after 1945, I argued in the previous chapter, a Jewish character carries this burden of representation, since he or she is either the signifier of a radical and irrecoverable "otherness," at once "sacred" and "inhuman" or conversely, a character's Jewishness is no more than a psychological attribute in an individual's fate, and thus not capable of assuming the weight of the knowledge of what was to be the collective as well as individual fate of so many millions of Jews at the hands of Germans. In this sense, the framing and reframing just discussed works both ways: depicting the Jew, it hides (the meaning of) her absence.

But even then, the question of representing German Jewish relations is imperfectly put if it does not factor in another problem. For this invisibility did not go in one direction only: from the "Germans" to the "Jews." Invisibility was the order of the day, also among the small Jewish communities who made Germany their home after 1945. Their members kept themselves doubly invisible: invisible to the Germans, for fear of rousing hostility and resentment, which might have hampered ongoing negotiations behind the scenes with the federal authorities about compensation and reparation. But Jews living in Germany made themselves invisible also because of the disapproval they knew they were exposed to in Israel and the United States, for continuing to live in Germany, the land of the murderers. It was the protest action led by the Jewish community in Frankfurt to force a ban on the performance of Fassbinder's play "Garbage, The City and Death" in 1985 that first broke the collective self-restraint on visibility.

Presence as Parapraxis

The question to be put to the directors of the New German Cinema would therefore have to have been a somewhat different one. Not why did you not show Jews in your films, but how were you able to show what was not there, especially if its not-being-there is not missed, and furthermore, aggravated by a self-imposed invisibility? This raises the additional problem: how can the cinema show this missing as missing, how can it "perform" this double missing, and come to terms with it? But even then, the matter of representing German-Jewish relations in the New German Cinema cannot be settled, unless it also includes the insisted upon, frequently resented, and never adequately answered "demand" on the part of the rest of the world, to give a response, take responsibility, make amends, or be accountable. This inadequacy of Germans—individually and collective, through their politicians and in the arts—in meeting this demand compounds and brings together several kinds of impossibility, for it provides another ever-present backdrop to the all too perfect legibility of this absence, with which I began.

I think German directors did supply possible—and intriguing—answers to these dilemmas, which is why, rather than looking at the representation of Jews in post-war German cinema, my project took the mutual entanglements between Germans and Jews *after* "Auschwitz" as its point of departure, and at the same time, once more examined at the Red Army Faction's (RAF) violent reaction to the earlier (1950s) phase of "repression," "amnesia" and "disavowal" of the father-generation, which was so often given as one of the reasons for the terrorist attacks, the kidnaps and murders that the sons and daughters then undertook in the 1970s. Even then, it was a dubious argument, but one that, for a time, did win them sympathizers among the young and intellectuals, not for their deeds, but for the shared sense that something needed to be uncovered.

These deadlocks around representation can—such is my main argument—only be opened up, if absence and presence are not (only) construed antithetically. The possibility of presence should be recognized within absence, and accordingly, it may only be within absence that one can begin to look for evidence of presence, not against it. Often, the name for such a presence within absence is *trauma*, but in a situation where one is dealing with (different kinds of) "victims" and (several generations of) "perpetrators," other forms of being active and passive, of absence and presence are also crucial: these multi-layered manifestations of agency I want to bring together under the single notion of *parapraxis*.

Why Parapraxis?

One of the traditional ways in which Germany's "coming to terms" with its Nazi past has been discussed in film and cultural studies is by invoking the Freudian distinction between mourning and melancholy, as ways of coping with loss. In particular, the term *mourning work* has been used, but mostly as a negative, an absence—articulated as the expected response to a demand (to mourn the loss of so many human beings), in respect to which Germans, both private and in public, were assumed to have failed in the first decades of the post-war period.[10] Failed mourning work is a concept that I promoted in this context,[11] but one I would wish to revise and modify, first by giving the notion of failure a different meaning and value, and second by challenging the primacy usually given to "mourning" over "melancholy."[12] My claim now is that the absence of the Holocaust is made present through some of its most significant consequences in the New German Cinema of the 1970s, provided one accepts that the figures of such presence-in-absence do not function according to either the repression/disavowal mode, nor conform to the model of mourning work as (successful) "working through": of loss, of decathecting from the internalized love object, and of letting go. Instead, one should imagine a different kind of mourning work, somewhere between the "not letting go" of melancholia, and the "acting out" of mourning, prior to "working through."[13] The reinterpretation of failure and the redefinition of mourning work as unsuccessful "working through" come together in what I am calling "presence as parapraxis," implied by and seen as a consequence of "absence as presence."

Why parapraxis? Parapraxis refers to a psychic phenomenon that Sigmund Freud introduced in his *Psychopathology of Everyday Life*, and is James Strachey's neologism for the German compound noun *Fehlleistung*. The German term is, as explained in the introduction, more relevant for my purposes, not least because *Fehl* can mean both failure and missing, and *Leistung* refers specifically to the performative aspect, as well as to the concept of "work," as in mourning work.[14] Freud's own definition is as follows:

> By parapraxis, I understand the occurrence in healthy and normal people of such events as forgetting words and names that are normally familiar

> to one, forgetting what one intends to do, making slips of the tongue and the pen, misleading, misreading, mislaying things and being unable to find them, losing things, making mistakes against one's better knowledge, and certain habitual gestures and movements. [...] Parapraxes are full blown psychical phenomenon and always have a meaning and an intention. They serve definite purposes, which owing to the prevailing psychological situation, cannot be expressed in any other way. These situations, as a rule, involve a psychical conflict which prevents the underlying intention from finding direct expression and diverts it along indirect paths.[15]

The phenomenon Freud is describing is sufficiently familiar as an everyday occurrence for it to have earned the generic name "Freudian slip." I use parapraxis, however, not primarily in the usual sense of the Freudian slip, as a "slip of the tongue," or a lapse in attention. Parapraxis implies also effort, a voluntary or involuntary persistence, usually one with unexpected or unintended results, including reversals of cause and effect, or displacements in time and space. For instance, one feature of parapraxis I highlight is the way it often seems to figure "the right thing at the wrong place, the wrong thing at the right time." An example of such an explicit parapraxis would be the final scenes of Fassbinder's THE MARRIAGE OF MARIA BRAUN (1980), when the heroine places a rose on a hat stand, and her handbag in the flower-vase, as prelude to intentionally/unintentionally causing the fatal explosion that kills her and her companions.

Yet the reasons why I have opted for this rather unusual term in order to come to grips with the instabilities, asymmetries, hidden power-relations, deferrals, returns and reversals of German "history" in the mode of "memory," and of memory as the traumatic, but necessary failure of "mastering the past" are more complicated and manifold.

First of all, shifting from "working through" to parapraxis would not discard the idea of either mourning or melancholia as (valid) forms of "coming to terms." On the contrary, it would clarify and expand their significance to include the other stages named in Freud's original formulation: "remembering, repeating," along with "working through," as well as giving a new meaning to the "not letting go" of melancholia. By giving especially the stubbornness of repetition a productive role, one might come to a new understanding of that area where "mourning work" as *acknowledgement* (rather than appropriation) of the pain of others appeared to have failed most spectacularly, namely in the (missing or failed) dialogue between Germans and Jews after 1945 and well into the 1980s. Parapraxis would turn this around, by accepting miscommunication as part of the "given" of such a dialogue. More than that: the constantly reiterated and (self-)proclaimed "failure" would paradoxically be among the most positive and hopeful signs, notably in respect of my central question. The absence of representation and the failure of mourning work would become the index of a presence, whose double negation in the films is their aesthetic (and maybe even political) achievement.

Second, the compound nature of the German term allows me to make several kinds of distinction: between *Fehlleistung* as "performed failure," and *Fehlleistung* as "failed performance," but also between "*Fehlleistung* as mourning work" and "mourning work as *Fehlleistung*." This may seem like juggling with words (and their components), but I trust that the relevance of making these distinctions becomes evident as the argument unfolds, as well as in the individual chapters dealing with specific examples, where the hypothesis is that the films I have examined implicitly take the first two stages of the process of grieving to be as necessary and indispensable as the third, which means that "remembering, repeating," too, have their textual effects and figurative presences. With regard to the "mourning work" associated with the Holocaust, we may collectively and as a national culture (after the first fifty years or so of "remembering"), have reached or become stuck at the stage of "repetition." It would indicate that the very ubiquity and omnipresence of the Holocaust as focus of attention and media phenomenon in the 1990s actively partakes in such mourning work, although in a way that makes its compulsive iteration symptomatic either for its in-completion (as "working through"), or for its "ethical" value (as melancholia's stubborn clinging to the lost object).

Assuming, therefore, that compulsive repetition in the form of parapraxis—a third, somewhat extended meaning of the term—is an integral part of this particular kind of mourning work, my further distinction becomes crucial. "Mourning work as parapraxis (i.e., failed performance)" would thus designate the officially prescribed acts of public mourning in West Germany. It all too often, but with predictable regularity, resulted in a kind of repetitive ubiquity of unintended mishaps and embarrassing *faux pas*—thereby exemplifying what I shall call *a politics of parapraxis*. "Parapraxis (i.e., performance of failure) as mourning work," on the other hand, would name the various counter-strategies that I see films and filmmakers adopting in their way of saying the unsayable, or representing that which cannot be directly represented, thereby performing a *poetics of parapraxis*.

To give some specific examples of the politics of parapraxis, one could point to the many incidents and occasions in the public life of the old and the new Federal Republic where politicians, diplomats and even writers provoked scandals by their statements, actions or utterance: from the "incident" caused by a German diplomat at a Russian Embassy reception in May 1955, who angered his hosts when he refused to toast to the liberation of Germany by the victorious Red Army in 1945 (as a patriot he saw it as a "defeat"), to the novelist Martin Walser, who, as late as 1998 and as publicly as in his acceptance speech of the Frankfurt Book Fair Peace Prize, meant to pay his respects to the memory of the Jews when he spoke of Auschwitz as the "moral stick" still used by the world to beat Germany. The latter prompted a violent, despairing but also predictable attack from Ignatz Bubis, the then Head of the Council of Jews in Germany.[16] In between these two dates lie a sheer unending catalogue of such public spats and scandals, of which the Helmut Kohl-Ronald Reagan visit to the Bitburg military cemetery in 1985, in which Reagan equated the German soldiers buried there with the victims of the Holocaust, and the speech by Philip Jenninger commemorating the so-called Kristallnacht in November 1988 wherein he attempted to explain the attraction of National Socialism without adequately disassociating himself from its ideas are perhaps the most egregious examples.[17]

In contrast (or as response) to this, elements of a *poetics of parapraxis* can be found in the New German Cinema, which in the 1970s has given several examples of "performed failure," where figurative tropes such as catachresis or zeugma, stylistic peculiarities such as repetition or *faux raccord* (mismatched) montage, as well as rhetorical strategies of reversal and irony all point to acts of "performative failure," whose misalignments, double-takes and "parallax" effects together constitute a kind of "mourning work-in-progress," an ongoing return and repetition around something which, perhaps only now and certainly only with hindsight, can be read and decipher differently.

Besides the works to which I devote separate chapters, there are films like In a Year of 13 Moons (R.W. Fassbinder), Germany in Autumn (A. Kluge et al.), The Patriot (A. Kluge), Hitler a Film from Germany (H.J. Syberberg), Fitzcarraldo (W. Herzog) and Images of the World and the Inscription of War (H. Farocki), where one is now struck by the often excessive, tragic or absurd ways of enacting failure or futility in many of the narrative premises, verbal discourse or individual scenes. Take, for instance, Fitzcarraldo's quest to build an opera house in the Amazon rainforest, while hauling a boat over a mountain; take the tragi-comic love of a male transvestite for a heterosexual man in In a Year of Thirteen Moons, or take Farocki's documentation of the Americans' failure to realize that their reconnaissance planes had photographed the death camps of Auschwitz and Birkenau as early as May 1944, but did not pay any attention to them because they were not looking for them. All would be examples of *Fehl-Leistungen*, constituting either the films' very premise or woven into the inner fabric of the films' narratives.

Thus, while the German public sphere demonstrated time and time again the uncanny force of failed performance, the New German Cinema seemed to be engaged in an equally remarkable exercise in the performance of failure, or as I would gloss it now, "successfully performed failure." Freud himself hinted at such a possibility: "It has repeatedly happened that a creative writer has made use of a slip of the tongue or some other parapraxis as an instrument for producing an imaginative effect" adding: "the author (could) intellectualize it by providing [parapraxis] with a sense so as to suit his own purposes."[18]

In several scenes from the films of Fassbinder, Kluge, Achternbusch but also Konrad Wolf's somewhat earlier film Sterne and Ingmar Bergman's

German-produced THE SERPENT'S EGG, I have tried to document the extent, but also function of such a veritable "poetics of parapraxis."[19] The main purpose, it would seem, is to forestall an all too literal legibility or psychologically motivated "realism," and to enact a more rebus-like mode of representation. The results are narratives, whose turning points are signposted with more or less overt moments of enigmatic visuals, perceptual discrepancies or cognitive dissonances: precisely, ways of figuring an absence as presence, but in the mode of parapraxis. In a second move, the viewer is invited to make sense of this puzzling incoherence, forcing him or her into an allegorical mode of reading, while holding the image or narrative information against the hitherto invisible backdrop of an embattled or contested history that makes the underlying realities palpable: as "unreconciled" or incomplete. What is not there can be made to appear by the enigmatic pull of an illegible presence. The unspoken and the not-seen, which I claim is typical for (part of) the New German Cinema, renders such parapraxes only legible against a double or triple frame of reference to Germany's history: first, the recentering of our understanding of the twentieth century around the universalized Holocaust discourse; second, the "negative symbiosis" of Germans and Jews after 1945, and finally, the "reaction to a reaction" by consecutive generations, in response to so-called Hot Autumn of 1977 (the most serious incidents of terrorism in the Federal Republic), an episode which, as I indicate in another chapter, is being rewritten every ten years, and forms the other side of a past that will not pass. In both public discourse and the cinema (e.g., films like DEUTSCHLAND IM HERBST, TODESSPIELE, DIE INNERE SICHERHEIT, BAADER or DER BAADER-MEINHOF KOMPLEX) the rise and demise of RAF functions as yet another layer of the reflexive-recursive memory of the Nazi period.

Parapraxis, then, describes the type of (symbolic) action that arises when a documentary or realist mode of representation—meant to give us the illusion of witnessing a state of affairs either by "being there," or from a presumed position of full knowledge—contains a remainder or registers a blur that troubles the implied transparency of the "facts." Parapraxis adds the counter-knowledge of their implications, and the doubts and self-doubt that are attached to the facts' apparent self-evidence.

Yet rather than being a nagging doubt that impedes or muffles action through hesitancy, this other reality pushes equally hard for purposive, if self-divided action. The energy of such parapractic action in this case comes from the urgency of an impossible dialogue where, across the official discourse of Germany "mastering the past," a mandate of accountability (with West Germany as moral representative and legal successor of the German Reich), confronts a demand for taking responsibility (as well as making financial reparations and amends)—each, as it were, rendering the other at once impossible, necessary, inaccessible, and unrepresentable. It is these deadlocks, I argue, that produce the *Fehlleistungen*, both in politics and in the films. Yet the two public spheres relate to each other in a-symmetric mirror-fashion: to the instances of failed performance of public life, the reflexivity of the films responds with performed failure. The latter would in turn be the allegorical modes of the former, refiguring *Fehl* (failure) and *Leistung* (performance) in inverse relation to each other. Loss becomes (hit-and-) miss, miss is mis-, and mis- is a symptom of the continuous work on the image flows and media feeding frenzies, the work on the non-chronological temporalities of history, the work on the discourses of guilt and responsibility, on the moments of omission and commission.

The Uses of Parapraxis

By proposing parapraxis as a poetics (and thus a form of symbolic action), I am aware of taking some risks. As a central concept in my attempt to understand how a film's mode of agency and address might instantiate dialog between parties that are not prepared to "listen from where the other speaks" (or indeed, to listen at all), *parapraxis* is my answer also to questions I have not fully posed: distinct but interrelated questions that relate, variously, to deadlocks in film studies (about embodiment and vision), in the "politics of representation" of cultural studies (about who can speak on behalf of another), and the history/memory-debate in the humanities more generally (about authenticity, evidence and truth). As this opens up fields much wider than I can address here and goes beyond the case of Germany and German cinema, I want to limit myself to a set of remarks that outline and explore not the debates and deadlocks themselves, but the more formal features of *parapraxis* that make me believe that it is indeed a conceptual instrument, rich in resonance as well as strong enough to carry the considerable burden I am placing on it.

First of all, I want to claim that *parapraxis* can constitute a valid or legitimate poetics, and, in line with Freud's own vocabulary, implies a formal system, a rhetoric and a set of tropes like zeugma, hyperbole or metonymic substitution. It acts as a "quid-pro-quo" (this for that), but under conditions where no equivalence can settle or stabilize itself. In such a parapractic poetics, the normal codes or conventions of representation are suspended, subverted, and the substitution process this for that is destabilized, as in the example of the right thing at the wrong place, or the wrong image at the right place. In addition, a mode of indirect speech, close to irony or catachresis, supports a rhetoric of indirection and substitution, the structure of an exchange that is both necessary and programmed for failure. I expand on this point of uneven and impossible exchange in chapter 10, "From Mastering the Past to Managing Guilt."

Second, as already indicated, I think parapraxis complements, if it does not altogether replace, other more familiar Freudian terms such as *repression* and *disavowal* which are in many ways quite problematic and clichéd concepts when used to explain the coexistence of two seemingly incompatible "speaking positions," or in my example, the seeming absence of Jewish characters from films made in Germany during the 1960s and 70s, and their corresponding over-representation since the 1990s. In other words, a history of Germans and Jews since 1945 needs to be able to account for the absence of the fate of the Jews from public consciousness in the 1950s, their displaced presence in the turbulent 1960s, the melodramatic public response to the Holocaust in the 1970s, and their stereotypical representation since the 1990s? In such a history, *repression* and *disavowal* do not allow for the option of *positively* figuring absence, in the mode that I have called "absence as presence," nor for its opposite, the too insistent display, like a permanently fondled fetish-object, while "presence as parapraxis" has the advantage of drawing attention to the dynamics of the supplement, the remainder and the gap, as well as to reversible positions of agency implied by failure and performance.

Third, as pointed out, parapraxis can usefully alter the terms of the debate around "collective memory" and "mastering the past" and the deadlocks it invariably produces in the German context, where the term *mourning work* always gives rise to the awkward question "whose victims"? Instead of responding solely to the irrecoverable loss and unexpiated wrongs suffered by the victims of the Holocaust, officially prescribed *Trauerarbeit* cannot but conjure up the Germans expelled from the East or killed in the firestorms of the bombing raids: victims as a consequence of or in retaliation for Nazism, but whose unmourned memory stubbornly returns. Parapraxis would here be the name of the deadlock where the missing willingness to offering solace and compassion to the victims and survivors of the Holocaust encounters the demand for expressions of regret and contriteness from the perpetrators, whose kin and descendants have their own grief and grievances to attend to. The chief example of such parapractic mourning work—one that pays tribute to both kinds of victimhood not by comparing them, but by enacting them performatively, in the manner of compulsive repetitions, cognitive realignments and tragic-grotesque inversions—are the writings and films of Alexander Kluge, to whom I devote a separate chapter.[20]

Fourth, insofar as parapraxis is a form of agency, but one manifesting the gaps between intentionality and rationality, while also pointing to the different temporalities or "timing" of an action, the term also wants to engage with notions of active and passive, voluntary agency and involuntary memory. By defining parapraxis not as the "slip of the tongue," or the lapse in attention, I focus on it as a kind of effort, a persistence, even a tragic-comic heroic "insistence": usually one with unexpected or unintended results, including typical reversals of cause and effect.

I am aware here of a possible misunderstanding regarding the use of the term *performativity*. While this notion has, in the wake of Judith Butler's *Bodies that Matter* (and its misreadings), been widely and enthusiastically embraced as a term of resistance and subversion against the generally naturalizing pressures and power of the socially or ideologically enforced construction of identities (of gender, race and ethnicity), this is not the way I read the "performance of failure" in the New German Cinema (and elsewhere). Whereas there is a tendency in the humanities today to make the body the ground of self-hood and self-worth, for which performativity is the appropriate mode of agency, parapraxis wants precisely to draw attention to the nonalignment of body and agency, granting neither the body nor performativity automatic autonomy or foundational priority.[21] At the limit, my idea of *parapraxis* is a critique of performativity, not its confirmation or celebration. It speaks to the literary scholar Anselm Haverkamp's hope for a form of cultural studies and hermeneutics "which is aware of the latency within every kind of (self-)evidence, and knows about the contingency attached to any kind of performativity, including one's own."[22]

Parapraxis, then, would be a critique of too positively constructivist a conception of performativity, because of its insistence on failure and slippage, and indeed contingency (that is, parapraxis as the contingency to which a subsequent situation retroactively attributes desire or intent).[23] Yet I would maintain that a parapractic poetics does entail a bodily or embodied mode of consciousness which also stands in a determinate relation to the embodiment of memory and trauma—mediated, however, through the signifier and its slippages, in language, sounds and in images.

Parapraxis as Stolperstein: Tripping, Slipping, Stumbling

When trying to bring together agency and memory, the semantics of parapraxis become especially revealing in light of the various terms coined by Freud's translators. In a review of the new Penguin *Freud* edition, Michael Wood singles out parapraxis as a particularly telling case of how translation is already an interpretation: "Paul Keegan in his introduction to *The Psychopathology of Everyday Life*, follows Bruno Bettelheim in complaining about versions of Freud's *Fehlleistung*, his word for what we know as a slip. It's true that the German word is a fine one, made up of the idea of missing or failing (*Fehl*) and the idea of achievement or performance (*Leistung*). Our achievement is to miss the target. And our miss is an achievement [...]. Now *parapraxis* doesn't get us very close to this, but 'slip' is terrific. It's stealthy where the German is explicit, and it performs the action it fails to name, the intention we'd like to believe is an accident."[24]

Wood has picked up on the reversibility potential of the German compound in much the same way I am exploiting it. For him, however, the English colloquial understanding of a Freudian slip are also pertinent. A slip in his sense would be translated back into German as *Ausrutscher*, which has both a literal meaning, namely slipping on a wet or icy surface, and thus entailing the failings of a body to keep balance, but also a metaphorical meaning, as does the English tripping up, usually explained in both English and German by the French word *faux pas*. Faux pas, on the other hand, in its literal meaning, is closely related to the Greek word *skandalos* (scandal), which literally means stumbling-block, which, when translated back into German, gives us *stolpern*, often used also metaphorically in the combination *ein Stolperstein*, in turn related to the metaphoric meaning of *ein Stein des Anstosses*, that is: a cause for offense, but also reminiscent of the philosophical use of *Anstoss* in Johann Gottlieb Fichte, which denotes the (internal) blockage, experienced as (external) check that sets in motion the formation of the I or the subject.[25] *Stolpern* in turn translates as *trébucher* in French, which is the term used by Marcel Proust for describing one of the triggers of memory in *A la recherche du temps perdu*, the uneven, wobbly cobblestone, on which Marcel trips in Venice, and which makes him decide to devote the rest of his life to recalling such moments in writing. If one adds that *Stolpersteine* (literally stumbling stones) is the name of a project by the Cologne artist Gunter Demnik, to commemorate all the victims of Nazi persecution, by placing small brass plates in the shape of cobblestones on the sidewalk in front of their last known address, then parapraxis as stumbling or tripping becomes a mnemotechnic reminder that is meant to make us stop in our tracks, and reflect. By interrupting our stride, the stumbling stone redirects our attention, bending purposiveness and intentionality towards remembrance and giving Holocaust memory a local habitation and a name.[26]

There is yet another reason for me to choose the term, which has to do with the degree to which parapraxis involves an act of attempted communication ("failed," or "successfully failed" as I have presented it). As Freud notes, parapraxis presupposes a dynamic link with the other, who is the one that alerts us to it:

> The occurrence of parapraxis requires the following to be the case:
>
> a) It must not exceed a certain measure, which, however much its limits are set by our own estimation, has to remain within the spectrum of normalcy.
>
> b) It must have clear signs of a momentary and temporary aberration. [For there to be parapraxis] we have at all times to consider ourselves capable of executing the action/ performance correctly. When corrected by another person, we must immediately recognize both the direction of the correction, and the mistake made by our own psychic apparatus.
>
> c) If we ourselves notice the parapraxis, we must not be conscious of its hidden motivation, but will be tempted to ascribe it to inattention, or to present it as purely contingent and accidental.[27]

In other words, only when pointed out or noticed by another does a mistake become a parapraxis, and therefore crucial to Freud's limiting conditions is the double structure of dialogue that he stipulates. On the one hand, a *parapraxis* implies a dialogue between me and myself, whose dynamics the *parapraxis* manifests in the very act of momentary failure ("we have at all times to consider ourselves capable of executing the action/performance correctly"). On the other hand, a *parapraxis* requires the presence of another person ("when we are corrected by another person, we must immediately recognize both the direction of the correction, and the mistake made by our own psychic apparatus"). Thus, Freud stipulates that a listener should notify the speaker of his slip, and that the speaker then has to be able to recognize the hidden logic and meaning. However, at the same time, the speaker will normally attribute his *parapraxis* to carelessness, inattention or contingency. In Freud's seemingly self-contradictory formulation, *parapraxis* as an inter-personal phenomenon thus becomes an enabler of dialogue, even in a potentially antagonistic situation, and even in the face of disavowal, while allowing for contingency and chance: all, however, in the mode of "failure and performance." To be told one has committed a Freudian slip is not agreeable: one has allowed the other to look behind the scenes, as it were, into one's own theater of the self. But this momentary exposure of the creaking machinery of self-control can open new conduits of communication where others are blocked, leading to new insight and understanding. What the poetics of parapraxis suggest is that such a dialogue is most "successful" when its unintended consequences and unspoken resentments enter into the speech situation itself, rather than be excluded or repressed. With respect to memory and disavowal, then, *it is not that the past is repressed, but it is the present situation that overwhelms*, and this "too much" of conflicted knowledge manifests itself as *parapraxis*. On the one hand, parapraxis is the form that trauma can take in the present. On the other hand, parapraxis is also a sign of the willingness to deal with its manifestations and consequences. Placed within the context of entering into a difficult dialogue—which always has to assume that the default value is failed communication—parapraxis becomes a theoretically more promising concept not only than "repression," "disavowal" but, in respect of the "politics of representation," more promising even than the always demanded and never delivered "correct" representation of (… the Jew, the Nazi, the victim, the bystander, the perpetrator).

Finally, *parapraxis*, while clearly derived from Freud, and what he called the "psychopathology of everyday life," can also be understood in the context of systems theory, where *parapraxis* constitutes an example of positive feedback, that is, a failure of internal self-regulation between a system and its environment. *Parapraxis* asks what the locus of agency is in any feedback loop, and answers that it is not a locus but a circuit, reversible and indeterminate. It is the noise that goes with the signal, while nonetheless making available a body as material support, and keeping a social or interpersonal space open for the public effects of this internally/externally directed, nonregulated agency. The apparent failure of self-regulation manifest in *parapraxes* becomes the very sign of possible change, a hopeful gesture that is open towards the other, in the very act of seeming to foreclose it.

Conclusion: Out of Sync and yet the Recto and Verso of Each Other

I have discussed and deconstructed the original German term for Freud's *parapraxis* at some length to make both a historical and a theoretical point. By splitting the word into its component parts, and showing the reversibility of the respective references, I wanted to arrive at what appeared to me a small but crucial distinction (*Fehlleistung* as failed performance, *Fehlleistung* as performed failure) between the *parapraxes* of public life, so often present at acts of commemoration and official state occasions, and a possible poetics or rhetoric of *parapraxis*, to be found in the films of Fassbinder, Kluge, Achternbusch, Farocki and others. In short, I wanted to draw attention to the oddly appropriate incongruities and mismatches, which these filmmakers either discovered in the fabric of social and interpersonal situations and their human agents, or which they produced through their filmic procedures of narrative plotting, editing and juxtaposition. While in the previous chapter I concentrated on the different kinds of "burden of representation" around the depiction of the Holocaust on film, especially from the perspective of German directors, I would argue, by way of concluding this chapter, that my formula for some of the films of the New German Cinema—"absence as presence, presence as parapraxis"—may also apply to other films, directors and other national cinemas, where similarly traumatic histories have to be negotiated in view of finding a "usable past" that permits each side to enter into dialogue or envisage a shared future. Thus, the concept of parapraxis has been applied to Palestinian cinema and to the films of the American director Sam Fuller. [28] I have extended it to a reading of recent Hollywood films that have race as their traumatic, absent-present referent.[29]

The potential for such a wider relevance underlines two aspects of parapraxis: first, it allows one to turn to the English meaning of the term, and view it as a "praxis beside itself" also in a temporal sense, as a praxis yet to come, where the failed performance would render visible and palpable the elements in place for a future action, with the double negative once again sustaining both necessity and urgency. Second, the term's usefulness and viability in historical contexts other than the Holocaust and Germany's "mastering the past" may clarify the question with which I began, namely whether there is something inherently parapractic in the cinema itself that finds in traumatic situations the objective correlative of its own functioning as a recording and a reproduction apparatus, when capturing the unique moment and replaying it forever: two modalities out of sync with each other, and yet the recto and verso of cinema. Cinematic representation always puts in play more information and data than can be contained by meaning-making and narrative, and as a form of embodied thought and performative speech, for which physical action will always be only a parapractic support, it needs absence as the space in which presence can emerge.

Notes

1. One of the main proponents of this debate has been Aleida Assmann, writer of numerous articles and books, notably *Erinnerungsräume. Formen und Wandlungen des kulturellen Gedächtnisses* (Munich: C. H. Beck, 1999).
2. This passage and a few other paragraphs are taken from "Absence as Presence, Presence as Parapraxis" in *Framework*, 49, no. 1 (Spring 2008), 106–20. My thanks to the editors for permission to republish these parts.
3. Films made in the GDR did feature Jews, but usually in the context of the "anti-fascist" struggle, which became the regime's official doctrine of resistance. For a more nuanced and historically researched account of this "absence" in the West and "presence" in the East, see the project and databank Cinematographie des Holocaust, jointly coordinated by the Fritz Bauer Institute Frankfurt, Cinegraph Hamburg and the Deutsche Filminstitut/Filmmuseum Frankfurt, and supported with publications such as C. Dillmann, R. Loewy (eds.), *Die Vergangenheit in der Gegenwart* (Frankfurt/M: DIF, 2001). The project's website is http://www.fritz-bauer-institut.de/cinematographie.htm
4. Dan Diner, "Negative Symbiose — Deutsche und Juden nach Auschwitz," *Babylon*, 1 (1986), 9–20.
5. Thomas Elsaesser, Subject Positions, Speaking Positions: from *Holocaust*, *Our Hitler*, and *Heimat* to *Shoah* and *Schindler's List*," in Vivian Sobchack (ed.), *The Persistence of History: Cinema, Television, and the Modern Event* (New York: Routledge, 1995), 145–83.
6. See Thomas Elsaesser, "Antigone Agonistes: Urban Guerrilla or Guerrilla Urbanism? The Red Army Faction, *Germany in Autumn* and *Death Game*" (http://www.rouge.com.au/4/antigone.html).
7. Susan Sontag, *Regarding the Pain of Others* (New York: Farrar, Straus and Giroux, 2002).
8. In the last two decades, there has hardly been a film or a television program made in Germany with a twentieth-century historical setting that did not have archive footage from the Holocaust, a witness from the camps, a survivor, or spokespersons from the Jewish Community. Similarly, the new Federal capital of Berlin presents itself to the world mainly through three symbolic sites: no longer the Brandenburg Gate, but the Reichstag with the new glass dome, no longer the Victory column but the restored synagogue in the Oranienburgerstrasse, and no longer the Kaiser Wilhelm Memorial Church but Daniel Libeskind's Jewish Museum.
9. Henryk M. Broder, *Der ewige Antisemit. Über Sinn und Funktion eines beständigen Gefühls* (Frankfurt/M: S. Fischer Verlag, 1986).
10. The assumption was mainly based on an extrapolation from Alexander and Margarethe Mitscherlich's influential study *Die Unfähigkeit zu Trauern* (München: Pieper, 1967), in English: *The Inability to Mourn* (New York: Grove Press, 1975). See also Eric Santner, *Stranded Objects: Mourning, Memory, and Film in Postwar Germany* (Ithaca, NY: Cornell University Press, 1993).
11. Thomas Elsaesser, "Primary Identification and the Historical Subject: Fassbinder and Germany," *Cinetracts*, 3, no. 3 (Fall 1980), 43–52.
12. The gender implications of Freud's distinction have been probed by Judith Butler, *The Psychic Life of Power* (Palo Alto: Stanford University Press, 1997), 132–51.
13. On giving a different value to "acting out," see also Dominick LaCapra, *History and Memory after Auschwitz* (Ithaca: Cornell University Press, 1998) and *Writing History, Writ-*

ing Trauma (Baltimore: Johns Hopkins University Press, 2001) as well as my comments on LaCapra in chapter 12 of this volume.

14. As will be argued in another chapter, "work" is also the concept of choice in Alexander Kluge, the filmmaker who, more than any other, inspired my exploration of the fruitful ambiguities of parapraxis.
15. Sigmund Freud, *Collected Papers of Sigmund Freud*, Vol. 13, 1913, 166–67.
16. Reference to the Martin Walser-Ignatz Bubis controversy can be found in the German weekly *Die Zeit*, September 14, 1999.
17. These and other examples are discussed in Thomas Elsaesser, "West Germany's Inability to Commemorate: Between Bitburg and Bergen Belsen," in *On Film*, 14 (Spring 1985), 9–16.
18. Freud, *The Psychopathology of Everyday Life*, 36.
19. The chapter on Bergman's SERPENT'S EGG can be found in Maaret Koskinen (ed.), *Ingmar Bergman Revisited: Performance, Cinema and the Arts* (London: Wallflower Press, 2008), 161–79.
20. See chapter 6, this volume, on Kluge.
21. For a discursive definition of body, see Judith Butler, *Bodies that Matter* (New York: Routledge, 1993), 186–88.
22. Quoted in Niels Werber, "Qual, Gier, Langeweile," review of Anselm Haverkamp's *Latenzzeit — Wissen im Nachkrieg* (Berlin: Kadmos, 2004) in *Frankfurter Rundschau* 24.03.2004 (http://homepage.ruhr-uni-bochum.de/niels.werber/Haverkamp.html).
23. Contingency might be worth insisting on, perhaps even against Freud's notion that every parapraxis is not only meaningful but also has unconscious intention. See Sebastiano Timpanaro, *The Freudian Slip* (London: New Left Books, 1976), a sustained critique of Freud's idea and method.
24. Michael Wood, "There is no Cure," *London Review of Books*, 28, no. 13 (July 6, 2006).
25. See, for instance, Christian Klotz: *Selbstbewußtsein und praktische Identität. Eine Untersuchung über Fichtes Wissenschaftslehre nova methodo* (Frankfurt: Surhrkamp, 2002).
26. On the subject of stumbling in Freud, the most pertinent and illuminating discussion is an essay by John Mowitt, who traces the genesis of *The Psychopathology of Everyday Life* to the topological disorientation experienced by the citizen of Vienna during the extensive modernization of their city around 1900. Mowitt draws the following conclusions: "In some yet-to-be-determined sense *I regard psychoanalysis itself as a parapraxis*, but for that very reason it is important to stress that *everyday life cannot be treated as the background out of which emerged the concept of parapraxis*. Rather, [...] virtually all of *The Psychopathology of Everyday Life* constitutes a writing of everyday life in Vienna [around 1900. Michel] de Certeau, who, three-quarters of a century later, came to appreciate the narrative character of walking, would thus appear to be, literally, following in the footsteps of Freud. [What] I want to stress [is] that it is precisely within the swarm of [his everyday] routines, these drives, that Freud recognized the faulty functioning binding him to his fellow citizens, a recognition that cleared the ground for the royal road he had contracted his science to pave. Even the concept of Bahnung or pathbreaking, which was to figure so prominently in *The Project [of a Scientific Psychology]*, by participating in the associative paradigm of circulation, would also thus appear to derive, at least in part, from Freud's effort to think the psyche and city in one space." John Mowitt, "Stumbling on Analysis: Psychoanalysis and Everyday Life," *Cultural Critique*, 52 (Fall 2002), 78–79.
27. Freud, *Psychopathologie des Alltagslebebens* [Psychopathology of Everyday Life], 201 (my translation).
28. See Nurith Gertz and George Khleifi, *Palestinian Cinema: Landscape, Trauma and Memory* (Edinburgh: Edinburgh University Press, 2008), 9 and Drehli Robnik, "Running on Failure: Post-Politics, Democracy and Parapraxis," *Senses of Cinema*, 55, July 2010 (http://sensesofcinema.com/2010/feature-articles/running-on-failure-post-fordism-

post-politics-democracy-and-parapraxis-in-thomas-elsaesser%C2%B4s-film-theory/).

29. Thomas Elsaesser, *Hollywood Heute* (Berlin: Bertz + Fischer, 2009), 97–115 (PULP FICTION), 163–80 (BACK TO THE FUTURE) and 181–90 (FORREST GUMP). See also Thomas Elsaesser, *Melodrama Trauma Mindgames: Affect and Memory in American Cinema* (New York: Routledge, forthcoming).

4

GENERATIONAL MEMORY

The RAF Afterlife in the New Century

The Dissolution of the RAF and Its Resurrection as Rebus Picture and Palimpsest

In an earlier essay devoted to the Red Army Faction (RAF) and Germany's Hot Autumn, I identified and discussed in detail a number of interrelated narratives: the student protest and political activism, notably in West Berlin and Frankfurt; the "return of the repressed" in Germany's recent past; and a younger generation's search for a viable national identity, while divided about the use of violence for political ends.[1] These narratives evolved in the films made in the wake of the events of 1977—films like GERMANY IN AUTUMN (1978), KNIFE IN THE HEAD (1978), THE GERMAN SISTERS (1981)—before the different strands became fused, consolidated and hardened into clichés. The narratives, in turn, were modified somewhat in the films and television programs since the 1990s, often restaging and reenacting key episodes: for instance, the focus shifted to the leading figures on both sides of the divide, rather than concentrating on the bystanders or sympathizers, as had been the case in the films of the late 1970s.

Nonetheless, it was surprising how quickly this violent, chaotic, and for the reputation of the Federal Republic, quite dangerous period became legible as a single drama with tragic overtones: initially across the rather literary pedigree of Hamlet, Oedipus and the Fatherless Society, on which most German commentators—and filmmakers, then and since—have fastened their interpretations.[2] *Hamlet* was soon countered and complemented by *Antigone*, putting the emphasis on the female protagonists of this high drama of state, society, the individual, resistance and the law. Twenty years later, I argued, the contours of tragedy were still visible, but now focused on the representatives of authority, the Claudius and Creon figures, as it were. Thus, the RAF history appeared, in the interval between 1977 and its "return" in 1997, as a palimpsest not so much of the political history of the post-war Federal Republic (BRD) as of Germany's intellectual history from Hegel and Hölderlin to Bert Brecht and Peter Weiss, which however proved to be more political than I had anticipated: the layers showed how the father-son axis of the Hamlet ghost story of literature had shifted to the father-daughter paradigm of Antigone in GERMANY IN AUTUMN; but the reversal of perspectives back to patriarchal authority, operated in DEATH GAMES, also revealed a new technocratic understanding of politics and the power of the state, when orchestrated by an information war and new communication media.

I also detected two subsidiary narratives, visible as rebus-pictures and legible like a watermark: one having to do with the changes in urban space that took place at about the same time, the other was the apparent collusion between terrorist violence, its twenty-four-hour news coverage by the media, and police surveillance and "homeland" security measures. In the narrative of "guerrilla urbanism"—the militant strand in the urban renewal projects of the 1960s and 70s—the RAF episode may have appeared marginal or even irrelevant, but my argument was that the way it played out nevertheless intervened indirectly in these political issues, because the RAF's use of public space for terrorist actions effectively redefined what was once the (democratically sanctioned) "politics of the street."[3] Their violent version of such politics had as one of its consequences the securitization (and privatization) of public space, leading to a general media-and-technology saturation of the built, lived and experienced environment, which has taken shape both above and below the level of the visible. Before the widespread use of surveillance cameras in shopping areas, and the penetration of public space by all manner of recording and communication devices, "augmenting" this reality with accessible and interpretable information, the RAF had already forced into the open, or rather had made palpable this new space of total control and instantaneous information. With their (failed) politics of "mobilizing the masses" by terrorizing shoppers and pedestrians, they highlighted the end of an era when people took to the street to demonstrate for political rights. With their actions—and the response they received—the RAF ushered in both the non-space of exclusion, and the media space of the twenty-four-hour news cycle and the state of permanent media emergency. The latter can also be seen as a legacy of fascism's ambivalently pleasurable subject effects of political spectacle (through the use of radio, loudspeakers, parades and flag-waving), and also its contemporary, updated reinvention by bringing spectacle into the living room, while giving public space over to consumerism and rigorously monitored surveillance, which—as has increasingly become apparent since the 1970s—can perfectly complement each other. It retroactively installs a new *visibility of secrecy*, namely the extent to which the RAF (episode) on both sides of the political divide prepared the militarized security state, while turning the formerly politicized public spheres of "the street" into the depoliticized

Disneyland of shopping malls, leisure areas and fitness centers: a double-sided phenomenon which elsewhere I have called an urban scene with zones of exclusion and inclusion "policed in equal measure by violence and fantasy."[4]

The periodic returns, even more so than the RAF itself, thus became a lens or prism across which to read the larger changes in Western societies under the impact of the media and communication revolution, of which these urban guerrillas/guerrilla urbanists were in some sense the negative vanguard. In this respect, certain parallels between the October 1977 and September 2001 force themselves on the observer: each event, in the subsequent move and counter-move logic, incrementally and irreversibly has changed the character of civil society. The mirror-effects of terrorism and the war on terror created ripple effects, until the temperature dropped, something went rigid in the body politic (whether for fear or out of paralysis), and became locked into permanent stasis. As with Kurt Vonnegut's "Ice-Nine" (and Alexander Kluge's "ice-age")—society froze into place, installing those networked grids of ubiquitous surveillance both Hollywood movies and high theory are so expert at depicting and deciphering.[5]

In other respects, the connotations of "terrorism" are hardly the same when one speaks of the bank robberies and kidnappings of the 1970s and compares them to the suicide bombings since 2001. The RAF, while claiming solidarity with international liberation movements, was primarily a domestic phenomenon, with roots and references mostly in recent German history; Al Qaeda saw itself as a worldwide movement, with religious roots and millennial aspirations. The RAF comprised a very small number of active members; Al Qaeda organized cells all over Europe, the Middle East and Asia. The ideology, such as it was, of the RAF was Marxist-Leninist; that of Al Qaeda was based on particularly literal readings of the Koran. The scale of devastation and the number of victims of the RAF also pale in comparison to the victims of Al Qaeda.

On the other hand, a case can be (and has been) made that despite these crucial differences, the RAF and Al Qaeda have elements in common that bear important lessons for our understanding.[6] Besides sharing in their methods the common anarchist heritage of "propaganda by deed" and in their message the vague projection of a future that will be entirely different from the present, the RAF and Al Qaeda also perfected the use of media, both in their own practices and by exploiting television's dependence on news, sensations and spectacular, traumatizing events and the memorable images they produce.[7]

This chapter, however, is above all about the periodic "returns" of the RAF, not in some other guise, or how its methods or message might have been carried forward by other terrorist organizations, but the way the RAF episode does not seem to be laid to rest in Germany itself, despite the many and momentous changes since 1970s, not least the end of the Cold War and German unification. Whether commemorated because of anniversaries or reactivated by unpredictable yet expected scandals, the RAF's return as national disaster and historical trauma in the form of extended media attention raises a question: to what extent can one still speak of "working through" and "mastering the past," in the Freudian sense? Or are the repetitions and reruns more a kind of "acting out" whose spectacular allure but also obsessive traits trumps any therapeutic-cathartic sense or intent? As explained in the introductory chapter and chapter 3, my hypothesis is that a *parapractic* logic presides over many of these returns, an assumption reinforced by the fact that a similar logic of repetitions and untoward returns, for a long time, both prior to the 1970s and since, has typified what can be called the counter-history to the RAF's own pre-history: the Holocaust in German media and memory. But if the RAF members saw the Nazi-father generation as their most justified target and immediate antagonist, it does not follow that they allied themselves with the Nazi victims, the Jews. On the contrary, they tended to side with those they saw as the victims of the victims of Germany's racial persecution. They professed themselves anti-Zionists, making common cause with the Palestinians, in a move that had all the signs of displacement (in space and time), reversal (of cause and effect) and disavowal (of the never fully examined German anti-Semitism). At the time of the student movements of the 1960s—the politicized activists' prelude to the RAF's armed underground activism—neither the fate of the Jews under the Nazis, nor the roots of German anti-Semitism were live issues. Even German-Jewish relations "after Auschwitz" were at best marginal concerns, if not altogether nontopics. It seemed as if the old denial, camouflaged as *ignorance* about the camps among the guilty fathers had, among the radicalized sons, mutated into repression, now manifesting itself as *indifference* towards the survivors.

However, it was the seemingly interminable catalogue of missteps and public embarrassments around the commemoration of Nazi crimes that first alerted me to the possibility that a dynamic other than that of repression, denial or indifference was at work. Like Gerd Koenen and Peter Sloterdijk a few years later, I was struck not only by the regularity with which these "affairs" or "scandals" occurred, but also by the libidinal investments, pointing to the deeper psychic needs the scandals seemed to fill.[8] But instead of fastening on what in the context of the Fassbinder-affair I called "Beyond Guilt and Debt (*Jenseits von Schuld und Schulden*),"[9] I opted for the term *parapraxis*, redefining as well as deconstructing Freud's original German term *Fehlleistung* (also used, as I discovered later, by Koenen, see later citation), which I discuss at length in chapter 3. In the case studies comprising the second part of this volume, which deal primarily with films and filmmakers from the 1970s and 1980s, I argue that the narrative structures, narrational strategies, and particular scenes show corresponding incongruities and mismatches. Once related to the question of how to represent the unrepresentable, and how to find a voice or images for that which has not found a voice or a narrative, the peculiarities of these films, irrespective of their ostensible topics, begin to make more sense. They serve a purpose, I argued, whether these idiosyncrasies of style maniferst themselves as temporal shifts and deferrals, reversals in agency, or merely register as non-sequiturs and contingent coincidences.

One purpose, it now seems to me, was the no doubt only half-conscious if not altogether unconscious wish to undo what had been done, without denying what has been done, and to augment the actual with the possibility the virtual "as-if," and the memory of what might have been ("if-only"). Such a "poetics of parapraxis" has been less evident in the films made in the new century, either on topics relating to the legacy of Auschwitz, or with respect to the RAF and its afterlife. I discuss some of the newer films and the narratives that have emerged in chapter 10, "From Mastering the Past to Mastering Guilt: Holocaust Memory in the New Century." This chapter is devoted to the afterlife of the RAF in the films made leading up to the thirtieth anniversary of the Hot Autumn, looking at what these works, especially those made after 9/11, tell us not only about what kind of shadow these events from more than a generation ago still cast, but also how they help illuminate the conjunction of terror and trauma, more generally, as part of a wider (European) predicament. Again, I want to make the case that it is not the depiction of the events of the 1970s in themselves, but the narratives that emerge from them or embed these events in larger historical contexts that make the films significant contributions to the ongoing memory discourse. It will turn out that the cinema since the 1990s has had to share this function of a palimpsest or litmus test with other art forms of the public sphere, so that the films since the 1990s are only one aspect of how the Federal Republic in its media debates, popular culture and memory discourses has engaged with the RAF, and across it, also with Nazism and the Holocaust.[10]

The RAF and Hamlet's Ghost Revisited

The various memory discourses and the commemorative turn in European culture (discussed in chapter 2) are the main reasons why the RAF, although in some ways now so remote and confined mainly to Germany, can nonetheless be a useful test case, in unwinding once more the spiral of terror and trauma, as well as unpacking the terms of the asymmetrical powers of escalation, retribution, reprisals and retaliation. In these cycles and mirror-relations, it is important to distinguish several periods, stages and sets of personalities also within the RAF. From 1967 to 1972, it named the small group of urban guerrillas around Andreas Baader, Gudrun Ensslin, Ulrike Meinhof, popularly known as the Baader-Meinhof Gang, who caught the public imagination with bank robberies, jail breaks and arson. After their imprisonment in Stuttgart-Stammheim in June 1972, a so-called second generation formed itself, now calling themselves the Red Army Faction, more loosely organized, but also more focused in their targets: usually high-profile public figures they kidnapped or assassinated in spectacular raids and hold-ups. The next phase was the Hot Autumn, when, in a carefully coordinated series of actions, four RAF members kidnapped Hanns Martin Schleyer, then President of the Confederation of German Employers' Associations and the Federation of German Industries, and a former SS officer, in Cologne (September 5, 1977) and had the PLO hijack a plane of German tourists in Majorca and detain them at Mogadishu airport in Somalia (October 13). Both hostage-takings were meant to force the German government to release RAF prisoners, including the ones remaining in Stammheim (Ulrike Meinhof having committed suicide in her cell in May 1976). The government of Helmut Schmidt stood firm and the Mogadishu plane was stormed by a German special unit (October 18), whereupon the Stammheim prisoners committed suicide (October 18), and the RAF cell killed their hostage (October 19).

However foolhardy and incompetent, reckless, inhuman, and ideologically inconsistent their actions, united mainly by a hatred of the state (and of the United States), the RAF was given—for a time, and by a sympathetic minority—the benefit of the doubt as an understandable if not justifiable, traumatized (over)reaction to official Germany's lingering and latent Nazi legacy.[11] Such rationalizations, themselves prepared for by a decade of student anti-fascist and anti-capitalist protest, created the moral-emotional climate for siding with the RAF, even extending, in one case, to condoning the killing of "symbolic" public figures.[12] If this seems hard to believe today, it was sustained by another specifically post-war German narrative, namely the sociopsychological matrix of violent revolt against the father-generation. As mentioned, the Oedipal drama was played out against the background of a Hamlet scenario, except in this case, the main Hamlet figure, Baader, had little self-doubt and no compunction whatsoever, when it came to direct action.

But Hamlet perfectly fitted the younger generation's obsession with the good-bad father-image, an Oedipal conflict that the RAF activists seemed to stage in a particularly flamboyant way, violently distancing themselves from the (Nazi) fathers, but seeming to overidentifying with them in a similarly violent fashion, in a mixture of wounded narcissism and self-hatred that followed a preordained pattern as much anthropological as it was Freudian in its mirroring function. If one thinks of filial rebellion as a founding act of a new community, as Freud did in *Totem and Taboo*, then the parricidal protest had an intergenerational as well as political-utopian point. But if one stresses the reverse mirror function—along the lines of "they were 'anti', in order to have a sense of belonging"—then it also hints at a potentially tragic double bind of a person who is only able to accept himself through forcing the respect of the (hated/feared/admired) authoritarian other. It forms the dramatic knot of a key novel from the period, Bernward Vesper's *Die Reise* (1977), the autobiographical story of a self-tormented student rebel trying to square up to his Nazi father and—finding the father too strong even in death—committing suicide. Made into a film of the same title by Markus Imhof in 1986, Vesper's narrative connects to the RAF through Gudrun Ensslin, Vesper's ex-girlfriend and mother of his son Felix (whose surname is Ensslin, rather than Vesper).[13]

The more general political-anthropological reading of such self-other conflicts play a role in (post-)colonial studies from Gregory Bateson, Margaret Mead and Mary Douglas to Frantz Fanon, Paul Gilroy, Gayatri Spivak and Homi K. Bhabha, insofar as the colonial master can exercise a similarly devastating role in double-binding the educated/ emancipated (and subaltern) colonial subject.[14]

Applied to the Federal Republic, the parricidal-suicidal scenario might have looked as follows: while the "anti-" (authoritarian, fascist, capitalist) stance was directed at the authoritarian rectitude, acquisitiveness and repressed guilt feelings of the father figure, the "sense of belonging" was less clearly articulated. It could, for example, include nostalgia for the authentic (if subsequently deemed criminal) camaraderie enjoyed by the fathers during the war; it could be envy of the material achievements of this generation thanks to the "economic miracle," becoming prosperous without ever having been fully held accountable; or it could be rivalry for the increasing international prestige of Chancellor Willy Brandt's government, conducting a successful *Ost-Politik* (opening up to—the then communist—Eastern Europe) through parliamentary politics and without subscribing to Marxist orthodoxy; it could even stage by proxy and as deferred reversal, the resistance to fascism the father-generation so egregiously failed to mount.[15]

Being "anti-" and at the same time wanting to "belong"[16] found its most successful, if ultimately even more problematic compromise in the anti-authoritarians' dogmatic insistence on Marxism's scientific truth. Playing on this need to belong of their members, the Maoist so-called K-groups were able to enforce party-line discipline, even in the face of the post-Stalinist revelations of the horrors of Gulags and show trials. A similar double negative may well have made the German radical left delude themselves about their anti-Zionism: retroactively relieving both the anti-Semitism of their fathers and their own post-Auschwitz guilt-feelings. By living parts of this tortured psycho-drama so much in the blaze of publicity, the RAF became the German family tragedy par excellence: not just fathers versus sons, but mothers, sisters, godfathers and grandsons caught up and embroiled, when one thinks of the Ensslin sisters, Gudrun's son Felix, Ulrike Meinhof's twin daughters, or Susanne Albrecht luring her sister's godfather Jürgen Ponto into a deadly trap.

The RAF can also serve as a case for how the idea of a generation possessing a unique identity was resurrected and corroborated, in spite of the protagonists' intentions. As Marxists, they would probably have denounced such a periodization scheme as "bourgeois."[17] But with the RAF members habitually finding themselves divided into different generations, the second generation was sufficiently awed and inspired by their predecessors' self-image for it to dictate the scope and ambition of their actions. When these, too, had been hunted down and put in prison, the remnants of the RAF became ever more self-serving and paranoid, as Fassbinder claimed in THE THIRD GENERATION (1979): a negative image that a documentary, Andres Veiel's BLACK BOX BRD (2001) sought to modify by giving a more nuanced and restrained portrait of one such member of the "third generation."

Generation, in the German post-war context, is a wholly overdetermined concept, loaded with special significance, both political and emotional. Not only does it assume that people, born within three to five years of each other, can form a coherent and cohesive group, with common personality traits, sets of beliefs, values, attitudes or aspirations, but that this group is also sufficiently distinct and different from others, born earlier, who, by this very fact, become the first generation, from which the second sets itself off in an act of self-definition and self-demarcation. In the German context, the act of demarcation and distanciation preceded the internal definition, since it was a matter for the sons (and daughters) of the Nazi fathers, to declare as clean a break as possible, in order to begin to cope with this terrible legacy. In the German context, therefore, the Oedipal (Hamlet/Antigone) definition of the generational paradigm determined and dominated the meaning given to the "68 generation." Elsewhere in Europe and the United States, the same generation drew its identity more from a new life style, coupled with a common set of beliefs than from a clearly defined Oedipal struggle.[18] The RAF's several "generations" were as much the result of external ascription as of internal self-differentiation, and marks the point where the political meaning of generation begins to blur. They make way for it to become a label and a marketing tool, to justify the relentless promotion of both newness and belonging, so typical of youth cultures.[19]

For a non-German public and the international press, the RAF's identity—and with it, the sympathy created for their motives—was crucially shaped less by their actions than by their imprisonment in Stammheim, from June 1972 onwards, after the original members' spree of arson, bank robberies and bombings of U.S. military installations was over.[20] That they were able, for full five years, in the run-up to their trial, to orchestrate a successful publicity campaign on their own behalf, speaks to the widespread unease, suspicion and distrust felt by the so-called student generation vis-à-vis the government, the criminal justice system and the police. They managed to link the term *solitary confinement* with *torture*, and *torture* with *Auschwitz*, thus aligning themselves with another narrative that could be (and was) mobilized, especially to enlist the support of such prominent French intellectuals as Jean Paul Sartre and Michel Foucault.[21]

Besides trying to turn the tables on their captors by presenting themselves as victims, the campaign conducted from prison also highlighted the RAF's media skills. While the photographs of burnt out cars and bombed buildings made them outlaw celebrities, the Baader audio tapes released to the press through his lawyers, along with the manifestos published in student journals or smuggled out of prison, assured the RAF of a phantom presence. By inventing mirror-mazes of victimhood and dissidence, by winning high-profile sympathizers for drug-addicted sociopaths, and drawing attention to (by foiling) the state's state-of-the-art surveillance technologies, the prisoners entered the nation's living rooms with sounds and images never seen or heard before. Their media products generated the hybrid spaces and the aural static—one might call it, anachronistically but not incorrectly, the "augmented reality" of the RAF—that, along with the public radio broadcasts and television images from the period, make up the legacy of the RAF today. In a genealogy of terrorism as a "war of images," which, thanks to Bin Laden's videotapes, has become a thoroughly familiar operational theater, the RAF can claim a well-deserved place—but so can its opponents.[22] Taking "propaganda by deed" to a new level, the RAF exploited the "society of the spectacle" for their own ends, to the point where the images they produced or gave rise to, became the main objectives of their actions, with the actual victims the collateral but necessary props for a successful staging.[23]

Ghosts: Images as Icons, Phantoms and Revenants

However, another reversal was also at work in assuring the RAF's troublesome legacy. The more the centrality of the Holocaust since the 1980s came to define Germany's sense of its recent past as obligating it with a special historical legacy, the more the origins and motives of the RAF became written into the national narrative of the Federal Republic on the side of *fascism's anti-capitalist afterlife* rather than on the side of the *anti-fascism's anti-capitalism* which the group so stridently professed.[24] What supported such a shift from Hitler's belated opposition, to "Hitler's children"[25] were a number of political changes, not least the collapse of Communism, and a swing of the pendulum against the generation of '68 more generally. Equally significant was the fact that the RAF's pro-Palestinian actions and anti-Israel stances increasingly refocused the debate about the group's political identity.[26] The approximation of West German left-wing anti-Zionism with neo-Nazi anti-Semitism further undermined any residual understanding there might still have been for the student left's political objectives, whether these were protesting against West Germany's collusion with repressive regimes (such as the demonstrations against the Shah of Iran's visit in 1967, which radicalized both Ulrike Meinhof and Gudrun Ensslin, and is usually cited as the origin of the RAF), or the widely popular support for the international liberation movements, demanding an end to military dictatorships in Latin America and of the West's collusion with these repressive regimes.

Also bracketed off were the RAF's connections to other left-leaning and violence-embracing political protest-movements in Italy and Japan during the same decade, which might have pointed to instructive parallels and common origins that united the sons and daughters of the twentieth century's three major fascist regimes (Franco's rule in Spain had only just come to an end).

Forgotten, too, were the broader international and less violent contexts of the anti-Vietnam War movement, the widespread support for protests against the stationing of U.S. Pershing atomic missiles on German soil, and the radical (anti-)psychiatry movement (the Socialist Patients' Collective), from which the RAF recruited its second generation. The direct and frequent links of RAF members to the armed groups of Palestinian guerrilla in Lebanon, Syria and North Africa tended to be treated as exotic anecdotes, highlighting the discrepancy between the disciplined fighters of the PLO and the sex-drug-and-rock-n-roll antics of the RAF, rather than as the last remnants of a utopia that had once fought for social justice and liberation from colonialism by believing in the "armed struggle."

And yet, despite this melting away of any form of sympathy for either their means or their message, the RAF continued to haunt even the united Germany into the 1990s and beyond. One telling index is that almost twice as many films and television docudramas about the RAF have been made since 1997, compared to the number produced during the heyday of the New German Cinema. The latter's political identity, moral seriousness and international appeal as a "national cinema," was practically defined with such films as Volker Schloendorff/Margarethe von Trotta's THE LOST HONOUR OF KATHARINA BLUM (1975), the omnibus film GERMANY IN AUTUMN (1978), Fassbinder's THE THIRD GENERATION (1979), von Trotta's THE GERMAN SISTERS (1981), Reinhardt Hauff's KNIFE IN THE HEAD (1979) and STAMMHEIM (1986), plus the already mentioned German-Swiss-made THE JOURNEY (Markus Imhof, 1986).

While the RAF as a film topic disappeared subsequently for a whole decade (1986–1997), one finds a veritable break in the levee from 1997 onwards: Hans Breloer's TODESSPIEL (DEATH GAMES); the omnibus film IM FADENKREUZ — DEUTSCHLAND & DIE RAF (1997); Christian Petzold's DIE INNERE SICHERHEIT (THE STATE I AM IN, 2000); Schloendorff's DIE STILLE NACH DEM SCHUSS (THE LEGEND OF RITA, 2000), Andres Veiel's BLACK BOX BRD (2001); Gerd Conradt's STARBUCK HOLGER MEINS (2001); Christopher Roth's BAADER (2002); Klaus Stern's ANDREAS BAADER — DER STAATSFEIND (ENEMY OF THE STATE, 2003); Johannes Unger and Sascha Adamek's ULRIKE MEINHOF — WEGE IN DEN TERROR (WAYS INTO TERROR, 2006), Uli Edel and Stefan Aust's DER BAADER MEINHOF KOMPLEX (2008), as well as another Ulrike Meinhof film, CHILDREN OF THE REVOLUTION (Shane O'Sullivan, 2010), a special edition of the popular *Tatort* detective-series with Ulrich Tukur *Wie einst Lily* (Achim von Borries, 2010) complemented by a second film by Andres Veiel, WER WENN NICHT WIR? (2011) which goes over some of the same narrative as Imhof's DIE REISE. In other words, these thirteen films/tv productions compare with only seven films between 1975 and 1986.

What the titles and topics suggest is that the RAF's afterlife was less determined by either the political content of their actions, or the moral stance taken in respect of their violent methods, but by the impact that their publicity strategies, their personality cult, and their war of images managed to make on how "terror" and "trauma" came to be understood also in the new century. This impact found its own metaphor, which we have already come across in Jacques Derrida, when he speaks of "the spectre of terror and trauma." For if trauma and terror describe the historical moment of the 1970s—the untimeliness and unpredictability with which a climate of fear and violence, of paranoia and persecution that everyone thought to belong to the Nazi past, suddenly returned and visited the present—then Derrida's mention of spectrality captures the subsequent history of resurrection and return, because a ghostlike aura of ungraspable, but palpable presence has persisted ever since. Wolfgang Kraushaar, along with Gerd Koenen the leading full-time professional RAF-historian, also invokes the image of a ghost, when trying to account for the "extremely neurotic response," that has added the RAF to the nation's other well-rehearsed "conflict scenarios":

> It is true: the RAF has vanished long ago and entered into the Federal Republic's history. At the same time, however, a ghost going by the same name appears to be stalking the land, still capable of causing considerable commotion and unease.[27]

Derrida had reintroduced Hamlet and his father's ghost when assessing the consequences of the Marxist vision of social justice having vanished so quickly with the end of the Cold War. *Specters of Marx*, significantly subtitled "the state of the debt, the work of mourning, and the New International," evidently harked back to Marx' own use of the term *specter* in *The Communist Manifesto*, but in listing ten plagues afflicting mankind in the present, Derrida also tried to counter, in the strongest possible terms, the idea that liberal democracy and capitalism had pacified the world. The language of ghosts and haunting thus carries clear overtones of accountability, justice and redress which for Derrida link the political movements of the 1960s and 1970s to unfinished tasks and persisting obligations.[28]

Ghosts (English in the original) was also the title of a book by Klaus Theweleit, reflecting on the ambiguous aliveness of the RAF, and aligning it with the unredeemed promises inherent in the social ideals of the generation he and they were part of. Written on the occasion of the twentieth anniversary of the Hot Autumn and published in 1998 as "three politically incorrect essays," Theweleit's book helped the "ghost" metaphor gain even wider currency, so much so that the notion of the RAF as a ghost has in the meantime itself become a revenant, whose appearance is as predictable in the debates as are the rest of the ever more recursive arguments and repeated clichés. By the time that Christian Petzold titled one of his films GESPENSTER (GHOSTS, 2005) the plot, unlike his DIE INNERE SICHERHEIT, did not have to feature any ex-RAF protagonists to conjure up the leaden anxiety and paranoia of the 1970s. If Kraushaar's "ghost stalking the land" wanted to evoke the uncanny part of the RAF that lives on in the form of public debates, art installations, films and television reenactments, it also provokes the question of how a violently anti-American protest group, practicing the politics of resistance and the armed struggle copied from the liberation- and guerrilla movements of Southeast Asia and Latin America, should mutate in public perception into copycats of American movie stars, acting out the plots of Hollywood B-movies?

To answer this, I want to persist with the metaphor a little longer, in order to track this mutation "from politics to pop" via the connotations of "ghost" in the RAF's afterlife into the twenty-first century. In contrast to Derrida's and Theweleit's ghosts, conferring a certain tragic pathos on the generation's historical double binds, the ghosts of the RAF's afterlife at first glance are above all the media (after-)images that their actions flashed on the nation's screens. More than documents, because of the "toxicity" of the icons and slogans, these images are also less than documentation, because they are so much part of a propaganda war of images fought by both sides.[29] Either way, these RAF ghost images have so far visited at least two generations: that of the former activists, fellow travelers, sympathizers, ex-members who left radical politics, rejoined post-bourgeois society, and have been, in their often leading political positions, revisited by their past allegiances. The second generation is that of their children, who either considered the 1970s as the last heroic period they were unlucky enough to just miss,[30] or who were captivated by the RAF as a potent soundscape and image-emporium, and who appropriated the icons and slogans of the "German Autumn" as style items and fashion accessories. The RAF history is thus undead from the perspective of several interested parties, whose divergent stakes can be identified, mostly along the lines of the same generational schema.[31]

"Undead" first of all, because the RAF, and the milieu of student protest from which it came, considered themselves to be the necessary response to another history they were convinced was undead: that of German fascism, which had been buried without having been exorcised, and of which the RAF could present itself as "the return of the repressed." Second, those directly involved or part of the broader movement that the RAF drew on (insofar as their motives if not their actions enjoyed some degree of support, solidarity and sympathy), were in the 1990s, themselves in positions of power and influence: they had quietly renounced their past, but their response necessarily remained ambivalent. They drew on it politically, rejecting its methods or morality, but still lived with this legacy, and often enough, it would return to haunt them. The spectrum of post-68 reentry candidates reached from "green" politicians to university professors, media entrepreneurs, software developers and publishers. In the case of prominent figures such as Joschka Fischer, Jürgen Trittin, Otto Schily, Daniel Cohn-Bendit, or the publisher Klaus Wagenbach, the past was dangerously undead: it could catch up with them at any moment, as it did for Fischer, who nearly lost his job as foreign minister, when blurry footage resurfaced of him hitting a policeman during a street demonstration in Frankfurt (passed to the press by no less an interested party than Bettina Röhl, daughter of Ulrike Meinhof and Klaus Rainer Röhl, another controversial publisher).[32] In the case of Cohn-Bendit, a misleadingly phrased passage in his autobiography about his time as a teacher of young boys found him accused of paedophilia.[33] Their pasts could stare them in the face, as in the case of the by then Minister of the Interior Schily, with the mocking grimace of the maverick Horst Mahler, a fellow-lawyer who joined the RAF, went underground, was eventually convicted and after several years in prison was granted early release, only to reemerge in the 1990s as a spokesman for a Neo-Nazi splinter group. Even Federal Chancellor Gerhard Schroeder had his youthful "sympathies" turned against him in later years.[34]

Reversals and returns of this kind is what the next generation had to come to terms with as well. To the dismay of their elders, it could take forms considered vulgar and in bad taste, often in the manner typical of popular culture appropriation, rather than with the obligatory critical distance or the required gravity of therapeutic "working through." Yet the more performative or playful modes of engagement surfacing in the 1980s should not *per se* be dismissed as frivolous:[35] reworking the RAF emblem of the five-pointed star, the letters "RAF" and the Heckler & Koch machinegun into a "Prada-Meinhof" logo on t-shirts and other accoutrements may seem the height of cynicism, but it is not without its own historical as well as semiotic (and dare I say, parapractic) logic.[36] It counters the deadly boring undeadness of public debates: weary of the endless repetitions of disavowal and affective investment, the for-and-against, on-the-one-hand/on-the-other, everyone competing for victim position, such aggressive in-your-face misappropriation resorts to a more direct and graphic expression of mismatch and incongruity, in the idioms that were designed to register precisely such clashes in perception, sensibility and values, namely, pop art, brand identity, advertising. These only repeat (and thus comment on), in the most authentic medium of inauthenticity, i.e., fashion, what in the 1970 was even more shockingly "normal": the screaming headlines of the tabloid *Bild-Zeitung*, the defamatory paranoia of editorials in serious papers like *Die Welt,* and the deliberately disorienting word-images collages on the front covers of *Quick* or *Stern*, West Germany's mass-circulation illustrated weeklies. Kraushaar, too, has drawn attention to the paradox of the RAF images:

> The difficulty lies in the fact that in the case of the RAF, a reality predominantly without images was being overcompensated by a media-driven image-world, that [...] counted, above all, on the shock-and-outrage factor of a preconditioned public sphere. The exorbitant amount that *Stern* paid to former RAF member Astrid Proll, in order to get its hands on the only existing private photographs of Baader and Ensslin (the photos that showed the couple in a Paris café towards the end of 1969) is a telling confirmation. [...] The RAF was strategically conquered and lastingly

> occupied through its images. It was this appropriation of a language of images by very diverse (partly state) powers that has shaped today's overall perception of the RAF phenomenon.[37]

Perhaps for the 1990s "Generation Golf," the RAF was indeed the 1970s super-group or rock band Germany never had. But what holds together the mythologies spun about Ensslin and Baader as Germany's very own Bonnie and Clyde are not only fast cars, girls and guns.[38] Those who grew up in the 1980s and 1990s were the first generation to be completely socialized via television: having been born "too late for sixty-eight," they became nonetheless sufficiently sophisticated and blasé in their use of media representations, to find their own ways of dealing with the contradictions and complexities that lay buried in these images. They also had to resituate themselves as Germans, now taught about the Nazi era and the Holocaust in schools, but so much so that their grandfathers may have tended to become intriguing fossils of "absolute evil" rather than its maligned incarnations, while their fathers' ambivalences about what it meant to be German gave little firm direction to their own compass of national identity, once more gyrating wildly after (re)unification, when the two Germanys quickly realized how little they had in common.

The pop appropriation of the RAF is thus in itself not an illegitimate way of trying to cut some of these Gordian knots, but an "acting out" in situations intuited as either deadlocked or disavowed: the RAF's history of movie-land violence, street-theater terror and acts of shameful inhumanity entailed enough taboos to tempt one into breaking them, by playing with them, *pour épater les bien-pensants* (to impress the self-righteous). What was being acted out was not so much any fascination for this kind of direct action, or the political program meant to justify the terrorist violence, but rather this earlier manipulation of images and signs by newspaper and television journalists as well as the police, with their insistence on plastering the mug-shot "Wanted" posters of terrorist on the walls of every post office or newsagent stand: all surely more calculatedly demagogic and propagandist than the display, thirty years later, of the RAF logo on underwear, headscarves or handbags. And this would be one of the lessons of the case study of the RAF's afterlife: aided and abetted by their apparent enemies, the popular press, the state apparatus and the police, the RAF were among the pioneers of terrorism as *graffiti warfare*, even as they thought of themselves as conducting *guerrilla warfare*.

Despite such domestication of the RAF ghost, it is understandable that many, especially since September 2001, would like this *Spuk* (phantom, specter) to finally go away, and for this ghost to be laid to rest. Since so much has been written about the national psycho-syndrome to which it belongs, the RAF can hardly be called "repressed." If it keeps returning, as in fact it does, this casts a more general doubt on the efficacy of the therapy usually prescribed, with "working through" and "mastering the past," themselves by now one of the most repetitive and clichéd notions in the whole debate.[39] Rather than speak of a "return of the repressed" or a "compulsion to repeat," my argument is that the periodic return of the RAF, in the form of media events, revelations, confessions and, of course, feature films and TV mini-series, has to do with their complex but contradictory media presence right from the start. The RAF remains not just undead, but symptomatically so because of the images that circulate about them, or rather, because of the discrepancy between the group's clandestine, hidden and underground existence—picture-shy and shadowy—and their actions, which were specifically designed to produce images: of destruction, chaos, mayhem, blood and death. The RAF threw bombs, but as in all subsequent terrorist actions, their machinegun burst of light and fire were also flashbulbs, helping to arrest the flow of ordinary life, and terminate lives, in order to expose an imaginary filmstrip that was to fix forever the moment that was theirs and has become collective history as well a popular memory. For since these images were not only repeated at the time, but found themselves reproduced over time, whenever mention was made of the RAF, they entered into cycles of iterations and replay—emblematic, suggestive, not letting go and not being let go—lodging themselves in the visual memory of a generation that had no direct experience of the RAF other than through their screen presence as the traumatic, but also powerfully iconic and thus sufficiently contradictory signifiers of action and violence in the media age.[40]

"Mythos RAF" or "*Vorstellung des Terrors*": Tracing the Nation's Excitability Graph

As will be argued in several chapters, I regard this "unfinished business," this "refusal to normalize," "this nondisposal" of the detritus of the '68 generation's history a special kind of challenge and opportunity. Not only for Germany after unification, which is set to continue to "work" on its several nonsynchronous histories anyway, but also for the way Europe's commemorative culture, has, in Derrida's sense, a peculiar debt and as yet unfulfilled obligation to the past that it carries into its future as a continent and political project, countering its slow subsidence into becoming merely a tourist destination for history as heritage. [41] It is where the arts, as well as the cinema, can realize their responsibilities, not least by indicating what sort of discourse is conceivable after 9/11, about events that in a nation's history mark the turning points, but also the (missed) opportunities that might yet bear fruit in a future all too easily discounted.

A demonstration of how terror and trauma still reverberate in Germany was provided by a Berlin exhibition in 2005, one of the more prominent restagings of the RAF-effect as afterlife. The exhibition was originally planned for 2003 under the title "Mythos RAF" but finally took place between January and March 2005 as "Zur Vorstellung des Terrors" (*Vorstellung* can mean idea or image but also performance, show, thus "The Idea & Image of the RAF"), at the Kunstwerke Berlin (and subsequently in Vienna), co-curated by Felix Ensslin, son of Gudrun Ensslin and Bernward Vesper. Eliciting a predictably mixed response, the pre-history, preparation and opening of the exhibition perfectly fitted the pattern already established by the RAF discourse many times over. Controversy, protest, press-campaigns, misunderstandings, mutual recriminations, revelations, cancellations, interferences, rescue operations followed each other, thereby once more confirming that the RAF embodies a public trauma and is a perpetual parapraxis, by virtue of the repetition compulsion it invariably provokes.[42]

Without giving an extended digest of the commentary it provoked, two points are relevant to the present context.[43] First, the exhibition heavily relied on the stock images and press photographs, serving as inspiration, caricatures and counterpoints for scores of artists trying to come to terms with the RAF legacy. The photos ranged from Rudi Dutschke's shoe to Siegfried Buback's Mercedes riddled with bullets, from the poster photo of the "prisoner" Hanns Martin Schleyer put out by his captors, to the skeletal Christ-like torso of Holger Meins and the forensic picture of the dead Ulrike Meinhof. The artists included Joseph Beuys and Martin Kippenberger, Jörg Immendorff and Sigmar Polke, Wolf Vostell and Thomas Ruff. Typical was the series of police photos collected of all the fallen on both sides, terrorists and their victims united in death (Hans Peter Feldmann, *Die Toten*), along with Gerhard Richter's blur paintings, titled *October 18, 1977*, immortalizing the police photos from Stammheim prison. It seems that for contemporary art, too, it is hard to find an "outside" to the inside of the media-generated images by which the RAF and its decade is remembered and continues to survive.

The second point is that the exhibition illustrated what Aleida Assmann in the wider context of memory culture in Germany has called the *Erregungsspur* ("excitability trace," analogous to "memory trace") that follows certain images or events, or as in this case, that terms like *terror, trauma* or *RAF* leave in their wake.[44] In other words, the controversy itself became part of the substance of the exhibition and even its primary performative dimension. As one commentator remarked: "After leaving the RAF exhibition at the Kunstwerke I could not help feeling that its pre-history [of protest, controversy and obstruction] was in every respect healthy and productive for the exhibition, and not only in answering the question of how to generate maximum attention." [45]

The lines of force mentioned at the outset of this chapter, where state and terrorists seemed to play each other's game of mutual implication and reciprocal escalation, were on full view in the exhibition as well, adding as it were, a third set of experienced players, the avant-garde artists (and their habitual nemesis, the bureaucrats of normality and the guardians of good taste). The artists, for the most part, were ranged on the side of revolt and rebellion, rather than the "forces of order," but their works also confirmed that the RAF's original terrain of physical violence and spectacular acts of terrorism, had, in the intervening years, become a "forest of symbols": a landscape of graphic signs, texts and images, readable as a revolving panorama, a slide- and picture gallery or as a cinematic loop, the non-stop show *Terror and Trauma—Made in Germany*. As such it was clearly a co-production: between *the RAF* (with their acts of targeted destruction yielding surreal images of twisted and burnt-out limousines in leafy villa suburbs), *the tabloid press* (with their front page photos and screaming headlines), *the police* (besides pasting the "Wanted" photo-IDs in public places, they videotaped demonstrations and funerals with camcorders), *television* (reporting live from the scenes in grainy, out of focus images, with failing soundtracks or jerky hand-held camera work) and now *the artists* (navigating their own degrees of distance and proximity). On display, through these images and artifacts, were also generations of obsolete technology, proving the point made earlier that parallel to and intertwined with the history of the RAF runs the history of the media technologies which their actions were recorded by and intended for.

If it was true that the RAF was a "vanguard of the communication revolution, riding high on exploiting the latest innovations of our mediatized society, national champions in the struggle over that scarcest of resources, attention,"[46] then this was equally true of the security forces, not to mention the professionals of the popular media, fast learning the new rules of the game. They all *had a ball* and *kept their eyes on the ball*: even in retrospect one could feel the adrenalin pumping through everyone's bodies, a sort of beat and rhythm, of syncopation and improvisation, caught up in the accelerating pace, the sudden reversal and final denouement on a dying fall, after the storming of the hijacked plane, the discovery of Schleyer's body, the Stammheim suicides and the Stuttgart funerals. Indeed, the artists contributing to the Kunstwerke exhibition might have felt a pang of envy, seeing the challenge they were up against. I myself, on leaving the exhibition, could not help being reminded of Karlheinz Stockhausen's infamous, envious impromptu comment on 9/11: "the greatest work of art ever."[47] The RAF had decidedly prepared such an unguarded admission.

In this polyphonic reading of a social text like the RAF history alongside the social body that collectively produces and reproduces it, the "scandals" of the Kunstwerke exhibition were thus more in tune with the meaning of the RAF for the Federal Republic than any single exhibit within the show could have been by and in itself. It suggests that an exhibition today, at least in the context of German history and memory, is merely another machine for bringing these parapraxes, i.e., these productive mishaps of preprogrammed outrage, response and counter-response to the surface. Exhibitions, too, create what Peter Sloterdijk, following Assmann, dubbed *Erregungsgemeinschaften* (communities of excitability), the emotional oscillations that seem to give Germans their most precious moments of identity and belonging. If correct, it would indicate that there is no reason why these commotions, but also the trans- and inscription of the history of the RAF (along with the parallel Holocaust history) should fade away or cease at any point soon:

> In actual fact, mastering the past has become a form of life for Germans. The debates or scandals, which ignite themselves almost every year when something or someone revises or radicalizes the generally agreed version of history, or when some intellectual parapraxis or provocation is committed, which are, of course, part of the game—such as: the Fassbinder-affair, [Reagan and Kohl's] Bitburg-visit, the historians' debate, Jenninger's speech, Syberberg's Wagnerian incantations, Botho Strauß's satyr-songs, the Goldhagen-debate, the Wehrmachts-exhibition, the Holocaust-memorial, Martin Walser's peace-prize lecture, his "Death of a Critic", Hohmann-lamento (to name only a few of the long list of incidents readily springing to mind)—, they could all be described, following Peter Sloterdijk, also as "rituals of constitutive instability", across which the society of the Federal Republic "achieves some of its strongest moments of the collective we."[48]

Besides confirming the parapractic logic animating these graphs and rhythms of excitability also briefly recapitulated at the beginning of this chapter (and giving a powerful indication what use a scandal might have for a community's internal cohesion), this passage by Gerd Koenen brings to mind another concept that could be helpful and relevant: that of the "immemorial," introduced by Jean François Lyotard. Defined as "that which can neither be remembered (represented to consciousness) nor forgotten (consigned to oblivion) [and] which returns, uncannily,"[49] it may well be Lyotard's definition of trauma, but applicable to supra-personal phenomena. If the RAF is still a traumatic phenomenon, and if Germany's key "immemorial" takes the form of "rituals of instability," performed by the media creating temporary but recurring "communities of excitability," then it signals that "trauma" is likely to be the very mode by which German society, even in the twenty-first century, most easily and indeed most comfortably (i.e., with the least narcissistic wound) communicates with itself. Repetition in this case would not be a return of the same, but a *mise en abyme* of the preceding events, or rather, a particular form of performing that which has preceded it, so that "scandal" is only another name for this internal mirroring and potential for infinite reversibility: it does not come to an end, unless, of course, another event or seismic shift reveals the repetition—whether compulsive or recursive—to have been merely the symptom of yet another, even more fundamental or foundational malaise.

Black Box or Overexposure: The RAF Films since 2000

It is the contention of this study that the cinema is one of the privileged sites—if not *the* privileged site—for enacting some of the mirror-relations and transferences that are part of this conjunction of terror and trauma in the formation of collective or public memory. Earlier described as a special concurrence of persistence, absence, displacement and return, which are present-day Germany's "ghosts" or German history's "afterlife," this material immemorial, this medial and discursive memory of the RAF has, as indicated, produced a surprising number of films. Above I listed a number of titles, comprising documentaries and feature films, usually made either for or with television, some by established professionals or aspiring *auteurs*, others first-time films or one-offs, and including one—THE BAADER MEINHOF COMPLEX—aimed at an international blockbuster market. What has been said so far about the inner dynamic and outer contradictions of the RAF's afterlife should help establish a conceptual framework, as well as criteria that give some guidance for how to locate the contribution made by these films since 1997. I refrain from sorting them in terms of their degrees of endorsement or condemnation for the RAF's actions, their lifestyle and professed aims. I also assume that one the contentious issues of some of the films from the late 1970s and 1980s, namely their focus on (innocent) bystanders becoming victims of the police or tabloid press and thus reluctant sympathizers, was no longer relevant to the filmmakers nor of interest to their audiences in the 1990s and beyond. Among the terror-trauma narratives that I have so far identified, four are of particular symptomatic value: first, the antagonistic cooperation between the different actors and players, in particular, between the security services and the terrorists; second, the understanding, now common currency, that terror (the RAF, propaganda by deed) and trauma (the repetition, returns and associated scandals) are media-effects; third, the changing positions of victims and perpetrators, either to suggest that here too, a possible reversal has taken place, or at least a shift in the direction of identifying elements of victimhood in every protagonist; and finally, the sense that these historic images and the archive footage have become the untranscendable horizon of public memory, the primary reality and court of final appeal, to the point of requiring reenactment in the idiom of documentary authenticity, should original material no longer be—or never have been—available.

I refrain from going through each of the titles listed, and instead indicate some of the intersections of the films with these narratives. My focus is how the films engage with the historical energies that generate this afterlife, as opposed to merely referencing the known tropes. With respect to a symbiotic mutual dependence having existed between the "forces of order" and the RAF, both BAADER and THE BAADER MEINHOF COMPLEX explicitly refer themselves to the documented "understanding from within" that Heinz Herold, then Head of the *Bundeskriminalamt* (the German FBI) claimed to have had with and for Andreas Baader. In THE BAADER MEINHOF COMPLEX this affords the opportunity of a bravura part for Bruno Ganz, still recognizable from playing Hitler in DER UNTERGANG/THE DOWNFALL, and thus giving a double layer of irony to his quasi-filial bond of recognition with Baader. Alas, Ganz' star turn does not mitigate or modify the film's very conventionally Manichean scheme of protagonists and antagonists. The cops do what they are meant to do, and the group's eventual undoing is mainly due to internal divisions and the psychopathology of the individual characters. By contrast, Christopher Roth's BAADER makes the Herold-Baader love-hate, father-son, recognition-respect dynamic its central structural device and narrative motor. Going well beyond the documented facts, Roth invents a scene where the two meet at night, admitting in so many words that they need each other. Also in flagrant disregard for the historical narrative, Roth's Baader has a showdown and shoot-out with Herold, and dies in his arms. As Roth told an interviewer: "at a certain point, the facts didn't interest me anymore, so I started telling my own story."[50] It is, of course, not at all his own story, but that of countless Hollywood movies and their Spaghetti Western pastiches. As reviewers pointed out, one can actually be more precise in identifying Michael Mann's HEAT, with Robert de Niro and Al Pacino, as the cinephile blueprint for BAADER, so that the film not only shows a Baader enamored with striking a pose, aping macho American actors and always looking over his shoulder into an imaginary mirror to make sure he is being seen to be cool; it also shows its director caught in many of the same mirror-reflections, hoping to turn this sordid tale into a really cool movie. BAADER reproduces the by 2003 prevalent cliché of the RAF as politically naïve, media-addicted and sexually voracious, making one wonder even more why such an odious and unappealing person should ever have enjoyed any kind of allegiance or sympathy. This Baader is such a self-indulgent, violent, narcissistic Al Pacino Scarface wannabe, that his incompetence and arrogance makes it difficult to believe in the premise borrowed from HEAT, namely that between a ruthless gangster and a ruthless cop a certain code of honor can prevail, and thus provide comfort of sorts not only in the face of the inevitable, but also in the fact that committing crimes and fighting crime may require each knowing the mindset of the other better than one's own.

The mutual dependence narrative is developed in quite different ways in Schloendorff's DIE STILLE NACH DEM SCHUSS (THE LEGEND OF RITA, 2000), because it poses another level of antagonism and complicity altogether, namely the potential of the RAF, declared anti-capitalists, as "useful idiots" (but also liabilities) for the security services of the German Democratic Republic, when assisting them in their espionage activities and infiltration of West Germany. Scripted by Wolfgang Koolhaase, one of the most seasoned of GDR screenwriters, THE LEGEND OF RITA condenses the documented cases of several RAF-women who, after being involved in bank robberies and fatal shoot-outs in West Berlin, eventually found cover and were given new identities in the GDR. Telling the 1970s past in flashbacks (referencing his own films of the time, as it were) Schloendorff concentrates on how someone who, having stepped outside the law and forfeited one life, accommodates herself with almost naïve idealism to another, only to have to realize that there is no going forward nor back, since the past inevitably catches up with her, as indeed does the future: first she is recognized by someone at work, when her photo is shown on West German television (watched by everyone in the East) and then, once the Wall comes down and the Stasi files are opened to the West German authorities, she is once more on the run, eventually being shot dead by a policeman, as she tries to evade a routine road block vehicle check. By featuring a strong woman protagonist (reminiscent also of von Trotta's films), The Legend of Rita tips the scales towards showing the human cost. Its central character suffers heroically (and, we come to believe, undeservedly), so that much of the politics—whether of the RAF or of the greater East-West conflict—remains background noise. Well-made and with its heart in the right place, The Legend of Rita could almost be a DEFA film from before the Fall of the Wall, which is what the English title hints at, by echoing the only internationally popular GDR movie The Legend of Paul and Paula (Heiner Carow, 1973).

In a similar vein of melodrama with a political theme, but more contemporary and coherent in the way it braids together the generic clichés of the thriller with many of the motifs now firmly established as belonging to the RAF narrative, a seemingly modest television offering (admittedly, made a decade later) gives a much more convincing picture of how the past can consume the present and swallow the future. "Wie einst Lilly" is a feature-length episode of the wildly successful *Tatort* weekly tv-crime series, directed by Achim von Borries and scripted by Christian Jeltsch. It is inspired by one of the notorious RAF cases, the assassination of Siegfried Buback, public prosecutor in Karlsruhe, and the second-generation terrorist Verena Becker, not only implicated in the case, but possibly an informant and double agent, working for the West German state, even as she participated in murder.[51] Detective Inspector Felix Murot is called to an idyllic lake somewhere in Hesse, where a body has been found in one of the boats for rent drifting on the lake. It looks like suicide, but once Murot begins to get clues about the identity of the man, doubts arise, and he finds himself drawn into a dangerous plot, involving a female ex-RAF member who, having hidden for many years in the GDR, returned to the West, there to run a secluded guesthouse. Her past, too, catches up with her, but so does Murot's, who—as it happens—used to be a left-wing militant close to comrades that had ties to the RAF. In a turn of events that is more reminiscent of Three Days of the Condor or The Parallax View, it emerges that Murot's own boss in the police is involved in the liquidation of the man in the boat, with conspiracy and corruption reaching to the highest levels. It is an efficient way of giving an easily recognizable genre identity to the mutual implication of several rivaling institutions and political systems, but the most imaginative moves are in the way the television feature manages to evoke the protagonists' different but strangely symmetrical political pasts via the memory of a love story, which returns in mere outlines through mistaken identities, identical locations and hallucinations brought on by persistent headaches. Terror in "Wie einst Lilly" may be mainly of the Hitchcockian kind of finding oneself hunted by both the police and the bad guys, but the theme of trauma is ingeniously pathologized (instead of being psychologized) through the benign brain tumor that Murot knows he ought to have removed, but cannot find the time or courage to have done. The film is full of references to the other RAF narratives, notably a pastor very much in the mold of Gudrun Ensslin's father, but those in the know also recognize Ulrich Tukur, the actor playing Murot, as having been Baader in Reinhardt Hauff's STAMMHEIM, while the ex-RAF woman returned from the East and now his landlady, conjuring up visions of his former love (with echoes of Hitchcock's VERTIGO), is played by Martina Gedeck, the Ulrike Meinhof from THE BAADER MEINHOF COMPLEX. By furthermore alluding in its title to LILI MARLEEN, both the Fassbinder retro-spectacle with Hanna Schygulla and the song made famous during WWII by Lale Andersen, the film adds further reflexive layers of conflicting memories and counterpoint feelings, while making sure that its story is embedded not just in Nazi and RAF media memory, but in German (and Hollywood) film history as well.

The narrative of uncanny parallels—across the generations, but also between political and class antagonists—is perhaps most subtly fleshed out in Andres Veiel's BLACK BOX BRD, a documentary that, with minimal reenactments, and slow motion (courtesy of Errol Morris's THIN BLUE LINE), is tracking the lives of two very different individuals. One is the victim of a particularly diabolical and brutal assassination, the other a RAF member of the "third generation," possibly implicated in the car bomb assassination, but himself shot dead in an exchange of fire at a railways station, which also killed a policeman. Ostensibly, Alfred Herrhauser and Wolfgang Grams have nothing in common. The former, a high-flying, politically prominent, impatient and ambitious director of Deutsche Bank in Frankfurt; the latter a musically talented, drop out, aspiring actor (but also thinking of becoming a forester or pastor, i.e., dedicating his life to caring for nature or other human beings) and eventually hard-core RAF member, living in hiding for nearly ten years with his girlfriend. But as Veiel interviews Trudl Herrhauser, the banker's second wife, and Grams' parents, an infinite sadness invades both narratives. Sorrow transcends even the opposition of victim and perpetrator, especially as it becomes clear that both Herrhauser and Grams had made decisions, which increasingly isolated them from their friends, colleagues and loved ones. "In these interviews, the unequivocal distribution of roles quickly dissolves. The attempt to clarify how someone becomes victim and another one a perpetrator invariably point to the general social background,"[52] but it does not reproduce the "them" and "us" which prevailed at the time the events recalled in the interviews took place. Using two less well-known figures and the regional setting of Frankfurt-Wiesbaden doubly displaces the perspectives in BLACK BOX BRD. It allows the two standard narratives of either the Baader-Ensslin-Meinhof drama, or the Schleyer kidnap-Mogadishu hijack-Stammheim suicide denouement to be present, but only through our implicit knowledge, thus giving these wasted lives and devastated families an added melancholy tenor of belatedness and futility.[53]

The shift away from the protagonists towards grief and feelings of loss among those left behind is also noticeable in STARBUCK HOLGER MEINS (Gerd Conrad, 2001), which tells the story of the RAF member and avant-garde political filmmaker Holger Meins, nicknamed "Starbuck," after the pilot of the *Pequod*, the whaling ship in Herman Melville's *Moby Dick*—a novel that served the first RAF generation as a kind of allegorical self-representation (with Baader, of course, in the role of Ahab). But the documentary leaves much of this to one side, and instead tries to reinstate Meins as an artist: filmmaker, painter, poet. By restricting the scope to Meins' creativity, and seemingly "personalizing" the RAF narrative, Conrad does try to give a positive portrait of a terrorist, but since most if not all who are likely to see the film are cognizant of the story it doesn't tell, it helps raise more questions, rather than putting forward a RAF apologia. Meins is above all remembered thanks to two iconic photographs: one when surrounded in a Frankfurt safe house by the police and captured in his underwear, the other in his coffin, long beard and folded hands, after dying as the result of a hunger strike in prison—the latter image often compared to the Christological photo of the dead Che Guevara or Mantegna's Christ. Also well-known and notorious, is footage from Meins' funeral, with prominent figures at his graveside in November 1974, such as Otto Schily, the future Minister of the Interior, who once called Meins' death "execution in installments," and Rudi Dutschke, still recovering from the assassination attempt on him in 1968, who raised his fist and shouted: "Holger, the struggle continues." Not unlike Grams, whose sense of justice and compassion led him to join the RAF, Meins' major film is the sympathetic and respectful portrait of a Berlin homeless man and rag picker, called OSKAR LANGENFELD (1967).

But the actual hero and emotional center of STARBUCK HOLGER MEINS is Wilhelm Meins, Holger's father. As with Grams' father, major attention is given to the father generation, now not as part of the hated Nazi perpetrators, too arrogant, stupid or cowardly to either revolt or repent, but as grieving, sorrowful figures, unable to comprehend what had befallen them, and desperate to understand their intransigent sons.[54] It heralds one of the major changes in the RAF afterlife: the perspective has become that of the next generation, looking at their "grandfathers" with compassion or pity. Although Meins senior died in 1986, the filmmaker had interviewed him in 1975 and 1982, at a time when such a film could not have been made. Conrad, himself a friend and fellow filmmaker of the same generation as Meins, had to wait twenty-five years—precisely the time span of generational change—before the footage could be used. Meins senior speaks about the degrading conditions in prison, and the cynical way he thought the authorities had encouraged his son to die: a sentiment which outraged Helmuth Schmidt, who in a speech in 1974 said that those who have no compunction about blowing up innocent people should not complain about being inconvenienced when held in prison while their innocence or guilt is being established in a court of law. By 2001, the idea that, somehow, both sides had claims to making the case for themselves as victims seemed much more acceptable.[55]

Die Innere Sicherheit

The breakthrough film that established the perspective on the RAF afterlife of the grandchildren, i.e., the children of the sons and daughters of the "Auschwitz generation" was Christian Petzold's Die Innere Sicherheit/The State I'm In (2000). Told from the point of view of the fifteen-year-old Jeanne, it is the story of an ex-RAF couple and their daughter, in hiding in Portugal under an assumed name for more than a decade, who want to come in from the cold. The three return to Germany as a foreign land, where they are mere ghosts, haunting their former associates, and haunted by a past entirely irrelevant to the present. Without money or papers, they make their way back to Hamburg, but unable to get help from former friends or sympathizers, they take desperate measures. Meanwhile, the daughter is ever more determined to have a life of her own, untainted by her parents' paranoia and fear. The danger this puts the family in grows once Jeanne gets to know young people of her age, and the freedoms they take for granted. Yearning for a settled, ordinary life, she falls in love with the boy she first met in Portugal, knowing that it means the end of her family. "In Petzold's tragic story about the reverberation of terror, love is the contradictory end of terror and at the same time the continuation of trauma. The daughter of the terrorists, who also wishes for a bourgeois life, survives their violent, self-inflicted end and must live on. But she won't be able to forget these traumatic events. And neither shall we."[56]

Long silences—between Jeanne and her parents, between the parents, and between Jeanne and her boyfriend—punctuate the film, as if to carve out a negative space for the echo chamber of the sound and fury, the violence, the shoot-outs, the screeching tires and the shouting that in other films connotes the RAF. Atmospherically, these muted moments convey the leaden weight of inner terror and the paralyzing sense of being trapped in one's own nightmares, but as allegory, the silences also hint at the reluctance of society at large to speak about the militants of the 1970s as anything other than criminals and terrorists. Petzold, rather than taking the view that all those who in the 1970s found themselves on the run must have been lawless egomaniacs, or conversely, portraying them as victims, has found a cinematic way of marking a gap, leaving a space, intimating an absence, without feeling the need to fill it, as the grieving fathers, mothers and wives do in Black Box BRD and Starbuck Holger Meins.

Petzold, a graduate of the Berlin Film Academy, is also a cinephile. There are a number of filmic references in Die Innere Sicherheit, most conspicuously a scene where Jeanne watches Alain Resnais' NIGHT AND FOG, which brings "Auschwitz" back into the viewer's mind, but perhaps more to the point, also cites Margarethe von Trotta's DIE BLEIERNE ZEIT (THE GERMAN SISTERS) where another young girl has to watch NIGHT AND FOG at school, but too sensitive to stomach such images, she runs to the toilet to throw up: Marianne being a fictionalized Gudrun Ensslin. Petzold's Jeanne has no such reaction, as if to fault the causal nexus implied by von Trotta, of guilt and repression in the father-generation, leading to the daughter's violence and lethal protest. Again, the emphasis is on the subsequent generation, but perhaps it also suggests that Petzold wants to distance his family from fitting into the usual genealogy of terror→trauma→trauma→terror.

There is a further cinematic intertext that Petzold draws on: unlike BAADER, which tries to imitate HEAT, in order to look cool, DIE INNERE SICHERHEIT is, coolly and unobtrusively, a *remake* of Sidney Lumet's RUNNING ON EMPTY (1988), about a couple with two boys on the run, wanted for having, in their college days, bombed a lab in their university developing Napalm for the U.S. military. The matter-of-factness between parents and children, as well as their wit and intelligence seems to have impressed and inspired Petzold, who takes from Lumet's film the basic moral premise, namely that these are people who once made a choice and are willing to live with the consequences. In RUNNING ON EMPTY the consequences are hardest on the mother, who has to let go of her son, so that he can have a future, while DIE INNERE SICHERHEIT distributes the emotional weight, as it were, more evenly, with the result being a tragic, rather than an open ending. Lumet's 60s radicals are a blend of East Coast intellectuals and West Coast hippies, but they do not seem to have to carry an entire generation's burden of failed causes the way that Petzold's couple does. To this extent, the *remake* is also a *revision*, shaded several degrees darker than the source, as well as a transposition into a recognizably German setting, just minimalist enough to sustain its credibility as a parable and theorem.

Petzold is also the leading filmmaker in what has come to be known as the new "Berlin School," a label that carries its own history and afterlife, paralleling and indeed intersecting with that of the RAF. Film historians might recall that there already was a "Berlin School" in the 1970s, also associated with the (West) Berlin Film Academy. It counted among its teachers the left-wing documentary maker Klaus Wildenhahn, and among its alumni were Christian Ziewer, Ingo Kratisch, Erika Runge and Theo Gallehr, the founders of the German workers' films of the 1970s, but also Harun Farocki, Hartmut Bitomsky and Holger Meins. Meins, as indicated, joined the RAF, while his colleague Farocki, one of the most politically committed directors in the 1980s, is credited on virtually all of Petzold's films as co-author or script-adviser, indicative of a mentor role that unites two generations of filmmakers and suggests a special loyalty on the part of Petzold regarding the legacy of the other Berlin School and its radical roots. In other words, DIE INNERE SICHERHEIT may well draw its detached, but compassionate perspective from Petzold's—and Farocki's—intimate knowledge of the intellectual milieu once close to the RAF. As a critic noted: DIE INNERE SICHERHEIT "brilliantly builds a bridge between the New German Cinema, whose filmmakers were not shy of showing their sympathy for the RAF, and the present, where it is becoming possible to see terrorism in a historical perspective."[57]

The Baader-Meinhof Complex

Also claiming both intimate knowledge of the RAF and a historical perspective on the events is Stefan Aust, author of the most widely read book dealing with the subject, *Der Baader-Meinhof Komplex*, first published in 1985 and by 2008 in its third updated and revised edition. Aust's book served as the basis for the 2008 blockbuster by the same title, produced by Bernd Eichinger and directed by Uli Edel, both of whom wrote the script together with Aust. After having produced two films on Hitler (HITLER — A FILM FROM GERMANY, 1977, and DOWNFALL, 2004), Eichinger wanted THE BAADER MEINHOF COMPLEX to be the definitive account of the first generation of the RAF, and the crucial decade from 1967 to 1977. Initially intended for the thirtieth anniversary of the "Hot Autumn," the film was written and budgeted for an international—including a U.S.—release, costing almost $20 million, half of which were federal and regional (i.e., tax-payers') subsidies. Considering the budget, it was not a commercial success, earning less than half a million in the United States, and just over six million dollars worldwide (which compares very poorly with the $93 million world-wide for DOWNFALL).

How did Eichinger and Edel present this so eminently cinematic subject to the world? What had gone wrong in the calculations of these savvy film industry pros, and does their failure tell us anything about the public's perception of terrorism in the twenty-first century in general and of the RAF's afterlife in particular?[58] The screenplay opts for a conventionally linear, chronological account, showing first how the two central female protagonists, Ulrike Meinhof and Gudrun Ensslin meet each other, and are drawn into the more violent wing of the student protest movement, each out of different, but deeply held moral convictions and under personal circumstances that have as much to do with their contempt for male authority and arrogance (a philandering husband in the case of Meinhof, a stern and moralizing father in the case of Ensslin) as with orthodox Marxist convictions about the class struggle or social justice. In Ensslin's case, Baader had entered her life almost out of nowhere. Sexual attraction fanned by emotional intensity and a black-and-white worldview seems to have been the combustible mix that drove her into the "armed struggle" and illegality. In the case of Meinhof, when helping Baader escape, an action that cost a guard his life, she finds herself, more or less by accident, at a point of no return, shown by having her literally jump out of a window.

The second part focuses on the group's spectacular exploits—bank robberies, bombings, the Fatah training camp in Jordan—before the action returns to Germany, with more bombings and assassinations, shootouts with the police, the violent deaths of several core members and eventually the capture of almost all the leading figures. The third part establishes that the RAF became ever more preoccupied with themselves, their safety, their survival, how to evade the increasingly tight net of police surveillance, and after capture, how to communicate with those still outside and coordinate their actions, which were now mainly aimed at freeing the prisoners, leaving little or nothing for the struggle to mobilize the masses for the overthrow of capitalism.

The film draws a clear line: from care for others and concern for the world, the RAF, once underground, became self-obsessed and increasingly violent, provoking a counter-violence which aggravated and intensified the paranoia and violence of the group, until their aggression mostly turned against each other, with Ulrike Meinhof growing isolated and increasingly depressive, until she commits suicide in her cell. Against the background of hunger strikes and protests over solitary confinement, the prisoners prepare and obstruct the ongoing trial hearings, letting it be known that they fear for their lives at the hands of the authorities. The film ends, after the kidnap, hijack and failed rescue operation, with the subsequent suicides and the killing of Schleyer.

In the relentlessness with which the events follow each other on screen, it is easy to lose sight of the overall thesis: the reversal from young idealists caring for others, to narcissists caring only about themselves. While a strong point in the overall concept, it also indicates the weakness and limits of the film: pathologizing the RAF, without taking the time to develop individual psychologies means simplifying the conflicting motives that flow from them. Here the title is misleading: Meinhof, besides a journalist, reformer and a filmmaker, was a *complex* personality by any measure, a "figure out of a Dostoevsky novel" as her foster mother once described her, which is why so many writers have felt the need to "get inside her." Once the film, like the two women, are hijacked by Baader, any complexity is lost, replaced by complex in the military or pathological sense. Only at the very end, when Meinhof's mental breakdown is shown, does one have a moment to reflect on the enormity of her tragic waste.

Unlike the majority of the films discussed, which take a retrospective, melancholy or ruminating approach to their respective characters and narratives, Der Baader Meinhof Komplex knows only the present tense and thus foregoes such reflexive dimensions, turning itself into an action thriller, which must convince thanks to its own inner logic, short of becoming a naïve exercise in mimetic doubling, by presuming to show "how it really happened." Repetition has become "remediation as transparency"—a seamlessly staged presentation, enacted in the form of "coverage," without the periodic "returns" of the RAF as the irritating itch in the nation's self-understanding, and without in the process taking on any symptomatic significance. This way, the Baader

MEINHOF COMPLEX never becomes the German Nation Complex that it so evidently also partakes in.

Although the action scenes show the Hollywood-style professionalism of Eichinger's team, critical reception in Germany mostly complained that the thirty-odd years between the events and their retelling yielded no new insights, other than evoke nostalgic feeling about period clothes, haircuts, beards, shades and cars. Made to look authentic by their sheer quantity, the props' insistent "look-at-me" tipped them towards camp and pastiche.[59] On the other hand, in evacuating the politics after the first fifteen minutes and psychopathologizing the protagonists, THE BAADER MEINHOF COMPLEX did reproduce the current consensus, especially about Baader, as a born criminal and psychopath, alternatively childish and violently macho, for whom the fashionable politics of the day were merely an excuse to cause anti-social mayhem, fornicate, steal and kill without having to feel pangs of conscience or face the disapproval of his peers and followers.[60]

Given that "every RAF film confronts the same dilemma: how to compete with the sensational images the RAF image machine has churned out over the years, without itself succumbing to the fascination still emanating from them,"[61] THE BAADER MEINHOF COMPLEX had few qualms about simulating the RAF "live," rather than capturing the fascination in a refracted afterlife. Yet what if this "live" was already a staged effect for and with the media, which, as mentioned, is ultimately the condition of contemporary terrorism as a "collaborative project"? In this respect, the film makes of itself another "player" in this "co-production," and a latecomer, arriving on the scene with the claim to "demystify" the (politics of the) RAF, when it is in the logic of this game that it can only remythify the (personalities of the) RAF: "stop seeing them the way they weren't" is the critical advice one of the RAF women shouts to eager followers, meant, presumably, to humanize "them" [i.e., Baader, Meinhof, Ensslin]. For the rest, what is visible on-screen painstakingly "matches" the image material known from thirty years of media coverage, setting off a succession of recognition *aha-effects*, pleasurable at first but tiresome over two hours; taken out of their real or manipulated contexts, and immersed in the internal logic of an action film, these images cannot but add another layer to the *frisson* of their fetish appeal.[62]

A tension remains nonetheless, and as a result, the narrative is disjointed, moving in fits and starts, almost every episode culminating with the reenactment or restaging of one the iconic photographs known from press-coverage at the time and kept in active memory by the media and RAF folklore ever since. Once the iconic moment is reached, the scene breaks off, the action moves elsewhere, or the film switches to another character or location. It has earned it the satirical title of "The RAF: Their Greatest Hits," or worse, its numbers principle has been likened to a "porn film," grinding from climax to climax.[63]

The negative reactions point to a structural problem the writers were apparently unable to solve: how much background knowledge can they assume in their audiences, what information do they have to supply? This well-known dilemma of the historical epic was in this case aggravated by the fact that a German team was making the film for world audiences, on a topic that only Germans are familiar with, but so familiar with it that the movie-going public will resent being retold what it already knows so well. For the German spectators the restaging of the iconic photographs might have been reminders, but by the same logic, they would then want something other than an action picture that ticks these well-known photos off, one by one. They should at the very least appear in a new light: but then the film would have had to be *about* these photographs, rather than use them as surreptitious staging posts and pit stops in its forward rush.

In other words, Eichinger and Edel felt they had to navigate between keeping a German audience on board by the thrill of the blow by blow spectacle, while supplying an international audience with enough historical information to distinguish between the large cast of characters (there are 123 speaking parts, according to the press release), as well as to piece together into a coherent plot the motives, goals, setbacks, triumphs and denouements. In the end, they made a film that sins in both directions: too many clichés and predictable scenes for the home spectators, too little context and in-depth motivation to make the characters seem real to a Hollywood audience. By trying to make a Hollywood blockbuster in Germany, they were in the end neither sufficiently "European" (in finding fresh images or reflexively doubling them), nor sufficiently "American" (in sticking with genre), which would have required tighter plotting, the weaving together of external action, internal motivation and "character," and above all, hiring someone capable of writing dialogue with subtext, nuance, innuendo and wit.

But perhaps the main issue to raise with THE BAADER MEINHOF COMPLEX is that it so clearly subscribes to a dramaturgy of heroes and anti-heroes, and treats the cycle of returns and the thirtieth anniversary as an obligation to "demystify the myths," which not only ends up doing the opposite, but brutally simplifies the multi-layered fabric of the myth. No wonder that the real-life survivors and descendants of the RAF's victims complained that their side of the story is given no space or voice whatsoever, and that far too much attention is lavished on the antics of the anti-heroes.[64] As indicated, most of the other RAF films from the last decade include at least one significant character whose perspective is that of another generation or who can legitimately show grief: an ethical stance that is symptomatic for the wider transformations taking place. These tend to bring perpetrators and victims closer together, a trend in media memory more generally, and especially in its televisual forms, indicative of the attempt to create out of the nation's different disasters a loose, but still connected transgenerational community of victims.

Conclusion

Extrapolating from my earlier essay on the RAF, which documented a paradigm change in the filmic response to the Hot Autumn, from the perspective of the sympathizers (in GERMANY IN AUTUMN) to the mechanics of managing a political crisis (in DEATH GAMES), this chapter, too, has tracked the representation of the RAF in German cinema. Choosing the subsequent, third decade, I noted how the afterlife of this violent but relatively brief episode has continued to be a sort of barometer or litmus test for reevaluating wider processes of change, notably in the way that social and political history is transmitted in the arts and the media as "memory." I also argued that while the RAF appears to "return" as media event at least once every decade, it is never in the same narrative: this time, for instance, the generational perspective had undergone an inexorable shift from the "children" (of the Nazi "perpetrator generation") to that of the "grandchildren," with a corresponding reassessment of the old "father generation," now perceived as "grandfathers" and looked at with a new curiosity, if not necessarily always more kindness, but also judging their own parent generation—that of the RAF—more coldly and dispassionately. Both the RAF children (Bettina Röhl, Felix Ensslin) and the children of their victims (Michael Buback, Hanns Eberhard Schleyer) were often less forgiving of the RAF generation and their sympathizers, although the daughter of Ulrike Meinhof and the son of Gudrun Ensslin were, at least in public, at opposing ends of this spectrum, while the sons of prominent victims—Buback and Schleyer, for instance—also took public stances, especially regarding the possible pardon or early release for individual RAF prisoners.[65] As a consequence, some of the films became more contemplative and melancholy, absorbing whatever energies they could from these figures, while other films treated them as remote and yet close as any Hollywood gangster story. In either case, it has become more difficult to see a "parapractic" memory at work in the films and filmmakers since the 1990s, replaced by either ready-made simplifications or by a more clear-cut distribution of points of view, with Petzold's films perhaps the only ones that signal a certain mastery of parapraxis through a new aesthetic minimalism that does not shortchange the embedded contradictions and countervailing emotional currents.

The generational turn—along with the enormous intellectual upgrade that the periodizing trope "generation" has received[66]—confirms that the fascination with the RAF has remained unbroken, peaking in a pop-cultural appropriation of their symbols and insignia, complete with themed albums and fashion lines.[67] Although possessing its own authentic potential, and, as indicated, reflecting the precise degree of authenticity and artifice in the RAF itself, the pop appropriation was generally read as a way of further "depoliticizing" the RAF, with the consequence of the mainstream media, too, offering more of a psychogram of the main protagonists than a historical analysis. Especially

Andreas Baader came to be seen mainly as a psychopath obsessed with the paraphernalia of celebrity status and Hollywood stardom, which made the RAF's anti-Americanism now seem more like an *envy-Americanism,* with Baader aping Brando tough guys and James Dean matinee idols. The Hollywood emphasis is strongest in the two films BAADER and THE BAADER MEINHOF COMPLEX, of which the latter prides itself on its authenticity and historical research, while the former happily admits to inventing its story around motifs taken from the life of the RAF leader.

It suggests that, in the light of 9/11, the RAF now acts as a kind of protective fetish, against the much worse and even less graspable forms of terrorism that came after: as if, with the RAF, terror and trauma were at a scale when one could still contain it politically, and comprehend it within a-political and pop-psychological categories. By contrast, 9/11 and its aftermath is still so much beset with taboos that no negotiated or agreed-upon narrative has yet emerged, as shown by the aesthetic (and box office) failure of films as varied as Oliver Stone's WORLD TRADE CENTER (2006), Paul Greengrass' UNITED 93 (2006) or Stephen Daldry's EXTREMELY LOUD AND INCREDIBLY CLOSE (2011). These "failures" go hand in hand with the ubiquity of (retroactive) premonitions, uncanny echoes, or indirect allusions to 9/11 in Hollywood movies, as if the United States were still in the "parapractic" phase of coping with the "trauma" of being both perpetrators and victims, with all the asymmetric power-relations, gaps and "immemorials" this entails.[68]

A perhaps minor, but lasting after-effect of the RAF is, as indicated, that in Germany the generational logic has become so firmly absorbed and woven into the periodization of its post-war history. Yet even here, a difference between the 1970s and 1990s is noticeable. While previously, it required a "second" generation to retroactively produce a "first" generation, from which the second could distance itself or against which it could define its own identity, fashion and the Zeitgeist are now forever producing new "generations" claiming a unique historical moment of identity formation.[69]

Speaking more broadly, one could say that the RAF's afterlife—in the films and in the wider media landscape—shows many of the classic signs of how communities selectively remember and forget, across different social dynamics of differentiation, plurality and localization, but also by seeking to identify moments of authenticity and direct emotional appeal, thereby simplifying historical processes for the sake a memorable trope. This would "normalize" even Germany's obsession with the RAF. At the same time, the RAF episode also benefitted (if that is the right word) from another more overarching tendency that has emerged in the memory discourse since the 1990s, namely the gradual transformation of such emotionally and historical charged binary oppositions as perpetrator versus victim, or bystander versus sympathizer, into another, seemingly no less loaded, but also more malleable and adaptable category, namely that of the *survivor*: a group to whom almost everyone could belong, on the basis of very different attributes, by the very fact of (still) being alive. In fact, "survivor" makes life itself a traumatic phenomenon, which says a lot about the state of Europe and its belief in its future, since "survivor" implies a figure turned backward as s/he moves forward.

The reasons for this shift in vocabulary, and the politics behind it, thus go well beyond the RAF, and may have contributed to its afterlife being no longer quite the ghost that once stalked the land. As Europe embarked on fashioning a new consensus on its history, it "came to terms" with the Holocaust, by a process that in the end had to include Germany not only as a perpetrator nation. As terror chose different weapons with suicide bombings, and the response took on a different scale with the "war on terror," the RAF diminished in symbolic significance also for Germans, shrinking to the image that prevails in THE BAADER MEINHOF COMPLEX, as no more than a bunch of colorful criminals and desperado outsiders with political pretensions. Yet if the tenth anniversary of 9/11 in 2011 opened more old wounds and gave rise to more doubting and discordant voices than at any previous U.S. anniversary, who knows whether another anniversary—or another film—of the RAF history will also reveal (or revive) some of the *tragedy* of these lives and of their "Generation 68," where currently they appear as little more than a farce.

Notes

1. Thomas Elsaesser, "Antigone Agonistes: Urban Guerrilla or Guerilla Urbanism?" (http://www.rouge.com.au/4/antigone.html).
2. The literature on the "Hot Autumn" or "Germany in Autumn" is extensive, as is the body of work analysing the afterlife. I draw primarily on German sources, notably Wolfgang Kraushaar, Gerd Koenen, Klaus Theweleit and Heinz Bude.
3. Guerilla urbanism in the 1970s and 1980s took different forms in different European countries: from the "Hausbesetzer" in Germany to the kraker-movement in the Netherlands and the squatters in Great Britain. Since the 1990s, it has become a global phenomenon of reclaiming public space. For a brief historical overview, see Jeffrey Hou's introduction to his edited collection *Insurgent Public Space: Guerrilla Urbanism and the Remaking of Contemporary Cities* (New York: Routledge, 2010), 6–16.
4. Thomas Elsaesser, *Harun Farocki. Working on the Sight-Lines* (Amsterdam: Amsterdam University Press, 2004), 34.
5. "Ice-Nine is a crystalline form of water so stable it never melts. A single crystal of Ice-Nine would crystalize every bit of water it touched. Unfortunately, the melting point of Ice-Nine was 114 degrees; once the entire planet locked up, it would probably never melt." Kurt Vonnegut, *Cat's Cradle* (New York: Random House, 1963), 46–48 (http://www.technovelgy.com/ct/content.asp?bnum=415). "[H.C. Andersen's Snow Queen] is a romantic fairytale, a fiction rather than a folk-tale, where nonetheless the metaphor of ice and ice-coldness stands for a deathly and fatal indifference." Reiner Stollmann/Alexander Kluge, *Die Entstehung des Schönheitssinns aus dem Eis* (Berlin: Kadmos, 2005), 13.
6. See, for instance, Bruce Hoffmann, "Putting German Terrorism in Perspective: An American Response," German Historical Institute (GHI), *Bulletin,* 43 (Fall 2008), 59–65.
7. See, for instance, Andreas Elter, *Propaganda der Tat: Die RAF und die Medien* (Frankfurt: Suhrkamp, 2008). "In addition to its destructive force, terrorism is 'always also' a com-

municative strategy whose actual target is the general public rather than the direct victims of an attack. Elter's desire to locate a 'comparable orchestration of horror through terrorists' in the wake of 9/11 leads him to the West German RAF, which he describes as the 'first group ... to make extensive use' of advances in electronic mass media. The extent to which the RAF was unique in this regard may be called into question, since the Weathermen, the Popular Front for the Liberation of Palestine, Black September, the Japanese Red Army, and the Italian Red Brigades all employed similar strategies in the 1970s. This observation does not, however, undermine the central thrust of Elter's argument. Concentrating on acts intended to function as 'propaganda of the deed,' Elter demonstrates convincingly not only that terrorists have depended upon the media as a transmitter and amplifier of 'fear and horror,' but that the entire strategy of propaganda of the deed has only emerged and evolved in conjunction with advances in media technologies." Alan Rosenfeld, H-Net (German), January 2010 (http://www.h-net.org/reviews/showrev.php?id=26329).

8. An earlier, more extensive discussion of this topic can be found in my *Fassbinder's Germany — History Identity Subject* (Amsterdam: Amsterdam University Press, 1996), 175–96.
9. Ibid., 315–46.
10. See especially chapter 7 on Rainer Werner Fassbinder and chapter 9 on Harun Farocki in this volume.
11. A sketch of the different types of sympathizers and fellow travelers is given in Wolfgang Kraushaar, "Das Milieu der sogenannten Unterstützer und Sympathisanten" (http://www.bpb.de/geschichte/deutsche-geschichte-nach-1945/geschichte-der-raf/49229/sympathisanten).
12. The most notorious document was the so-called Mescalero manifesto, expressing satisfaction (*klammheimliche Freude*) over the death of Siegfried Buback. See Peter Brückner: *Die Mescalero-Affäre: ein Lehrstück für Aufklärung und politische Kultur* (Hannover: Internationalismus Buchladen u. Verlagsgesellschaft, 1977).
13. Felix Ensslin, born in 1967 is an author, curator, theater director and philosophy professor. See http://de.wikipedia.org/wiki/Felix_Ensslin
14. In the public statement at their trial in Stammheim, the RAF defendants frequently referred themselves to Fanon. See Martin Hoffmann (ed.), *Rote Armee Fraktion, Texte und Materialien zur Geschichte der RAF* (Berlin 1997), 238. Vesper himself quoted Stokely Carmichael's "Go home, kill your father and mother, hang yourself."
15. The younger generation—according to Koenen's (self-)interpretation—"Die Jungen—were obsessed by the thought of giving historical weight to their own biographies, while their parents could at least point to their endurance during the war and their achievements of rebuilding Germany after the war. This is why the sons and daughters were so ready to fantasize themselves into war-like situations, either against the background of the Third (atomic) World War or the Third World Liberation Wars." Gabriele Metzler, "Irrungen, Wirrungen — Die Selbst(er)findung einer Generation," *Frankfurter Allgemeine Zeitung*, July 2, 2001, Review of G. Koenen, *Das rote Jahrzehnt. Unsere kleine deutsche Kulturrevolution 1967–1977* (Köln: Kiepenheuer & Witsch, 2001). The same suggestion of a revolt by negative proxy is made in Heinz Bude, *Das Altern einer Generation* (Frankfurt am Main: Suhrkamp, 1995), 25.
16. This was also the case made by Christopher Hitchens: "The propaganda of the terrorists, on the few occasions when they could be bothered to cobble together a manifesto, showed an almost neurotic need to 'resist authority' in a way that their parents' generation had so terribly failed to do. And this was also a brilliant way of placing the authorities on the defensive and luring them into a moral trap." "Once Upon a Time," *Vanity Fair*, August 17, 2009.
17. The debate over the generational paradigm in Germany has been intense, vivid and central to several major research initiatives. One of the most important ones was coordinated by Sigrid Weigel at the Zentrum für Literaturforschung Berlin, where she was

also in charge of several major publications. Her central thesis is that "generation" has become an interpretative template ("Deutungsmuster") to the degree that other forms of periodization have lost their validity. Its advantage is that it allows for affirming a unity of experiences and attributes, while also positing a radical break with those who precede the group or cohort in question. At the same time, generation is such a semantically rich and pliable notion that it can serve as a placeholder for all kinds of rapid identity formations, and has become something like a symbolic form, accommodating both self-ascription and othering, but also playing a key role in the memory discourse of Germany since 1945. Sigrid Weigel, "Generation" as a Symbolic Form: On the Genealogical Discourse of Memory since 1945," *The Germanic Review* 77 (2002), 264–77.

18. In the United States, this generation is called "baby-boomers," tellingly named from the point of view of the parents, rather than the sons and daughters' perspective on their elders.
19. In the meantime, the generational paradigm has become so ubiquitous in the media for designating the generation of '68 that new explanatory models are being sought for the phenomenon and its consequences ("Generation Golf," "Berlin Generation"): "The most important feature of a generation is that adjacent birth-years understand themselves as sharing an experience-based identity." Heinz Bude, *Deutsches Allgemeines Sonntagsblatt*, November 13, 1998. "Where identity is based on class, there is a sense of tradition and supra-individual style; where there is social mobility, it's easy for the mechanisms of generational identity and sub-cultures to take over." Gustav Seibt, *Die Zeit*, March 2, 2000.
20. For younger Germans, the sympathy barometer peaked a little earlier: an often quoted statistic claimed that in 1971 one in five West Germans under the age of thirty said that they felt "a certain sympathy" for the Baader-Meinhof group. See "Jeder fünfte denkt etwa so wie Mescalero: Berlins Wissenschaftssenator Peter Glotz über Sympathisanten und die Situation an den Hochschulen. *Der Spiegel,* 41, 1977 (special issue on "Terrorism's Sympathizers"; http://www.spiegel.de/spiegel/print/d-40859179.html).
21. See the essays assembled in the "German issue" of *Semiotext(e)*, edited by Sylvere Lotringer (originally published in 1982, and reissued by MIT Press in 2009).
22. "Astrid Proll became a picture editor and released a 'family album' of the RAF under the title of the Grimm fairy tale 'Hans und Grete.' Brigitte Mohnhaupt works as a photographer, and Christian Klar is offered an education as stage designer by Claus Peymann after his release in 2009. As most of the RAF terrorists were professional media practitioners when diving into the political underground, they were fully conscious of their use of emblematic elements in the setting of victim photographs, in their snapshots among themselves, in their appearances before court, in the imagery of their prison life, and, most of all, in the allegoric utilisation of the RAF logo and typography." Rolf Sachsse, "On the logocracy of the RAF emblem" (http://old.rietveldacademie.nl/index.php?id=1452).
23. Apart from the influence of Guy Debord's *Society of the Spectacle* (1967), the main inspiration for the RAF's media strategy was Carlos Marighella's *Minimanual of the Urban Guerrilla* (1969), whose section on "Information" argues that modern mass media can be manipulated to serve the ends of counter-movements and thus provide an effective weapon of terrorist propaganda (http://www.marxists.org/archive/marighella-carlos/1969/06/minimanual-urban-guerrilla/index.htm).
24. "That the fascist mass movement in Germany was itself born of the spirit of resistance and driven by a socially rebellious, anti-establishment, anti-capitalist resentment; that this affective syndrome was able to recharge itself through anti-Semitism, the Aryan Nation and the Master Race; that this highly contaminated anti-capitalism finally turned against 'international finance capital' in the form of the 'rich Jew,' whose belongings one could ruthlessly appropriate without shame or guilt—all this we didn't

want to know before Götz Aly, in his book *Hitler's Beneficiaries* provided us with the evidence." (http://web.psychosozial-verlag.de/psychosozial/details-rezension.php?isbn=3-89806-352-6&id=35&p_id=352)

25. The phrase comes from an early book by Jillian Becker, *Hitler's Children: The Story of the Baader-Meinhof Terrorist Gang* (Philadelphia: Lippincott, 1977), but was later moved one generation along in Hans-Jürgen Wirth, *Hitlers Enkel—oder Kinder der Demokratie? Die 68er-Generation, die RAF und die Fischer-Debatte* (Giessen: Psychosozial-Verlag, 2001).
26. For a history of anti-Israel actions and anti-Semitic sentiment among the radical left preceding the RAF, see Wolfgang Kraushaar, *Die Bombe im jüdischen Gemeindehaus* (Hamburg: Hamburger Edition, 2005).
27. Wolfgang Kraushaar, "Zwischen Popkultur, Politik und Zeitgeschichte. Von der Schwierigkeit, die RAF zu historisieren," Zeithistorische Forschungen/Studies in Contemporary History, Online-edition, 1 (2004), H. 2 (http://www.zeithistorische-forschungen.de/16126041-Kraushaar-2-2004).
28. Jacques Derrida would give the Hamlet-ghost configuration new international validity with the coinage of "hauntology" in his *Specters of Marx. The State of the Debt, the Work of Mourning & the New International* (London: Routledge, 1994), although he was of course referring himself to the opening sentence of Marx' & Engels' *Communist Manifesto*.
29. An intriguing sidelight is thrown on the media background and artistic ambitions of some of the RAF members by a grim anecdote from the early 1970s: "In December 1971, the sculptor Dierk Hoff got an unexpected visit at his inner-city Frankfurt studio. Two young men were at the door: one of them was Holger Meins, a student at the Berlin Film Academy; the other called himself 'Lester'—his real name was Jan-Carl Raspe. After smoking a few joints and talking about 'hippies and subculture,' the two men asked if Hoff could help them build props for a film they were working on. He agreed, in principle. What props? Meins showed him a picture of a hand grenade. Hoff asked what sort of film they were trying to make. 'Eine Art Revolutionsfiktion,' Meins replied. 'A kind of revolutionary fiction.' By the time that Meins and Raspe were arrested as part of the Baader-Meinhof gang in June 1972, Hoff's "props" had been used in five major bomb attacks in West Germany which left six people dead and at least 45 seriously injured. Fiction had turned into reality in the most violent way thinkable." Philip Oltermann, "The Well-Read Terror," *The Guardian*, November 15, 2008.
30. "The 78er, those who are now in their forties, were too late for the revolutions of the sixties, but in the 80s, they found themselves in front of the locked doors of the reform society that did not seem to need them. [...] as members of a historically irrelevant in-between generation, they fell through the imaginary grate of the Zeitgeist. [...] They had no label, no identity." Reinhard Mohr, *Zaungäste. Die Generation, die nach der Revolte kam* (Frankfurt a/M: Fischer, 1992), 2.
31. "The social contribution of [the Generation Golf ...] is the definition of one's own existence across advertising slogans and fashion brands." Florian Illes, "Generation Golf," *Leipziger Volkszeitung*, May 4, 2000.
32. See Wolfgang Kraushaar, *Fischer in Frankfurt* (Hamburg: Hamburger Edition, 2001) for a detailed history of the Frankfurt context for many of these activists.
33. The accusations of paedophilia, also launched by Bettina Röhl, became especially virulent in France, though not when Daniel Cohn-Bendit published his memoir, *Le Grand Bazar* (Paris: Belfond, 1975), but twenty-five years later, after he became a Member of the European Parliament and leader of the French Green Party. At that time *Libération* in France, *Bild-Zeitung* in Germany, *La Reppublica* in Italy and *The Independent* in Britain published supposedly salacious extracts. See Kate Connolly, "Sixties hero revealed as kindergarten sex author," *The Observer/Guardian*, January 28, 2001.
34. "And the Baader-Meinhof sympathisers and lawyers? Why, one was Gerhard Schröeder, who became German Chancellor; another became the Interior Minister responsible for

counter-terrorism in Schroeder's government. And, as elsewhere in Europe, the others are now firmly ensconced in a 'liberal' establishment that, on closer inspection, does not seem 'liberal' at all." Michael Burleigh, "The Clowns of Terror," *Daily Mail*, March 7, 2008.

35. "How can it be that historical episodes that shocked a whole generation, become the plaything of the next generation?" Martin Warnke, "Warum ausstellen, was alle schon kennen?" *Art*, no. 12 (December 2003), 78.
36. The Prada-Meinhof label was a British import: "In spring 2001, the fashion company Prada releases a collection under the title 'Prada Meinhof'—a clear assonance to the 'Baader Meinhof Group' which was the criminalist name of the self-attributed 'RAF' (Rote Armee Fraktion—Red Army Faction). Just two years prior, an exhibition at the ICA London established the use of both the name and the emblem of the German terrorists as a part of the radical chic then fashionable." Rolf Sachsse, "On the logocracy of the RAF emblem" (http://old.rietveldacademie.nl/index.php?id=1452).
37. Kraushaar, "Zwischen Popkultur, Politik und Zeitgeschichte."
38. An essay devoted to the pop cult around the RAF in the various media such as film, literature, theater, music and fashion magazines can be found on a website specially dedicated to the RAF and its afterlife (http://www.rafinfo.de/archiv/files/RAF-Pop.pdf).
39. "For several decades now there can be no question of a 'cowardly repression' [of the Holocaust]—more like a vital act of appropriation. [...] But the peculiar narcissistic bond the Germans have with Auschwitz, their obsessive desire to 'master' and 'work through' their own past—that permanent source of self-mortification—does not stop there. For when we Germans today readily acknowledge that the victims [of Nazism] retained a deeper loyalty to their 'portable fatherland' i.e. German literature and culture, than our perpetrator parents, who betrayed it in the most shameful way, our identification with the victims puts us on their side, makes us belong to them, and so we, too, are 'survivors', and at the same time, we are reborn, reborn Germans." Gerd Koenen, "Mythen des 20. Jahrhunderts," in Doron Rabinovici, Ulrich Speck and Natan Sznaider (Hg.) *Neuer Antisemitismus? Eine globale Debatte* (Frankfurt/M: Suhrkamp. 2004), online at http://www.gerd-koenen.de/artikel_kommentare.htm#a4
40. See also Jean Baudrillard, "Requiem for the Media," *For a Critique of the Political Economy of the Sign* (St. Louis: Telos Press, 1981), 168–78.
41. The State Art Collections Dresden advertised its loan acquisition of Gerhard Richter's Stammheim series of painting *October 18, 1977* on its website as follows: "In a city like Dresden, scarred by death and suffering in 1945, and in light of the current debate on terrorism, the work of Gerhard Richter can serve like no other to ask once more how especially works of art can get closer to subjects of recent history, outside the rigidified patterns of explanation, when their proper place and our mastery of them still eludes us [...]. Gerhard Richter himself has declared: 'The death of the terrorists and all the events relating to them, before and after, name a monstrosity that touched me, and even if I repressed it for a time, it came to preoccupy me like some unfinished business'." (http://www.skd-dresden.de/de/ausstellungen/aktuell/Gerhard_Richter___18_Oktober_1977.html)
42. Starting with *Bild* ("Why does Berlin pay 100.000 Euro for an outrageous exhibition devoted to the RAF?") and regional newspapers (Ludolf Schulte, "Streit um erste RAF-Ausstellung," in *Düsseldorfer Stadtpost*, 15.5.2003) the whole sprectrum of media outlets and politicians—including the Minister of the Interior and the Federal Chancellor - was mobilized to stop the exhibition from taking place ("Politiker wollen Terror-Ausstellung stoppen," *Bild-Zeitung*, 23.7.2003). See Christoph Stölzl, "Was soll denn da gezeigt werden?" in *Der Tagesspiegel*, 2.8.2003.
43. Wolfgang Kraushaar, whom I have been citing several times, was—as representative of the Hamburg Institute for Social Research—actively involved in the preparations

around the exhibition. See also the critical commentary by Gerd Koenen, who also for a time acted as consultant for the curators: "Black Box RAF: Zur symbolischen und realen Geschichte des linken Terrorismus in Deutschland," *Kommune*, Heft 2/2005, also on Koenen's Homepage http://www.gerd-koenen.de/artikel_kommentare.htm#a5

44. Aleida Assmann and Ute Frevert, *Geschichtsvergessenheit — Geschichtsversessenheit: Vom Umgang mit deutschen Vergangenheiten nach 1945* (Stuttgart: Deutsche Verlags-Anstalt, 1999), 3.
45. http://www.art-in-berlin.de/incbmeld.php?id=705&-Kunstwerke
46. Christian Semler, "Es war die Verheissung," *die tageszeitung*, April 24, 2001.
47. Asked to clarify whether he had meant to equate art and crime, Stockhausen replied "It is a crime because the people were not agreed. They didn't go to the 'concert.' That is clear. And no one gave them notice that they might pass away ['draufgehen': "snuff it"]. What happened there spiritually, this jump out of security, out of the everyday, out of life, that happens sometimes poco a poco in art. Otherwise art is nothing." "Stockhausen provoziert Eklat mit Äußerungen zu USA," Associated Press, September 18, 2001.
48. Gerd Koenen, "Rituale der Labilität — Wozu eine Ausstellung über die RAF?" *Süddeutsche Zeitung*, 26/27 Juli 2003. (http://www.gerd-koenen.de/artikel_kommentare.htm#a1)
49. Cited in Bill Readings, *Introducing Lyotard: Art and Politics*. (London: Routledge, 1991; 2nd. ed. 1992), p. xxxii.
50. "I didn't find the reality all that interesting ... at a certain point I put all of that aside and told a story of my own," quoted in Ulrich Behrens, *Follow Me Now* (http://behrens-freiburg.de/html/body_baader.html).
51. For more information on Verena Becker and the reopening of the Buback case, see *Der Spiegel Online*, April 23, 2007 (http://www.spiegel.de/international/germany/0,1518,478928,00.html) and (in German) http://www.tagesspiegel.de/zeitung/die-verlorene-ehre-der-verena-becker/839738.html.
52. Georg Seesslen, *Das Todesspiel: Die RAF im Film*, WDR 5 (Radio), April 27, 2007.
53. The director published a book to go with the film, documenting his research. Andres Veiel, *Black Box BRD: Alfred Herrhausen, die Deutsche Bank, die RAF, und Wolfgang Grams* (Stuttgart: Deutsche Verlags-Anstalt, 2003).
54. In Black Box BRD, there is even a suggestion that the father *does* understand the son's silent withdrawal and subversive actions: "Curiously enough, father Grams [ex-SS man] and son [ex-RAF member] did find common ground after all — in the illegality of going underground. [...] In what must be the most scary scene in the film, we see a father, who completely understands his son's silence over what he is planning and what he has done. It wasn't all that different during the war." Claus Christian Malzahn, "Republikflucht der Romanciers," *Der Spiegel*, May 3, 2005 (http://www.spiegel.de/kultur/literatur/ost-literaten-republikflucht-der-romanciers-a-354469.html).
55. On this afterlife, see also Werner Bohleber, "Das Fortwirken des Nationalsozialismus in der zweiten und dritten Generation nach Auschwitz," *Babylon*, 7 (1990), 70–83.
56. Georg Seesslen, *Das Todesspiel: Die RAF im Film.*
57. Michael Althen, "Im Reich der Schatten: Christian Petzolds Filme" (http://www.goethe.de/kue/flm/far/de4055772.htm).
58. Not all reviews of The Baader-Meinhof Complex were negative. Especially among the Anglo-Saxon commentators, several had nothing but praise for the film, or rather their detestation of the RAF found in the film a suitable vehicle. This would be the case of Michael Burleigh, Christopher Hitchens and Jeffrey Herf. Herf, for instance, writes, regarding the rumor of the Stammheim deaths having been assassinations rather than suicides: "*Der Baader-Meinhof Komplex* places on the big screen the truth about these self-inflicted deaths, which RAF supporters transformed into a politically useful story of martyrdom at the hands of the allegedly fascist state." J. Herf, "Unpleas-

ant Truths," *The New Republic*, December 30, 2008 (http://www.newrepublic.com/article/books-and-arts/unpleasant-truths).

59. "Every object in every image is eager to tell us about its historical provenance." Diedrich Diederichsen's remark in a review of *Das Wunder von Bern* (Sönke Wortmann, 2003) also applies to DER BAADER MEINHOF KOMPLEX (http://www.filmzentrale.com/rezis/wundervonberndd.htm).
60. Good examples of this consensus are Hitchens' "Once Upon a Time" and Burleigh's "Clowns of Terror."
61. Matthias Dell, "Der Baader Meinhof Kompott," *Freitag*, September 26, 2008 (http://www.freitag.de/autoren/der-freitag/das-baader-meinhof-kompott).
62. "... and at some point, a young man is shot down, and then a rather smartly dressed woman comes along, lifts the young man's head, a photographer snaps a picture, in the background we see a car with the licence plate B-WM 960—and that's 'June 2nd,' that's 'the death of Benno Ohnesorg.' In a 'Memory' game you'd have scored a point by now. But what has been scored by the film?" Ibid.
63. Ibid.
64. See the well-known interview with one of the ex-RAF members, allegedly the assassin of both Martin Schleyer and Siegfried Buback, Stefan Wisnewski, "Wir waren so unheimlich konsequent ... Ein Gespräch zur Geschichte der RAF," *die tageszeitung*, October 11, 1997.
65. See Michael Buback, *Der zweite Tod meines Vaters* (Munich: Droemer, 2008).
66. For an overview, see Sigrid Weigel, "Families, Phantoms, and the Discourse of 'Generations' as a Politics of the Past: Problems of Provenance: Rejecting and Longing for Origins," in Stefan Berger, Linas Eriksonas and Andrew Mycock (eds.), *Narrating the Nation. The Representation of National Histories in Different Genres* (Oxford: Berghahn Books, 2008), 133–51.
67. Philip Oltermann mentions "Baader-Meinhof-themed concept albums and songs" by Luke Haines, Brian Eno, Marianne Faithfull and Chumbawamba. See Oltermann, "The Well-Read Terror."
68. See Caryn James, "Quiet, but unmistakable, echoes of 9/11 work their way onto the screen," *New York Times*, May 14, 2007. "Successful" but indirect 9/11 films include Michael Moore's anti-Bush pamphlet FAHRENHEIT 9/11 (2004), Alejandro Gonzalez Inarritu's BABEL (2006) and James Marsh's documentary MAN ON A WIRE (2008).
69. Although said to have been inspired by Douglas Coupland's *Generation X: Tales for an Accelerated Culture* (London: St Martin's Opress, 1991), generational paradigms are also home-grown in Germany: see Florian Illies, *Generation Golf. Eine Inspektion* (Frankfurt: Fischer, 2001); *Generation Commodore 64*: Christian Stöcker, "Die Generation C64 schlägt zurück," *Spiegel* online 2. June 2, 2009; *Null Bock Generation* (http://de.wikipedia.org/wiki/Null-Bock-Generation), *Generation Prekär* (http://de.wikipedia.org/wiki/Generation_Praktikum). An intellectually ambitious German website is called Single-Generation (http://www.single-generation.de/) while the "Generation 89" is a Europe-wide, officially sponsored initiative: "The project 'Generation '89' proposes to commemorate the fall of the communist systems in Europe, through the lens of young people born in 1989." (http://www.generation89.eu/)

PART II

Parapractic Poetics in German Films and Cinema

5

RESCUED IN VAIN

Parapraxis and Deferred Action in Konrad Wolf's Stars

Konrad Wolf's STERNE (SVEZDI/STARS, 1959) is one of the better known (though less often seen) films produced in the former GDR. As an early treatment of the reaction of an "ordinary" German to the concentration camps and the deportation of Jews, the film reflects the "clean conscience" of the state-owned DEFA film studios in the process of coming to terms with the Nazi past (*Vergangenheitsbewältigung*). But Wolf's film is also about love, self-sacrifice and resistance, and uses filmic idioms reminiscent of classic melodrama and Italian Neorealism, as well as the first stirrings of European auteur cinema. Despite the almost sacrosanct aura surrounding this film, we should not hesitate to reexamine it, however, treating certain junctures in its plot structure as a sort of palimpsest—that is, as a specific layering of moments, a sedimentation of known images and historical references, whose political and hermeneutic function, I argue, can be read anew in retrospect. Today these temporal layers appear in a new light in view of the migration of, and dialogue between visual motifs, which is typical of contemporary memory discourse and which, in turn, characterizes the general memory culture that has grown up around the Holocaust since the 1990s, not only in Germany, but in Europe as a whole. This process of layering, sedimentation, migration and return—typical of "media memory" in post-1989 Europe—is here already present in a film made in 1959, in a country that, as the saying goes, has disappeared from the map.

In revisiting STARS by examining its flashback structure and the question of agency—that is, the motivation and actions of its protagonists—it becomes clear that the film does not correspond to the psychoanalytic model of "working-through," in terms of which *Vergangenheitsbewältigung* tends to be discussed. In contrast, my suggestion is to interpret the film performatively, not only in the poststructuralist sense of the word, but also in the sense of a Freudian slip or parapraxis. Parapraxis (*Fehlleistung*) can be understood as an apparent mistake of speech, action or behavior, which, on closer inspection, reveals another layer of meaning. As argued in the previous chapter, the German term situates itself in a dual register, depending on where one puts the emphasis: it can signify either "failed performance" or "performance of failure." The latter would retain the positive connotations of performance and refer to a special poetics of ambivalence, needed for narratives or films that try to address the consequences of catastrophically bad decisions in a way that, nonetheless, allows the protagonists of disaster their own motivations without either justifying or condemning them in light of what, in retrospect, would seem to have been the "wrong" decision. To parapraxis in this sense apply the words of Paul Ricoeur, "The point [of historiography] is to first accord the past its own future."[1]

Conceptually, this "poetics of parapraxis" is an extension and elaboration of the idea of a "historical imaginary," which plays a central role in my book on the cinema of the Weimar Republic.[2] Insofar as both concepts deal with the implicit or unconscious knowledge of a work about the historicity of its own cinematic means and effects, a poetics of parapraxis is the opposite of pastiche or ironic reflexivity. Its chief characteristic is the respective double inscription (and, along with it, the trace of possible discrepancies) of time and place, of intention and agency, of authenticity and citation, of knowledge and ignorance. Such a poetics of parapraxis has exemplary relevance with respect to Konrad Wolf, whose acute awareness of deferred action (*Nachträglichkeit*) and asynchronicity throughout his work once persuaded Michael Wedel and myself to compare STARS to Nazi aesthetics and the first post-war West German productions: "STARS … is an archetypal melodrama of the victim and victimization that, in a typically German pattern predating Wolf, … casts women as victims in order to test the male protagonist's capacity for change, while the women are tested for their endurance in suffering."[3]

Although not entirely wrong, this rather harsh judgment overlooked certain crucial nuances within the stereotypical story elements, which lend the film a new relevance. In particular, its significance today derives from our current experience in a united Germany and Europe, where televisual and cinematic media-memory tends to assume a superior moral position, derived entirely in hindsight. The question to ask, then, is to what extent does STARS—a representative production of East German cinema, after all—make its contribution to *Vergangenheitsbewältigung*, as defined above, precisely by already challenging this easy wisdom in hindsight, opting for a "performance of failure," rather than representing an example of a "failed performance" as our negative remarks about its gender-bias apologetics seemed to imply.

A central role is played in the film by the idea of a past that continues to inscribe itself, not in the present of the plotline, but rather in the future of historical events. This yields a more complex relationship to the historical moment of the film's creation (1959), now placed in the framework of our current knowledge of these historical events (as well as of the GDR's history) and the post-1989 memory culture, called either "postmemory" or "prosthetic memory."[4] In brief, my new reading of STARS is prompted by an "archaeology" of our contemporary mode of representing history in film and on television, of how public recollection and commemoration is inflected by the memory of images, especially as this history relates to fascism, socialism, Germany's Nazi past and the persecution of Jews.

Konrad Wolf and STARS

STARS was a German-Bulgarian coproduction which was offered to Konrad Wolf after the treatment, written by the Bulgarian novelist and screenwriter Angel Wagenstein, had already been completed.[5] The story concerns a German corporal who, in 1943, bitter and convinced of the senselessness of war after having been on the eastern front, is sent to oversee a mechanics' garage in a Bulgarian town. When a transport of Sephardic Jews from Greece is temporarily housed in the town's school, he meets a young Jewish woman who asks him to bring a doctor for a pregnant woman.

At first he is indifferent to their plight and refuses; her accusation that all Germans are wolves, however, is troubling enough to persuade him to get medicine and a doctor. A sense of attachment and burgeoning love between the two slowly leads him to change sides. When he finally brings himself to arrange for a hiding place for the young woman, to save her from death in Auschwitz, he is too late. The transport has already left; he sees the last cars disappear into the night, while she looks out from between the bars of one of the boxcars. In a short final sequence, we see the corporal offer his services to the Bulgarian partisan leader as a go-between for arms deliveries to the communist resistance.

The film has attracted numerous interpretations, which often refer—at least figuratively—to Wolf's own biography.[6] It is not difficult to recognize in Walter, the protagonist, and Ruth, the Greek Jew, a constellation of characters that recurs in Wolf's films (Frohmeyer-Lissy in LISSY, 1957), Mamlock-Rolf in PROFESSOR MAMLOCK, 1961), and Manfred-Rita in DER GETEILTE HIMMEL (DIVIDED HEAVEN, 1964). Walter calls to mind other male protagonists in Wolf's work, particularly in terms of the inner conflict they endure about their identity as Germans and their divided self when it comes to a sense of loyalty, duty and moral responsibility. At no point and in no place in the film does Walter truly feel at home: neither in the *Wehrmacht*, nor in the pub with his buddy Kurt; neither among the interned Jews, nor among the Bulgarians who work for the Germans, although he speaks their language, he feels as indifferent to them as he does to the war. Least of all does he belong among the communist partisans, who can hardly trust him, as a German soldier: for them he remains a German and, as soon as he helps them, becomes a "traitor to his own people."

This accusation had also been leveled against Wolf, following his return from Moscow in the late 1940s. The allegation of having changed sides—viewed either positively as resistance or negatively as treason—plays a central role in the literature on Wolf.[7] When understood in negative terms, as identity confusion and a source of uncertainty and indecision, it can also be interpreted in a positive sense, however, as the deeper reason for a particular quality of Wolf's films, a capacity for being true to oneself and showing moral rectitude. Sensitive and remarkably clear-sighted about personal dilemmas throughout his work, in his life, too, he had to negotiate radically irreconcilable elements. For instance, he had to find a viable position between the contradictory demands made on him by his triple identity as a German, a (Russian) communist, and a Jew. Always liable to find himself on the "wrong" side (of history), caught between so many different fronts, he had to assume complicity for actions in which he took no part, or found himself an actor in events whose consequences only caught up with him in retrospect. These agonizing strains were the source of Konrad Wolf's creative inspiration and may well guarantee the continuing relevance of his oeuvre today. The same biographical dislocations would therefore also fuel the dynamics that make the concept of "performative parapraxis" pertinent to Wolf's films, giving us one of the reasons why this director still fascinates us today as a European auteur filmmaker, while also directing our attention to the specific question of how both personal history—that of the director, as well as of the screenwriter—and the history of cinema inscribe themselves into STARS.[8]

Historical and Political Contexts

Presented as the Bulgarian contribution at the 1959 Cannes Film Festival, STARS won the Special Jury Prize. It was, one will recall, the year of the *nouvelle vague*, with Truffaut winning the Best Director award for LES QUATRE CENTS COUPS (THE 400 BLOWS). STARS not only made Konrad Wolf famous, it also caused a diplomatic incident in German-German relations. The film is a historical document, if only because of the fact that a work by a German director could, after an official protest from a German foreign office appealing to the so-called Hallstein Doctrine, only be shown at this international film festival as a Bulgarian, not a German film.

A further political dimension can be ascribed to STARS insofar as it was one of DEFA's first co-productions with a "socialist brother-land" and, through its prize at Cannes, brought the East German film studio considerable international legitimacy in both East and West.[9] In the European context, its historical meaning is ultimately that it is the first film by a German director in which Auschwitz and the persecution of Jews are directly thematized. Even though films such as OSTATNI ETAP (THE LAST STOP), produced by the Polish director Wanda Jakubowska in 1948, had been shown in both the GDR and FRG, no other German director had dared come as close to this sensitive topic as Wolf. This circumstance still gives *Stars* an exceptional status and perhaps further explains why the film has most often been treated with particular reverence by critics.

If I recall these contradictory, but in the end productive historical dimensions of STARS, it is to argue that the film, seen against multiple backgrounds, requires an equally multiple—dislocated and parapractic—perspective:

- First, rather than merely historicize the film's reception history, an immanent reading should be given to the fact that it was subsequent events which endowed STARS with the special significance it now has and that these retroactive revisions are now part of the historical meaning of the film. In other words, the film is part of a particular "historical imaginary" because, in its case, the present was able to change its own past, especially when seen in light of the unification of Germany in 1990 and the resulting double status of the GDR within this new/old country, as object of disavowal as well as of nostalgia and regret.
- Second, there is the central role the Holocaust is now playing as a defining moment in the identity of the European Union. As a consequence of such a recentering of the Second World War, several of Konrad Wolf's films can now be understood more generally as memory documents and monuments within the present memory culture of Europe's "divided memories," particularly in the face of EU expansion to the East and the aftermath of the Balkan Wars.[10]
- Third, in a certain sense reaching back to my first point, but now within a European perspective, is the question of how Wolf's films serve as sediments of a future memory culture about another trauma and touch on the political core of the post-war period, which we—because it is too close to us—are perhaps still unable to formulate correctly (although it is, of course, constantly being discussed and narrated): namely, the trauma of the "betrayal" of the idea of a better, different, more just world—betrayed in equal measure by the Stalinist version of socialism and by its victorious opponent, liberal market capitalism.

While this indicates the metahistorical and conceptual horizons of why a new reading and revision of STARS is both suitable and challenging at this point in time, the concrete historical references to the time of the film's production can likewise not be overlooked. One is faced, on one hand, with the political situation around 1959: the film was made after the 1956 Hungarian Revolution and the Suez Crisis, but before the Eichmann trial in Jerusalem and the Auschwitz trial in Frankfurt, and also before the construction of the Berlin Wall (which Wolf thematized in DIVIDED HEAVEN, 1964). On the other hand, the significance of the debates that took place in the late 1950s about the function of the feature film in the GDR, where the question of how DEFA films ought to engage with the "contemporary problems of people in the GDR" was repeatedly raised, cannot be underestimated. When one considers that SONNENSUCHER (SUN SEEKERS, 1958/71), the film produced by Wolf directly before STARS, was banned by the censors because it dealt with problematic aspects of the relationship between the Soviet Union and the GDR, it seems symptomatic that his acceptance of the subsequent project should avoid contemporary East German issues, focusing instead on the Second World War and a period when, according to official GDR doctrine, the Soviet Union heroically conquered fascism and liberated Germany.[11]

What traces remain of these historical circumstances in the film, and what future does it outline for those aspects we now can, and must read into the film as deferred action, or *action après coup,* given our knowledge in hindsight? The question already points to the palimpsest-like character of films that engage with history in general and, more specifically, with the persecution of the Jews. How do such films cope with the knowledge that they can neither withhold, nor impart to their protagonists? What do they do with the inevitability of the catastrophe they would just as soon have not taken place? *The parapractic core of such films is that the unavoidable becomes the (un)representable and the (un)representable becomes the unimaginable.* Particularly in the case of the Holocaust it seems paradoxical that this catastrophe, apostrophized time and again as the (un)representable per se, has proven, over the last thirty years, to be perhaps the most narrativized event (in literature and film) of the entire twentieth century—so much so that a whole iconography surrounding the Holocaust has emerged, with its own genres, sub-genres and predetermined interpretative frameworks. In this sense, the clichéd elements of STARS, critiqued in our earlier essay, are also the effect of another type of temporally displaced action, according to which Wolf's film seems clichéd in retrospect because of the many films that were produced later and that lodged their images so deeply into our subconscious over the course of the 1980s—repetition as a motor of knowledge in ignorance.

If we now consider the film from its own political and historical position, it presents itself as a particularly good example of what I described as the mode of "working through" the past, albeit specific to the dominant ideology of the socialist countries around 1960, rather than to the needs and desires of the West German *Vergangenheitsbewältigung* of the 1970s and 1980s. Viewing STARS as a variant of the *Bildungsroman*, we encounter a protagonist who is sensitive yet irresolute and whose striking nihilism reveals not only his defeatism with regard to the war, but also the hard shell surrounding the soft core of his idealism. Through an external demand, or rather a provocation ("All Germans are the same.... wolves!"—another self-referential pun, in view of the director of the film), Walter is confronted with his own indecision, finally faces up to the choices he must make and finds his way into determined antifascism and—by implication—militant socialism.

From this perspective, East German critics were able to confirm that "Wolf, Wagenstein and Werner Bergmann [the cameraman] draw on artistic devices that are as simple as they are clear and convert the linear plot into memorable images."[12] Read in this way, the sacrifice of the woman acquires meaning—not unlike, one might argue, in a Hollywood Western (a genre both imitated and turned inside out in many a DEFA production), where the woman must sacrifice herself so that the man can become a man. In Hollywood's case, however, it is the demimondaine from the saloon or brothel who clears the way for the teacher, whereas here it is the teacher who sacrifices herself so the hero can commit himself to socialism.

I am consciously employing this somewhat casual form of comparison not only to outline a basic cinematic structure, which in this case is common to DEFA and Hollywood cinema alike, but also to indicate that the events in STARS, or rather in the historical field of reference surrounding the film, are more complicated and layered than the laudatory critics would suggest. It is evident that a reading of the fable that focuses entirely on the maturation process of the male protagonist—from an indifferent *Wehrmacht* soldier, through love and doubt, to an antifascist saboteur and militant communist—downplays the monstrosity of the extermination of the Jews. The genocide occupies a subordinate role in such a reading of the plot, not only dramatically, but also ideologically. Since Marx, as we know, the Jewish question took second place, or even had no place in the struggle for socialism. Particularly among communists, Jews were all too often labeled as the class enemy, and even the murderous anti-Semitism of the Nazi regime was described as "irrelevant" in comparison to the class struggle. Against this background, Wolf's detailed depiction of the transport, his sophisticated portrayal of the group's plight, and his portrait of the officer Kurt, capable of any atrocity despite his jovial bonhomie, are noteworthy acts of independence and courage, not least in a political sense. Despite my complaints that his Jewish figures are not free of clichés—they include, for example, only feeble old men, worried mothers and children, and the intellectuals among them wear glasses and read Heinrich Heine—the sheer, interminable tracking shot along the faces of the Jews assembled for roll call leaves a lasting impression as a scene of great documentary power and depth of feeling. As one East German reviewer remarked in 1959: "One of the high points of the film (and of the oeuvre of Konrad Wolf as a whole) is the long camera shot over the deported Jews from Greece. [...] In these scenes the visual imagery is so intense that a blush of shame creeps across one's face."[13]

A further instance of the film's historical and ideological complexity is in the choice of setting and moment at which the plot takes place: October 1943. At this point in time, Bulgaria was still allied with Hitler's bloated Third Reich. We are therefore dealing with what was, for the Bulgarians of 1959, a very painful period in their history: the focus is not on scenes of foreign occupation, but rather of collaboration (the police interrogation, for example). When one considers the film from this perspective, it comes as no surprise to learn that STARS was never shown in Bulgaria, even though the partisans play an important role in it. Just imagine: a film that won prizes at Cannes as a Bulgarian entry is banned in its own country because it depicts the Bulgarians as collaborators and Nazi Germans as all-too-human. As this impression was no coincidence, however, and the reactions to the film must have been anticipated by all the parties involved, it seems to be less an irony of history than a kind of consciously staged performance of failure.

This is the more remarkable in that a further historically crucial point is never mentioned in the film: namely, that Bulgaria (which, in this respect, is only comparable to Denmark and stands in stark contrast to other occupied countries, such as France or the Netherlands) refused to hand over Bulgarian Jews to the Germans. From our current perspective, it is precisely this question—how European states treated their Jewish fellow citizens—that is decisive in our understanding of our shared history as "Europeans." It moreover influences our attitude towards new EU countries, in particular Poland, the Czech Republic and Hungary, who, as members of the EU, must demonstrate how they are addressing their respective histories of anti-Semitism. Under these circumstances, yet another significant historical event seems like a parapraxis. In 1992, at the commemoration in Berlin of the tenth anniversary of Konrad Wolf's death, Wagenstein reported that, after a single television broadcast in 1989, STARS had once again been banned in his homeland because it allegedly glamorized the communist partisans, who—from the perspective of a new Bulgaria with a renewed sense of nationalism—seemed not much different from terrorists. Wagenstein also reported that in the town of Bansko, the location of the film, a monument erected in memory of a poet and partisan leader had been demolished during the anti-communist purges of 1991.[14]

Transcending the specific context of its genesis, as well as the biographies of its makers, STERNE therefore remains an exceptionally vivid historical document, whose productivity springs precisely from those contradictions inherent in European history itself—from the misunderstandings or, as I call them here, the constructive parapraxes of its memory work.

Visual Imagery

Turning to the visual imagery of the film, one is struck by the many occasions that convey a sense of *déjà vu*. It begins with the women and children being loaded into railway cars at the start of the film and continues, through the shots of detainees at the barbed wire, to the emotionally and thematically central image of Ruth, the Jewish girl, clinging to the bars of the window as the transport pulls out of the station. Here, factual material derived from the historical record is overlaid and combined with images that have become iconic. As to the historical record, the following quotation helps clarify the situation of the Greek Jews in Bulgaria:

> During the war, German-allied Bulgaria did not deport Bulgarian Jews. Bulgaria did, however, deport non-Bulgarian Jews from the territories it had annexed from Yugoslavia and Greece. In March 1943, Bulgarian authorities arrested all the Jews in Macedonia and Thrace. In Macedonia, formerly part of Yugoslavia, Bulgarian officials interned 7,000 Jews in a transit camp in Skopje. In Thrace, formerly a Bulgarian-occupied province of Greece, about 4,000 Jews were deported to Bulgarian assembly points at Gorna Dzhumaya and Dupnitsa and handed over to the Germans. In all, Bulgaria deported over 11,000 Jews to German-held territory. Jews were deported from Kavala, Seres, and Drama in Bulgarian-occupied Macedonia. Some 3,000 Jews were taken to Drama and herded onto trains without food or water for transport to a camp in Gorna Dzumaya. The Jews were probably then taken to the Bulgarian port of Lom on the Danube River, where they boarded ships for Vienna. From there, the Nazis deported them to the Treblinka extermination camp. In 1945, the Jewish population of Bulgaria was still about 50,000, its pre-war level. Next to the rescue of Danish Jews, Bulgarian Jewry's escape from deportation and extermination represents the most significant exception of any Jewish population in Nazi-occupied Europe. Beginning in 1948, however, more than 35,000 Bulgarian Jews chose to emigrate to the new state of Israel.[15]

A photograph of one of these transports of Greek Jews from Bulgaria has survived, which was circulated widely at that time and bears a remarkable resemblance to the opening images of Wolf's film.

The more important iconographic source for STARS, however, was undoubtedly Alain Resnais' NUIT ET BROUILLARD (NIGHT AND FOG, 1955), whose lasting impression Konrad Wolf emphasized in an interview given in 1964.[16] The image of barbed wire, for example, which is a leitmotif throughout STARS can also be found in Resnais' film, but is typical of photos taken during the liberation of the camps rather than during internment.[17] Another substantial borrowing from NIGHT AND FOG is clearly found in the famous passage in STARS where the Jews are leaving the transit camps. In Resnais' film, this involves footage (not specifically identified in the film) originating from Westerbork, the biggest reception camp in the Netherlands. It is from a film commissioned by the German Commandant Albert Konrad Gemmeker to send to Berlin as documentary evidence of orderly and efficient deportation techniques. The footage was shot by Rudolf Breslauer, a Jewish prisoner from Munich who had fled to the Netherlands with his wife and three children, but was rounded up in Utrecht. A further case of performed failure: Gemmeker had his work documented because he was proud of it; today, however, the same footage is considered a document of German fanaticism and barbarity. Did Breslauer hope to save himself and his family with his services? The unconstrained atmosphere in the camp speaks against this and ignorance renders it all the more grim for us viewers in retrospect: the film was shot in May 1944; in September 1944, he and his entire family were deported to Auschwitz and immediately murdered. By some standards a collaborator, Breslauer is for us today a hero of the Jewish resistance because he helped to document the heartless reality of Westerbork and the transports.[18]

In particular, the image of the Jewish girl at the door of a railway car has become iconic. It has been reproduced hundreds of times, used as the title of a book and, particularly in the Netherlands, been elevated alongside Anne Frank to a symbol of the Holocaust in general. When one compares Wolf's central thematic motif—the Jewish woman at the boxcar window—with the icon of the Holocaust in Resnais' film, one is struck not only by the similarities, but also by the differences: in Resnais, the anonymous victim represents millions; in Wolf, the altruistic love and self-sacrifice of the personalized angel of mercy call the man to moral duty and political choice.

The melodramatic charge of the image in Wolf's film, in turn, relates in a particularly productive manner to a discovery that only came to light in 1994—that the Dutch icon of the Holocaust does not depict a Jewish victim. The transport filmed by Breslauer in Westerbork, which Resnais spliced into his film about French political prisoners in Buchenwald, and Wolf transformed into the symbol of a failed rescue attempt in STARS, also contained several railway cars with non-Jewish victims, in particular Sinti and Roma (gypsy) people living in the Netherlands who were picked up in May 1944. Journalist Aad Wagenaar has shown in meticulous detail that the unknown girl actually has a name and a story. She was Settela Steinbach and came from the area around Aachen and Maastricht, on the German-Dutch border:

> Anna Maria (Settela) Steinbach (Dec. 23, 1934–July 31, 1944) was a Dutch girl who was gassed in Auschwitz. For a long time she stood as an icon of the Dutch persecution of the Jews, until it was discovered in 1994 that she was not Jewish, as had previously been assumed, but rather belonged to the Sinti branch of the Romani people. Steinbach was born in Buchten near Born in southern Limburg as the daughter of a trader and violinist. On May 16, 1944, a raid was ordered throughout the Netherlands against the Roma. Steinbach was rounded up in Eindhoven. That same day she arrived in Camp Westerbork along with 577 others, of whom 279 were subsequently allowed to leave because, although they lived in caravans, they were not Roma. In Westerbork, Steinbach's head was shaved as a preventative measure against head lice. Her mother tore off a piece of a sheet for her to cover her head. On May 19, she was deported to Auschwitz-Birkenau, along with 244 other Roma, on a train that also contained railcars with Jewish prisoners. As the doors of the boxcar in

> which she would be transported were closed, she briefly glanced outside at a dog running past. This image was captured by Rudolf Breslauer....[19]

Thus a chain of mistaken assumptions, unacknowledged appropriations, cultural prejudices and symbols taken out of context, but all the more effective for it—in short, a whole series of performative parapraxes—nevertheless leads to an important discovery and a vital recognition. Hidden behind every train there can be a further transport, one genocide may obscure another, only to then reveal it in a new form. The images do not simply come to a standstill at some point in history; they travel with us—they accompany us and sometimes even overtake us.[20]

It also indicates the presence of a media-specific memory of the Holocaust, which is likewise activated—as I have tried to show, nolens volens—through a reading of STARS. This media-specific memory, I suggest, exhibits several characteristics alongside the use of images whose iconic meaning is already established from the outset. Paradoxically—thanks to the ever ready and repeated repertoire of images drawn from an almost inexhaustible supply of photographs, individual film stills and newspaper images that these atrocities have bequeathed to us—such media-memory, like Freud's unconscious, seems to know no temporal "before" and "after" and is therefore bound to no permanently fixed causality. Likewise, the location of these images is unspecified with respect to the past and future. Their cultural presence becomes a sort of "virtual" dimension, in which images circulate in suspended agitation, capable at any point of redefining their meaning: they can hit the spectator like a sudden shock, or open up an altogether new path into the past. This might explain why media images can repeatedly rewrite cultural memory. In other words, through the visual and linguistic elements inscribed in media images a particular form of potentiality—singular in its reference, but multiple in its reverberations—comes into being. It once more underlines the constitutive asynchronicity of the historical imaginary and purposive performances of failure mentioned above. What struck me in particular, during repeated viewings of STARS, is that it is precisely in these suspended and suspending temporal levels that the discrete layers of meaning embedded in the futile attempt of the male protagonist to save the Jewish woman can fully deploy themselves.

Temporal Layering, or Sheets of Time in STARS

My thesis, then, is that STARS, through the intertwining knots of history, its twists and turns, its reversals and rewritings not only presents itself to us differently from how it was perhaps originally intended; as a film that has been viewed as paradigmatic of East German or Central European *Vergangenheitsbewältigung*, it also accesses something like a historical unconscious—the historical imaginary—nested in the images themselves and identical neither with the auteur(s), nor with their original public. This unconscious knowledge, written into the "memory images" of the film, shows that history is not archived in images as in a strongbox, or fixed in the same way as the indexical bond ties the photographic to reality. On the contrary, it suggests that history continues to act, is continually resurrected, like Dracula, much more powerfully through images than text (and is also open to reinterpretation, of course). For this reason, historical images do not help us deal with the past, in the manner of "working through" loss or mourning. On the contrary, it is the past in these images that threatens to overcome us, and often in quite unexpected ways: closer to living memory than to history, and closer to trauma than memory.

How, then, does STARS succeed in keeping this past alive and continuing to exert friction energy, as Alexander Kluge would say?[21] Paradoxically, it is not in the form to which we are accustomed in western European auteur films—namely, through a so-called open ending, in which the hero is sent off into an uncertain future. Wolf cannot and does not wish to indulge in an open ending, à la Michelangelo Antonioni; instead, he chooses narrative forms and visual techniques which suggest several temporal levels that are neither interdependent, nor mutually exclusive. I would call them the temporal levels of too-late and too-early and thereby return to my title-topos of a "rescue in vain," now seen as a performance of failure or parapraxis. Four modalities or themes of hoped for, yet impossible "rewinding" can be discerned in STARS: the future as past; the voice of God; the appeal to the virtual spectator; and the temporalities of a foreclosed future.

The future as (a still recurring) past: Let us ask ourselves again: what is the core of the story which Wolf is telling us? Is it really that, in 1943, it was more useful to help the communists to victory, than to save a group of Greek Sephardic Jews? That might have been the right political choice for a German communist, but Walter is not a communist. He is an artist who has not yet achieved a great deal, who is soft-hearted towards all manner of people, including the Bulgarians and Jews, and harbors an intuitive sense of sympathy, but is nevertheless mostly indecisive in his behavior and actions. Or does the moral lie in the possibility that rescuing the woman one loves is less important than fighting on the side of foreign partisans against one's own compatriots? And why would this alternative be the logical consequence of the futile rescue attempt? Is fighting on the side of the partisans more a form of atonement for a subjectively-felt complicity in the death of the beloved, as if one could compensate for the other, or even as if two "wrongs," or parapraxes, could make a right? Could restore some justice to the world, as in ancient tragedy? Yet Ruth did not want to be saved in this way at all: she had already absolved Walter from his guilt before he had thought of a concrete escape plan, equating the value of her life with that of her community. ("Every star belongs in its constellation … [and] everyone has a star in the sky. And when it breaks from its place, the person perishes.") Moreover, Wolf shows how difficult it is for Ruth, because of her contact with

Walter, to hold her ground within the Jewish community and not be cast out as a spy or traitor.

What makes STARS so unconventional in this respect is that the film clearly sustains all these possibilities, and thereby subjects its hero to a more detailed scrutiny of the motivation and efficacy of his actions, long before Walter ultimately arrives at the politically correct decision. The episode with the medicine is a striking example of this: Walter wants to help the Jews and therefore lets the partisan leader Petko have valuable army medicines. The latter smuggles them to the partisans, however, with a boy from the village, who is promptly captured by the police in the forest. As Walter himself must admit, his good intentions harmed both the Jews, who are humiliated at roll call and have their food rations withdrawn for three days, and the partisans, whose clandestine network has been uncovered and compromised. Walter rationalizes his failure, as though this is, even in advance, the reason why his attempt to rescue Ruth can only lead to further calamity. In both cases he concludes: "I didn't mean for it to be like this, I didn't want it to be like this." This would indicate that Walter knows he will fail from the outset and that the film's entire plot actually unfolds under the sign of the foreknowledge of this failure. Melancholic and nihilistic as he appears in the opening scenes, it is clear that his actions, his change of heart, even his love are in vain and that right from the start everything he does comes, as it were, "too late."

This "too late" has echoed down the decades ever since. And, in the film itself, it is only from this position of deferred action that the flashback structure becomes comprehensible, even compellingly necessary, since only this temporality of recall can make palpable to the viewer the possibility that the future is nothing other than the past, which inevitably recurs because it is not yet understood. The narrative of STARS is therefore not comparable to the flashback structure of films such as Andrzey Munk's fragmentary PASAŻERKA (PASSENGER, 1961/63) or Sidney Lumet's THE PAWNBROKER (1964). When Walter picks up the Star of David lying in the mud and tries once again to run behind the train, the film refers us to the return of what the Star of David will one day signify for Germans as well. It seems as though this star will be waiting for him, wherever Walter happens to return from his partisan combat. Thus, one of the most striking images of the film remains that of a hero who is constantly chasing after events, or even—as is expressly emphasized both in the commentary and on screen—that of a hero *visibly limping after history*.

An equally startling displacement of the film's temporal levels can be observed in the roll call scene mentioned above. Dramatically, this is a moment of extreme tension, of terrible foreboding and trepidation regarding the fate of those assembled. Then, however, there begins a piece of music that already mourns and weeps for these faces and figures, as if the Jews only existed in the memory traces of their future murder. Thus, amidst action taking place in the present, Wolf switches into the pluperfect: a glance from the future into the irretrievable past. A similar tense of im-possibility is activated in the Yiddish song itself: the lyrics of "*S'brennt*" ("It is burning") cry out for help because the *shtetl* is on fire—but also know that the *shtetl* will continue burning, even if help should arrive. Here too, the futility of rescue is a central motif.

In this sense, the film never takes place in any conceivable form of an imaginable "present" (whether 1943 or 1959), which would open towards the future. Instead, right from start it is a film of remembering, a film which must conceive of itself from beyond its present, in the suspension between a traumatic past and a deceptively insecure future, in a time that is neither utopian, nor purely cyclical. This position is clearly outlined in one of the opening scenes. Walter and his friend Kurt are sunning themselves on a hill above the town. They are relieved to have escaped the hell of Leningrad and are now simply awaiting the end of the war, which even Kurt, the committed and—as we later learn—sadistic Nazi, believes to be lost. In contrast to Kurt's cynicism, Walter's nihilism recalls what Alexander and Margarete Mitscherlich identified in the postwar generation as the "inability to mourn," or the melancholy of those who, in the Freudian sense, have lost their ego-ideal and can no longer derive meaning from the world.[22] In this way the film becomes a *memento mori*, not only for the Jews who lost their lives in such a horrific manner, but also for those who lost their souls in the process: the Germans.

The Voice of God. This loss of the subject's temporally anchored point of reference—given that for Germans of Walter's (and Wolf's) generation, the past had already appropriated the future, explains why the film has a narratorial voice-over, in addition to its flashback structure. Where does this voice come from, and to whom does it belong? It remains anonymous and disembodied; it is not embedded in the diegetic world of the characters; it is at times benevolent, at others disdainful, sometimes ironic; and it usually speaks from a position of retrospective omniscience, although it claims not to know who this German soldier named Walter really was. It speaks German with a Bulgarian accent, but clearly does not belong to the partisan leader. Since it is not visible as a person on-screen, it ought really to be assigned to the church tower and its symbolism, to which Walter refers in his sketches at the outset. This church is repeatedly shown in the picture, and from its bell tower the town, the camp and Walter's futile attempts to reach the moving train are observed as if by a silent witness. The off-screen voice would thus actually be something like the proverbial "Voice of God" of conventional documentary film commentary, albeit taken here literally as a voice *sub specie aeternitatis,* which nevertheless can or will not help these protagonists. Abandoned by man and by the Christian God, this story of a futile rescue attempt becomes something like an attempt to "rescue the futile"; all the utopias, the effort and sacrifices for a better, more just future—or, more precisely, the desperate endeavors to secure a future at all—are concurrently awaiting rescue, and to no avail.

The Appeal to the Virtual Spectator. In Wolf's STARS, this anticipation of a "rescue of the futile" is translated into a highly remarkable compositional style, which tends to stage the action along a diagonal, often with extreme close-ups in the foreground and an equally extreme vanishing point situated far back in the depth of field. It almost seems as though Wolf has modeled his film on CITIZEN KANE (1941, dir. Orson Welles), which, after what I claimed about the use of the flashback structure, should not seem quite as disconcerting as at first sight. Werner Bergmann's camera style can perhaps best be described as deconstructing Gregg Toland's deep staging, as it seems to exaggerate Welles' baroque spaces into moments of mannered expressionism, forcing the audience to reflect on its own spectatorial position. Are we being addressed as voyeurs, or as witnesses? Where, in this mise en scène, is our optical point of view, and thus our locatable place within the space of the fiction? The foreground—in particular when the two leading actors turn directly to the camera in close-up shots—refers to the hope of a blossoming romance, whereas the background encompasses all that the two lovers want and need to leave behind. If one looks even more closely at what is being negotiated here, and in particular what is placed in the space of the spectator, it becomes apparent that this extreme form of frontal staging does not refer to the profilmic space, but rather to the fact that space once again represents a temporal dimension, albeit no longer the future or past, but rather the respective "present" and presence of the spectator and his/her knowledge about both the past and the (now-historic and failed) future. Whatever we might think of the lovers' hopes when voiced directly into the camera, the direction of this address already contains the knowledge of the futility of this hope. And vice versa: when Walter decides to follow the partisan leader, Wolf shows him not approaching the camera, but rather vanishing into the depths of field, becoming increasingly small and inconsequential, and thereby undermines the expectation that the hero is promised a better future as a result of his decision.

Temporalities of a Foreclosed Future. Most of the scenes displaying this curious movement—between a future that has already become past, and a past that is yet to arrive—play very close to the camera. The film marks out a temporal trajectory along the spatial axis of an extreme foreground and the emphatic staging across the diagonal (which leads into infinite space). As such, it implicitly answers the question: What is the direction/decision that its protagonist will take? But by metaphoric extension, it also asks (and answers): what destination and fate await the Jews on the train (entering a tunnel whose shape recalls the ovens at Auschwitz)? In these scenes, the film moves on a temporal axis of an impossible, already foreclosed future, as the foregrounded close-ups do not communicate closeness or intimacy, but rather function as an appeal. The anxious face of Ruth, the baffled features of Walter address the present, on behalf of a past that burdens the characters with an unbearable future. It is as if we, the

Nachgeborenen (those born after), were to be their judges, but also the ones who might undo what the protagonists already know about the futility, as well as necessity of any doing-as-undoing, and thus making us part of what has indeed proven to be a vicious circle of guilt and disavowal, of regret and restitution, of rescue without redemption.

From Germany to Europe

My reading of STARS in terms of performative parapraxis and "futile rescue/rescuing the futile" leads me to conclude that the usual questions about the autobiographical elements in Konrad Wolf's work—the fact that he was frequently forced to change sides, and the fateful role he played as a double agent for the noble idea of socialism—should be expanded to include a European dimension, as someone who anticipated the memory wars yet to come. On the one hand, his preoccupation with the (un)representability of time links him to the European auteur cinema of the 1960s, in particular to Alain Resnais (and, of course, the post-Holocaust "time-image," as Gilles Deleuze defined it).[23] On the other hand, the ambivalence that Wolf repeatedly expressed towards the films of Resnais (in particular HIROSHIMA MON AMOUR, 1959) and L'ANNÉE DERNIÈRE À MARIENBAD (LAST YEAR AT MARIENBAD, 1960) becomes more comprehensible precisely because of the many parallels to Resnais, as well as a crucial difference. For in Wolf's work asynchronicity is not a psychological motif rooted in the interpersonal dimension of consciousness and memory, but rather has political underpinnings: to be precise, the "politics of memory" as a key to European identity. The tragedy, for Wolf, is that the hope for a better future always leads to the suspension of the present, which, as a result, risks always being overtaken by the past. The knowledge of deferral and delay attending upon action, as much as causality and consequence, is therefore one of the more authentically political aspects of STARS, not only in relation to Konrad Wolf's biography and life history, but also for the history of the country he sought to serve with his work.

This would mean that Konrad Wolf's personal fate—as a remigrant in both senses and both directions, from West to East and East to West—makes him all the more representative today, or rather only now renders him representative of the GDR, in a way that could never have happened in his lifetime, despite his prominent position in the political and cultural hierarchy of the GDR. Precisely in light of the "disappearance" of the GDR and the suspension of its history, Wolf and his films are growing in importance. From his work we can learn what it means to expose oneself to those contradictions and temporal ruptures which emerge when one dedicates one's work fully to the legacy of German history and the rescue of the "soul of Germany." In the words of Walter Benjamin, echoing Karl Kraus and taken up by Alexander Kluge (and which, in my interpretation, reverberate in the uncanny deep space photography of

Stars): The more closely one examines Konrad Wolf's films, the more distant becomes the answering gaze, not only of Konrad Wolf, not only of "Germany," but also of "Europe."

Notes

1. See Paul Ricoeur, *Gedächtnis, Geschichte, Vergessen* (Munich: Wilhelm Fink Verlag, 2004).
2. Thomas Elsaesser, *Weimar Cinema and After: Germany's Historical Imaginary* (London: Routledge, 2000).
3. Thomas Elsaesser and Michael Wedel, "Defining DEFA's Historical Imaginary: The Films of Konrad Wolf," *New German Critique*, 82 (Winter 2001), 13.
4. Marianne Hirsch, *Family Frames: Photography, Narrative, and Postmemory*. (Cambridge, MA: Harvard University Press, 1997); Alison Landsberg, *Prosthetic Memory: The Transformation of American Remembrance in the Age of Mass Culture* (New York: Columbia University Press, 2004).
5. Angel Wagenstein, "Die ersten und die letzten Jahre mit Konrad Wolf," *Beiträge zur Film- und Fernsehwissenschaft*, 28 (1987), 15–38.
6. See, for example, Marc Silberman, "Remembering History: The Filmmaker Konrad Wolf," *New German Critique*, 49 (Winter 1990), 163–91; Gertrud Koch, "On the Disappearance of the Dead among the Living: The Holocaust and the Confusion of Identities in the Films of Konrad Wolf," *New German Critique*, 60 (Winter 1993), 57–75.
7. Konrad Schwalbe, "*Sterne* (1959): Um den Anspruch auf Leben, Liebe, über Vaterlandsverräter, Kameradenmörder," *Konrad Wolf: Neue Sichten auf seine Filme, Beiträge zur Film- und Fernsehwissenschaft*, 39 (1990), 65–71.
8. Much of what has been said about Konrad Wolf's biography, as a life torn between divided nationalities and political loyalties, applies a fortiori to Angel Wagenstein as well. See, for instance, an article on the intertwining of fiction and autobiography in his literary work (http://www.thenation.com/article/schlepics-fiction-angel-wagenstein).
9. Ellen Mollenschott, "*Sterne* – Der erste deutsch-bulgarische Gemeinschaftsfilm," *Neues Deutschland*, 29. 3 (1959), 6.
10. For an account of Germany's "divided memories," see Jeffrey Herf, *Divided Memory: The Nazi Past in the Two Germanys* (Cambridge, MA: Harvard University Press, 1997). On the question of Europe's divided memories, see, among many others, James Marks, "1989: Divided Memories East and West" (http://www.historyandpolicy.org/opinion/opinion_18.html).
11. Barton Byg, "Konrad Wolf — From Anti-Fascism to Gegenwartsfilm," *Studies in GDR Culture and Society 5. Selected Papers from the Tenth New Hampshire Symposium on the German Democratic Republic*, ed. Margery Gerber. (Lanham, MD: University Press of America, 1985), 115–24.
12. Mollenschott, *Sterne*.
13. Hans-Dieter Tok, "Sterne," 1959; reprinted in *Regiestühle. Zoltán Fábri, Akira Kurosawa, Andrzej Munk, Alain Resnais, Michail Romm, Francesco Rosi, Konrad Wolf*. (Berlin [DDR]): Henschel-Verlag, 1972), 111–28.
14. Angel Wagenstein, "Rede für Konrad Wolf," *Film und Fernsehen*, 5 (1995), 5.
15. *United States Holocaust Memorial Museum*, September 27, 2008 (http://www.ushmm.org/wlc/article.php?lang=en&ModuleId=10005451); compare also Michael Bar-Zohar, *Beyond Hitler's Grasp: the Heroic Rescue of Bulgaria's Jews* (Avon, MA: Adam Media Corporation, 1998).
16. Ulrich Gregor & Heinz Ungureit, "Konrad Wolf," *Wie sie filmen: Fünfzehn Gespräche mit Regisseuren der Gegenwart*, ed. Ulrich Gregor. (Gütersloh: Sigbert Mohn, 1966), 336.
17. The sequences at the barbed wire used by Resnais come from footage filmed by the

Allies, that is, when the camps were liberated. It is unlikely that during the war such proximity between those behind and in front of the wire would have been tolerated. Wolf's barbed wire serves above all a symbolic function.

18. For a detailed analysis of the Westerbork film, Breslauer's fate and Gemeker's motives, see chapter 9 "Rewind after Replay."
19. Aad Wagenaar, *Settela — Het meisje heft haar naam terug* (Amsterdam: Uitgeverij De Arbeiderspers, 1995). Compare also *Wikipedia,* October 7, 2008 (http://en.wikipedia.org/wiki/Settela_Steinbach).
20. On the Settela case, see also Thomas Elsaesser, "One Train May Be Hiding Another" (http://www.latrobe.edu.au/screeningthepast/classics/rr0499/terr6b.htm).
21. See Klaus Eder, *Alexander Kluge, Ulmer Dramaturgien: Reibungsverluste* (Munich: Hanser, 1980).
22. Alexander Mitscherlich and Margarete Mitscherlich, *The Inability to Mourn: Principles of Collective Behavior* (New York: Grove Press/Random House, 1975).
23. Gilles Deleuze, *Cinema 2: The Time Image* (Minneapolis: University of Minnesota Press, 1989).

6

THE PERSISTENT RESISTANCE OF ALEXANDER KLUGE

As a filmmaker with a modest but loyal transatlantic following, Alexander Kluge's oeuvre and career are markedly different from those of other European directors venerated by cinephiles.[1] He belongs to the same generation as Jean Luc Godard, Jean Marie Straub, and Theo Angelopoulos, but trained as a lawyer before making his first film in 1960. In Germany, he is equally if not more famous as a short story writer, television personality and the author of several volumes of sociology. To film historians, he is the legal brain and policy shaper behind the New German Cinema of the sixties and seventies, having been the driving force behind the famous Oberhausen Manifesto of 1962 and the government film-funding legislation that followed.[2] In 1964 he co-founded West Germany's first film school (at the Ulm Institute for Design) and in 1972 he published, in his capacity as professor of sociology at the University of Frankfurt, a book with Oskar Negt, which became a classic for the student generation of '68, *Public Sphere and Experience*, a radicalized rejoinder to Jürgen Habermas's equally classic 1962 *The Structural Transformation of the Public Sphere*. Co-author of other critical and political analyses, including a book-length study of the European film industry, Kluge remained, for more than two decades, the undisputed master-strategist of the parliamentary lobby and the chief architect of a state film subsidy system based around the concept of the *Autorenfilm* (auteur film)—before becoming, in the eighties, one of its fiercest critics.[3]

Between 1966 and 1983 he directed some twenty films, of which about six have remained in active memory: Yesterday Girl (1966), Artists Under the Big Top: Perplexed (1968), Occasional Work of a Female Slave (1974), the framing segment of Germany in Autumn (1978), The Patriot (1979), and The Power of Feelings (1983). On these titles rests his reputation as a filmmaker, although for his fans, a few more remain to be rediscovered, such as THE MIDDLE OF THE ROAD IS A VERY DEAD END (1974), STRONGMAN FERDINAND (1976), and THE BLIND DIRECTOR (1985).

By 1985 Kluge had changed tack, having entered into what many saw as a Faustian bargain with commercial television to produce late-night cultural magazine shows. *The Hour of the Filmmakers: Film Histories*, *Ten to Eleven*, *News and Stories*, and *Prime Time: Late Edition* are programs that have been sponsored by, among others, the Japanese advertising firm Dentsu, and supervised by Kluge with a consortium headed by the German newsmagazine *Der Spiegel*.[4] They feature half-hour mini-films, ciné-essays, and interviews on subjects as diverse as the guillotine and montage cinema, opera and Greek mythology, a sampling of a scene from Godard's CONTEMPT, an interview about the Roman historian Tacitus with playwright Heiner Müller, or "Fidel Castro, the Last of the Mohicans." This output has averaged two half-hour programs per week over the last twenty-five years, complementing a filmography of altogether thirty films (features and documentary shorts), in addition to a thousand short stories that run to ten volumes and a further sixteen works of nonfiction.

Faced with such relentless productivity in so many media, one's first reaction is awe, followed perhaps by skepticism and incredulity. For besides the books, the films, and the hundreds of hours of television, there are also newspaper articles, polemics, interviews, press conferences, and public lectures: If Kluge has become something of a myth, an institution even, one could be forgiven for also sensing something almost monstrous in so much talent. His energy never flags, his curiosity is inexhaustible, and no occasion is too ephemeral to ignite his enthusiasm for reform or creative engagement. Unlike that other German filmmaker of seemingly superhuman productivity, R.W. Fassbinder, Kluge has proven himself a marathon man, still going strong after more than fifty years on the front line; predating the generation of '68, he has outlived even their pessimistic afterlife and (self-)defeat.

The sheer size of Kluge's oeuvre makes it enigmatic, and not only because the man himself has chosen to remain so utterly private. He credibly maintains that filmmaking is only one way of pursuing his activist's agenda, and compared to the work of younger compatriots like Fassbinder, Herzog, and Wenders, his features look deliberately improvised—brilliant compilations of aperçus and astonishing montages of bits and pieces rather than self-sustaining masterpieces (one of his last films, from 1986, was actually called MISCELLANEOUS NEWS). Finally, in contrast to two filmmakers of his own generation, Edgar Reitz and Hans-Jürgen Syberberg, Kluge seems free of the obsessive urge to undertake works of the *longue durée* like HEIMAT or OUR HITLER. Instead, he has chosen case studies of remarkable or odd individuals, like Anita G., the heroine of YESTERDAY GIRL; Ferdinand Rieche, the security chief of STRONGMAN FERDINAND; or the contrasting fate of two women, one an East German spy, the other a prostitute and shoplifter in THE MIDDLE OF THE ROAD IS A VERY DEAD

End. If asked, Kluge might argue that his filmmaking had always been work in progress, with each film more of a means to an end than a goal in itself—the documentation of a contingent history, not of himself as artist, nor necessarily that of his characters, but of the historical body called "Germany," belated nation and premature state, alternately bloated and divided, with which the filmmaker has been engaged in an unending and unhappy dialogue, like an old couple for whom tenderness, aggression, and mutual dependence have become indistinguishable.

The close links between Kluge's literary output and his film scenarios suggests that a web-like network binds his other activities to his cinema work and vice versa: many of his film protagonists first appeared in the story collections *Case Histories* (1962), *Learning Process with a Deadly Outcome* (1973), and *The Uncanniness of Time* (1977). Some films are the result of utilizing the out-takes from a previous film; others feel like slightly hysterical self-parodies. The director has even reworked and reedited films in response to public discussions with audiences. But if the films are off-cuts from an ongoing dialogue, the pieces of the jigsaw puzzle fit into an overall design that is by necessity both self-directed and remote-controlled. Kluge's working method is best described in Harun Farocki's words as a *Verbund*, or "synergy network." A symbiotic or mutually implicating arrangement of input and output, Kluge's *Verbund* is at once a Dada collage and a *Gesamtkunstwerk*, where newspaper clippings, photos, snatches of popular music, Wagner, Verdi, home movies, and *objets trouvés* serve as material for installations in a permanent museum of human idiocy, idiosyncrasy, and heroic persistence. His work is furthermore held together as much by the structural contradiction of remaining an artist while servicing a culture industry as by the exigencies of grappling with several media simultaneously. Like Brecht, Kluge has wanted to intervene from within, rather than, in the manner of Adorno, critiquing from without (to contrast two of Kluge's own master thinkers).[5]

Despite the public attention he generates through television (though he is never on screen in his shows, only a voice-off), Kluge is enigmatic also in the eccentric impersonality of his working method. Unlike others in the film business, he has never sought the limelight nor presented himself as a visionary artist with a personal mission—the latter being the all-too-Germanic vice of other New German Cinema auteurs. What is striking are the many collaborative projects and collective signatures, not only on manifestos and press releases, but also with the omnibus films Germany in Autumn (1978), The Candidate (1980), and War and Peace (1982), as well as one short and one feature, made in conjunction with, amongst others, Ulrich Schamoni, Edgar Reitz, Volker Schlöndorff, Margarethe von Trotta, and Fassbinder. Kluge often handed his television slots over to friends like Ula Stoeckl, Alfred Edel, and Günter Gaus. Shaped by the collectivist ethos of the sixties, with a deep distrust of specialization and an abiding antipathy towards any division of labor, Kluge is an ideal advocate of cooperation. But in practice, he is the auteur as autocrat; even the most sprawling enterprises with which he is involved reverberate with the quirky logic of his mind—while being held in the steel grip of his formidable intellect, reclaiming as idiosyncrasy and stubbornness the very dispersal of authorship and self-expression that the collectivist projects and the different media outlets would otherwise imply.

Where, then, in this massive output, this eccentric personality, this shadowy, publicity-shy presence, can one finally locate a center? Is there a real Alexander Kluge, or merely a dazzling, and to some observers, irritating succession of disguises, masks, masquerades, and performance pieces? To adapt a phrase originally taken from Walter Benjamin (who took it from Karl Kraus) and quoted at the beginning of THE PATRIOT: "The longer one looks at [him], the farther [he] looks back at you." The inventor of the *Autorenfilm* challenges all the usual assumptions of auteurism that would sanction the reading of his work thematically or as existential self-expression. On the other hand, given Kluge's own voluminous commentaries on his (cinematic) intentions, (reformist) aims and (didactic) methods, his views on everything and anything, his obsessive-compulsive return to certain phrases and references, it is tempting to quote the director on his own behalf and assume a strong autobiographical core. But it is a temptation (initially) to be resisted. Reading Kluge and viewing his films can leave one with the blurry feeling of watching a spinning top only to realize that his self-analysis only deepens the enigma. What exactly does he mean by sound bites like "film theory is film politics," "public sphere is the productivity of the senses," "opera is the power-house of feelings"? In the end, one abiding concern remains clearly discernible in everything he does: the why and where of his nation, his country and its history.

How could it be otherwise? For *any* German of his generation, history looms large, usually contracted to the twelve years of Nazi rule, its consequences and aftermath. Not so in Kluge, at least at first glance. In the Dada *Gesamtkunstwerk* that is his oeuvre, the grand design is laid out in the second book he wrote with Oskar Negt, *Geschichte und Eigensinn* (*History and Idiosyncrasy*).[6] Translating literally as "self-sense," the *Eigensinn* of the title can mean anything from obstinacy and persistence to resistance and self-determination. From Tacitus' account of Arminius' Teutoburg Forest victory to the Battle of Stalingrad, via the Stauffer Kings, Martin Luther's Reformation, Thomas Münzer and the Peasants' Wars, to the German Romantics and their contact with first the French Revolution and then the France of Napoleon, Kluge and Negt survey Germany's nearly two-thousand-year history not in order to extrapolate the German mentality or a putative national identity, but to observe generations of Germans at work, at battle and in their sleep, having nightmares in their fairy tales, passing on ballads and folk sayings, building cities and inventing the postal service.

And yet over the book's 1,250 pages, the Nazi regime, WW II and the

Holocaust are barely mentioned. Instead, according to Kluge, the dead of those two thousand years now look at the living and utter the words "that's not at all what we had in mind."[7] This phrase echoes in THE PATRIOT and THE POWER OF FEELINGS through the sometimes scurrilous, sometimes distressing catalogue of futile efforts of Kluge's protagonists to forge a destiny out of accidents—"a hundred thousand reasons which afterwards are called fate."[8] Kluge's preoccupation with history turns out to serve as a kind of "dream-screen" for an intense working over and obsessive return to the only question that seems to matter: "how could it have come to this?" where "this" is never named. In *Geschichte und Eigensinn*, Kluge and Negt opt for an answer of sorts in a Brothers Grimm fairy tale, *Das eigensinnige Kind* (*The Wilful Child*) about a young girl who repeatedly disobeys her mother. She eventually dies, but even buried underground, her resisting hand digs its way up until the mother herself has to go out to the graveyard and chastise it with a rod. This terrible, but mysterious tale becomes a sort of *leitmotif* hinting at forms of resistance, but also self-destructive obduracy, that for Kluge becomes a kind of archetype for the sort of political action he both admires and fears, embodied as it is in female rebels against authority and the power of the state. The Wilful Child is Germany's own Antigone, who leads to the terrorism of the Red Army Faction, to Ulrike Meinhof and Gudrun Ensslin—in short to the Hot Autumn of 1977.[9]

Gabi Teichert, the history teacher in THE PATRIOT had already appeared in GERMANY IN AUTUMN (the documentary record of those six September–October weeks) suggesting subterranean links between the violent underground of Germany's protest generation and Kluge and Negt's efforts to "read" the country's two thousand years of destructive/self-destructive "patriotism" across Kluge's own coming to terms with political radicalism and the emerging feminist movement. Female *Eigensinn*, it seems, has to carry a lot of historical baggage, as well as a moral burden in Kluge: it stands for the ethical act of refusal par excellence (Antigone); for the way the popular imagination can work through historical trauma and memorize its history lessons; for legitimate liberation from (patriarchal) oppression; as well as for violence well beyond protest and entirely outside the law. Awed admiration for this peculiar obstinacy and persistence infuses several of Kluge's films from the 1970s, and their air of baffled urgency gives them a topicality worth revisiting today, when "terrorism" and "suicide" have taken on a quite different meaning and political charge.

The fairy tale of the obstinate girl also throws into sharper relief another peculiarity of Kluge's work, besides the gender of his protagonists, who are—with few exceptions—female. All are compulsively hyperactive, constantly at work on something, full of schemes, life plans, grand designs. Their relentless motor-sensory apparatus is set to red alert, while their mental navigation is determined by self-directed admonitions such as "I'll just make the extra effort." Is Kluge making fun of them? The viewer cannot be sure. To say that his protagonists are accident-prone would be an understatement: the dynamics of their lives have an inner momentum that turns their best intentions into their worst enemies, but it also makes them look stupid, sometimes irritatingly so. What critic Wolfram Schütte has called "the conceptual slapstick of Kluge's characters"[10] reflects an irrepressibly well-intentioned decisionism, responsible not only for the miscalculations that bring the characters down, but also for putting up the roadblocks to which the miscalculations are intended as the preemptive response.

Kluge, too, always seems in a hurry in his films, rarely letting a scene develop its own dramatic weight before butting in with a voiceover or cutting to a completely different location or moment in time. He shares with his heroines this restless, impatient spirit, without which his satire might be more compassionate, but this would contradict his self-appointed role as chronicler of the nation's little people and custodian of their dreams. Peel away the layer of concern and empathy, and a salvage operation of a different kind is revealed, for which the lives caught on celluloid and in Kluge's prose narratives are mere coils of energy, headed for entropy. In all the life stories and biographies that Kluge puts before us in such profligate profusion, much the same principle prevails: desires, hopes, and wishes, seen from the vantage point of their eventual futility, take on a terrible mechanical quality. For not only are the characters' motives and intentions exposed as pitiable, their lives seem like impersonations of life, templates and ready-mades, formed and fashioned elsewhere, and for another purpose. They may have acted like saints, ordinary mortals, or monsters, but especially in the short stories, they are miniaturized and serialized, they are more like wind-up toys, marching on and on, with Kluge watching them plummet or fizzle, or freeze-framing them when their time is up. It makes the characters both tragic and ridiculous, at once perpetrators and victims. This compulsion to repeat, the motor behind the characters' initiative and survival, could be called the dark side of *Eigensinn*, when obstinacy, perseverance, and even resistance have become a "program," perfectly executed and replicated once installed. Repetition turns these "drive-creatures" into phantoms of their own life-plans, which is why it is ultimately irrelevant whether Kluge has faked his documents and merely invented their biographies: for these lives there can be no "original."

One is left with a paradox and a conundrum. On the one hand, Kluge's films are part of the New German cinema's mourning work, not unlike those of Syberberg, or early Herzog: speaking about the unspeakable by endlessly speaking about something else, unable to mourn "the others" because not permitted to mourn "our own," and thus always risking self-pity. On the other hand, Kluge's cinema is in a hurry, with time-lapse and fast-forward motion among his most distinctive stylistic signatures. Is Kluge rushing to get to the future, in order from there to look back at the present and perhaps finally give the past a happy ending—and thereby overcome the infinite sadness of "that is not what we had in mind at all"? If so, it suggests a possible answer to our initial enigma, namely how the cinema fits into his patchwork *Gesamtkunstwerk*: Kluge may have become a filmmaker because he wanted to be a time-traveler and he needed to be time-traveler in order to cope with the many deferred actions and hypotheticals (if only ... what if ...?) that make narrating German history such a tragic undertaking. It would explain why Kluge's commitment to the cinema does not require him to make films, and why he can be faithful to the redemptive power of cinema as a time machine even when abstaining from filmmaking. Such time travel is as much a matter of displacements in moral perspective and rearrangements in mental space as it is a science-fiction trope: in either case, however, it is a quintessentially cinematic way of living time, memory and history.

Kluge and Parapraxis

Another, and in the present context preferred term for this cinematic way of living German history as a memory loop is "parapraxis"—as mourning work, and on several fronts. Indeed, it was Kluge's films that first gave me the idea that there might be a distinct logic to the particular melancholy of the fragment that pervades not just his work, but his life project—a logic I then began to recognize in other films and directors of the New German Cinema. In his case, too, the general absence of Jewish protagonists did not go unremarked, especially outside Germany. Jörg Drews, for instance, as a visiting professor at the University of California Irvine once noted: "What does it mean, incidentally, that in [Kluge's] *The Patriot* the murder of the Jews appears to be entirely excluded from Gabi Teichert's excavations of German history—a fact noted with great amazement by my American students?"[11]

Yet if one starts from the premise that in Kluge's work the Holocaust is present, though in the mode of parapraxis, i.e., "performed failure," then Drews' question does begin to find a possible answer. In fact, it opens up a field of reference that encompasses almost all of Kluge's films and more, as it also includes his scholarly publications and his short story prose works. I have in mind above all the following films and texts: *Lebensläufe mit tödlichem Ausgang/Attendance List for a Funeral* (short stories, 1968), IN GEFAHR UND GRÖSSTER NOT... (film, 1972), DIE PATRIOTIN/THE PATRIOT (essay film, 1979), *Geschichte und Eigensinn* (sociological work, written with Oskar Negt, 1981), DIE MACHT DER GEFÜHLE/THE POWER OF FEELINGS (film, 1983) and *Die Macht der Gefühle* (book, 1984). One can consider these works as a giant socio-ethnographic meditation and interpretation-machine about the modes of productivity typical for human labor, creativity and affectivity over the centuries. But with equal justification and pertinence, Kluge's work belongs in the context of the paradigm of "absence as presence, presence as parapraxis," that is, as a kind of documentation not so much of what is missing, but of what constantly misfires, goes awry and misses its intended goal or target. This central thematic and semantic complex in Kluge revolves around the concepts of *Geschichte* (history) and *Eigensinn* (obstinacy, resistance): the title, as indicated, of his magnum opus as a social historian. Accordingly, a number of very specific characteristics can be noted in Kluge's work that relate to this complex:

- the restless, manic urge for action and activity in his protagonists, as if they found themselves in a permanent state of emergency;
- the compulsion to repeat, which affects not only Kluge's fictional characters but also typifies his own work, often a kind of looped reprise of a limited number of themes-and-variations, always incomplete, proudly presented as a permanent work-in-progress;
- the cinematic device of time-lapse photography (e.g., in UNHEIMLICHKEIT DER ZEIT/THE BLIND DIRECTOR, 1985);
- a special form of mimicry, of dead-pan humor and disguise, especially in his pervasive (and to many critics, intensely irritating) voice-over commentary.

THE POWER OF FEELINGS

Emblematic in this respect is an episode in THE POWER OF FEELINGS, announced by Kluge's voice-over as "*gerettet durch fremde Schuld*" (saved thanks to someone else's fault/guilty act), in which a woman, slumped unconscious in her car parked close to some trees, is raped by a commercial traveler who happens to park his car next to hers. However, by raping her, he accidentally saves her life, because—abandoned by her lover—she had swallowed an overdose of sleeping pills and was intending to commit suicide. What does this strange scene signify? Its anecdotal-episodic appearance in the film (after a brief court-case, we never see either the woman or her rapist again) is altogether typical for the apparently frivolous-farcical nature of Kluge's film. Yet once one considers it under the heading of *Fehlleistung*, and turns this bizarre parable and improbable fictional construction by 180 degrees, so to speak, one arrives at an intriguingly different, alternative situation. Instead of "rescued through someone else's guilty act"—"Schuld," it will be remembered, carries a particular semantic burden—the inverse possibility arises, namely of someone incurring guilt and putting himself in the wrong, by *not* rescuing someone in mortal danger. Held against the background of the presence-in-absence of the German response to the Holocaust, the reference of the scene would then be, for instance, to the guilt (feelings) of those who failed to come to the rescue of Jews during the years of confiscation, expulsion and deportation: one of the central sins of omission in the relation between German Jews and ordinary Germans during the so-called Third Reich, and a point of grievance ever since.

The purpose of the reversal of the historical situation as (para)practiced by Kluge would be that it allows for a "virtual" or utopian dimension, nurturing the insanely forlorn hope that in the forever deferred and therefore always ongoing trial of the German nation regarding the responsibility for the Holocaust, the victim—typically imaged as a raped woman—might testify on behalf of the guilty party, by claiming not to have seen/noticed/been aware of having been raped. In other words, the dialogue tentatively initiated in this scene is the hope that the Jews might absolve the Germans by yet another form of "uneven exchange"[12]—yet at what price: murder becomes attempted suicide, the Jewish people become "feminized," and genocide becomes a sort of unconscious rape. As if to underline the transgressively absurd nature of this proposition, Kluge's voice-over, commenting on a no less improbable hostage-taking and kidnap, which follows this scene, asserts: "What is an even stronger bond than marriage?—an act of murder, if everyone knows about the fact that everyone else is implicated." ("Was bindet stärker noch als eine Ehe?—Ein Mord, wenn jeder von der Tat des anderen weiss.") Again, if the German-Jewish cultural and civic cohabitation across several hundred years qualifies as a "marriage," bonding through murderous collusion and mutual implication is often cited as what kept both Nazi cadres and ordinary citizen acquiescent in the face of acts they knew to be crimes.

If such a reading of the film's enigmatic word-play or "conceptual slapstick" seems far-fetched, one might consider another scene in The Power of Feelings, in which Kluge provides a further metastatement and commentary on his own method in yet another trial scene. A housewife is accused of having grievously wounded her husband with a shotgun. The judges are trying to establish what her motive was and whether she acted in self-defense, which she denies [sic]. Then, one of the judges laboriously twists and turns the imagined fire arm, in the hope of understanding how it was possible for the heroine to shoot her husband when, according to her, she only wanted to produce a loud enough bang to shut him up. Here, the physical gestures of aligning weapon and target, and not succeeding in doing so, are like a graphic illustration of the kinds of cognitive twists and misalignments which constitute Kluge's argumentative method.

These and many similar scenes, inconsequential episodes and anecdotal constellations in Kluge's films would qualify for what elsewhere I have called a "parapractical poetics." Their purpose, it would seem, is to forestall an all too literal legibility, and to construct a more rebus-like mode of representation: something is being said and not said at the same time. In a second move, the viewer is invited to make legible this very opacity, but is not given the foil or context directly. Yet when held against the dominant historical trope of the entire post-1945 era, i.e., the always present demand to "master the past" by giving account of how this dreadful history was possible, then Kluge's figures take on contours, and their erratic movements form part of a distinct pattern. That this "coming to terms" largely excluded what one would now consider the appropriate discourse on the Holocaust or the terms of a dialogue on anti-Semitism, merely intensifies the hermeneutic enigma of what it is that Kluge needs to say, and what takes him such a monstrous productivity to say it.

Kluge is therefore a good example of why the absence, of which Drews' students complain, cannot simply be filled by a presence, and why "absence as presence" is not the same as, indeed exceeds the tropes of repression, denial and disavowal, usually adduced to explain the blind spots and gaps in the account that German films give of the Nazi past. As pointed out in an earlier chapter, when arguing from our (present) position of the Holocaust's ubiquity, the charge of its invisibility in the "Germany" films of the 1970s risks missing the works' most significant dimension. The unspoken and the not-seen, which I claim as typical for (part of) the New German Cinema, makes such "presence as parapraxis" only legible when held against a double frame of reference. Kluge's method enacts this double frame of reference, precisely by appearing so disorienting and confusingly "unframed."

"Fehlleistung" as *"Eigensinn"*

In this light, even a sociological-philosophical work like the monumental *Geschichte und Eigensinn* receives a further, historically specifiable level of reference. The fact that Kluge and Negt base themselves on the anthropology of the early Marx has often been interpreted as if the authors had intended to add to *Das Kapital* the volume never written on "the subjective factor." And indeed, in its size, binding, lettering and color scheme, *Geschichte und Eigensinn* camouflages itself and mimics the (East) German edition of the MEGA, the *Marx-Engels Gesamtausgabe*, widely purchased (but rarely read) by students in the early 1970s. From the present perspective, however, these preoccupations with human labor and its subjective components of emotion, affectivity and the unconscious seem in some sense the pretext—one is tempted to call it the protective cover, the mimicry, the dissimulation—for another interest, namely the already mentioned obsession with German history as a whole (and not only the post-war period) now interpreted as a series of parapraxes, which the authors call "2000 years of productive relations as present in the [German] public sphere." Kluge and Negt label this driving force, this symptomatic power behind production *Eigensinn*, that is obstinacy or obduracy, which I am suggesting, approximates *Fehlleistung*, once taken into the political, as well as the poetic realm.[13] For what Kluge and Negt name and document across more than a thousand pages is the peculiar, historically specific and apparently endlessly self-blocking and deadlocking ways in which Germans over the centuries have buried themselves in work only never to have a sense of achievement, have dreamt of hidden treasures only to wake up to dreadful ogres, have built themselves a homeland only never to feel at home, and a Heimat, only to become "unheimlich" (uncanny) to themselves as well as to the rest of humanity, and to have imagined the most utopian futures for mankind, only to end up wrecking their own one for generations to come.

German history emerges as a constant, uninterrupted laboratory of energy, ingenuity and work, considered under the (positive) aspects of *Eigensinn*, but which also produces the negative fallout, for such is the nature of Germany's "political unconscious" (to borrow a term from Fredric Jameson) that each episode of "going its own way" invariably seems to lead down yet another path of disaster. The outcome of these labors of generations upon generations of Germans is, according to Kluge and Negt, that the dead now look at the living in utter consternation:

> For the last 2000 years, human beings have been working on a territory we now call Germany, fashioning a single product: German history [...]. If we could interview these dead generations who have worked on this product, whether the result of their work had been appropriated [...] differently from their intentions [...], and if all the dead had an overview over what the subsequent dead had done, then we could only assume the reply to be unanimous: it's impossible to approve of the result. Their answer would be: "that's not at all what we have had in mind."[14]

It is this phrase that stays in one's memory after seeing Kluge's films, and it is echoed in The Patriot as well as in The Power of Feelings as the sometimes hilarious, sometimes distressing catalogue of futile efforts to forge a destiny out of accidents: "hunderttausend Gründe, die hinterher Schicksal heissen (a hundred thousand reasons which afterwards are called fate)."[15] Such an effort to bend contingency into the shape of destiny not only illustrates the gap between what was intended and what turns out to be the result:

> The individual experiences reality not as the historical fiction that it is, but for real, as fate. However, reality is not fate, but made by the work of generations of people who all the time want and wanted something, but who [invariably] achieved something else.[16]

Clearly, the phrase "that is not at all what we have had in mind" expresses both horror and regret in equal measure, while it cites at once the seeing eye and the self-protecting gesture of not wanting to recognize the blindingly obvious. One could call it the very definition of Germany's "Medusa's mirror,"[17] the "not-to-be-looked-at-ness" of its recent history, and thus outlines very precisely the thing it cannot name, the tragedy of the (German) Jews' relation to (German) history. It gives a valuable clue as to why Kluge and Negt so persistently work over these 2000 years: their theme are not millennia in a strict sense, but the Thousand Year Reich, the central catastrophe of the twentieth century, started by Germany and which all but destroyed it: "in April, 1945, the 1000 year old city of Magdeburg burnt to the ground in less than two days."[18] The misalignment of time itself is another of these *Fehlleistungen*, and it includes not only Kluge's grief over the destruction of the city of Magdeburg (which here also stands for his home town of Halberstadt, also burnt down in a matter of hours in the last days of the war—a personal disaster to which he devoted another book), but all other forms of destruction, whose senselessness finds in this catastrophic mismatch of "1000 years" and "two days" its definite commemorative symbol. Thus, Kluge's preemptive preoccupation with history, no less than his preemptive preoccupation with labor and production serves as a kind of "dream-screen" for an intense "working over," but also an obsessive return to the only questions that seem to matter: "how could it have come to this? What does it mean that it came to this?"

The first answer, which may not be an answer at all, is contained in the title already mentioned and which programmatically heads Kluge's second collection of short stories: *Lernprozesse mit tödlichem Ausgang* (learning-processes with a deadly outcome). What would it mean to accept that German history has been a series of learning processes, all of them with deadly outcomes? That the dead had lived in vain, that Hitler and the war had not only robbed the present—Kluge's own—generation of its future, but as it were, had once more murdered the dead, because the shame over what Germans did has, so to speak, worked its way backward into history. This fact becomes for Kluge and Negt the starting point of any reflection about the present, but also about its representation.

In *Geschichte und Eigensinn*, Kluge and Negt focus on finding a way out of this terrible dilemma, by inventing a sort of hypothetical or virtual temporality, one in which the possibility can be envisaged that these deaths could at least be comprehended and thus, retroactively, be given a meaning: on condition that the present is not seen as the end-point, the *terminus ad quem*, but itself appears already as a past, of which the future would act as the present: a sort of time-travel into the temporality of the future anterior. Bertold Brecht once said that it is not Mother Courage who has to learn. Rather, it is the spectator who has to learn from Mother Courage *not* learning. The question would then be not only how a nation learns or does not learn from what happens in its history, but what *Nachträglichkeit* or belatedness might make it at all possible to envisage a present, from which to draw the utopian faith to carry on, the resources for further "working on the future": this would be the possibly positive meaning of *Eigensinn*, the perseverance of parapraxis, the stubborn resilience of pushing the fast-forward button, and of using time-lapse photography, so often deployed by Kluge in order to gain a vantage point on the present from the anticipated perspective of the future anterior. Kluge, like his characters, is always (metaphorically) in a hurry, mostly so that he can look at the present from a position where it is already the past. Like so many heroes of science fiction, he becomes the chrono-naut, hoping to make the time-travelers' paradox (that one can enter the past only on condition that one does not change it) turn to the benefit of a history that Hitler has set on a course inexorably running backward.[19]

Trauma, Scar and Wound: Parapraxis as Embodied Mimicry

This opens up yet another perspective, present in *Geschichte und Eigensinn* and THE POWER OF FEELINGS. As Kluge enigmatically puts it: "Die Narbe arbeitet nicht wie die Wunde (a scar does not work like a wound)."[20] The corresponding scene in THE POWER OF FEELINGS is that of a British Royal Air Force officer, offering—instead of apologies for the firestorms of Dresden, Hamburg, Magdeburg, or Halberstadt—an oddly clinical simile about the conditions under which a wound can heal without leaving a scar. The officer speaks of the firestorm as of a necessary wound, tearing open the scar tissue of a grown city in order to make it bleed, because only fresh blood can clean a wound and commence the healing process. Strangely incongruous and inappropriate to the terrible damage inflicted on Germany's venerable cities and its civilian population, the metaphor at least gains in plausibility if applied to the "scarred" (the word Kluge's officer uses is "scabby") relationship between Germans and Jews after 1945, scarred and scabby by the misunderstandings, mistakes and tactlessness, which have kept the "skin" (i.e., contact and context of the encounter) at once oversensitive and overexposed. Across the film as a whole, Kluge extends a peculiar conceptual-semantic field around notions of labor, work, memory, pain, fire, ice and warfare, which, on the one hand, has everything to do with what one would call "mourning work," a process that thanks to the notions of scar and wound, now becomes wholly embodied and body-related. On the other hand, it perfectly demonstrates what Kluge means by "die Gewalt des Zusammenhangs" (the violence of contexts), invariably referring to trauma and vulnerability, repetition and the location of lost traces.

In THE PATRIOT, where some of these complex filiations of the violence of contexts are worked out in greatest detail, it is the knee-joint of a dead German soldier—the body part standing for the whole, but at the same time, emphasizing the joint, the relation rather than an essence—that is made to voice this demand for mourning work, in scenes whose pathos would be unbearable, were the conceit, and Kluge's manner of handling it, not so whimsical. This particular knee refers to a famous nonsense poem by Christian Morgenstern, "Ein Knie geht um die Welt" (a knee goes out to conquer the world) which, applied to a German WW II soldier, cannot but evoke the world-conquering hubris of Germany's territorial ambitions.

Yet the whimsicality is also a purposively performed parapraxis, now in the form of dissemblance. For it takes very little to see what sort of displacements, gaps and reversals have taken place around this pars-pro-toto of the German knee. One only has to substitute for the knee of Soldier Wieland a solitary shoe, a pair of glasses, a comb or a tooth, and to imagine what this passage would be like if it was these part-objects, so familiar from the archive footage of the camps, that had suddenly decided they no longer wanted to be silent.

But, then, if one takes a close look at the pictures, these seem to be the "right images," but at the "wrong place." Do these prisoners of war that are looking at us, not belong to the images we have become used to see from the camps or from the rounding up of ghetto inhabitants, rather than from the trek of hungry Germans, marched into Soviet camps after the defeat at Stalingrad? And why does this scene start with a deceptively idyllic picture of the Wartburg, the home of Martin Luther, one of pre-Hitler Germany's most notorious and vociferous anti-Semites, if not to name something the more insistently by *not* naming it?

The same shock of recognition-in-misprision overcame me, when noticing the images from near the opening of another of Kluge's films, the 1972 IN GEFAHR UND GRÖSSTER NOT BRINGT DER MITTELWEG DEN TOD, set in Frankfurt during the student movement and the housing riots. Do these workers silently digging the streets not look like forced foreign labor, again facing the camera with the wordless hostility of those having to bear the indignity of being classified, registered, objectified by the gaze of a camera? As one of the heroines so aptly muses in what stands as the motto at the very beginning of the film: "Inge Maier hatte das Gefühl, sie sei in den falschen Film geraten ("[looking at these street scenes] Inge Maier had the feeling of having strayed into the wrong movie"). To have persisted with so much *Eigensinn* in making "the wrong movie" for the past thirty-five years is surely Kluge's greatest contribution to the mourning work of post-war Germany, for it is through these artfully deliberate and yet nevertheless deeply disturbing parapraxes that Kluge outlines how a possible dialogue between Germans and Jews, between Germany and "its Jews" might designate itself, however negatively its "Gestalt" may have to be inferred, and however deferred or delayed its redemptive presence may still have to remain.

Considered in this light, Kluge's film theory as film politics becomes the politics of memory and commemoration, in the full knowledge of the cinema's impossible role as a medium of history—which on film can never quite come alive, just as it is never quite dead—and its inability to put the past to rest, since each viewing reopens the wound. As the constantly renewed experience of loss, "truth 24 frames a second" is necessarily a melancholy truth. But if the melancholy that emanates from his films derives in part from the knowledge that he is mourning the "wrong" Germans—a dead soldier frozen in Stalingrad in THE PATRIOT; the civilians burnt in the firestorms of Hamburg, Halberstadt, or Magdeburg in THE POWER OF FEELINGS—then this marathon perseverance of *Eigensinn* gains its energy from the hope of righting that wrong at another time, in another place.

In 1995, five years after German unification, Kluge published, by way of obituary and tribute to his friend, the conversations he had had on his TV program with Heiner Müller, the East German playwright, under the title: *Ich schulde der Welt einen Toten* ("I owe the world the [one] dead"),[21] which is a promissory note of a debt that needs to be heeded not only by Germans, East or West. Elsewhere, too, in the aftermath of a war or worse, such melancholy mimicry as found in Kluge's films, his television programs and literary output, may be the mourning work preliminary to recognizing the debt the living have not only towards the future, but to the past as well.

Notes

1. See, for instance, the special issue on Kluge in *October*, no. 46 (Fall 1988), with essays, among others, by Fred Jameson, Andreas Huyssen and Stuart Liebman. On Kluge's reception in the United States, see Peter C. Lutze, *Alexander Kluge, The Last Modernist* (Detroit: Wayne State University Press, 1998). A more recent volume is Tara Forrest's (ed.), *Alexander Kluge: Raw Material for the Imagination* (Amsterdam: Amsterdam University Press, 2012).
2. For a more detailed account, see Eric Rentschler (ed.), *West German Filmmakers on Film: Visions and Voices* (New York: Holmes & Meier, 1988) and Thomas Elsaesser, *New German Cinema: A History* (New Brunswick, NJ: Rutgers University Press, 1989).
3. Alexander Kluge, *Bestandsaufnahme: Die Utopie Film* (Frankfurt am Main: Zweitausendeins, 1983).
4. Alexander Kluge, "Why Should Film and Television Cooperate?," *October*, no. 46 and Christian Schulte and Winfried Sibers (eds.), *Kluges Fernsehen: Alexander Kluges Kulturmagazine* (Frankfurt am Main: Suhrkamp, 2002).
5. The third master thinker would be Ernst Bloch. Kluge's analysis of why fascism had been so successful in mobilizing the libidinal energies of the working class derived from Frankfurt School thinking about the mass media, while his conception of a counter-cinema revives the more "optimistic" outlook on how to reclaim popular culture for emancipation from Ernst Bloch's love of operetta, Karl May novels and sentimental popular chansons. See, for instance, Ernst Bloch, "On Fairytale, Colportage and Legend," in *Heritage of Our Times* (Berkeley: California University Press, 1991), 153–68.
6. Alexander Kluge (with Oskar Negt), *Geschichte und Eigensinn* volumes 1–3 (Frankfurt am Main: Suhrkamp Verlag, 1981). For an early commentary, see Eric Rentschler, "Kluge, Film History, and *Eigensinn*: A Taking of Stock from the Distance," *New German Critique*, no. 31 (Winter 1981), 109–24.
7. See below, pp. 183–84 for a fuller discussion of this passage.
8. Alexander Kluge, *Die Macht der Gefühle* (Frankfurt: Zweitausendeins, 1984), 5.
9. *Geschichte und Eigensinn* opens with a description of the "German Autumn" (1977), which is also the topic of Kluge's most famous omnibus film, DEUTSCHLAND IM HERBST/GERMANY IN AUTUMN (1977). The parallel of "Das eigensinnige Kind" with Antigone is elaborated on pp. 767–69.
10. Wolfram Schütte, "Alexander Kluges 'Angriff der Gegenwart auf die übrige Zeit.'" *Frankfurter Rundschau* (August 11, 1985).
11. Jörg Drews, "Leseprozesse mit tödlichem Ausgang," *text & kritik*, no. 85–86 (1985), 31.
12. See my discussion of uneven exchange in Thomas Elsaesser, *Fassbinder's Germany: History Identity Subject* (Amsterdam: Amsterdam University Press, 1996), 253–56.
13. The volume is divided into three sections: "The Historical Organization of Labor Power," "Germany as Productive Public Sphere" and "The Violence of Context."

"Labor" includes its opposite, fantasy and desires, as well as the history of the senses in their somatic and cognitive relation to abstract labor and modes of production.

14. Alexander Kluge and Oskar Negt, *Geschichte und Eigensinn* (Frankfurt: Zweitausendeins, 1981), 500–01.
15. Kluge, *Die Macht der Gefühle*, 5.
16. Alexander Kluge, *Gelegenheitsarbeit einer Sklavin: Zur realistischen Methode* (Frankfurt: Suhrkamp, 1973), 215.
17. For an elaboration of this idea, see August Closs, *Medusa's Mirror: Studies in German Literature* (London: Cresset Press, 1962).
18. Kluge and Negt, "Stadt/Bomben," *Geschichte und Eigensinn*, 719.
19. Such a rewind recalls Kurt Vonnegut's *Slaughterhouse Five*, about the firestorms caused by RAF bombers in Dresden in 1944, and Martin Amis' book about Auschwitz doctors, *Time's Arrow*. It is also how one may read the scene at the beginning of THE POWER OF FEELINGS when a singer is asked by an interviewer why, even after the eighty-four performances, is he in denial over the fact that the opera *Rigoletto* has a tragic ending? The singer replies: "It might have been different, and maybe once, it will be different." In other words, even in the face of an already-written "text" (or repeatedly experienced past), he holds on to a hypothetical dimension, which might also be called a "test-scenario." Is it stupidity, disavowal of reality or does the encounter give the usually "tragic" learning processes of Kluge a seemingly counter-intuitive, but necessary "utopian" dimension, where hope-against-hope asserts itself in the face of a fatal outcome and disaster?
20. Kluge and Negt, *Geschichte und Eigensinn*, 125.
21. Alexander Kluge/Heiner Müller, *Ich schulde der Welt einen Toten* (Hamburg: Rotbuch, 1995).

7

RETROACTIVE CAUSALITY AND THE PRESENT

Fassbinder's The Third Generation

A Year in History

June 2012 marked the thirtieth anniversary of Rainer Werner Fassbinder's premature and unexpected demise. In retrospect, it was "the year of a death foretold," because 1982 has, over time, become a watershed for German historians and film historians in several different ways. It is the year that saw the end to the social democratic coalition that had formed the West German government for the preceding decade, first under Willy Brandt and then Helmut Schmidt: the bold opening up to the East (under Brandt) and an unprecedented crackdown on civil liberties in the West (under Schmidt). They were succeeded by a conservative government under Helmut Kohl, who consolidated the security state, but also pursued a policy of détente vis-à-vis the Soviet Union that after 1989 yielded the dividend of a (surprisingly speedy) German unification.

What made 1982 a fatal year for the New German cinema was that the death of its creative center and beating heart, as Fassbinder was called in the obituaries, coincided with a change in funding policy that tilted the various state and federal subsidies decisively in favor of more "commercial" productions: a change, which, at least for a decade and a half, made German cinema, once more, all but invisible on the international scene.

Since 2012 also marked the fiftieth anniversary of the Oberhausen Manifesto (February 28, 1962), generally celebrated as the birth date of the New German Cinema,[1] of which Fassbinder to this day remains the most widely recognized "unrepresentative representative," it is only fitting that a retrospective such as this one should also ponder more generally the significance of crisscrossing time frames, intersecting dates and overlapping time lines. For German film historians, the years 1962 to 1982 have become something like a separate epoch, unified by a number of distinctive features, to which the death of Fassbinder has given both an exclamation mark and a closing bracket. It is worth recalling that the word "epoch" comes from Greek *epochē* and *epechein*, meaning pause, cessation, and a holding back or closing off—in other words, a punctuation mark, a break, as well as a fixed point, from which to make a retrospective turn. The present chapter chooses another year—1979—and the film by Fassbinder that most directly "responded" to a precise moment in history, namely THE THIRD GENERATION, in order to probe questions of the historical moment, and the extent to which, here too, a parapractic logic can be discerned.

Specific dates and anniversaries also bring into focus other attempts at tracking with films how political trajectories and cultural trends traverse each other, or find themselves bundled together in the symptomatic cipher of a single year.[2] For instance, at Yale University, the Film Studies Department has been devoting annual retrospectives to the years 1945, 1956, 1989, and, of course, 1968.[3] The historical significance of the year chosen was predefined: these were all turning points in post-war European history. The challenge was not to cinematically "illustrate" their political significance, but to unearth films that seemed at first sight removed from the retroactive weight given the crisis year in question, but which, on closer inspection, revealed other lines of genealogy, either leading to dead-ends or surviving underground, to subsequently surface again in a different constellation, or in other ways proving itself to have become symptomatic.

I also recall a chapter I co-wrote on the month of July for a volume, which for each month of 1929 pinpointed a particular event that retrospectively became significant, because a momentous development could be traced back to its first appearance. Called *1929: Contributions to an Archaeology of New Media,*[4] the book marked milestones of that year for photography, radio, television and computation. For instance, 1929 saw the first application of Hollerith cards for the automatic sorting of data and information. The year also elicited chapters on Aby Warburg, presenting his Mnemosyne Atlas; on the first television transmission in Germany; the premiere of Billy Wilder and Robert Siodmak's PEOPLE ON SUNDAY; a spiritist séance conducted by Georges Melies in Paris; Bert Berecht's radio experiments in Baden-Baden; and Walter Ruttmann editing the first German sound film, MELODY OF THE WORLD.

Such archaeological enterprises play with two opposites—contingency and predestination—as if to challenge fate to show its invisible hand. Once the year in question has been selected, the specific topics and events that match the predefined parameters almost choose themselves: proof, if nothing else, of the productivity of creative constraints and arbitrarily imposed limitations that the sociologist Jon Elster has credited with being the counter-intuitive, but ultimately most rational response one can make when faced with too many options, an overload of stimuli or—as in this case—the infinite complexity and multi-layered map of historical determinants for a phenomenon such as the audio-visual and technical media, including the cinema.[5]

The "1929" book project took its cue from another well-known study of a single year, Hans Ulrich Gumbrecht's *In 1926,*[6] where a literary scholar undertakes a kind of science-fiction time travel. Transported back to the year 1926, he immerses himself in the rush of experiences that made people feel like they were "living on the edge of time." As Gumbrecht admits, there is nothing particularly remarkable about 1926, if measured by the standard history books, which prefer "political" watersheds like 1789 or 1848, 1917 (the Russian Revolution) or 1933 (the year Hitler came to power). It is not even the year of the Wall Street crash (1929), which many now believe was the trigger of so much that was to follow also elsewhere in the world, given that its effects paved the way not only for the United States to become the dominant world power, but arguably prefigured that, during the second half of the twentieth century, finance capitalism would take over from political ideologies and the real world economy, as the motor force of history.

Yet as Gumbrecht summarizes it, 1926 was "the year that A. A. Milne published *Winnie-the-Pooh* and Alfred Hitchcock released his first successful film, THE LODGER. A set of modern masters was at work—Jorge Luis Borges, Babe Ruth, Leni Riefenstahl, Ernest Hemingway, Josephine Baker, Greta Garbo, Franz Kafka, and Gertrude Stein—while factory workers, secretaries, engineers, architects, and Argentine cattle-ranchers were performing their daily tasks."[7]

In contrast to traditional historians, Gumbrecht mixes the retrospectively extraordinary, such as Martin Heidegger publishing *Sein und Zeit*, or Fritz Lang spending most of the year shooting METROPOLIS, with the portentously ordinary, indexing the novelties of the day such as "bars, boxing, movie palaces, elevators, automobiles, airplanes, hair gel, bullfighting, film stardom, dance crazes." It is to his credit that Gumbrecht does not restrict himself to Europe alone. From the vantage points of Berlin, Buenos Aires, Paris and New York, he traverses Spain, Italy, France, and Latin America. Thus, "we learn what it is to be an 'ugly American' in Paris by experiencing the first mass influx of American tourists into Europe. We visit assembly lines in Chicago, Detroit and Philadelphia. We relive a celebrated boxing match and see how Jack Dempsey was beaten, yet walked away having won the hearts of the fans. We hear the voice of Adolf Hitler condemning tight pants on young men."[8] Gumbrecht narrates these events and snippets as a living network of sensations and ephemeral intensities, evoking the excitement of "being there" during another era. It is an audiovisual tour that tries to engage all our senses, while resolutely confining itself to the stylistic resources of literature and the expressive means of the written word—in short, its evocative power results from a creative constraint of self-imposed limitations: a compilation movie made of words.

For what makes Gumbrecht's method remarkable is that it presents itself as an assemblage or montage, a collection of short sketches that can be read in any randomly chosen sequence, using the traditional form of the book, but written against the sequential logic of the book, in order to produce the effect of a kaleidoscope, which—each time it is shaken—mixes the splinters differently. It is a book that demonstrates the limits of the book, being not only "at the edge of time," but also "at the edge" of those media that most vigorously challenged "in 1926" the hegemony of literature: above all, the cinema, but also foreshadowing the zapping culture of television and random access media we know today—from Facebook to YouTube, from databases to video games.[9]

In other words, taking a particular year, and reconstructing through its heterogeneous elements a "topography of historical simultaneity," hoping to capture the anatomy of an epoch, its zeitgeist or its tipping point event, is as tempting as it is treacherous. We find what we are looking for, in a vicious circle of tautologies. Or maybe there is a heuristic value after all? Does history have a way of writing its own scripts? Skimming the surface *and* digging into the layers of a single year often does produce unexpected connections, which suggests that parallels in temporal sequence can yield illuminating contiguities of meaning, if arranged in a multi-directional space. But such a habit of mind is also historically conditioned and in this respect, typically contemporary: it reaffirms the *spatial turn* in the humanities, that is, it reflects our current preference for "cognitive mapping" of temporal phenomena, and thus it implicitly accepts our loss of belief in the "dynamic forces" of history, the forward and onward sweep, but also the loss of belief in the possibility of radical ruptures, abandoning the expectation that the new could either emerge ex-nihilo, or that *change* could be a performative act, either individually or collectively. It commits us to an "allegorical" reading of the ruins of our utopias and hopes, but it may also testify to a need to slow things down, because they have rushed by too fast.

The Moment, the *Longue Durée* and the Power of Retroactive Causality

It is this malleability and even reversibility of time, mapped on a consistent extension of space, that brings cinema into conflict with conventional ideas about history, as relentlessly pushing in one direction, by a chain of cause and effect. If cinema and history turn out to be mutually incompatible ways of understanding and rendering the world, then the twentieth century—the century of cinema—will have offered a sustained challenge to historiography, not on the basis of how accurately a film renders "the facts," but by a different understanding of temporality, of which the preoccupation with memory, trauma and the various memory regimes become one prominent symptom.

So thoroughly have the peculiar temporal logics of the cinema been universalized and become second nature that we invariably treat much of the past—and especially the history of the last hundred years—as if it was a film. We rewind or rerun it in a loop, passing its photographs, sound bites and moving images before us in slow motion, the way that an artist like Douglas Gordon takes a classic Hollywood movie like PSYCHO or THE SEARCHERS, and slows it down to the point where the instant turns to monumental stasis.[10] Similarly, the filmmaker Terrence Malick, in THE TREE OF LIFE (2011), suspends ineffable moments of childhood, so that they can be savored in the dilation of their particularity, while speeding up the millions of years of our universe into a ten-minute montage of swirling gases and galaxies.

What certain films that deal with twentieth-century German history, and notably with the Nazi period, the Holocaust and its different forms of afterlife have in common—I am thinking of Hans Jürgen Syberberg's OUR HITLER, Edgar Reitz's HEIMAT, Claude Lanzmann's SHOAH as well as Fassbinder's BERLIN ALEXANDERPLATZ—is their inordinate length: seven, fifteen, nine and sixteen hours respectively. While "epic" is the word that usually comes to mind, the effect is also that of a slow motion (*zeitlupe*), as if this terrible and interminable period between 1933 and 1945 was so compressed, so multi-layered, but also such an insane acceleration of history, that it took most of the second half of the twentieth century to reexamine, to *process* (never mind, to comprehend) these twelve years, and put them under the magnifying glass of the slow motion action replay.

Alexander Kluge's films often literalize this metaphor of an "anamorphosis in time" by using slow-motion or time-lapse photography, most strikingly in THE BLIND DIRECTOR (DER ANGRIFF DER GEGENWART AUF DIE ÜBRIGE ZEIT, 1985), emulating how, for Kluge, a single moment can consume everything that went before and came after (*wie ein einziger Augenblick alles Vorher und Nachher verschlingen kann*).[11]

Kluge's remark about the moment consuming everything before and after puts him on one side of the ongoing debate about history and memory in the twentieth century. His side favors radical breaks, aligns itself with Walter Benjamin's "messianic time" and Alain Badiou's notion of the "event." It contrasts with the idea that an ever-finer mesh of causal factors, drawn from all areas of life, including climate and geography, is what weaves the web of the slowly emerging constellations we later call a history. Such histories as Syberberg, Reitz or Fassbinder wanted to tell needed large and extended time frames to reveal their significance for the "here-and-now" of when they were made. The contrast between the flash of the moment (Kluge's *Augenblick*) and deep time (the *longue durée*)[12] throws an interesting light on the secret connections in Germany's postwar society between *commemoration* and *trauma*, under whose double sign of *recurrence* and *repetition* so many of its national, transnational but also biographical anniversaries now tend to take place.

For if trauma confirms the event's singular significance, by an absence (or rather, by the event's presence as trauma, experienced retroactively, striking suddenly and seemingly at random), then the culture's obsession with anniversaries would be the mirror reversal of the event's suddenness. It would be the performance of a fetish-action, meant to protect oneself from the apparent arbitrariness of the event by ritualizing its unpredictability into periodicity, and taming its disruptive force by the regularity of its recurrence.

Yet the opposition between "moment" and "deep time" also hides another contrasting pair, this time concerned with causes as much as consequences. A notable shift seems to have occurred, analogous to the spatial turn, and maybe occasioned by it: namely the move away from linear causality to some other model capable explaining how events come about. Especially commemorative occasions behave according to a form of *retroactive causality*, where the effect (i.e., the present state of affairs) imagines or generates from within itself the causes to which it owes its existence, allowing it thereby to presuppose the proleptic (anticipatory) anchor-function of the date it commemorates or celebrates.[13] This retroactive causality—inspired by Freud's *Nachträglichkeit* or belatedness—has taken over from *overdetermination*, the preferred model of causality in the 1960s and 1970s, especially among Marxists, keen to locate the contradictions that would drive the historical process onward and forward. Overdetermination (also a Freudian term) was understood to acknowledge multiple—including contradictory—forces to act simultaneously upon any given situation, each factor or force being either necessary to bring about a certain state of affairs, or preventing it from becoming a catalyst for (political) change.[14]

The more the idea of retroactive causality has gained ground since the 1990s, as a way to understand collective memory and account for the recurring cycles of crises, the more overdetermination has become a problematic concept, not only because the belief in contradiction as the energizer of history has all but disappeared. Overdetermination also runs counter to the play of predestination and contingency I mentioned earlier, which now serve to cope with risk and uncertainty. Our sensitivity to risk has made us tolerant for all kinds of counterfactual understandings of the past, so that, rather than assuming a single chain or a cluster of contending events converging on a determinate outcome, we like to build forking paths into our causal trajectories, indulging in regretful "if-onlys" and allowing us to make room for hypothetical "what-ifs": options also much favored in digital media environments, such as computer games, but especially popular in contemporary cinema, either in the form of forking paths and multiple possibilities (e.g. Blind Chance, Run Lola Run, Sliding Doors) or as networks of contingent encounters and fatal coincidences (as in Short Cuts, Magnolia, Crash or Babel).

Fassbinder was one of the earliest directors to understand the powerful pull of retroactive causality, for instance in the BRD trilogy or in The Merchant of Four Seasons, where the present is not so much overshadowed by the past;

rather, characters create pasts to explain to themselves the misery they feel and suffer in the present. But Fassbinder was also a film director and storyteller who had a keen sense of forking paths, who worked with coincidences in order to highlight the roads not taken (and thus to sharpen our appreciation of counter-factual possibilities), in films as desperately fatalistic as the The Marriage of Maria Braun, as intricately hypothetical as Welt am Draht, as prophetic-proleptic as The Third Generation, and as historically situated as Lili Marleen. Perhaps his reliance on coincidences was too quickly assigned to his preference for melodrama, and should now be reevaluated in the light of probability theory, "six degrees of separation" and the "butterfly effect." What is certain is that his way of indicating that the significance of a particular event can only be evaluated in retrospect was through strategically placed anachronisms: they were designed to jolt us out of any nostalgic reverie or sentimental self-oblivion; they challenged us into thinking about what the past has to tell the present, either as a reminder of what lingers and still festers, or as part of the past's never redeemed or fulfilled promise.

More generally, one could describe the present dilemma of our "culture of commemoration" as follows: it demonstrate a *belief in history* (that is why we pick a date from the past) as well as *skepticism towards history* (that is why we now read the past transversally, or spatially, rather than in linear fashion). But the dilation, such as manifest in the replay, and the topographical metaphors that map succession backwards, sideways and forward, nonetheless serve a spirit that *acknowledges contingency* (the forking path: things could have happened otherwise, nothing in human history is inevitable) and yet also *puts its faith* in contingency, as the only way to bring about desired change: after all, lateral links make up the network society, we tend to depend on chance encounters for our emotional lives, and we benefit from the small world syndrome or "six degrees of separation": they have become our spur to innovation, and they foster our still flickering hope of a future not yet foreclosed by the relentless replay of so many pasts.

It is this dilemma or paradox that I want to explore around the case of Fassbinder in the hope of redefining how we can understand his work's historicity: meaning that his films are very precisely of their time, place and moment, *and* they constitute a kind of feedback system, open towards the future, which is our present, as well as doubling back to reinscribe our present in a history. Such a historicity would be the effect of *something appearing in retrospect as prescient and prophetic*: a sort of short-circuiting of causality and consequence in the convergence of retroactive recognition. Yet if with hindsight we can designate something as prophetic, we open a closed loop: we do not discover some sort of necessary causality, though it might seem so. Rather: a moment in the past reveals itself as especially pregnant and prescient for the future, in order to endorse that our present not only has a past, but that this past can empower us to face an uncertain future. It is a historicity that strongly confirms a contemporary predicament: the more we are traumatized by the present, the more we remember the past.

This would give us the definition of an event's parapractic relation to history, but it would also be my primary claim to Fassbinder's relevance and topicality: not that he predicted a specific event or outcome; rather that he—perhaps better than any modern filmmaker besides Bunuel—understood the logic of why we have to replay the past, in order to even imagine a future, and why we have to see the present—any present—in terms of history, in order not to be swallowed by the eternal presence of the past that the very existence of the cinema has brought into the world. The conditions that define a particular film's historicity—given the cinema's profusion of period detail and precise locatedness, amidst the generalized a-temporality I have just alluded to—will therefore bear the signs of these contradictory coordinates. To single out three criteria that in film history have often characterized a future "classic," but which I shall here extend to historically prescient events in general: (a) the *unlikeliness* of the event in question happening, (b) its *openness* and indeterminacy at the time of its occurrence, and (c) its *remaining unrecognized* in the prevailing *constellation of incompatibilities*.

1979: Contingent Date, Negative Conjuncture or Future Constellation?

I can now turn to 1979, to Fassbinder's THE THIRD GENERATION, and the conditions of its historicity. In what sense, does my choice of this date satisfy any of the criteria of the "historical moment"? At first sight, it does not seem such a propitious year for radical breaks, singular events, or potential turning points, especially not in Germany, where it is the Hot Autumn of 1977 that was the landmark event, defining powerful lines of force way beyond its brief duration and in a sense, consuming what preceded it and much of what was to follow. But look up 1979 on Wikipedia, and you will find that on March 28, the Three Mile Island Nuclear Accident happened—at the time the most serious in the history of nuclear energy; on April 1, the people of Iran voted for a new constitution which would see Ayatollah Khomeini become the Supreme Leader; on April 11 the President of Uganda, protégé of the West, Idi Amin, and one of the worst leaders of post-colonial Africa, was forced into exile; also in April, Rhodesia became Zimbabwe, with Robert Mugabe as its first (and so far only) president; on May 4 Margaret Thatcher became the first woman Prime minister of Great Britain; on July 16; Saddam Hussein became president of Iraq; on June 18 the United States and the Soviet Union signed the 2nd Strategic Arms Limitation Treaty; on July 19, the Sandinista entered Managua and formed a revolutionary government; on December 24, the Soviet Army invaded Afghanistan; and on the same day, the European Space Agency successfully launched the first Ariane rocket.

Reading these primarily political events, one is tempted to reconstruct a causal nexus of interrelated events, most of which point in one direction, especially with hindsight: discernible are the outlines of a shift, which signals the reassertion of powerfully autocratic and conservative tendencies, both in Europe and the Middle East, mixed with the dying aspirations of the revolutionary movements that began in the 1960s: the Sandinista success in Nicaragua would be undermined by the CIA and the Reagan administration's support for the Contra's, the Iranian Revolution would lead to a repressive theocracy, Mugabe would turn out to be an autocrat and near dictator, and America's support for Saddam Hussein, as well as for the Mujahedin in Afghanistan against the Soviet invasion would come to haunt successive U.S. presidents to this day.

The events would be a good example of overdetermination, for the list, as I have presented it here, can easily confirm *the end of revolutionary aspirations* of the previous two decades, and thus the reason for paralysis and stasis. It would even provide a contingent but cumulatively persuasive historical logic for the contradictory effects of decolonization, while contextualizing the failed aspirations of May '68, including the turn to violence in the case of the Red Army Faction (RAF). On the one hand, one is tempted to (yet again) invoke Walter Benjamin's "Angel of History": "His face is turned towards the past. Where we see the appearance of a chain of events, he sees one single catastrophe, which unceasingly piles rubble on top of rubble and hurls it before his feet."[15]

Read however, from the opposite end of the temporal arrow, not with the angel contemplating the mounting mass of rubble, nor with the "storm from Paradise" mistaken as "progress," but from our present, post-9/11 world, the contingent events of 1979 chart a constellation we recognize only too well: the constellation is readable as the confluence of forces that put in place *the elements of the surveillance state*. Consider the following: in a counter-current to the political disasters which the list charts, it is easy to draw up a list of major technical "breakthroughs," such as the invention of the compact disc, the introduction of the Sony Walkman, Apple's marketing of the Visicalc spreadsheet as the first computational business application, and IBM's first attempt at developing the personal computer, all of which also belong to the *epochē* of 1979. If one adds to this the massive surge in satellite technology, of which the launch of the Ariane rocket is both a symptom and a result, then the year 1979 can credibly claim to be pivotal in the other tendency that still dominates our lives today, namely the relentless growth of the surveillance state (the *recto* of which post 9/11 terrorism is the *verso*). Once again, when viewed from our own ambiguous position (or Benjamin's dialectic of disaster and progress), the cumulative effect of computing power, compact storage, space research and autocratic governments ushers in what at first appeared as an ad hoc alliance, in response to "terrorism." It was Michel Foucault who first systematically examined this alliance, and formulated it as both an epistemic break and the transformation of elements rooted in the European Enlightenment, from Jean Jacques Rousseau's demands for self-disclosure and social transparency to Jeremy Bentham's self-policing Panopticon.

Foucault's thinking thus combined the confluence of forces with the historical specificity of the "moment." In many of his writing from that period—*Discipline and Punish* was published in English 1979, and his lectures on governmentality and the birth of bio-politics were held at the College de France in 1978–79—he examined such coming together of seemingly distinct and at first sight disparate phenomena under the notion of *dispositif*, which Foucault defined as "a heterogeneous ensemble of material and discursive practices whose configuration is historically specific." The surveillance and security paradigm—what Gilles Deleuze a few years later would summarize in his "Postscript on the Control Societies"[16]—is precisely this: a *dispositif* in Foucault's sense, an ensemble, where "power," "paranoia" and also "pleasure" come together in a peculiarly unique combination. It is this paradox of paranoia, power and pleasure, that Fassbinder recognized lucidly and intuitively, not least in his contribution to GERMANY IN AUTUMN. Foucault's *dispositif* and Fassbinder's instantiation of it thus belong to the specific markers of the "historicity" of 1979—and our peculiar proximity to it, some thirty-five years later.

Before elaborating on this *dispositif* and the way it is given body and dynamic in THE THIRD GENERATION, it is worth reminding oneself of how Fassbinder saw his own historical moment, and how his films as a whole configure a very particular relation of cinema to twentieth-century German history. He once said in an interview: "How do I fit into my country's history? Why am I German?" and many of his films can be seen as implicitly seeking an answer to these questions. As so many of his generation who were born between 1942 and 1948, his childhood and adolescence were marked by the legacy of Nazi dictatorship, and also like many others, he grew up without a father, leaving him with a doubly fraught relation to authority. Yet unlike those whose writings and films stood also under the sign of "mastering the past," Fassbinder did not use oedipal revolt as the trope and master-narrative of his film. Partly, because in his choice of historical epochs, he reached back further than the Nazi years, while also extending it into the present. He wanted to start with the 1840s, to the rise of the German bourgeoisie and the root of modern anti-Semitism by filming Gustav Freytag's *Soll und Haben*. The project having been cancelled by the television company that had commissioned it, Fassbinder began his chronicle of modern Germany with the decline of Prussianism in FONTANE'S EFFI BRIEST; following this are the turmoil of the Weimar Republic (BERLIN ALEXANDERPLATZ), the rise of National Socialism (DESPAIR — EIN REISE INS LICHT), Hitler's war (LILI MARLEEN), the rubble years (DIE EHE DER MARIA BRAUN), the "economic miracle" (LOLA), the late 50s (VERONIKA VOSS) and early 60s (DER HÄNDLER DER VIER JAHRESZEITEN), the presence of the so-called guest workers (ANGST ESSEN SEELE AUF), the "hot autumn" of

1977 (DEUTSCHLAND IM HERBST) and the end of the Red Army Faction (DIE DRITTE GENERATION).

To call him chronicler of post-war Germany—and thus put him on the side of historicism, i.e., preferring continuities over breaks—would be misleading, if it did not stress how in each film, he captured the crisis moments and seized on the turning points of the period and history in question, bound up with the modest, often failing, hopes and dreams expressed from the vantage point of the petit-bourgeoisie, the conformists, anti-heroes and asocial figures on the margins of a German society at war with itself until the 1970s for at least one hundred years.

The key factor to remember, however, is that Fassbinder "wrote" German history by rewriting it as "film history," not via remakes of classics or even adapting realist novels (with one or two significant exceptions), but in the sense that in all his films the mass media of the twentieth century play a uniquely determining part. Radio and the gramophone, the written word, the cinema and television are material presences and historical forces in his films, reflecting the ambiguity already noted, where a potentially or actually authoritarian society aligns itself with media-technologies as instruments of wielding a new kind of power. It means that the breaks and crisis points are also refigured as the birth-pangs of possible new beginning, so that recurring tropes like prostitution, the black market, (homo)sexual relationships and commune-, group- or gang-like living arrangement are depicted as sites and practices where the exchange rates of human commerce are still open, where the moral and emotional currencies can be or should be constantly renegotiated. This ever renewed openness in Fassbinder's films, present at the formal and deep-structural level, however fatal and pessimistic his stories seem to end, is part of Fassbinder's legacy for the present, where we think ourselves as open and non-deterministic, but only because our culture no longer has the power to imagine a future that might be different from the present.

"I Don't Throw Bombs, I Make Films"

On the poster advertising THE THIRD GENERATION, a handwritten note proclaims "I Don't Throw Bombs, I Make Films." It was used in the publicity material distributed by the *Filmverlag der Autoren* at the Cannes Film Festival, in May 1979, and is Fassbinder's reply, taken from an interview from 1977, to a question that implied that he was siding with the terrorists, on the basis of his very autobiographical contribution to the omnibus film GERMANY IN AUTUMN.

It is perhaps worth underlining that Fassbinder did not have to wait until the events in 1977 that culminated in the making of GERMANY IN AUTUMN in order to understand that political activism always contains an element of provocation and that in Germany, too, violence and counter-violence had a way of escalating each other. He also understood that one of the aims of the RAF was to provoke the government into taking the "iron fist" of the security apparatus out of the velvet glove of liberal democracy, in the hope that the population would be persuaded that underneath the surface of a mature West-European country, there still lurked the specter of fascism: a strategy common at the time among radical fringe groups also in the United States (the Weathermen, the Symbionese Liberation Army), Italy (the Red Brigades) and Japan (the Japanese Red Army, or *Nihon Sekigun*). Fassbinder, it is fair to say, was intellectually attracted to the ruthless radicalism of the Baader-Meinhof group. As an anti-bourgeois outsider, who sympathized with the anarchism of Bakunin—and Bakunin plays an important, if paradoxical role in THE THIRD GENERATION, along with Arthur Schopenhauer's *World as Will and Representation*—Fassbinder was nonetheless only too aware that the brutality of the RAF's actions would isolate them from any political efficacy and deprive them of mass-support. By saying "I don't throw bombs, I make films," he demanded the right to be judged by his work, and not by his personal opinions, wanting to keep faith with his own political project, which was to make films that provoked questions, not violence.

Karlheinz Böhm, known for his role as Peeping Tom in Michael Powell's film by that title, and who played the sadistic husband in Fassbinder's MARTHA (1974), an arrogant homosexual in FOX AND HIS FRIENDS (1975), and a communist in MOTHER KÜSTER'S TRIP TO HEAVEN (1975), once asked Fassbinder where he stood politically: "I went to him and said: 'I've just read your script of *Mother Küster*. I like it, but there's one thing I don't understand: I know you're against the right, I know you're against the left, you're against the extremists, the ones from below, the ones from above, you're against political parties, against established religion—so what exactly are you for?' Fassbinder looked at me for a while, and then he said: 'I think I just notice when it doesn't smell right, whether it's on the right or the left, above or below, I couldn't care less. It's just, when I notice that it stinks, I fire in all directions'."[17]

This "firing in all directions" is worth keeping in mind: it is the opposite of having no views at all, or claiming an artist's prerogative to stay neutral or objective. But it also means that for Fassbinder, it was not a matter of "exposing" in his films either the illiberal West German state or even to "condemn" the RAF, but to demonstrate in action certain political mechanisms, to examine the role of the media and media technologies, and to lay bare the parallels in the emotional dynamics at the personal level. His films dealing with historical periods or topical issues are especially apt at pointing out unexamined contradictions as well as pointing to unexpected connections, focusing on the inner workings of German post-war society, whose recent history had made it especially vulnerable to extremism, but also to paranoia, and the seductive submission to authority and strong leadership.

In one sense, the plot of THE THIRD GENERATION is ingeniously simple, linear and straightforward. A loose group of urban guerrillas, all of them middle class and almost all of them with day-time, respectable jobs, form a kind of underground cell, mainly it seems, to escape their bored unfulfilled lives, and as a kind of parlor game, somewhere between playing charades, card games and Monopoly. They are constantly making arrangements of secret meetings, or they telephone each other with coded messages and passwords, until one of them is brutally assassinated, whereupon they suspect that they have been infiltrated and betrayed to the police, start to panic and decide to strike. They kidnap the Berlin director of an American computer company, not realizing that this is in fact part of the trap into which they have been lured, and which will cost most of them their lives.

A more laconic summary is provided by Fassbinder himself: "On the one side, there is an industrialist (Eddie Constantine), on the other a policeman (Hark Bohm). Together they decide to form a terrorist cell, the first man because it will be useful for his business ventures, the second to justify his repressive activities. Their idea is very simple: nowadays it is capitalism that brings forth terrorism, to boost itself and strengthen its system of hegemony."[18]

This is both accurate and misleading, in that it leaves out the network effects and media interfaces, reducing the power-relations to their shortest link. Yet the "historicity" of Fassbinder's film lies precisely in this tension between the intricate generational, gendered and technologically mediated networks that Fassbinder lines up (there are father figures like Lurz, the industrialist, but also the grandfather Gast, and a father-in-law who has an affair with his son's wife) and the brutal simplicity of the power-structures that mastermind them (police protection for the industrialist, who pays a homosexual to play agent provocateur in an anarchist cell). Historicity is here understood as a "time exposure" of heterogeneous forces at work, a sort of "snapshot" of incompatibilities, captured at a precise moment in time, the winter of 1978/79, and in a precise place, West Berlin. Little could he know how this "place" was to change out of all recognition during the next generation, but the very self-evidence of his Cold War Berlin in the late 1970s now gives the film a dense documentary texture.

Among the character constellation, the peculiar dynamic derives from the sense that the centripetal impulses (fear and paranoia as corroding factors in human relationships) and the centrifugal forces (fear and paranoia as a political weapon used by terrorism to undermine and by the state to consolidate political legitimacy) are poised in a paradoxical equilibrium. This in turn is amplified but made even more volatile, by Fassbinder immersing all parties—police, would-be terrorists and the industrialist—in the atmosphere of twenty-four-hour news cycles and permanent states of exception, made possible by media technologies and their network effects. He is, in other words, offering a "paranoid" interpretation of our own network society, where everything connects and mutually interacts—part of the very *dispositif* and episteme earlier identified with the year 1979 and the name of Michel Foucault, but also offering a historical commentary on something we only appreciate now, as if our future was already his past.

Yet from a more conventional vantage point, say, an *auteurist* perspective, THE THIRD GENERATION joins many other Fassbinder films and merely reiterates or varies some of the director's most predominant themes throughout his work. Among these we could name:

- The *asymmetrical, often sado-masochistic, but also highly volatile and thus reversible power-relations* among the members of a tightly knit group: Whether a multi-generational family (THE MARRIAGE OF MARIA BRAUN), a professional team (BEWARE OF A HOLY WHORE), a group of homosexuals (FOX AND HIS FRIENDS), a utopian commune (THE TRIP TO NIKLASHAUSEN) or as in the case of THE THIRD GENERATION, a self-styled conspiratorial "terrorist" cell, there has not been a filmmaker since Fassbinder who can orchestrate group dynamics as complexly and incisively. This becomes even more striking when one considers that ensemble films, of the kind pioneered by Robert Altman with NASHVILLE, reprised with SHORT CUTS and PT Anderson's MAGNOLIA, or multi-strand narratives like Alejandro González Iñárritu's AMORES PERROS and BABEL have become something like the norm of contemporary art-house cinema. Perhaps the only film that comes close to presenting a similarly intricate web is Lars von Trier's THE IDIOTS, a sort of Danish remake of THE THIRD GENERATION, insofar as both directors emphasize how the ideals of the '68 generation about sexual liberation or anti-bourgeois emancipation in general can take on a dynamic that leads invariably to forms of authoritarian rule, reflecting at the micro-level what I indicated about the year 1979 at the macro-level of world politics.
- The *convergence of different forms of addiction and dependency*: The film draws analogies between drug dependency, sexual dependency, and media addiction. The former nexus is well known from many of Fassbinder's films, such as THE BITTER TEARS OF PETRA VON KANT, LILI MARLEEN or VERONICA VOSS, as indeed is the role of the mass media in fostering such addiction. A startling condensation of the media as a drug is a shot in THE THIRD GENERATION, in which Fassbinder draws a link between the film's oversaturation of ambient sound and Ilse's—one of the doomed characters—craving for drugs: we see Ilse with her arm outstretched reaching towards a radio antenna that looks like a heroin needle, as if she needed to be connected the world and to others, by any means, however desperate or desultory.
- The *insistence on the "cash-nexus" holding human relations together*, irrespective of how rich or poor the protagonists are, and irrespective of whether they genuinely love one another or not: money is the only true measure of self-worth, recognition and self-esteem. By fervently and openly embracing this otherwise disguised ideological motivation, Fassbinder's protagonists implicitly subvert the value system which forces them to "sell themselves." However, underneath this seemingly materialist deconstruction of hypoc-

risy and double standards, there is another economy of exchange in Fassbinder, one that is based on giving to excess, of sacrificing without demand, of self-sacrifice and the pure gesture of handing over to the other what is most precious to the self.

This may at first sight appear as mere masochism, but in the end, is the only kind of self-transcendence or salvation known in Fassbinder's world. Several of the characters in The Third Generation are capable of such gestures of giving, even if the film barely pauses to mark their moment of ecstatic sacrifice, notably Franz Walsch, who knowingly lets himself be shot by the police. The fact that the character is played by Günther Kaufmann gives a hint, for those who know Fassbinder's work, of the element of idealization behind such self-sacrifice.[19] "Giving" in advance of receiving, "choosing" ahead of being targeted is the micro-ethics of Fassbinder's macro theme: how to assert agency in situations governed by multiple temporalities, each of which is under the sway of retro-action. In Fassbinder, to act is to take charge of the effects in the hope that they will bring forth their own causes, thus creating the historicity of the singular event out of the otherwise closed feedback loops of mutual antagonism and mutual dependency.

Such a retroactive breaking open of a closed loop is, according to Slavoj Žižek's argument, "the only way to save historicity from the fall into historicism"—the latter being a linear succession of "historical epochs" that have to be thought of as "a series of ultimately failed attempts to deal with the same 'unhistorical' traumatic kernel."[20]

The Generation Paradox

What, then, would be the "un-historical traumatic kernel" that allows Fassbinder's films to acquire the kind of "historicity" I am tentatively ascribing to it? In one sense, it is contained in the very personal obsessions and quasi transhistorical themes I have just enumerated, all of which revolve around acts of symbolic exchange and asymmetrical but reversible power-relations. But in another sense, the traumatic kernel might be hidden in the title itself, which draws attention to the trope of "generation" as an increasingly prevalent but also problematic gesture of redemptive historiography in the way that especially Germany endlessly works on its past, in order to derive from it the grounds for a present that can not only legitimate the future, but redeem the past.

I have already discussed in an earlier chapter how the generational paradigm has become constitutive of the shape of Germany's cultural memory, in its efforts to arrive at a viable past. Yet it is easy to see how contradictory, but also how convenient the use of "generation" is, when applied to the historical moment and to historical succession. First of all, it signals a break with the Marxist notion of causality and determination, no longer identifying either the class struggle or the inherent contradictions of the mode of production as the driving forces of the historical process. It wants to retain, however, the group element of the "collective historical subject," against the "great man/single actor" theory of historical agency, as it has previously tempted so many Germans, who saw in Hitler first their salvation and then the source and origin of all evil.

Yet the generational paradigm also breaks with any notion of progress or telos in the Enlightenment sense; it has no grand narrative to offer, other than biology, and thus can be seen as one of the many ways the latter part of the twentieth century is turning towards "natural history," "evolutionary psychology" and the environment as ways of charting human time in relation to geology or to the paradoxes of astrophysical space-time. But generation is also an inherently contradictory way of sensing oneself both in time and exempt from its consequences. For the "generation" paradigm is either framed negatively, as a fatal legacy or curse, in the biblical sense: the sins of fathers are to be visited upon the subsequent generations,[21] or the paradigm is lifted out of time, insofar as a generation is deemed to have a unique outlook on life shaped by shared experiences, and thus separate from the rest. This would be Karl Mannheim's definition, emerging out of the First World War, of a group or cohort who, at an early age, participates in, experiences or is traumatized by the same historical events of a given time-period.[22] This generational concept was revived in the early 1970s to retroactively designate a particular group who had been old enough to experience the Nazi period first-hand, but felt themselves sufficiently young to be exempt from personal responsibility, and to be able to claim for themselves a *Stunde Null*, or zero hour, i.e., a resetting of the historical clock and a new beginning after 1945. They came to be known as the *Flakhelfer-Generation* (boy-soldiers manning anti-aircraft guns in the last months of the war): they were born between 1926 and 1929 and included Günther Grass, Hans-Dietrich Genscher (Minister of Foreign Affairs), the philosophers Jürgen Habermas and Niklas Luhmann and Josef Alois Ratzinger (ex-Pope Benedict XVI), as well as many writers of the Group 47, such as Martin Walser and Siegfried Lenz.[23] Best known is the phrase by another prominent member of the *Flakhelfer-Generation*, Chancellor Helmut Kohl, who, on a state visit to Israel, reclaimed for himself "the blessing of a late birth" (die Gnade der späten Geburt).[24]

As discussed in the chapter on the RAF afterlife, there have been several "generations" since, yet the notion of generation has also regained traction recently, once more in the sense mentioned above, as a burden or curse, insofar as the present economic and political crisis in Europe should lead to a feeling of guilt (*Schuld*) for burdening future generations with the *Schulden* (debts) of the present one: Not necessarily because their future is bright and might be blighted, but because the future as such has become both precious (there are not enough being born) and precarious (there is less and less for them to inherit or to look forward to).

It is telling that Fassbinder has given different explanations for the title The Third Generation, which retrospectively both reinforces this new trope of historical succession and determination, and deconstructs it, by multiplying the frames of reference. In a newspaper essay for the *Frankfurter Rundschau* published while he was shooting the film (December 2, 1978), Fassbinder reasoned that "The Third Generation" can mean:

1. [The First Generation] The German bourgeoisie from 1848 to 1933;
2. [The Second Generation] Our grandfathers, how they experienced the Third Reich and how they remember it;
3. [The Third Generation] Our fathers, who had an opportunity after the war to set up a state that could have been more humane and free than any had ever been before, and [look] what became of this opportunity in the end.[25]

This generational scheme is in line with Fassbinder's overall ambitious plan that I sketched earlier, of making as many films as needed, in order to tell the history of Modern Germany from the failed revolution of 1848 to the semi-revolution of the Weimar Republic, the pseudo-revolution of the Third Reich and the aborted revolution in 1945, which could—a hundred years later—have ushered in this free and humane society that the generation of German Romantics from Kant and Hölderlin to Kleist and Fichte had dreamed of and imagined. Here "generation" is what Žižek meant by historicism, i.e., the succession of "historical epochs" that turn into a series of ultimately failed attempts to deal with the same core problem—how to create a more just world, by redeeming the promise and vision of an earlier epoch.

Yet The Third Generation is more often interpreted in light of another statement made by Fassbinder, after the film had been completed: "The first generation was that of '68 idealists, who thought they could change the world with words and demonstrations in the street [he presumably is thinking of Rudi Dutschke and Daniel Cohn-Bendit, whom we see arguing with an interviewer on the television set in one of the pivotal scenes of the film]. The second generation, the Baader-Meinhof group, who moved from legality to the armed struggle and into total illegality. The third generation is today's, who just indulges in action without thinking, without either ideology or politics, and who, probably without knowing it, are like puppets whose strings are pulled by others."[26]

We can see how the "traumatic kernel" here revolves around the paradox of agency and autonomy: on the one hand, the very point of identifying a generation is to be able to assign to it a distinct form of agency, within a succession and a history. But the "third generation" here is one that is effectively perverted in its agency, by being unwittingly manipulated. Sharing a particular past experience may create a generation whose identity constitutes itself around a trauma, which in turn renders the agency illusory: unable to break out of the loop, the gesture that was meant to liberate turns out to be part of the trap, of which the very notion of a *redemptive historicity*, i.e., a messianic moment, a radical rupture or the spontaneous event, *was the bait.*

The Event and Its Retroactive Recognition

The question, therefore, is how this trap of the generational paradox nonetheless strengthens the claims of THE THIRD GENERATION to stand both at and for the intersection of the forces I earlier identified with "1979"? Perhaps by a certain reflexive doubling, which enacts a mise en abyme of the traumatic kernel. For just as "generation" in Germany has become the code word for an unredeemed past, of which it is the failed repetition, so the revolutionary aspirations and post-colonial liberation movements might be said to have been diverted, hijacked or turned on their head by disruptive media technologies and neoliberal globalization. Politically speaking, 1979 would prove *in advance* that the hopes placed in 1989 were misplaced, and that the "new world order" (of post 9/11) had already begun to take shape by 1979.[27] This is more than hindsight; it is a way of retroactively charging "1979" (and Fassbinder's film of that year) with of the status of "historicity," i.e., representing a past that impacts upon the present, insofar as this present is able to recognize something of itself in this past and thus effectively create this past as a memory for its own present, and thereby reinserting the differently rupturing agency of the "event."

Let me briefly return to some of characteristics of the "historicity of the event" already mentioned earlier: its *unexpectedness* and unpredictability, its *open form*, its *remaining unrecognized* in the *constellation of incompatible elements*, and its *retroactive causality*, i.e., the way the event might be said to open the closed loop of the actual by retroactively making room for other possibilities. How does Fassbinder's film relate to any or all of these criteria?

My case for THE THIRD GENERATION possessing the retroactive power of prediction that defines its historicity rests on several features: First, its open form (which includes the chaotic way it was made, and the fact that it almost did not get made at all, given the many obstacles that stood in its way). Second, its deployment of space as both an architectural category and an aural category (conveying a sense of urban paranoia that is both viscerally present and conceptually abstract, the latter allowing for different scenarios to project themselves into its narrative space.[28] And third, its temporality as a feedback loop: in one direction tight, claustrophobic, "negative" and self-regulating, while in the other direction, the loop is "positive," amplifying, proliferating and "out of control."

The film was originally to have been financed with television money (by Westdeutsche Rundfunk [WDR], Fassbinder's regular co-producer), but the broadcasting company cancelled at the last minute, for fear of touching with terrorism too sensitive an issue. The Berlin Senate, which at that time gave subsidies to films utilizing Berlin locations and facilities, also withdrew their financial support, and even refused to give permission to shoot inside the Schöneberger Rathaus, a key location in the plot. Fassbinder, who allegedly only heard about these negative decisions days before he was due to start shooting, wanted to cancel, but was encouraged by Juliane Lorenz and Harry Baer to go ahead, investing his own money, and by arranging a hasty co-production deal with the Filmverlag der Autoren. The crew was cut to a minimum, with several of the actors taking on production responsibilities, just as Fassbinder decided to be both director and cameraman, in order to save money and speed up the shooting schedule.

As to it being unrecognized at the time, THE THIRD GENERATION fared very badly with the press and had hardly any distribution in Germany. Fassbinder himself quickly moved on to other projects. Yet there have been few films in his *oeuvre* that have been more enthusiastically "rediscovered," written about and reevaluated than THE THIRD GENERATION, indicative of the kinds of historicity of something that is past, but only releases its energies and potential when reframed by another event.[29] Or to put in more technical language, the film's distribution of chance events only reveals its "bias" (or direction) contingent upon future context.

That the film qualifies as an open form also in this sense is testified by anyone who sees it for the first time. THE THIRD GENERATION presents itself as a baffling puzzle of intertwined relationships and cross-purpose affiliations, of unexplained loyalties and equally mysterious betrayals. It makes enormous demands on the viewer, first because of the many characters one must keep track of: there are more than a dozen, and each is so individually drawn, each undergoes subtle or sudden changes within him/herself, but also changes in the dynamic relation they have to each other. Using the title of one of Fassbinder's other films, one could say that is a Chinese roulette inside a series of Russian dolls, which is to say, Russian roulette inside Chinese boxes.

Contributing to the sense of a topsy-turvy world generated by multiple incompatibilities never quite ripening into full-fledged contradictions is that THE THIRD GENERATION pointedly includes in its plot the German *Fasching* as a moment of the carnivalesque within the (mis)rule of law, but also showing its necessary obverse, the scapegoating, though random and pointless, which follows such transgressions and mostly seems to include among the victims the innocent as well as the guilty. The very artificiality of the plot's basic premise and situation, its model character as parable or fairy tale, set against the elliptical tightness of the plot, give the most cartoonish kind of identity to the characters, yet the electronic and audio-visual presence in which they are immersed creates its own interchangeability, randomness of movement and opaque aquatic slipperiness.

The second main reason for its predictive power is the mise en scène, with an inordinately demanding sense of space, including the labyrinthine interiors, hinting at the complexity of the film's power-relations. "False" or disorienting shot-reverse-shots, odd angles, mirror shots, peep-holes and curtains, long corridors with doors upon doors, and the peculiar topography of large Berlin apartments all serve to underline worlds that are spatially separated and yet connect by their inner contiguity and emotional dependencies. By rendering addiction and dependency in spatial terms, THE THIRD GENERATION conducts a micro-analysis of power and its various networks or *dispositifs* on the side of those in power (global finance and industry supported by the state) and those opposing them (the terrorist cell).

However, the very term *opposition* has here lost its validity, and Fassbinder was one of the first to realize that such direct confrontations—whether between capitalists and progressives, between Left and Right—and other equally prearranged battlegrounds no longer exist, and that the concept of resistance and opposition have to be revised, because those who oppose the powers-that-be are often the ones most useful to the powers-that-be. Consequently, the frictions and resistances by which such a society balances interest groups and its actors are more difficult to pin down, replaced as the old binary oppositions have been by the micro-structures of dis-loyalty, of double-crossing, of submission, overidentification and disaffection. These are now the circuits by which the "system" begets its own "other" and also, communicates with its "other." Hence, the complicated lines of force that link the characters in THE THIRD GENERATION, where Hanna Schygulla is the industrialist's secretary, a member of the cell, and the policeman's daughter-in-law, with whom she has a self-hating affair. Volker Spengler, the leader of the terrorist cell, has in fact been bought by the other side and betrays his comrades, but when cross-dressing, is himself curiously vulnerable and insecure, as if he had stepped out of the world of another, quite different Fassbinder film, namely IN A YEAR OF THIRTEEN MOONS, where he plays a very confused and deeply troubled transsexual.

The most spectacular form of reversibility is the relation between the characters played by Bulle Ogier (Hilde) and Roaul Gimenez (Paul), the macho specialist, improbably come back from a training camp in South Africa. A feminist historian in her daytime job, and fiercely independent and articulate, Hilde is raped by Paul the first night he stays in her home, but when we next seem them, they are a couple besotted with each other. Hilde allows herself to be humiliated by Paul, but before we can fully recover from the shock at either Hilde's hypocrisy or Paul's misogynist sexism, Paul is gunned down in a restaurant, Mafia style, whereupon Hilde merely shrugs her shoulders and says, "Maybe it's better that way; it saves him from further self-torment."

For Fassbinder, then, left-wing politics became a viable subject only at the point, when extremism was caught up in the mirror-maze of its own double, when political analysis and paranoid projection coincided, and when the militants helped create the enemy they had set out to combat, and vice versa, when the liberal State needed its illiberal children in much the way that Apple or Microsoft need the hackers to alert them to the bugs in their software and the leaks in their security systems. What struck Fassbinder, especially in the mid-1970s during the most turbulent years of the Federal Republic, was that in the sphere of the political, the most uncompromisingly critical stance (the view from without) could well turn out to be the most complicit one: playing right into the hands of "the enemy," with fear, suspicion or distrust merely the feedback the system needed to sustain itself, an "anticipation" of what Adam Curtis, in the BBC television series (discussed in the introduction), called "The Rise of the Politics of Fear" and Naomi Klein was to baptize the *Shock Doctrine* three years later.

Aural Terrorism

The third element that creates an uncanny sense of prescience is the way Fassbinder's deploys sound, mixing overlapping dialogue, canned music, street noise, live song and speech from different audio sources (e.g., snatches of radio and television as moving wallpaper, as well as a taped monologue by a suicidal woman that Hilde listens to obsessively). The incessant acoustic carpet give these interpenetrating and mutually interfering worlds a unique sonic density of noise and static, while depriving the characters of any interiority, identity and coherence. It is as much the sounds, as it is the words that demonstrate the duplicity ("These remarks don't fit you," says the policeman) or nullity of every character ("What do you see when you look in the mirror?" replies the industrialist: "Not much"). As body and voice drift apart or find themselves haphazardly synchronized (Fassbinder makes it very obvious that Eddie Constantine is dubbed), it is the "flat" monitor world, lacking depth, that becomes the only surface on which proximity and distance, sex and affection, political ideology and personal loyalty can be renegotiated, in a space that is entirely made up of an electronic topography of sound, music, noise and filtered, milky and fogged images, in a wintry and cold Berlin, rendered palpably present.

In an interview, Fassbinder called the media saturation he tried to achieve in the film a form of "aural terrorism" (*Schallterror*),[30] hinting at the way the cacophony of mass media signals produces its own form of disinformation, to which correspond both addiction and its antidote: cynicism. By mimetically reproducing the assault on the senses, Fassbinder gives the film its double reflexivity, but also acknowledges a complicity between the world of the media—omnipresent in all of Fassbinder—and the characters' motives and passions. These appear to thrive on and energize themselves from being so wholly immersed in sounds and sights, underlining how spaces are always interfered with and disrupted in Fassbinder. Thus, while outwardly (the daytime image) German society in THE THIRD GENERATION appears solid, immobile and—in the landscape of pre-unification Berlin—(made of) concrete, a change of location, of light and perspective reverses the terms, and a curiously liquid world envelops the viewer, more like an aquarium, constant movement behind glass, transparent but enclosed, claustrophobic and untouchable.

Given the attention devoted to sound and the unique soundscape that is THE THIRD GENERATION, the fact that Sony launched their first Walkman onto the market that year sets off further ripples of retroactive prescience. Fassbinder's film is in good company: 1979 is also the year of Coppola's APOCALYPSE NOW, which, together with STAR WARS, profoundly changed the way that mainstream cinema became saturated with sound, almost at the expense of images. But APOCALYPSE NOW was itself a reaction and response to the new sound experience, of which first the Walkman and then the iPod would become the enduring icons. The picture of a person wearing headphones in public is the very embodiment of political resignation, heralding one of the more far-reaching redistributions of what is private and what public since the French Revolution, now focused on the inner sound, as if providing the homeopathic answer to the "aural-terror" documented by Fassbinder. The pervasive response to this crisis of a public sphere invaded and ambushed by noise masquerading as information, was to take refuge in oneself, provoking the kind of depoliticization, of which THE THIRD GENERATION is both the final act of revolt and first act of submission.

The Open Loop

This brings me to my last criterion of historicity, that of the retrospective prescience and the loop of anticipated fear and foreboding. Here a kind of reciprocal relation between terrorism and its traumatic aftermath is established which lies at the heart of the argument that Fassbinder is putting forward in THE THIRD GENERATION. It is not causal but viral, and names the already mentioned asymmetrical, but nonetheless intertwined power relations at stake which propagate by contagion. When the industrialist Lurz and the policeman Gans share the joke that underpins the film, namely that it was capitalism itself that had invented terrorism, in order to force the state to better protect capitalism's interests, a reviewer, ten years ago added: "Sounds much like what W. has done in Amerika since 9/11."[31] Today, one would say, with some justification, "politicians have invented the debt-crisis, to better protect the interests of finance capitalism."

That Fassbinder's THE THIRD GENERATION should be such a kaleidoscopic film is appropriate for the parapractic historicity I have been trying to distil from the film, because on the one hand it affirms the fragmented and contingent nature of every moment in the present, and therefore also in the past—everything that happens could have been otherwise—leaving the counter-factual and the counter-intuitive in play, while not diminishing the tension in which it stands to historicity as the decisive moment, which it retrieves in every act of retroactively attributed prescience. The film's powerfully paranoiac overall structure—capitalism and its security apparatus is masterminding the terrorist menace, while being itself masterminded and possibly self-deluded—emphatically affirms and insists that nothing is an accident, and that "actions have consequences," to use a phrase from David Lynch's INLAND EMPIRE (a film that, in this respect at least, out-Fassbinders Fassbinder) and at the same time, these consequences seem to form a loop, and possibly even a Moebius strip, which also brings Fassbinder closer to Lynch than one might have hitherto suspected: an effect of different retroactive causality, which makes Fassbinder in this instance "Lynchean," while still allowing Lynch to be a follower of Fassbinder.

What can one conclude? Each scene—and often even each image—of THE THIRD GENERATION is so densely layered and packed with references to the political or topical contexts that what seems fragmented merely appears as such, because it is one strand in a tapestry of topological and temporal references woven into the film, which—viewed from a certain angle—freeze into quite a coherent historical snapshot of West Germany at that time, while also pointing to the future, where events like the ones we have witnessed since (9/11, the "war on terror") give THE THIRD GENERATION a new urgency, by reviving some of its more outrageous conceits, as if life was not only imitating art, but as if the past had already anticipated the future, and that a year like 1979—perhaps even more than overdetermined dates like 1968 or 1989—was the horizon we are approaching as we move further away. It give us one more reason to take seriously, but also to examine critically, the commemorative turn of our culture, at the same time as we are instantiating the circular dilemmas of this turn, reiterating the loops but maybe also opening them up to a more parapractic slippage.

The paradox I have been exploring is this: the historicity of the single event, the special moment or the key year is the effect of a loop: revealing with hindsight its prophetic, predictive prescience, whereby the tautology effectively functions as a breakthrough moment: *the present needs the past more for its future than the past needs the presence for its survival.*

I have tried to show how one can construct such a loop for the more or less arbitrarily chosen year of 1979, and for a film that Fassbinder made that year almost by accident. Yet my intention has not been to deconstruct such "historicity" as merely an optical trick or perspectival illusion. On the contrary, repetition, under the special conditions of the open loop (*parapraxis* by another name) may be the only way the "new" can be made to emerge, which is to say, it may be the only ground from which one can indeed envisage a future that is both legitimated by the past and liberated from it.

Notes

1. http://www.spiegel.de/spiegel/print/d-13684768.html. See also http://www.oberhausener-manifest.com/
2. Stefan Andriopoulos and Bernhard J. Dotzler (eds.), *1929: Beiträge zur Archäologie der Medien* (Frankfurt am Main: Suhrkamp, 2002).
3. http://www.yale.edu/macmillan/europeanstudies/1968.htm
4. Andriopoulos and Dotzler, *1929.*
5. Jon Elster, *Ulysses Unbound: Studies in Rationality, Precommitment, and Constraints* (Cambridge, UK: Cambridge University Press, 2000).
6. Hans Ulrich Gumbrecht *In 1926: Living at the Edge of Time* (Cambridge, MA: Harvard University Press, 1997).
7. Ibid., back cover.
8. Ibid.
9. "Do not try 'to start from the beginning,' for this book has no beginning in the sense that narratives or arguments have beginnings. Start with any of the fifty-one entries in any of the three sections [...] (the alphabetical order of the subheadings shows that there isn't any hierarchy among them). [...] From each entry a web of cross-references will take you to other, related entries." Ibid., ix.
10. Douglas Gordon, *24 Hour Psycho* (1993) and *Five Year Drive By* (1995).
11. "Splitter der Wirklichkeit, die aber doch allesamt streng den einen Gedanken verfolgen, wie ein einziger Augenblick alles Vorher und Nachher verschlingen kann" (http://www.kluge-alexander.de/filmemacher/der-angriff-der-gegenwart-auf-die-uebrige-zeit/print.html).
12. For a lucid introduction to the Annalistes' longue duree and its critics, see Peter Burke, *The French Historical Revolution: The Annales School 1929–89* (Stanford: Stanford University Press, 1990).
13. Retroactive causality is also a topic in modern science. To quote from the abstract of a relevant paper: "Physical laws are inherently time symmetric. It is generally assumed that the fact that we experience only one direction of time development is related to constraints like those imposed on the universe at the time of the 'big bang'. [In this paper] the consequences of a less restricted view on time are discussed. It is argued that a) there is empirical evidence that effects can precede causes (or more precisely: that distributions of chance events might be biased contingent on future context), b) there is no necessary logical paradox related to these phenomena, c) that these findings might be interpreted as an extension of the recent interpretation of Quantum Physics but d) that the implications are far-reaching as far as the western scientific paradigm is concerned." Dick J. Bierman, "A world with retroactive causation," *Systematica*, 7 (1988), 6. See also the bibliography listed under "Retrokausalität" (http://home.arcor.de/klaus.scharff/time/retro.htm).
14. The classic text was Louis Althusser, "Contradiction and Overtdetermination," written in 1962, and published in English in *For Marx,* trans. Ben Brewster (London: Allen Lane, 1969), 87–128.
15. Walter Benjamin, "Über den Begriff der Geschichte: These IX" in *Gesammelte Schriften* I:2 (Frankfurt: Suhrkamp Verlag, 1974); in English: Walter Benjamin, *Illuminations* (ed.), trans. H. Zohn (London: J. Cape, 1970), 259–60.

16. Gilles Deleuze, "Postscript on the Societies of Control," October, no. 59 (Winter 1992), 3–7.
17. Karlheinz Böhm, "Fliessbandarbeit ist schwerer," in Juliane Lorenz (ed.), *Das ganz normale Chaos* (Berlin: Henschel, 1995), 319.
18. R.W. Fassbinder, *The Anarchy of the Imagination* (Baltimore: Johns Hopkins University Press, 1992), 125–26.
19. Fassbinder often signed as Franz Walsch when he worked on his films in a role additional to that of director, e.g., as cameraman or editor.
20. Slavoj Žižek, *Enjoy Your Symptom* (London: Verso, 1992/2001), 94.
21. See the poster from a 1929 campaign against the Versailles treaty, warning: "Bis in die dritte Generation müsst Ihr fronen" ("you'll be slaves until the third generation"). It showed a slave driver at the center of a circular winch, to which are chained a father, a son, and a grandfather. *German Historical Museum*, Berlin (http://www.dhm.de/lemo/objekte/pict/p74-3797/index.html)
22. Karl Mannheim, "The Problem of Generations" in P. Kecskemeti (ed.), *Essays on the Sociology of Knowledge by Karl Mannheim* (New York: Routledge & Kegan Paul, 1952), 276-322.
23. On the case of Günter Grass as *Flakhelfer*, see Nathan Thornburgh, "Günter Grass' silence," *Time Magazine*, August 14, 2006 (http://www.time.com/time/arts/article/0,8599,1226380,00.html). For a critical history of the Gruppe 47, see Stephan Braese, *Bestandsaufnahme — Studien zur Gruppe 47* (Philologische Studien und Quellen, Heft 157, Berlin, 1999).
24. http://www.dradio.de/dlr/sendungen/kalender/227514/
25. Reprinted in R.W. Fassbinder, *The Anarchy of the Imagination* (eds.), M. Töteberg and L. Lensing (Baltimore, Johns Hopkins University Press, 1992), 123.
26. R.W. Fassbinder, *Die Anarchie der Phantasie*, (ed.) Michael Töteberg (Hamburg: Fischer Verlag, 1991), 106.
27. It is a point similar to the one I made at the end of an essay on Bergman's The Serpent's Egg, made two years earlier, but also in Germany, and also under the impact of the peculiar haunted historicity of the RAF. See T.E. "Ingmar Bergman's The Serpent's Egg: Reflections of Reflections on retro-Fashion," in Maaret Koskinen (ed.), *Ingmar Bergman Revisited. Performance, Cinema and the Arts* (London: Wallflower Press, 2008), 161–79.
28. This is well observed by David Chirico: "The rebels of *Die dritte Generation/The Third Generation* (1979), no longer grounded in a distinct physical space, plan for revolution within a series of telescoping, rectilinear environments that are joined together only by a Langian network of televisions, phones and computers. [. . .] It is worth noting that [it] is easily Fassbinder's most Langian film: a group of underground criminals—even if they are buffoons—is controlled, ironically, by a distant Mabuse. The witlessness of the revolutionaries is not the only subject here; we are also offered a demonstration of how images are generated for TV—and the obscure, subterranean murmur of television pervades every scene." David Chirico, "In a month of thirteen films: A Fassbinder diary," *Studies in European Cinema*, 7, no. 1 (September 2010), 41–42.
29. Among other recent scholarly reassessments of The Third Generation are Frances Guerin, "A Generation Later and Still Unrepresentable? Fassbinder and the Red Army Faction," in Brigitte Peucker (ed.), *A Fassbinder Companion* (Oxford: Wiley-Blackwell, 2012), 441–60. The film's presence on the web can be gauged by the following entries:
http://jclarkmedia.com/fassbinder/fassbinder35.html
http://sensesofcinema.com/2011/cteq/the-third-generation/
http://www.critical-film.com/reviews/T/Third_Generation/Third_Generation.html
http://www.follow-me-now.de/html/fassbinder_iii.html

http://monoursblanc.com/2008/07/13/the-third-generation-rainer-werner-fassbinder-1979/
http://homepages.sover.net/~ozus/thirdgeneration.htm

30. R.W. Fassbinder, *Die Anarchie der Phantasie*, 106.
31. D. Schwartz, "The Third Generation," *Ozus' World Movie Reviews* (May 23, 2006; http://homepages.sover.net/~ozus/thirdgeneration.htm).

8

MOURNING AS MIMICRY AND MASQUERADE

Herbert Achternbusch's THE LAST HOLE

"... Yet if it could not be put in a comic way, would it be worth the effort?"

—Herbert Achternbusch[1]

Camp Comedy

The worldwide success of Roberto Benigni's LIFE IS BEAUTIFUL (1997), endorsed by an Oscar for best foreign film, and the almost equally well-received TRAIN OF LIFE (Radu Mihaileanu, 1998) convinced philosopher Slavoj Žižek that the time had come to formulate some general principles on the topic of "Camp Comedy."[2] Žižek did not take up the issue, frequently raised but to him falsely framed, of the very representability of the Holocaust.[3] Instead, he first attended to the question of genre: which of the classical genres lends itself most readily, and which is least appropriate, to a filmic rendering of the concentration camp experience? Again, Žižek was not interested in classifying all the European and Hollywood films so far produced on the topic, which by now number in the many hundreds.[4] Rather, he started out from a kind of symptomatology that wanted to probe why the subject had become fit for comedy in the 1990s, when not a single credible tragedy on this truly tragic topic had been made over the previous fifty years. In this respect, Žižek considered Stephen Spielberg's SCHINDLER'S LIST (1993), whatever its merits otherwise, a failure in its attempt to construct a tragic dilemma between "duty" and "desire" for camp commandant Amon Goeth.[5] On the other hand, Žižek defended productions such as LIFE IS BEAUTIFUL against accusations that any film which puts a comic spin on life in the ghettos or the labor camps can only have been made in ignorance of the full scale and scope of the Holocaust—partial ignorance arguably still prevailing at the time that Charles Chaplin's THE GREAT DICTATOR (1942) and Ernst Lubitsch's occupation comedy TO BE OR NOT TO BE (1942) were made.

Žižek's answer to the question "Why Holocaust comedies now?" was as paradoxical as it was meant to be polemical: precisely because during the 1980s and 1990s the Holocaust stood for "evil incarnate," so absolute that it cannot be narrated, visualized, or understood (Jean Francois Lyotard: "the Holocaust destroyed the very instruments by which it could be measured"[6]; Claude Lanzmann: "that is the point: it cannot be understood"),[7] comedy becomes the only authentic, and with it, topical form of representation. Comedy here functions not so much as the opposite of tragedy, in the sense that both genres take as their starting point some irreconcilable or incommensurate aspect of human experience, but comedy understood as the genre of the survivor, providing a psychic protective shield. By deferring trauma, while at the same time inscribing its marks the more indelibly, comedy represents a livable compromise in the face of the otherwise insupportable. But Žižek introduces a further twist: Holocaust laughter or "camp comedy" is now (i.e. since the 1990s) the protective shield not in the sense of a Medusa shield, the direct sight of which is too dreadful for the onlooker. Instead it serves as a "fantasmatic" guard against a different kind of insight: that the metaphysical, quasi-sacral status attributed to the Holocaust has de-historicized and de-politicized it: "Paradoxical as it may sound, the rise of the holocaust comedy is correlative to the elevation of the holocaust itself into the metaphysical, diabolical Evil—the ultimate traumatic point at which the objectifying of historical knowledge breaks down and even witnesses concede words fail them."[8] In other words, according to Žižek, the return of the category of 'evil' in the public political discourse risks becoming the ideological cover for a generalized culture of victimization. Invoking the Holocaust as mankind's moral catastrophe tends to suspend individual or collective responsibility for what happens in the world today. Žižek gave the examples of Rwanda, Bosnia and Palestine: "Is the holocaust not the supreme proof that to be human is to be a victim, not an active political agent and that proclaiming oneself a victim is the sine qua non of speaking with authority?"[9] If only victims are entitled to credibility and authenticity, then the endless round of misery and suffering in this world closes in upon itself, absolving us of responsibility: even for our own lives.

Behind camp comedy, therefore, stands not so much the inability to mourn the victims of gas chambers and extermination camps, nor is it prompted by an attempt to trivialize their fate. Rather it documents, and thus truthfully records, the inability of contemporary spectators to look themselves in the eye, pointing to the subterfuges and disavowals necessary to survive in the face of so much suffering and injustice. We need a protective shield to lie to ourselves about our direct as well as indirect role in the course of history. This is why so many contemporary films—Žižek includes in this category also the Hollywood-remake of JACOB THE LIAR (Peter Kassovitz, 1999)—tell their Holocaust story as the staging of an inoffensive (Žižek: "benign," punning on Roberto Benigni) *life-lie* which, in keeping with the spirit of comedy, guarantees survival and thus becomes a "survivors' lie" (inversely mirroring "survivors' guilt"). What makes Holocaust comedies possible as a genre is the necessity to conceive of oneself simultaneously as a victim and a survivor, and to cover up the contradictory "ground" for these two subject positions, by recovering a foil and a form that keeps in play radically incompatible options, while nevertheless leading them to a satisfactory—and for our European, postmodern societies, consensual—solution: precisely the anthropological function of comedy: to reconcile the community with its own contradictions.

Herbert Achternbusch: Against the Cinema and Television

I would like to take Žižek's idea and test it against Herbert Achternbusch's THE LAST HOLE (1981). Achternbusch was born Herbert Schild in Munich in 1938. A prolific painter, writer and playwright, he came to the cinema as a detour from writing, at a time (and after having a bit part in one of Volker Schlöndorff's television films) when the revival of filmmaking in Germany seemed to offer better access to a public and a public sphere than theater. His oblique entry into the New German Cinema (from which he always vehemently dissociated himself), as well as lack of a budget, led Achternbusch to practice a form of filmmaking that subverted the pressure emanating from the consensus of German independent cinema, made for and by television. Instead, he deliberately cultivated some of the more archaic, artisanal and anachronistic uses of the medium, in essence making home movies with his friends and neighbors as actors. Even *Cahiers du cinema*, in their Berlin film festival report from 1981, devoted a meager paragraph to Achternbusch's DER NEGER ERWIN (THE NIGGER ERWIN, 1980) with the lapidary comment: "This film is indefensible in its form as well as its subject."[10]

Virtually unknown outside Germany, THE LAST HOLE was shot thirty years ago, at a time when the Holocaust had not yet become *the* media topic par excellence in West Germany and when all manner of its representation (other than documentary) were still taboo being or dismissed outright as either tasteless or sentimental. It was also made a decade before the new world order of the post-Cold War period declared the end of history and with it regarded political activism as obsolete and futile. In this respect, therefore, Žižek's post-1990 political symptomatology does not yet apply, but for reasons I hope will become clear, his analytical frame seems helpful in unlocking some of the features of this odd, but brilliant film.

Formally, as well as in content, THE LAST HOLE deliberately occupies—and dismantles from within—the contradictory ground shared by victim and survivor. This is especially notable insofar as Achternbusch's film does not present Jewish victims of the Nazis, but rather starts from the Germans as perpetrators, concentrating not on a (Jewish) survivor, but on Germans as survivors and the next generation as victims. It is precisely this shift of interest from (Jewish) victimhood and survival to (German) perpetrators and descendants that bring the questions of ignorance and knowledge, conscience, denial and guilt more sharply into focus, as well as making them more paradoxical. This prompts the further question as to whether THE LAST HOLE should indeed be labeled a comedy or whether another generic assignation is ultimately more adequate. A possible answer is found in Hanno Loewy's genre theory pertaining to Holocaust films, which I shall contrast with Žižek's theory.[11]

In the German-German generational confrontation, the subject position of "victim" remains central in Achternbusch's film, despite the change of perspective away from German-Jewish relations. In order to highlight, rather than fudge these slippages, Achternbusch borrows some common topoi from the New German Cinema on the subject of "coming to terms with the past," such as the theme of "fathers and sons/fatherless sons" (prominent in Kluge, Fassbinder, Wenders, Herzog) and the motif of "flight-exile-return" (Reitz, Wenders). Particularly striking is the yearning for a reunion between mother and son, common in Fassbinder and Wenders, but which also underpins the emotional structure of Benigni's film. The function of these topoi is not to point to some deep psychological (or autobiographical) truth, or to build a causal (historical) nexus from which the plot derives its energy (as might be argued in the case of the directors' named). Rather, the constellations are cited by Achternbusch and superimposed onto another storyline, which counters their emotional pathos as well as their narratological role as an *emplotment* of the larger history.[12] Tragic affects and melodramatic effects give rise to moments of absurdity, dark humor, and grotesque embarrassment, rather than to the generalized *Weltschmerz* (melancholy and sense of loss) typical of other directors of the New German Cinema during the 1970s and 1980s.

The motif of the life-lie is also present in THE LAST HOLE, though doubly displaced. First, Achternbusch borrows a recurrent character from the immediate post-war period (the *Trümmerfilme*) about Germany coming to terms with its past: a former Nazi, often with a stolen or fictive identity, tries to blend in with bourgeois normality until confronted by a Jewish victim who also travels incognito so as to better hunt down the perpetrators.[13] But Achternbusch's aliases (as with Benigni, the director plays the central character) neither serve the avenger in unmasking the culprit, nor do they give rise to a back-and-forth game of deception, confusion, and pretense, as in Ernst Lubitsch's TO BE OR NOT TO BE (1942). Instead disguise underlines the tragic-comic divisions and painful-absurd confusions of the Self, as it overidentifies with the Other. If such overidentification is generally the result of emotional entanglements between the sexes, it can also dramatize the pitfalls of therapeutic negotiations of guilt, with transference veering between incrimination and exculpation, and undermining both. While none of the protagonists are Jewish, the high stakes gamble of the film is that the mutual dependence of the central couple in The Last Hole—sustained by a life-long habit of bickering and talking past each other—can be accepted as an adequate fictional foil for the historical relation between Jews and Germans. Such is Achternbusch's strategy that the spectator is torn between accepting and dismissing this allegorical ploy, when the "negative symbiosis" (see below) is marked by so much suffering and injustice, and not just by mutually binding and entangling misunderstandings.

A Love Affair with Fatal Consequences

At this point, a plot summary of the first few scenes from The last Hole is in order: "A woman in a bikini called Susn takes a watering can to moisten the floor in an attic; a man called Nil is sitting in an armchair. The love between these two seems to have faded. Following a prolonged, cantankerous banter, he fends off her unwanted kiss by stabbing her. In a restaurant a man going by the name of 'Green Asshole' is trying to convince his skeptical counterpart, Stupid Cloud, of his skills when killing and skinning rabbits. But matters are not so straightforward when it comes to [killing] someone like Nil: 'In order to do away with a person, you need the police.' The two men take their leave [as they put on their caps]; it is obvious that they are policemen. Nil is sitting at another table. Susn, his fiancé (whom he had stabbed in the first scene), works here as a waitress. She brings him a beer. Nil 'is a professional beer-drinker.' He talks of '6 million.' She thinks he has won 6 million D-marks, and falls in love with him and his money. What Nil is thinking of, however, are the '6 million murdered Jews' whom he keeps from his mind during the day by drowning them with 40 pints of beer but who return at night to haunt him in his dreams."[14]

In the scenes that follow, Nil (played by Achternbusch) now lives like a rabbit in a burrow in the open fields. He is smoked out by the two policemen, on the lookout for Susn's murderer. In the ensuing confusion, and blinded by the clouds of smoke, Stupid Cloud accidentally shoots and kills Green Asshole. When he later realizes his error, Stupid Cloud carries off Nil, as if he was a corpse, and takes him to the nearest tavern. There, in the men's room, the two reach an agreement. Since they are now both wanted murderers, they ought to flee together. They choose Genoa as their secret destination. But before departing, Nil goes to see a doctor to help him forget the Jews. The doctor advises him to drink schnapps instead of beer ("2 cl for every Jew") and calculates that he will have to prescribe 300,000 liters of schnapps for Nil. But when his calculations do not come out even, the doctor has the solution at hand. He tells Nil that, as a concentration camp doctor, his father once killed a Jew whom he failed subsequently to enter into the records. After this helpful suggestion but also inadvertent admission by the doctor, Nil casts off his disguise, presenting himself as a private detective, charged with hunting down former Nazis. But instead of being exposed as a war criminal, the doctor throws him out ("Nil: 'Another murderer!'—'My father: a German pig?' asks the outraged doctor before showing Nil the door.").

Nil is also looking for "the first and last Susn." Eventually he tracks her down in a nightclub, where she works and lives as a prostitute in an attic above the club. Nil finds her in bed with a client, whom he throws out of the window ("If you can screw [*vögeln*], you can also fly [like a bird, i.e., *Vogel*]") and then asks Susn to come with them to Genoa. Nil, Susn and Stupid Cloud all meet on the train. While Stupid Cloud complains about the quality of Italian food and Susn talks about her love for Nil, Nil slowly and methodically downs his prescribed doses of schnapps out of a giant bottle.

The railway tracks suddenly lead straight into the sea, soon after Stupid Cloud has the terrifying vision of a blazing oven that turns out to be the Stromboli volcano. There, at the base of the crater, the three run into Barbara, a woman from Germany who could no longer stand living there. While "the last Susn" recites a long farewell letter that Nil had addressed to her, Nil, kitted out with a lab coat, a steel helmet and two tennis racquets, starts digging into the lava ground in search of dead Jews. After uncovering a skull, Nil hops like a rabbit up the crater slope, eventually hurling himself into the volcano, as did Empedocles in Hölderlin's eponymous poem.

THE LAST HOLE, as may be seen from the synopsis, is first and foremost a story of unhappy love, with an absurd, rather than a tragic ending. If one were to tell it according to a more classically linear narrative schema, it would be a film about a man who kills his female partner, then teams up with a policeman turned murderer, goes looking for his first love, and flees with both of them to Italy, where he commits suicide on a volcanic island. The plot of this mixture between a love story turned bad, and a road-movie adventure turned history lesson, with an anticlimactic, tragic-absurd ending, would fit quite well into the brief spell of Hollywood independent cinema of the 1970s, following EASY RIDER (1969) and preceding JAWS (1975). One could easily imagine the same material being put to effective use by Monte Hellman, Bob Rafelson, Tom Gries, or Jerry Schatzberg. The fact that a love story combines here with a dimly suggested detective story also makes these events typical of European auteur cinema, especially since the two narratives have little to do with each other. It is even possible to be more specific and read into the reference to Stromboli and into the motif of a couple's trip to Italy an implicit connection with two films made by Roberto Rossellini with Ingrid Bergman in the lead role: STROMBOLI (1949) and VIAGGIO IN ITALIA (1953). These genre associations with European auteur cinema and New Hollywood cinema are in keeping with the director's acknowledged cinephilia[15] and the ostensibly improvisatory form of Achternbusch's film and themes. However important, they are finally not very illuminating, because they do not take into account any of the film's many specific strategies for making spectators feel unsettled and lose their footing. The same disorientation holds true for the various elements disrupting the temporal flow, the non-sequiturs in the chain of causality, and the (il) logic of the action in THE LAST HOLE, not to mention the patently absurd plot-premises and the many (bad) puns that both drive the film and send it off on so many tangents. Stories, anecdotes and fragments are nested into one another in such an involuted fashion that one may well ask, in good Achternbusch fashion, whether there is still a "nest" into which they all fit.

The Work of Mourning: Father and Sons Not Reconciled?

My aim is not only to identify the genre that might most adequately describe THE LAST HOLE, but to analyze how this odd combination of love story, adventure movie and detective plot—each one a pathetic "failure"—might be interpreted as a covert form of mourning and, as such, make a contribution—and an unusually touching and sensitive one at that—to the subject of "working through" the legacy and the memory of the Holocaust, from the German perspective. Without going over the ground of "mourning work" versus the "inability to mourn" in the discussion about the aftermath of the Nazi regime,[16] two aspects should be retained: first, in order to share the mourning of an other, one must be able to empathize with the other's loss, which is to say the other's loss must not only be felt as a loss, which, as I have been trying to show in another chapter, was by no means a given in the case of post-war Germany. In addition, however, one must be able to grieve for one's own lost object: in other words, such an act of empathy may require a transfer from the other's lost one to one's own, whoever or whatever that might be. Mourning work for "Germans" with regards to "Jews" thus implies either that the Germans see the Jews as part of themselves, or that they can imagine a similar situation of loss. Either case, from a discursive point of view, requires a stand-in and necessitates a rhetoric of metaphor/metonymy. To mourn the loss of a loved one after having killed her (the "Susn" in the attic), and to do so in the very presence of this loved one (the "Susn" of the journey) might fulfill these difficult conditions of transfer, substitute and identity. Secondly, the Germans' inability to mourn for the Jewish victims of the Holocaust has been posited as a fact, and correlated with the injunction against grieving for their own losses, and especially the loss of their ego ideal, invested in the Führer.[17] One historical compromise, allowing the next generation of Germans to overcome this dilemma of blocked mourning versus insufficient empathy, was to identify with the Jewish victims, but to do so, either on the basis of also seeing oneself as victims (the forced expulsion of Germans from Central and Eastern Europe after 1945), or of overidentification: another way of appropriating the victim position of the other. Whether the projection was based on having been the victims of Hitler's diabolical art of seduction, of the fatal logic of German history since Napoleon, of the Soviet Army, raping and plundering, of mass-expulsions from the East, or of British bombings and the firestorms over German cities, depended in each case on the political bias and moral conviction of the respective groups or persons. Their sons and daughters, by contrast, identified with the Jewish victims of the Holocaust, all the more so if they perceived themselves as victims of their family history or of "patriarchy." As these descendants of the perpetrators tried to distance themselves from the preceding "father-generation," they produced a variety of subject-positions, most of which were in the mode of wounded narcissism—another topic much discussed in the psychosocial literature.[18] However, this "settling of accounts" between the generation of descendants and the father-generation yielded a very rich harvest in West German literature and the New German Cinema of the mid-1970s and early 1980s, but was rarely brought to a polemic point as directly as in Achternbusch's film. In his farewell letter Nil writes: "I had to find out what is inside the Germans, and I'm telling you, it's murder, most industrious murder." So vehement and almost hysterical is this rejection of "Germans" and "the land of murderers" that one suspects Achternbusch is citing here the cliché slogans of the Red Army Faction (RAF) about the "Nazi criminals" inside the federal government, about the "murderers" who lurk underneath the robe of the state apparatus, as well as putting on the "Hamlet" stance so frequently invoked at the time, [19] and discussed in a previous chapter.

What became evident, in the years immediately following the RAF, was that such a radical distanciation from "the murderers among us" could not settle the question of German accountability, nor assuage the guilt complex it had instilled in the generation of '68. In their quality as descendants, the sons and daughters perceived themselves as victims, but compensated for the asymmetry of this improbable subject position through an overidentification with other victims (of oppression, of discrimination, or other socially marginal groups), helping to shape the social agenda of the anti-authoritarian or anti-imperialist struggles in the 1980s and the green movement in the 1990s. For this reason, Achternbusch repeatedly—to THE LAST HOLE one must add HEILT HITLER (1984) and HADES (1995)—returns to the apparently irresolvable conflict of under- and overidentification, of disavowal and display, i.e., of the first generation (of perpetrators), trying to pass themselves off as innocent and ignorant (of Nazi crimes), and of the second generation (of victims), who expose their guilt feelings like a badge of honor. Against this confusing background of contending loyalties and contradictory subject positions, THE LAST HOLE must be understood as a sort of "counter-project": subverting both the consensus of silence on the right, and the self-righteousness of anger and revolt on the left.

By opting for Strindbergmanesque "Scenes from a Marriage," instead of the usual "father-son" Hamlet constellation, Achternbusch raises the stakes in the relation between victim and perpetrator to a new level of psychic complexity, where the driving force is not the (narcissistic) subject position of victim, but an intersubjectivity that each partner experiences as a painful and deadlocked over-identification with the other. Also made explicit by this change of focus from generational succession to the heterosexual couple is the (male) fantasy of merging with the mother imago, which in father-son-stories remains the affective but pre-oedipal, and therefore foundational but always implicit vanishing point of the oedipal struggle.

Going back to Žižek's analysis of LIFE IS BEAUTIFUL, the "German" compromise of overidentification throws a new light on Benigni's father-son constellation. What makes his film a comedy (in the technical sense, and as a structural antipode to tragedy) is the type of *emplotment* according to which the action progresses from potentially tragic misunderstandings to a reconciliation of misunderstanding at another level: in LIFE IS BEAUTIFUL, the narrative moves from (deliberate) misunderstanding to (inadvertent) redemption. It traces a development from the victim (father) to the survivor (son), the latter mitigating the (senseless) death of so many million at the hands of the Nazis, thanks to the death of his father, made meaningful by saving his son and returning him to his mother. In SCHINDLER'S LIST a similar *emplotment* of victimhood leading to salvation rallies the extended family of the "Schindler Jews" round Schindler's grave, i.e., the dead totemic father, across generations. According to Žižek, the price for this redemptive gesture—especially in LIFE IS BEAUTIFUL—is, however, too high: the solution proposed is not viable because behind it, there lurks an even greater catastrophe, from the evolutionary perspective. A father who fashions reality as a life-lie for his son and gives it a consistency only by systematically proposing a counterfactual interpretation does not enable the child to enter into the symbolic order. Instead, he turns his son into a schizophrenic, leaving him to languish in the pre-oedipal phase, with all its paranoid demons and missing differentiation between Self and Other that it entails.

Such a post-Lacanian reading of the father-son relationship is useful for understanding Germany's way of working through the Nazi past, insofar as the life-lie logic pertains not only to victims but may also apply to perpetrators, as they pass not the content, but the form of disavowal to their children. To give another example of the logic of overidentification within an oedipal constellation, in the 1950s, much of Germany's official right—from Konrad Adenauer's Christian Democracts to the Axel Springer press—began to express their pro-Israel stance in the form of ostentatiously flaunted philo-Semitism, to which the "sons and daughter" generation responded with an equally ostentatious pro-Palestinian anti-Zionism (now, somewhat vindictively, "unmasked" as anti-Semitism).[20] Empathy with the other expressed itself through national symbols worn as fashion items.[21] But even this turn to bodily-mimetic identification could not erase the sense of guilt, inadequately expressed und thus never expiated. Instead, another double-bind emerged surrounding the positions of victim and perpetrator, as illustrated by Markus Imhof's film DIE REISE (1986), based on Bernward Vesper's novel by the same title. The autobiographical story of the son of a famous Nazi writer, who had joined the radical left around Gudrun Ensslin, only to find himself dumped by her for the even more ruthlessly radical Andreas Baader, DIE REISE depicts a "homecoming" to his father's house, where he commits suicide. Here, the feeling of being a victim, while belonging to a family/nation of perpetrators, puts the dilemma in its starkest form: the choice is between murder or suicide, violence against the self or terror towards others—seemingly the only options left for putting an end to the unbearable schizo-position, brought about by the collapse of the symbolic order on which a life-lie patriarchy rests. An even better-known example of the same dilemma can be found in DEUTSCHLAND IM HERBST (1977). Here the double father-son constellation between Hans Martin Schleyer and his son, on the one hand, and between Field Marshal Erwin Rommel and his son on the other, is pitted against the rebelling RAF sons (and daughters), while the respective spheres of public and private, of politics and family matters find themselves reversed in the process.[22]

According to Žižek's mode of analysis, only if the sons had, as it were, reinvented their Nazi fathers as monstrous perpetrators of unspeakable crimes also within the direct family context, would they have been able to cast themselves guiltlessly as victims, or as avenging angels. Žižek demonstrates this mechanism of retroactive projection of criminal behavior onto the father, as a way of clearing the ground for the sons to regain some measure of agency by way of the well-known Dogma-film FESTEN (1999), this time unconnected to the Holocaust subtext. Thomas Vinterberg reconstructs the monstrous father, along the lines of the *false memory syndrome*, in a deliberately clichéd, tongue-in-cheek revelatory narrative, unmasking him as a rapist and child-abuser. Both Benigni's and Vinterberg's fathers are sentimental fictions, functioning as psychic shields, to protect the subject from the greater danger of a fatherless society. But Žižek's conclusion is itself meant to be a provocation: when it comes to shoring up male identity, in the absence of a viable symbolic order, it is better to have an abusive father, as fantasized in Vinterberg's film, than a playful one, as imagined in Benigni's film!

Throughout the decades many other German filmmakers, among them Margarethe von Trotta, Helma Sanders-Brahms, Bernhard Sinkel, Volker Schlöndorff, Nico Hoffmann, Roland Suso Richter, have addressed this ambivalence of the father figure.[23] Set against this double historical background—on the one hand, the overstrained father-son conflict and Hamlet-situation in the New German Cinema from the 1970s through the 1990s, and, on the other hand,

Žižek's post-oedipal reading from the late 1990s, now within the context of post-Wall European cinema—Achternbusch's (dissenting) contribution to this topic can be assessed anew.

Negative Symbiosis

In Nil's case there is no son to speak of, but a (marriage) partner. However, a stereotypical father gains prominence in The last Hole, in the figure of the psychiatrist-neurologist, whom Nil consults for treatment of his recurring nightmare. But rather than unambiguously representing the generation of perpetrators, he is introduced as the son of a concentration camp doctor, mitigating his potential function as a father figure, and turning him into generational co-equal, as well as the catalyst for an absurd arithmetical operation. The scene begins with a typical inversion: Nil complains about the dead Jews, but only so as to better forget them. Successful in repressing their memory with beer during the day, he cannot make them disappear altogether: a prescription should help him keep them away also night. At the same time, Nil sees himself as a scapegoat, a stand-in and witness, rather than as a Holocaust-denier. If no one else remembers, "someone has to serve the cause of justice." Whereas the doctor does not see in Nil's situation as anything other than an arithmetical problem, for which he "may have something in store [*auf Lager*, literally in the camp]," what tortures Nil is the lack of conscience among his fellow citizens. Matter-of-fact and committed to his bureaucratic routine, the doctor connects more directly to the problematic of guilt and atonement: his business-as-usual stance is more hostile to any reconciliation than would be repression, denial or life-lie disavowal. Not even a representative of the "banality-of-evil" school, he is a counter-figure to all those symbolic villains that people other German directors' work, often weighed with Biblical analogies, as for instance in early Werner Herzog films. By portraying Nil's (feelings of) guilt as something pathological that needs to be treated by a doctor, when in fact it should be the lack of such feelings that necessitates therapy, Achternbusch's reversal of this disparity marks him out as a Swiftean satirist. Furthermore, he resists the temptation of using a metaphor to describe the relationship between Germans and Jews. Instead, the victims are named directly ("6 million"), but at the same time they become a signifier, whose reference is displaced several times over: Susn from the tavern thinks Nil is talking about his winnings in a lottery; in the doctor's office, a grotesque counting maneuver is proposed, whereby the 6 million are divided by 0.2, upon which the "remainder" is made to disappear through recourse to a paternal deus ex machina. Finally, for Stupid Cloud, Nil's travel companion, the figure reminds him of the "six million foreign words [*Fremdwörter*]" that gave him such a hard time in school, as if he was quoting Theodor W. Adorno's dictum that foreign words are "the Jews of language."[24]

Achternbusch's preferred filmic composition is that of the tableau (i.e., a fixed camera shot framing a character ensemble). Given that he plays the main protagonist, this might be explained by the circumstances of production, but especially in the scenes set in the village tavern or at the bar, the tableau shot comes to stand for the immobility, indeed catatonia and amnesia of the community as a whole, with regard to "the past in the present." Ever so often shreds of memory arise, momentarily or abruptly, from the surly silence, the redundant banter, and the obstinate staring into empty space. There is the scene, for instance, where an elderly woman, talking into her beer mug, reminisces about a sound that still haunts her: the scuffling of shoes on the staircase and on the pavement outside. It takes her back to the day, when her sick neighbor, too weak to walk on her own, was dragged down the stairs and into the street, to be carried off with the transports of the local Jews. Presumably, the woman had looked away, but she had not been able to shut her ears off, which is why the memory that haunts her now is associated with the scuffling sound of shoes.

Such treacherously revealing moments of bodily memory are rare. More often, Achternbusch's characters get tangled up in language. They stumble on words and twist idioms; officials (such as the police) suspect (or kill) the wrong person and commit slips of the tongue; verbal mishaps are the protagonists' most telling achievements: parapraxes (or "performed failures") power the plot. They advance—inadvertently, but determinedly—the task of uncovering taboos; they touch on traumas that are worked through by a self-administered talking cure of rubble-babble. The people propping up the bar in Achternbusch's film are so eloquently mute, because they are no longer able to tell stories about their own history, as awkward memories intrude like unwanted guests at the table reserved for the locals.

THE LAST HOLE is a collection of bad puns and atrocious visual gags which, in their grotesque exaggerations and misalignments, address the central dilemma, while constantly avoiding it: namely how Germans might find a morally valid "currency" that can acknowledge guilt or accountability, without attempting to calculate it in the form of "accounts" that can be settled. Like Fassbinder before him, Achternbusch addresses the incommensurability in the relation between post-war Germans and the victims of Nazi persecution through inappropriate puns, slippery situations and unfunny gags, walking a fine line between giving offense and offering proof of the very impossibility that "justice is being served."[25]

In THE LAST HOLE the narrative lurches forward more than it progresses, stumbling and skipping, getting its drift from skewed comparisons (rabbits/people), abstruse arithmetical acrobatics (measuring the memory of murdered Jews in centiliters of schnapps), and polemical equations (police/murderer). Achternbusch resorts to malapropisms or twisted clichés, like "life sentence" for "life-long," "inmate" for "mate," "the last hole" for "the black hole," as if desperate to prevent his story from turning into an allegory. On a Kamikaze mission, the puns in bad taste are meant to sabotage the possibility that with such a delicate topic, out of considerations of reticence and tact, the film might be misunderstood as coming down on the side of insight and understanding, forgiveness and reconciliation, or of providing poetic justice of sorts after all.

In line with the assumption of the other chapters (i.e., that the very absence of direct references or representations of Jews in the New German Cinema gives their fate its traumatic-traumatizing presence), the insistence on Freudian slips, combined with the obsessive literalness of figures of speech (*auf Lager haben*, which, as indicated, translates literally to have something "in the camp") means that Achternbusch intended to add another example to the type of films, where absence is figured as presence, and presence becomes parapraxis.[26] Because even though he does take up the Holocaust more directly than most, the persistence of its afterlife is that of a disruptive presence, taking the form of bungled actions and blunders, of more or less absurd twists or, on the verbal level, the slippages of meaning and reference, all of which combine to generate out of the "too much past" such effects as the "last hole" becoming a "black hole."

The spoonerisms and literalized metaphors mostly signal the "failed" work of memory in Achternbusch's film. But they can also open more benevolent lines of lyrical associations and surreal montages, mixing bathos and pathos around the central couple's difficult romance. For instance, Nil's name invites poetic outpourings and trivial comparisons: It designates the powerfully fertile river Nile, in his case dried up long ago, which is why Susn is watering the attic floor, as if to make Nil's passion for her flow again. The same river metaphor is taken up by Nil himself in his exchange with "the last Susn," this time given lyrical-erotic rather than directly sexual connotations. For the sake of her health, Susn should go to Egypt, but she has no money. Resigning herself to the situation, she claims that Germany is a desert anyway, whereupon Nil retorts: "Let me be your Nile." Later, when he turns up in her room above the nightclub, she greets him, saying: "You are the endless Nile, who made me wait for such an endlessly long time, and whom I have loved for such an eternity." Water imagery pervades the entire film, opening up associations that leads from water to beer and further to schnapps, but water also connotes oblivion (the river Lethe), the wide open sea (where the journey ends) and death. Generally speaking, water, air, fire (e.g., in the childhood memory of the first night with Susn in front of the fire) and earth (the burrow where Nil lives like a rabbit), taken together, build an elemental system of coordinates for personal memory and for a possible redemption, an eco-system which plays an anchoring role for the characters' identity, but also fails them in the end. Extending beyond the personal, water is also associated with the Jews. In the opening scene in the attic, Nil tells Susan: "This not a kiss, this is something wet from your mouth to mine. For me a kiss is something else. Do you know what a kiss is for me? A few Jews having made drawings in Auschwitz, *that* is a kiss for me." This unexpected link is the first—disconcerting—attempt to draw an (absurd) analogy between the fraught relationship of Germans and Jews, and the emotionally charged play of attraction and repulsion of the erotic couple. Their love-hate relationship, where each tries to take the other moral prisoner, serves as the affective grounding of quite another, more painful, more fateful bond—the post-Auschwitz "dialogue" between Germans and (German) Jews, held together by what has been called the "negative symbiosis."[27] With this Achternbusch aligns, but also distances himself from other filmic examples that depict this German-Jewish "negative symbiosis" in the form of a couple's love relationship: one thinks of the one between two men as portrayed in Fassbinder's IN A YEAR OF THIRTEEN MOONS (1978), where the links are both oblique (as a double projection of victimhood, occasioned by a sex-change) and direct (as part of one of the character's biography). Both Achternbusch and Fassbinder's figuration, however, are entirely different from subsequent attempts to explore the relation between Germans and Jews, when an actual or fictional love story between a "gentile" and a "Jew" is made, retrospectively, to bear the burden of a symbol, each partner "standing for" his/her race or religion, as in Josef Vilsmeier's COMEDIAN HARMONISTS (1997), Dani Levy's MESCHUGGE (1998), Max Färberböck's AIMÉE UND JAGUAR (1998) or Margarethe von Trotta's ROSENSTRASSE (2003).

Unlike these conciliatory films of the 1990s, where the potentially tragic stories are brought to a happy ending thanks to a "survivor" figure dispensing forgiveness, THE LAST HOLE builds on a deeply dysfunctional and destructive couple situation. Wanting to represent both the relation between victim and perpetrator and the dynamics between self-declared victims in altogether different dramaturgical terms, Achternbusch sets up long passages of quasi-monological exchange between the protagonists. The spectator is treated to three extended insights into the corrosive-destructive (but also banal-absurd) consequences of their mutual (self-)imprisonment, each time varying the emphasis and the point of view: once in the opening scene in the attic, a second time on the train to Genoa during the monologue of "the last Susn," and finally in Nil's goodbye letter to Susn, which she reads out aloud at the end of the film. The first confrontation gives us the perspective of both partners (in their cantankerous dialogue that culminates with a murder), then Susn's perspective (in her desperate monologue on the train, which culminates in her reliving the time she punched Nil so hard that he bled, in order to stir him from his presumptuous aloofness and provoke him into a counterattack), while the final confrontation comes from Nil's perspective, but mediated through her voice speaking his words (in the equally dismal and hopeless monologue that combines a torrent of hatred with a declaration of love, at the end of which he gives up his search for her although she is standing right in front of him). Not surprisingly, it turns out that in each encounter both partners perceive themselves as victims, but each of them is seen by the other as a perpetrator. Susn's role is played by different actresses, so that even after Nil stabbed her in the first scene, she can still appear in the next scene as the waitress serving him at the bar. It makes evident the repetition compulsion inherent in the relation, as well as the shifting temporal registers and the inversion of addressor and addressee, most glaringly in the third encounter on Stromboli, where "the last Susn" reads Nil a letter which he himself had written to her and in which he says goodbye to her with the words: "It would be nice to see you again one more time!"

The tragicomic impossibility of finding a path to the other—reminiscent of and modeled on the compressed, uncommunicative monologues in Samuel Beckett's or Harold Pinter's plays—implicitly becomes an alternative to the Hamlet-situation in the New German Cinema of the 1970s (or to the Romeo-and-Juliet-motif of subsequent films in the 1990s). These analogies make sense not least because German directors still look to the classical repertoire of genres and dramaturgical models for paradigms that will best address the inexistent understanding and defective communication between Germans and Jews in the aftermath of the Holocaust. The possibility offers itself here for a "tragic" representation of historical anti-Semitism and of genocide from the Germans' point of view: assuming that perpetrators and victims are emotionally and existentially connected to each another, one would have to talk about a sort of tragic "flaw" or "transgression," followed by a "recognition," however belated in nature. The "negative symbiosis" mentioned above refers to claims that Jews and Germans have, for two centuries of co-existence and assimilation, represented each other's "fate": the symbiosis of each being the other's other. If this were indeed the case, then the tragic irony would be that, in their insane attempt to break free from this fate through mass murder and extermination, Germans managed only to link their future and their identity as a nation even more unavoidably to that of the Jewish people, instead of continuing to co-exist side by side as two ethnicities or peoples within one (German) nation. This would be the "negative" that has to be added to symbiosis: after Auschwitz and because of Auschwitz.

As an interpretative matrix, the idea of negative symbiosis, when applied to Achternbusch's film, might help explain why in The last Hole (the second) Susn is still alive, even after (the first) Susn has already been killed by Nil. Murder (of the Jews) does not resolve (for Germans) the "problem" of having to look the other in the eye; on the contrary, the other stays there, in Achternbusch's pun "a life-long/as a life-sentence." Related to this is the fact that the (third) "last Susn" barely feels alive when Nil finds her in her tavern room and takes her along to Italy: "I am so weak that I cannot die anymore. (...) Everything perishes much too slowly." What could have lent itself to an allegorical interpretation of survival (after Auschwitz) as death-in-life is referred back to the yearnings and disappointments of this emotionally scarred relationship whose three different love objects carry the same name because they revolve around the same "void."

Guilt, Atonement, and Susn

Such allegorizing attempts would seem unseemly and even intolerable if they did not apply a certain mimicry, i.e., if they were not staged through the rhetorical repertoire of hyperbole, satire, inversion and parody. Comparable to Fassbinder's play *Der Müll, die Stadt und der Tod* (1976), which caused so much outrage, Achternbusch could be said to skirt dangerously close to anti-Semitic clichés, so as to occupy an affectively charged terrain, and to gain historically just about plausible traction for his ironic reversals. As suggested previously, these reversals aim to establish a different type of connection between guilt and atonement, and between victim and perpetrator—putting the deadlocks of the "mastering the past" on another basis, by recasting also the voluntary-involuntary entanglement of the subsequent generation, in guilt, responsibility and accountability for acts they neither committed nor disavow.

By pairing this story of a love affair gone awry with an adventure story of fugitives from justice on the run, Achternbusch joins Nil and Susn's acts of murderous love, to two murderers' (successful) attempt to escape the consequences of their deeds, adding as a twist that one of the victim is still "alive" and the other murder is the outcome of a parapractic mix-up in the fog of bungling zeal. Just as chronology is suspended in the love affair, creating a confusion over what is "before" and what "after," opening up a kind of belatedness of cause and effect, so the identity of the characters and their (power-) relation to each other becomes reversible and interchangeable. With the consequence that on the train to Genoa, all three—the perpetrators and the victims are on the run, confounding our sense of who at any point, is positioned where, on the scale of guilt, and underlining instead the mutually antagonistic, but also reciprocal relationship of perpetrator/victim/survivor that sustains each of them and binds him/her to the others. Nil is Susn's murderer; she in turn is both victim and survivor, and, through her survival, also embodies Nil's guilt. Nil himself is a survivor of the police intervention, but not by virtue of saving himself, rather by virtue of someone else—the policeman Stupid Cloud—assuming the guilt of the perpetrator. Nil is therefore "saved through the culpability of someone else" (as Alexander Kluge characterizes an equally "absurd" but tellingly appropriate parapractic situation in Die Macht der Gefühle). Susn, for her part, is both victim and guilt incarnate, having survived the thousand deaths of Nil's lack of affection, and stayed, to remind him of it every day. Stupid Cloud becomes a perpetrator in spite of his sense of duty as officer of the law: possibly Achternbusch's way of commenting on the "only following orders" excuse of the "ordinary German," so often invoked in the first post-war trials. The Last Hole—in an apparently absurdist and trivializing guise—revolves around a constellation in which guilt and atonement, crime and retribution, perpetrator and victim are so enmeshed that there seems no way out, at least not on this level. The repetition of situations similar in structure, but each with its own context, could be read as an attempt to embed into this dead-end affair of pitiful losers from the Bavarian *hinterland* a narrative of quit different gravity, without one noticing it at first.

A case in point is that the journey to Genoa and on to Stromboli evokes other, quite different train journeys and their "stations": from the barber who suddenly appears to give Stupid Cloud a haircut, to the terrifying vision of the "torn sun" in the blazing oven; from the train tracks that stop dead in the sea, to Nil wearing a white lab coat and a steel helmet; from the skull buried in volcanic ash, to Nil's final act, his eager leap into the smoldering mouth of the volcano. These are, strictly speaking, neither allegories nor metaphors: the episodes, incidents, locations and locutions follow each other in a narrative chain, where the surreal and the banal, dream and slapstick, farce and pathos interlock in all their incongruity, yet their non-sequiturs manage to accumulate a strange inevitability. For however absurd the individual circumstances, overall a melancholy, lugubrious or anguished intensity prevails, never lifting the tense irritability and sullen aggression that only serves to underscore the intangibility of reference: what it might mean or is meant to signify. The seemingly never-ending train journey embodies (by testing the viewers' endurance) what Stupid Cloud claims to have seen: a vision of something "so horrible that you will not be able to bear it." Yet whatever knowledge or foreboding any of the three may share, the film keeps it from the audience. Legitimate authority and the law being suspended, these characters are in purgatory, unable to locate the crime that would fit the punishment they are already undergoing. Nil the Nazi hunter, who poses as a psychiatric patient in order to track down his "634th case of a German pig," later writes in his letter to Susn that he only pretended to be a private investigator so as to be able to look for her in Germany's rubble: an explanation in reverse, which chimes in with Nil's answer, when asked why he is digging with two tennis racquets: "because I don't have a partner." The detective story, in other words, although ostensibly giving the love story and the adventure story their common, intertwining thread, zigzags and doubles-back, losing all momentum of propelling the action forward towards a resolution. Instead, text and pretext, tenor and vehicle may change places or reverse order at any given moment.

A detective, whose investigation cannot but lead to (the death of) his own person: in The Last Hole, too, the outlines of both Oedipus and Hamlet's dilemma are hard to miss. But unlike other instances in the New German Cinema already mentioned, Achternbusch makes far more explicit how and why this aggression towards the father is so often turned inward, becomes melancholy and suicidal: it is the—barred—fantasy of returning to the mother, which is the hidden spring, and as indicated, also the driving fantasy underlying Benigni's LIFE IS BEAUTIFUL. The fact that for Nil all women bear the same name ("Susn") is a clear sign, and should, on another interpretive level, be taken as an indication that Nil's love object is not a partner or mate, but the male projection, barely disguised, of the maternal imago, in all its ambivalence. So far so much in line with the New German Cinema in general, where the hatred against fathers or their complete absence as an affective anchorage are the two sides of a yearning to re-unite with the mother. Wim Wenders' films consistently revolve around this issue (think of WRONG MOVEMENT, ALICE IN THE CITIES, PARIS TEXAS, UNTIL THE END OF THE WORLD), but in an oblique way, which is why, in his early films, few if any of the women are love interests for the male hero. Fassbinder's "women's films," perhaps not surprisingly, show an intuitive, but no less ambivalent identification with strong female characters, while the presence of Fassbinder's own mother in so many of the films is something like a signature touch and complements the director's own cameo appearances. Alexander Kluge once called for a staging of the "primal scene" of his generation, when he suggested that WDR should commission a series of films under the title "Our Parents' Marriages." The proposal came to pass, in fact, at least to the extent that Kluge shot DIE PATRIOTIN, Fassbinder DIE EHE DER MARIA BRAUN, Jeanine Meerapfel MALOU, and Helma Sanders-Brahms DEUTSCHLAND BLEICHE MUTTER. Sanders-Brahms borrowed the metaphor of The Nation as a sorely tried or even raped mother from Brecht, but it is much older than that, of course, in the discourse of nineteenth-century nation states, and re-appears in parodic fashion in Volker Schlöndorff's Günter Grass adaptation DIE BLECHTROMMEL. In Helke Sander's FREIER-BEFREITE (1992), the same metaphor is being taken literally, as she documents with interviews and statistics the hundreds of thousands of actual rape cases, committed by the Allied Forces immediately after their victory in 1945.

At first glance, it seems that in THE LAST HOLE, too, the guilty conscience towards Jews is warded off by the protective shield of a hate-filled rejection of the fathers, the oedipal rage having to compensate for inaction, while the mother's body and her historical role as victim has to stand for the Jewish victims, for whom "truth and reconciliation" remained at best the symptomatic failed communication of the many kinds of parapraxes that this study tries to track. Yet in Achternbusch's film, the mother's image is so prominent, and so traumatic in its own right, as it fuses the hero's self-loathing with his lament over the loss of his beloved, that such ostentatiously flaunted over-identification precludes any possibility of it serving as the pathos-form of reconciliation.[28]

The Mother Figure in Achternbusch: Norman Bates at the Ammersee

Achternbusch's other films and writings demonstrate how openly incestuous, and thus part of "the personal as the political," the fusion with the mother has always been in his work. In THE LAST HOLE, Nil and Susn's odyssey of mutually inflicted pain displays all the asymmetry of the heterosexual couple: what the man is looking for in the woman is an ideal image resembling the mother, whereas the woman tries to obtain from the man a confirmation of her otherness and of her love for him as something unique. Failure, in the form of disappointment, is thus inscribed in the very terms of their encounter. In his play *Ella* (1978), by contrast, Achternbusch focuses on the relationship between mother and son. One stage direction, for instance, reads: "Ella is sitting in the foreground (…), watching the daily news on TV. Or is it Preminger's *River of no Return*? (…) Josef is her son. He sports a homemade wig from chicken feathers and is wearing a household apron. There is no doubt that he is his own mother. (…) *Ella* is a sequel to Hitchcock's *Psycho*."[29]

The emotions flowing into such a scene are a typical combination of cinephile and autobiographic memories, the latter staged even more fully in the play *Mein Herbert* (1985/6). A former professional swimmer, Achternbusch's mother participated in the Olympic Games of 1936 but did not win a medal—which for this very reason becomes a distinction in the son's eyes. In 1974, she committed suicide, and Achternbusch has dedicated several of his film to her, among others DIE ATLANTIKSCHWIMMER (1975) and DIE OLYMPIASIEGERIN (1983). Time and again in his writings he speaks of how much his mother's death has influenced his filmmaking. Further confirmation of this proud identification with the mother can be found in his diary about the making of his first film: "Never will my mother be my wife! I resemble her most when I laugh. In 1974 a shot tore apart her beautiful face. When they hastily buried the few grams of her ashes, I winced as if, as a newborn, I had ended up on my uncle's abortion tray after all. (…) Not having to be happy is what consoles me most. Later on I became a painter, and my mother bought me paints. (…) What would I have become without her? From her funeral I drove straight into my first day's shoot on DAS ANDECHSER GEFÜHL. (…) Margarethe von Trotta, the lead actress, gave me courage. On a good day, she looks like my mother. Then I shot ATLANTIKSCHWIMMER. (…) Much in need of a rest, as if on my first day in this world—it was hard work to protect my ideas from the clutches of the culture-vultures—, I put on my mother's clothes, took her little purse, her money and her son together with his friends and went to the bar by the Würmbad,[30] where people I knew from my childhood get together. (… Another time, standing) by the Atlantic Ocean I took my mother's hair, which I had cleaned of all the blood, and held it as I would a woman. Stunning girl, worthy of admiration more than of lament. How strange: a girl as a man. She resembles me most when I laugh. I cannot cry because I have lost all emotion while waiting for my mother. I write and make films in order to feel lust. Apart from that nothing becomes an image."[31]

Through this insistence on the image as a maternal instance, and his intensely erotic identification with the dead mother, Achternbusch defines cinema and his own filmmaking as a personal form of mourning-work, paired with passionate idealization. Loss and absence are reclaimed through an image, but an image whose power of seduction (or rather, whose "reality") is so strong that only mimetic embodiment and material re-enactment can still this hunger for possession, beyond fetish and "representation". Projection, overidentification and self-effacement are staged in such a painfully explicit way that suicide is nothing else but the final merger and fusion with "the image."

What stands out in The Last Hole, where the parallelisms between filmmaking and mourning-work are merely implied, but where the suicide is flamboyantly enacted, are the different temporal registers as a result of the unresolved tension between the search for—and ultimately the finding of—the mother figure ("the last Susn") and Nil's death on the Stromboli Island. As Susn's monologue on the train reveals in a brutally direct yet touching manner, Nil represents for her the lover with whom she identifies to the point of self-abandonment, whereas he needs "the last Susn" to be both desirable and unattainable, as we find out from his farewell letter. But as a classical mother figure, Susn demonstrates, *ex negativo* as it were, why the "normal" oedipal resolution of incestuous desire, namely the substitution of the mother by another love object, no longer works. The desperately intense presence of the mother image preserves a precious remainder of temporal belatedness—the "then" in the "now"—which in the substitution of attachment from mother to lover translates into the emotional distance that will forever separate Nil from Susn. The discontinuous and anecdotal narrative, with its gaps and inconsistencies, but held together by the constant squabbling of the partners, fuels an indeterminacy of time in the act of repetition which, despite the linear structure of the trip, creates the impression that several pasts are superimposed upon a present that never quite becomes actual. When Nil sees ghosts and dead people in his shaving mirror, or when he fights against shirts and bed sheets, one can relate the respective fissures and repetitions to his frame of mind, in and out of time, since Nil perceives the world never in the here-and-now, but always midpoint between his guilt-relieving inebriation and guilt-induced sleeplessness, buffeted between nightmares and hallucinations.

For the long final scene of the film, when the farewell letter is read aloud, Achternbusch has discovered a perfect topography, which further strives to remove the action from any psychological interpretation, however much several Freudian readings beckon. Having the last Susn recite the suicide note in the presence of the future victim/perpetrator of the act is, of course, Nil's supreme narcissistic revenge, gratifying an infantile fantasy of witnessing one's own death, while enjoying the sight of those who once scorned and misunderstood the deceased, and are now overcome with hot grief and bitter regret. Such fantasies of wounded narcissism can be found in other films of the New German Cinema, most explicitly in Hans, the main character of Fassbinder's HÄNDLER DER VIER JAHRESZEITEN (1972). But Nil's presence-in-absence can also be read as a traumatic moment, in which the subject observes himself, but is powerless to act, as if in a dream. The inversion here consists in the fact that the scene is shown from the dead man's perspective, rather than the (still) living man being the observer of a subject-about-to-die, as is the case in Sigmund Freud's story of the child who calls out: "Father, can you not see that I am burning?"

The perspective of the dead man—the posthumous point of view would be, as it were, the non-psychological take—is suggested by the geometry of the final shot in THE LAST HOLE: the two persons in the foreground (Stupid Cloud and Barbara) are holding the letter-amulet, while "the last Susn" draws near from the direction of the sea, her sight-line perfectly aligned with that of the camera, which "sees" these three characters forming a triangle from Nil's point of view—who in the meantime has vanished up the slope of the volcano—i.e., from the perspective of a man who is no longer alive but not yet dead either. The formalism of the composition is strengthened by the fact that the camera is located on the very spot where the viewer knows the skull to be that Nil had dug out earlier from the lava ash, so that when Susn reads out the letter, she is in fact looking at the skull. Nil has now fused with the dead of the past and merged with his own future self, or as he writes: "As a suicide, I belong to the mountain of the dead, made up of the victims, because I refuse to belong to the self-righteous Germans." The logic of the film requires such an ending which preserves the temporally and spatially displaced, and thus permanently suspended communication between "the last Susn" and Nil, while re-affirming that between them stands an unburied (or dug-out) skull, no doubt the supernumerary dead (the indivisible remainder) from the doctor's arithmetical acrobatics.

Suspended between remembered hope and a yearned-for recollection, the Susn-Nil love story maintains its own kind of reality, in its very pain, anger and ecstatic grief ("I looked for you—you, the tenderness, the insight (...) and the pride to help me endure this life with dignity"). But given the time-out-of-time, with its many kinds of "too-late" and "not-yet," their encounters also consist of a series of screen memories, through which one can make out the contours of another realty, always hidden, and another memory, always present. For instance, remembering their first get-together, Nil says that they both looked into the blazing oven all night long and he asked her: "Shall I put some more coal on?" Banal as the bathos of such a scene may be, it is followed up with a monologue by Susn, which ends: "I died for you. But because you didn't kill me, I wished a little Hitler on you for two days, to force you out through the chimney."

The Last Hole: Abyss of the Self or Groundless Ground for Optimism?

"Blood round, blood hole/Bleeding hole/Swallow me whole," shouts Nil at the very beginning, anticipating his suicidal leap into the Stromboli volcano at the end. Susn, her passion rekindled, ardently asks Nil to let her be his "last hole." Grave or maternal womb, female sex organ or Kafkaesque burrow, the "mound hole" of the hermit, or the rabbit hole from *Alice in Wonderland*, transporting the hero into a "topsy-turvy world": whatever the possibilities the title refers to, it always involves an abyss, the loss of any kind of ground on which the protagonists can base their identity, or relate to each other. The memory landscape of The Last Hole translates this groundlessness into its own temporal mode, whose apocalyptic tense not so much refers to the end of time as to an after-time, which no longer follows the laws of chronology or of linear sequence. But in the German context, such after-time is always already "historical" time, become trauma-and-bad-memory time, for as the motto of another Achternbusch film (Der Junge Mönch, 1978) has it: "[The story] begins, when everything is in ruins."

"Things collapse much too slowly," says Susn about her life, and then about Nil: "When nothing works out anymore, that's when he comes back to me." One has to imagine the characters of The Last Hole existing in a time "after": when all conceivable disasters have already taken place, when every possible move is already too late, when all the world is in a post-mortem condition. Although this seems to confirm why Achternbusch's hero is called Nil, now as a derivation of *nihil*, i.e., nothing, it is probably not necessary to see only the resignation and the nihilism in his name. Rather, it stands also for the heroic (though, of course, failed) attempt at "ex nihilo" self-creation, faced with the groundless ground of a moral universe lacking all bearings and an abyss of guilt and recrimination that swallows all hope and determination. Already in the 1970s Achternbusch coined a phrase, for which he does not always receive credit, given how well known it became subsequently: "You don't have a chance, but use it" (Die Atlantikschwimmer, 1976). During the economic crisis of the mid-1980s, it became the slogan of the Generation X (called *Sponti* in West Germany), meant to express frustration with a future that held only unemployment, and with the glibness of politicians who tend to fob off the young with patronizing encouragements. In the first years after German unification, it was again much in use not only by leftist anarchists but also among right-wing extremists. Such divergent contexts shed light on the anarchism of a director who has a special gift for absurd verbal contortions that reveal a new truth, in this case the possibility that the negative judgment society passes on its younger generation can also create unexpected leverage.[32]

How do these detours through Achternbusch's post-Apocalyptic imagination, bad puns, marital misery and the world of Sponti anarchism help clarify the question of genre—and Holocaust comedy—with which I began? My claim has been that THE LAST HOLE performs, in its very form and prior to any specific content, the mechanisms of the "fantasmatic protective shield" that, according to Žižek, might explain the turn to comedy, when confronting the memory (and bad conscience) of a nation of perpetrators (or bystanders). Achternbusch demonstrates how cause-and-effect reversals and verbal slip-ups camouflage but also lay bare motives and attitudes that would otherwise not manifest themselves. What is remarkable is that he did so, more than a decade before the memory of the Holocaust became a pan-European preoccupation. In the context of "representing" the Holocaust in and through the cinema, the issue of genre inevitably raises the question of what social purpose such a "mastering of the past" is meant to serve. Genres are, generally speaking, the shared interfaces, the sensory membranes or pre-defined filters that a community (or nation) recognizes, when communicating with itself across the leading media or art forms of the day, be they theater, the novel, television, or film. Genre is the vehicle whereby social norms, valid in and for a given time, are reinforced, but, where these norms are pushed to the limits, can be put to the test and if necessary, renegotiated, thanks to the "liberties" permitted in the realm of art. Or, as Achternbusch himself sums it all up in a more elegant and succinct manner: "THE LAST HOLE/It's Your Goal/Every Form/Is Ab-norm/Every Look/A mere Out-look/But whose?" ("Das letzte Loch/Versuch es doch/Jede Form/Ist abnorm/Jede Erscheinung/Ist eine Meinung/Von wem?").

If one follows Hanno Loewy, who more than anyone else has dedicated himself to categorizing and analyzing the genres of Holocaust cinema in general and of German films about "mastering the past" in particular, one notes a certain convergence with Žižek, insofar as Loewy, too, believes that neither for Jewish survivors, their descendants, nor for Germans, can the Holocaust be the subject of tragedy. Attempts at tragedy, for Loewy, only ever manage to express an underlying "longing for the tragic."[33] Instead, a preferred genre when Hollywood takes up the topic, is "romance," usually couched in (male-centered) stories of coming of age/loss of "innocence" (which in psychoanalytic vocabulary, would be submission under the symbolic order by accepting castration). SCHINDLER'S LIST is a case in point, if "romance" is here understood as an adventure story in which the hero is put to the test several times before proving himself in the fight against evil. From a German perspective, therefore, the Holocaust can hardly be a suitable subject for romance either. Instead, Loewy concludes that German films about "working through" or "mastering the past" oscillate between the "arrogated tragedy" and the "surrogate-comedy," the latter comprising all films in which a reconciliation of sorts, either across generations or between descendants, starts to develop, i.e., precisely the model that Achternbusch sets his film up against.

Perhaps a true comedy could only be made from the perspective of Jews affected by the Holocaust, with the proviso that it would have to have the structure of a Jewish joke, which means it would belong to the genre of satire. Loewy cites Theodor Reik, who wrote the following about Jewish jokes: "behind the comic façade [there is] not only something serious, which is present in the wit of other nations too, but sheer horror." Loewy comments that this would be "the wit of one who puts a mask on death and laughs this very mask in the face."[34] Insofar as Achternbusch is also capable of such a gesture and insofar as the motto "it begins, when everything is in ruins" has some of the death-defying sarcasm of Reik's description of Jewish jokes, the director's balancing acts on the brink of the abyss in The Last Hole, together with the verbal acrobatics and vertiginous non-sense à la Karl Valentin, do indeed qualify as satire, even if this satire extends its frame of reference well beyond the common experience of a couple's relationship and tries to tackle with the resources of absurdity a different register of unrepresentability.

Žižek defines comedy as the genre that allows not only life to triumph, but a particular kind of creaturely life, one that also accommodates the baser instincts and banal bodily needs. Speaking of the S-M camp comedy Seven Beauties (Pasqualino Settebellezze, Lina Wertmuller, 1976), he comments:

> What makes Seven Beauties so disturbing is that when the film's comic rendering of the resourceful persistence of life reaches its limit, we get not the usual pathetic dignity but the nausea of degenerate mortality. Though both comedy and tragedy deal with immortality, the forms of immortality they present are incompatible. In the tragic predicament the hero sacrifices his terrestrial life to the cause, but his very defeat is his triumph, conferring him with eternal commemoration. Comedy, by contrast, presents the indestructibility of vulgar, opportunistic, terrestrial life. This is why the ultimate comic scene is false death: the solemn funeral during which the allegedly dead awakens and asks what the hell is going on.[35]

With respect to films about the Holocaust, Žižek argues that if their vantage point cannot be "heroic sacrifice," it cannot be "opportunistic, terrestrial life" either, but only another vanishing point, beyond tragedy and comedy. It is at this juncture that he cites the concept of *homo sacer*, used, according to Giorgio Agamben, in Roman law to describe a person, stripped of all human virtues and vices, and denied all civil and spiritual rights. As an extreme state of objective worthlessness and subjective abjection, Agamben recognized the *homo sacer* in certain concentration camp prisoners known as the "Muslims," i.e. those who had given up the will to live but were still alive, who neither protested against their condition nor testified to its horror. Žižek draws from their state a conclusion also for his genre theory:

> The Muslims are so destitute they can no longer be considered "tragic": they have abandoned the minimum of dignity, reduced to the shell of a person, emptied of the spark of spirit. If we try to present them as tragic, the effect will be comic, as when one tries to read tragic dignity into a meaningless, idiotic persistence. On the other hand, though the Muslims act in a way that is usually the stuff of comedy (automatic, mindless repetitive gestures, impassive pursuit of food, etc.), if we try to present them as comic characters, the effect will be tragic, as when the spectacle of someone cruelly baiting a helpless victim (say, putting obstacles in the path of a blind person to watch him or her stumble) generates sympathy for the victim's tragic predicament instead of laughter. [...] The Muslim is the zero point at which the opposition between tragedy and comedy, between the sublime and the ridiculous, between dignity and derision is suspended, the point at which one pole directly passes into its opposite. [...] We enter the domain that is outside, or rather beneath, the elementary opposition of the dignified hierarchical structure of authority and its carnivalesque reverse, of the original and its parody, its mocking repetition. Can one imagine a film rendering this?[36]

Mimicry of Mourning, or a Sense of the Absurd Is Essential if One Wants to Stay Sober

Whether Achternbusch's film fully rises to this rhetorical challenge is not my main concern. However, *mutatis mutandis*, i.e., given the altered circumstances and the non-existent budget, The Last Hole is aware of the dilemma, and to this extent I would argue, is moving in the direction indicated by Žižek, i.e., beyond the dignified hierarchy of tragedy *and* its carnivalesque obverse, without thereby abandoning its own fundamental urgency and seriousness. Conversely, going back to Loewy's understanding of the genre, The Last Hole qualifies as a satire because it cites and parodies many of the clichés of the New German Cinema in the 1970s, when filmmakers solemnly assigned themselves the task of "mastering the past," and "representing the better Germany."[37] Achternbusch masked his own seriousness beneath knockabout farce, non-sequitur actions that at best literalized bad puns, and the self-pitying whine of a suicidal drunk, given to misogynist tirades, creating a counter-persona, played by himself. But from where does he speak, where does he take the right to make fun of every other kind of seriousness? The non-satirical part of Achternbusch's project is if anything even more problematic: for the generation born after the war, any personal experience of being victim, survivor or perpetrator will not have come from the war or genocide, neither of which they were party to. But a love affair turned ugly is well within a young person's horizon, even a relation that has all the hallmarks of being a "life-sentence"—one that is "impossible" not because of any perversity, but because of the dynamics of mutual interdependence, lived to the point where each cannot be with the other, and each cannot be without the other. Whether such a relationship—often the stuff of comedy as well as tragedy, depending on class, medium, or national temper—can serve as a template to generate an authentic mode and a viable genre, across which the German-Jewish negative symbiosis is not so much "represented" but can discover its own impossibility is questionable. It does, however, stand in sharp and deliberate contrast to the insistent call for "dialogue" in the public life of the then Federal Republic, as well as its successor, the "Berlin Republic," where the demand for dialogue has produced—ritually and habitually—mostly media-events: staged or spontaneous generational verbal wrestling matches between old (Ignaz Bubis/Martin Walser) and young (Michael Friedmann/Jürgen Möllemann), each seeing themselves as tragically misunderstood, but looking from the outside like any of the many "odd couples" of television situation comedies.[38]

THE LAST HOLE, then, is not a parody (of debates that were yet to take place) but the negatively-positively, aggressively-tenderly polarized mirror image of a particular deep structure of dependency and antagonism, of interdependence and non-communication. It accepts these asymmetric, but potentially complementary relations as given, while showing how such mutuality situates itself on separate and incommensurate levels of affect, discourse and action. Achternbusch rejects the idea of "dialogue": hence his depiction of them as nothing other than successive monologues, out of phase with each other. He scoffs at the pious hope of reconciliation, shown to be merely a temporary stalemate, brought about by attrition, weariness and exhaustion. This skepticism is bracing in its honesty, but also disheartening for the same reason. Concentrating on what he takes to be one of the most common experiences of painful and intricate "otherness," namely the solitude in the relation between sexes, he strips it of all individual psychology, and places it in a topography and a history where it echoes in powerfully suggestive, but also mysteriously alien ways. At first sight, the outcome is a bloody and cruel tale of mutually inflicted pain, of disappointment and anger, of a man searching in vain for the image of his mother, and a woman spending her nights in waiting, suffering a thousand deaths, while lending herself to other men, and, finally, a man sacrificing himself in the consuming fire of a volcano, as if to expiate for another kind of furnace. The "as if" here does not signify either allegory or any other relation of demonstrative substitution, but rather the opposite: a camouflage, an enactment which at once preserves and bodily mimics what it covers over and thereby renders invisible.

For if we read the numerous slips of the tongue, the verbal twists and absurdities in this story as mimicry of the unrepresentable, as covert forms of something that cannot manifest itself otherwise because there is no adequate language, narrative or genre for its expression, then the film's many acts of mourning an impossible love relationship can indeed, without risking a false analogy, be a mimicry, that is a "negative presence" covering for the absence of mourning those who perished in a completely different fire.

If getting drunk to drown one's sorrows is too common a cliché not to register as such, its absurd reversal as an active form of forgetting that which you are incapable of remembering with dignity and respect, then Nil's recipe for a cure is not some travesty of a guilty conscience, but precisely, a camouflage or masquerade of the absence of mourning in a situation that renders this absence a scandal. The insistence on precise measuring ("2 cl per Jew") and bureaucratic hairsplitting ("one Jew is left over") literalizes—and what is mimicry if not literalization—the inadequacy and asymmetry which so fatally flawed the counting up of "our" victims against "theirs" that once was considered normal by historians in Germany during the 1980s, when fending off demands to come clean on the issue of guilt, reconciliation and commemoration, and that has not died down since.[39]

This is one version, the one put forward in this chapter. The other would be that Achternbusch is merely reworking one of the pet themes of his work: how a man and a woman cannot live together and cannot live apart. This time, however, he would be deploying his "heteronormativity" in order to come to terms with the German-Jewish question that still haunts present-day Germany. Achternbusch is well aware of the risk, and THE LAST HOLE sets itself up for both interpretations, indeed it encourages their reversibility. Such might be the purpose of a central ambiguity around which the film explicitly pivots: is Nil disguising himself as a detective (and unhappy lover), in order to expose Nazi crimes, or does he disguise himself as a Nazi hunter (and oedipal detective), in order to find his "first love" in the "last Susn"?

"No cover, why no cover?" asks Susn, after her long-suffering despair makes her wish Nil "a little Hitler to force [him] through the chimney." But in Achternbusch's film there is plenty of cover, even for the things that are deliberately left uncovered. One could speak of mimicry and masquerade providing cover in two dimensions: "working on the relationship" as the cover-version of the (unperformed or interminable) work of mourning on German-Jewish relations, or conversely, making German-Jewish non-dialogue the performative template of working through one's love life, but now according to the victim-perpetrator scheme of the negative symbiosis.

The ambivalent instabilities of these maneuvers of mimicry and masquerade, when it comes to historical mourning work, would in turn be proof positive of how ungrounded are the grounds on which the "life-sentence" and the "after-life" of the Holocaust for Germans must manifest itself, in order to be truthful, rather than resort to another "life-lie" for self-protection, prematurely gratifying the wish for eventual redemption.

Notes

1. Taken from HADES, cited in *The Films of Herbert Achternbusch:* (http://www.xenix.ch/archiv/juni98/achtern.html).
2. Slavoj Žižek, "Camp Comedy," *Sight and Sound* (April 2000), 26–29; also available online under: http://www.bfi.org.uk/signtandsound/200_04/camp.html, 1–5.
3. See, for instance, the essays brought together in Saul Friedländer (ed.), *Probing the Limits of Representation* (Cambridge, MA: Harvard University Press, 1992).
4. For the most complete filmographic record of the Holocaust, see the website of the Fritz Bauer Institute's special research project and database "Cinematography of the Holocaust" (http://www.fritz-bauer-institut.de/cine/cine_e.htm).
5. "What is so thoroughly false is the way in which the scene between the concentration-camp commander and his Jewish kitchen help tries to render the 'mind of the Nazi'—here, the split between [erotic—T.E.] attraction and [racist—T.E.] repulsion—as his direct psychological self-experience: a deceptive 'humanization' in that it is wrong to assume that Nazi executioners experienced the contradictions of their racist attitudes in the form of psychological doubt." Žižek, "Camp Comedy," 27. Compare this to the purposely non-psychological dramatization of the contradictions entailed by the Nazi-led "Final Solution" in Frank Pierson's TV film CONSPIRACY (USA/GB 2001), which is based on the protocol of the Wannsee conference.
6. Jean Francois Lyotard's phrase is quoted in Geoffrey Hartmann, *The Longest Shadow* (Basingstoke: Palgrave Macmillan, 2002), 1, who goes on to say: "We are deep into the process of creating new instruments to record and express what happened. The instruments themselves, the means of expression are now, as it were, born of trauma."
7. Claude Lanzmann, "The Obscenity of Understanding: An Evening with Claude Lanzmann," *American Imago,* 48 (Winter 1991), 481.
8. Žižek, "Camp Comedy," 26.
9. Ibid.
10. *Cahiers du cinema,* no. 132 (April 1981), 42.
11. Hanno Loewy, "Tragische Märchen? Deutsche Generationsdramen," in Institut für Deutsche Geschichte der Universität Tel Aviv (ed.): *Tel Aviver Jahrbuch für deutsche Geschichte* (Göttingen, 2003), 311–34, and his "Fiktion und Mimesis. Holocaust und Genre im Film" in Margrit Frölich, Hanno Loewy and Heinz Steinert (eds.), *Lachen über Hitler -Auschwitzgelächter?* (Munich: text + kritik, 2003), 37–64.
12. The concept of "emplotment" is taken from Hayden White. See Hayden White, "Historical Emplotment and the Problem of Truth," in Saul Friedländer (ed.), *Probing the Limits of Representation* (Cambridge, MA: Harvard University Press, 1992), 37–53.
13. Telling examples can be found in DER VERLORENE (Peter Lorre, 1954) and DIE MÜCKE (Walter Reisch, 1955).
14. The quotation is taken from Johannes Gawert, "DAS LETZTE LOCH." in Richard Joos, Isolde Mozer, and Richard Stang (eds.), *Deutsche Geschichte ab 1945: Zwischen Vergangenheitsbewältigung und utopischen Entwürfen, Filmanalytische Materialien* (Frankfurt am Main, 1990), 32f.
15. Achternbusch has claimed that watching the opening scene of John Ford's THE GRAPES OF WRATH had made him want to make movies. Herbert Achternbusch, *Die Atlantikschwimmer* (Frankfurt: Suhrkamp, 1978), 121.
16. See, for instance, Eric Santner, *Stranded Objects: Mourning, Memory, and Film in Postwar Germany* (Ithaca: Cornell University Press, 1993).

17. This thesis was put forward by Alexander and Margarethe Mitscherlich, in their much discussed book, *The Inability to Mourn: Principles of Collective Behavior* (New York: Grove Press, 1975).
18. For a study, influenced by Mitscherlich, and broadened to encompass much of the Western world, see Christopher Lasch: *The Culture of Narcissism* (New York: Norton, 1979).
19. Michael Schneider, *Den Kopf verkehrt aufgesetzt, oder die melancholische Linke* (Darmstadt, Neuwied: Luchterhand, 1981), 8–79.
20. See Wolfgang Kraushaar, *Die Bombe im Jüdischen Gemeindehaus* (Hamburg: Hamburger Edition, 2005).
21. One can think here of the *keffiya*, the Palestinian headscarf worn as a stylish-militant accessory by many "sympathizers" in the 1970s, as well as of the *Bundeswehr*, the Federal German Army, training with the IDF, the Israeli Defence Force.
22. For more on the RAF, the German Autumn, and their reinterpretation in the 1990s, see "Antigone Agonistes. Urban Guerilla or Guerilla Urbanism" (http://www.rouge.com.au/4/antigone.html).
23. See Loewy, "Tragische Märchen?" 311–34.
24. T.W. Adorno, "Fremdwörter sind die Juden der Sprache (foreign words are the Jews of a language)," *Minima Moralia: Reflexionen aus dem beschädigten Leben (Gesammelte Schriften vol. 4)* (Frankfurt/M: Suhrkamp, 1980), 123.
25. See the chapter on IN EINEM JAHR MIT 13 MONDEN in Thomas Elsaesser, *Rainer Werner Fassbinder*. (Berlin: Bertz & Fischer, 2001), 315–46.
26. Thomas Elsaesser, "Die Gegenwärtigkeit des Holocaust im Neuen Deutschen Film," in Deutsches Filminstitut (ed.), *Die Vergangenheit in der Gegenwart. Konfrontationen mit den Folgen des Holocaust im deutschen Nachkriegsfilm*. (Frankfurt am Main: Deutsches Filminstitut, 2001), 54–67.
27. This concept is taken from Dan Diner, "*Negative Symbiosis*. Deutsche und Juden nach Auschwitz," *Babylon*, 1 (1986), 9–20.
28. Hanno Loewy has provided a similar reading of the motif of the mother in films of the 1980s and 1990s, i.e., after the heyday of the New German Cinema. About Bernhard Sinkel's VÄTER UND SÖHNE (1986), for instance, Loewy comments: "What the fable of the film pushes towards is (...) a search for the paradisiac state before the Fall—in this case: being symbiotically reunited with the mother." And about Nico Hoffmann's LAND DER VÄTER, LAND DER SÖHNE (1987), he writes: "But the mother's pangs of conscience are indispensable for the plot, in order to keep the door open for a reconciliation with the son." Finally, about Roland Suso Richter's NICHTS ALS DIE WAHRHEIT (1999), he says: "the fatherless Rohm does not find his father. But the emotional fusion with the mother ultimately reunites him also with his—pregnant—wife." Loewy, "Tragische Märchen?", 318, 320, 323.
29. Achternbusch, *Die Atlantikschwimmer*, 329.
30. The municipal beach and pool by the river Würm/Ammersee, near Achternbusch's home town of Andechs in Bavaria.
31. Achternbusch, *Die Atlantikschwimmer*, 253–54.
32. See Josef Bierbichler, Harald Martenstein, and Christoph Schlingensief (eds.), *Bensheimer Rede/Engagement und Skandal* (Berlin: Alexander Publishing House, 1998). "Was that politics? Or just theatre after all? Actor Sepp Bierbichler and journalist Harald Martenstein are looking for an answer to this question in a lengthy, meandering conversation with Christoph Schlingensief. They fail, of course. Intentionally." *Der Tagesspiegel* (July 10, 1998).
33. Loewy, "Tragische Märchen?" 313.
34. Loewy, "Fiktion und Mimesis," 62.
35. Žižek, "Camp Comedy," 2.
36. Ibid.

37. Achternbusch wrote a very caustic piece about New German Cinema directors performing as good-will ambassadors of the better Germany on the Goethe Institute circuit: "America: A Report for the Goethe Institute," *Semiotext(e): The German Issue*, IV no. 2 (1982), 6–15.
38. See chapter 3 "The Poetics and Politics of Parapraxis," for details of these debates.
39. The controversy over how to commemorate the victims of Nazism, and who were its victims came once more to the fore around the Berlin Memorial for the Murdered Jews of Europe. See Karen E. Till, *The New Berlin. Memory, Politics, Place* (Minneapolis: University of Minnesota Press, 2005).

9

REWIND AFTER REPLAY AND POSTPONEMENT IN HARUN FAROCKI'S RESPITE

il est des témoins qui ne rencontrent jamais l'audience capable de les écouter et de les entendre.[1]

Puzzled and Perplexed

In October 2006, Harun Farocki and I had almost missed each other in the Index Gallery, Stockholm, at a crowded reception in his honor after the opening of *Gegen-Musik* (*Counter Music,* 2004). In the subsequent e-mail exchange, Farocki wanted to know what I could tell him about a film made at Westerbork, the transit camp run by the SS during Nazi Occupation of the Netherlands.[2] I replied by telling him about Cherry Duyns' HET GESICHT VAN HET VERLEDEN (1994), a documentary about the camp footage shot by Rudolf Breslauer and about Aad Wagenaar's (successful) quest to identify the name of film's iconic image, known as *het meisje* (girl), also detailed in his book *Settela — het meisje heft haar naam terug* (1995, English translation, *Settela* 2005). I also sent him an essay I had published in 1996 on both Duyns' film and Wagenaar's detective work, titled *One Train May be Hiding Another.*[3]

A year later, at the Greene Naftali Gallery in New York—another opening of a Farocki installation, this time *Deep Play* (2007)—Farocki presented me with a package of DVDs, comprising a good part of his oeuvre. I was delighted and quite moved. Among the DVDs was also AUFSCHUB (RESPITE, 2007). On re-seeing this (to me, familiar) Westerbork material, and reading Farocki's "silent film" commentary, my first response was puzzlement, tinged with perplexity. No mention of Cherry Duyns' film, barely a word about Aad Wagenaar. Yet one of the crucial discoveries made by two forensic experts at the Rijksvoorlichtingsdienst (who appear in both Duyns' film and Wagenaar's book), namely the precise date of the convoy, thanks to the chalked initials and date of birth on the suitcase of the sick woman being deported on a handcart—is also a key discovery in RESPITE.[4]

The Westerbork footage is among the most familiar pieces of archival footage that the Nazis have left of their otherwise so clandestinely planned and executed deportation and destruction of Europe's Jews. It is unique in that it shows in relentless detail one particular transport of Jews to Auschwitz, wittingly or unwittingly testifying, in heartbreaking fashion, to the deception perpetrated by the Nazi and the self-deception of their victims, as those who stay behind shake hands and bid farewell to those in the trains, while other unfortunate passengers help the guards bolt the doors of their boxcars. What was less known, at least to the public outside the Netherlands, was that this much-used authentic footage of the deportation had been extracted from a considerably larger documentation of Westerbork camp life, whose origin, intent and purpose was quite different from what it now appears to be, and even contradicting the uses it has so often been put to since. These gaps and misalignments are prominent among the themes that RESPITE addresses.

Farocki is justly known for his pioneering use of found footage, from often anonymous and usually very diverse sources. He has an uncanny and extraordinary gift for establishing links and building connections that no one had thought of, or had dared to draw before.[5] By these criteria, even the extended Westerbork footage is not "found footage" and its makers are not anonymous. Nor does Farocki claim this to be the case: a prefatory intertitle establishes the basic facts of the material's provenance and putative author(s).[6] And yet the issue of appropriation, recycling and the migration of iconic images—together with the reasons for the increasing use of found footage by artists, its ethics and aesthetics—is here raised in much more complex and perplexing ways than, say, when Farocki acquired surveillance footage from Californian prisons (ICH GLAUBTE GEFANGENE ZU SEHEN/I THOUGHT I WAS SEEING CONVICTS, 2000) or featured scenes from the last interrogation of Nicolae Ceausescu and his wife before they were executed (VIDEOGRAMME EINER REVOLUTION/VIDEOGRAMS OF A REVOLUTION, 1992).

In his e-mail to me, Farocki is aware that part of the Breslauer-Gemmeker film had been used in Alain Resnais' NIGHT AND FOG, and he probably knew or learned about the findings of Sylvie Lindenperg.[7] These have further problematized a debate that Farocki was already familiar with from the reception of his own film IMAGES OF THE WORLD AND INSCRIPTION OF WAR, i.e., the ethics of using (often unattributed) visual material relating to the Holocaust, especially when these are film-sequences and photographs taken by the (German) occupiers and perpetrators or even when taken by the (American, British or Russian) liberators of the camps. In IMAGES, Farocki explicitly thematizes the dilemma of sharing an alien point of view: that of the aerial photographers of the U.S. Army, on reconnaissance mission, contrasted with the gaze of an

SS guard, on his post at the Birkenau ramp. Among the pictures the guard took that day, Farocki selects the one of a young woman, casting a brief glance in the direction of the camera, arguing that in this particular instance, part of the disconcerting fascination comes from the apparent normalcy of the "man-looking, woman-being-looked-at" situation, occurring in such extreme circumstances. When the film was first shown in the United States, feminist critics queried the "objectifying" use of the photo of the female detainee, as well as the "ventriloquizing" use of a female voice-over who speaks Farocki's commentary.[8]

Thus, one might have expected Farocki to confront the question of appropriation and the alien gaze also in RESPITE. It is particularly acute in the case of the Westerbork footage, principally for three reasons: first, one of the main points of Aad Wagenaar's book and Cherry Duyns' film was to document the misappropriation of this one particular image, that of the girl with the headscarf, in the open door of a carriage, who had become a symbol of the suffering of Dutch Jews at the hands of the Germans. In this role she had been much-used as text illustration, as book cover and poster girl from the 1960s to the 1990s. When Wagenaar established beyond doubt that "the Jewish Girl" was not Jewish but a Sinti, from Romani (gypsy) people, and that she had a name—Settela Steinbach—her function as icon of the Jewish Holocaust was jeopardized, if not altogether undermined. An image had been appropriated, for the best possible motives, but thereby unwittingly contributing to obliterating another Holocaust perpetrated by the Nazi: the genocide of the Sinti and Roma.[9]

The second reason why appropriation is a sensitive issue in this case are the essentially opposed and yet paradoxically convergent motives of he who ordered the footage to be shot (camp Commandant Arnold Gemmeker),[10] and he who shot the footage (the inmate and professional photographer Rudolf Breslauer). In the very uneven power-structure that bound these two men together—each trying to prove something, though not necessarily to each other—the loaded terms *collaboration*, *collusion* and *cooperation* take on the full tragic force which they acquired during World War II. Then, German officials enlisted Jews to administer, police or act as middlemen in the running of the ghettos and concentration camps, and even put Jews in charge of drawing up the lists of those who were to be deported on the trains headed to Auschwitz-Birkenau, Ravensbrück or Sobibor, as seems to have been the case also in Westerbork, where—Farocki draws attention to them—the *Fliegende Kolonnen* featured prominently as part of the camp's *Ordnungsdienst,* the Jewish police and administrative services responsible for almost all aspects of camp life. Who, therefore, do the images belong to, who is their "author" and through whose eyes are we looking as we watch the film?[11]

The third reason to raise the issue of appropriation is that the two-minute sequence which Resnais took from the nearly eighty minutes' worth of footage shot by Breslauer, and which he decontextualized by reediting it, adding images from another transport in Poland, has in turn been further decontextualized and anonymized. One comes across the sequence almost daily, as it is routinely inserted in television docudramas or even news bulletins every time a producer needs to evoke the deportation and the trains, and has only a few seconds to encapsulate them.[12]

Hiding Behind a Camera

These multiple layers of appropriations in the history of the Westerbork film, however, are not the primary focus of my comments here.[13] Nor was my initial perplexity caused by Farocki's omissions or possible misappropriation of previous research (filmed or otherwise) on the Breslauer-Gemmeker material. I was puzzled because, knowing Farocki's work, I assumed there must be a strategy behind his making a film that adds to our memory of the Holocaust, while doing so in a mode of "forgetting." A second viewing confirmed that RESPITE is indeed about the question of appropriation, but in a manner I had not anticipated. It is unexpected, because I think neither the ethics of appropriation, nor the aesthetics of found footage are at issue. Instead, appropriation—understood here as the transfer of knowledge, cultural memory, images or symbols from one generation to another, or as the making one's own what once belonged to another—finds itself filtered through a process of reflexive identification and self-implication. This self-implication demands that the memory of the Holocaust today not only needs to assert itself against ignorance, but also must prevail against its apparent opposite, too much knowledge. To vary a notorious saying: such memory may have to navigate between the "known knowns" (what we remember) and the "unknown knowns" (what we decide to ignore), in order to carve out the space of the "unknown unknowns" (the knowledge we might have if we neither knew what we knew, nor ignored what we knew).[14] What if RESPITE were proposing an epistemology of forgetting, that is, what if it posed the question of the kind of knowledge we can derive from no longer knowing what we think we know, and by extension, what it would mean to appropriate Breslauer's ignorance, rather than his knowledge?

Before trying to address this possibility, I need to backtrack to what it was that presumably attracted Farocki to the Westerbork material. The e-mail gives an admirably succinct clue: "double work as respite [i.e., suspension of work]." Farocki continues his examination of the ethics of work (or rather, the work ethic) of the twentieth century. The Breslauer-Gemmeker cooperation provides him with a unique —and uniquely poignant[15]—example of how work can be thought of not as production or progress, but as a delay and deferral, or *Aufschub*, as the somewhat crisper German title puts it, which means postponement as much as it is a respite. *Aufgeschoben ist nicht aufgehoben* goes a familiar phrase, to indicate that if I defer a promise or an action, it does not mean that it is cancelled. One of the pivots of the film is the idea that those who are making the film and those who perform in it are engaged in *delaying tactics*: the more they dismantle airplane parts, recycle batteries, strip electric wires and till the land (and, as Farocki was pleased to discover, the more Breslauer can film them doing so in *slow motion*), the more they can demonstrate their usefulness. And the more useful they are to the German war effort, the longer they hope to stay in the camp, while the film itself not only uses slow-motion, but in its somewhat disorganized, casual and non-linear manner also practices its own kind of deferral, trying to stave off the inevitable: the order to board next Tuesday's train.

But this inevitability is part of the knowledge gained from hindsight, not necessarily shared by the protagonists. As Farocki ventures, there might have been the notion that work in Westerbork was desirable simply because *better the devil you know*: "everyone tried to stay in Westerbork, maybe not because they knew what awaited them if they were ordered to leave for 'work-detail in the East', but because they knew that here at least, they had enough to eat."[16] Gemmeker, who made a point of treating his inmates "correctly" neither beating or verbally abusing them, had his own reasons for colluding with the decoy-and-delay exercise that Farocki thinks Breslauer was engaged in. Unlike Hans Günther, the SS officer in Prague who when commissioning Kurt Gerron to make a film in and about Theresienstadt, set out to camouflage the reality of camp life in order to deceive the Danish Red Cross,[17] Gemmeker wanted to prove to his masters in Berlin what an exemplary camp he ran, how efficiently both work and leisure were organized, and how orderly the weekly transports were dispatched. But he too, had an ulterior motive, and was anxious for a respite, indeed a reprieve: under no circumstances did he want to face the prospect of being posted to one of the death-camps in the East, generally seen as punishment among SS officers.[18]

This doubleness of motives, asynchronicity of coordinated actions and divergence of intended and unintended consequences together manage to create so many separate narrative trajectories, which nonetheless generate unexpected connections and startling intersections. It makes Respite an obvious sequel, or rather, supplement, to Farocki's best-known film to date: Images of the World and the Inscription of War (1988). Critics have taken it as such and pointed to some obvious similarities.[19] Both films, for instance, share a key date: May 1944—the month of the Allied reconnaissance flights over Auschwitz-Birkenau that play such a central role in Images; but equally the month in which Breslauer shot his film and the train departed for the selfsame destination of Auschwitz. Also, Images brings together two sets of photographs from apparently different contexts: one the U.S. reconnaissance photos, kept for decades in a bureaucratic filing cabinet; the other the trophy photos of an SS guard, kept in the so-called Auschwitz Album, retrieved by accident and also made public only decades later. One set are technical images taken from above—too far and following a grid, through which fell unnoticed the human beings lining up to be killed. The other set of photos are sentimental keepsakes, taken from ground-level, too close to register the enormity, because they frame views intended for an album of souvenirs (i.e., future memories), and therefore unframed by any moral concern for the here-and-now of context and situation. Each set documents—in spite of itself—that which it did not set out to show: the "known unknowns" of retrospection. In RESPITE, even though the images belong to one location and one event, the intention and execution, as it were, are also at variance with each other: the very efficiency of the organization that Gemmeker wanted to present to Berlin is undercut by Breslauer's meandering and impressionistic footage. While never presented to the gaze of the Big Other in Berlin, the film (which remained unfinished and unscreened) nonetheless "reached its destination,"[20] and did serve as a document, thereby redeeming its creator and indicting its instigator. Only when Alain Resnais took charge of the editing, and produced the sequence now so often shown, did one see the relentless and incriminating ruthlessness of the transports. It brought out Gemmeker's optical unconscious, as it were, more directly than Breslauer's no doubt, but in the process, it made the Commandant, who all along claimed ignorance of the fate his charges were headed to, condemn himself through his own vanity: "Why did the German camp command even think of making the film? Did they not realize that especially the scenes of the transports would reinforce the abominable image of the system which they served?" After the war the film was used as evidence during the trial against Gemmeker; "it was evidence that the Nazi themselves had created."[21]

Finally, both films feature a highly transgressive image: that of a woman, looking at the camera, returning the look. In RESPITE, Farocki, faced with the face of *het meisje*, speculates that Breslauer avoided close-ups of the people getting into the trains, out of respect for the victim's dignity. This is almost as if he was responding to the accusation, already mentioned, voiced about the young woman's face in IMAGES being violated by the camera's close up. There, Farocki's hands frame the shot, isolating her gaze, while the voice-over wonders what this gaze might speak of: a woman, aware of her beauty, catching sight for an instance of a man looking at her, stepping out of time and place into an eternal presence, while the other prisoners recede that much further into oblivion and anonymity.

The shot of Farocki's hands framing the shot has itself become iconic—reproduced on book covers, and making up the DVD-sleeve. Might it be, like the door shutting on *het meisje*, that the hands preserve the sense of presence while also distancing the face, poised and pictured in the moment where imminent death is the condition for the most palpable evidence of life? To me, this framing gesture now suggests also another association: it rhymes with a remark Farocki made many years later, in Montreal, at a conference in October 2007, when, after Philippe Despoix's presentation, the filmmaker commented on an ad for cameras from 1940–41, which suggested that *Wehrmacht* soldiers should carry one with them to the front, because it would protect them from bullets. Yes, Farocki said, that is actually true, behind a camera I do feel strangely invulnerable.[22] An odd sort of relay began to open up for me: perhaps Rudolf Breslauer felt that putting himself behind a camera in the camp gave him, too, some kind of invulnerability or protection from being devoured by the machinery of death;[23] and that Farocki, in turn, had put himself behind the camera of Breslauer, appropriating his predecessor's eye by respecting the (dis-)order of the material, rather than reediting it (as Resnais had done). In an act part-homage and part-critique, RESPITE imagines what it must have been like to look at the camp at that moment in time, without the knowledge that hindsight (and scholarly, commemorative or forensic research) had conferred on it since. Found footage filmmaking as recycling is "refound" footage, in Freud's sense of the word,[24] and here mirrors, in *mise en abyme* fashion, the recycling which is documented in the film itself, both serving as delaying tactic: for does not *doppelte Arbeit als Aufschub* (double work as deferral) also name and therefore implicate Farocki himself and his method? He too wants to postpone the inevitable—the knowledge of the Holocaust that came after.

Action Replay: The Dead Demand a Rewind

This special reflexive implication in the subjects of his films had always struck me as one of the outstanding virtues of Farocki's filmmaking.[25] His guiding principle of the *Verbund* (lit: interconnected network) is based on feedback and mutual interdependence, initially born out of economic necessity, he once explained, as much as derived from his own work ethics and politics.[26] While thinking further about the link between appropriation and self-implication in RESPITE, I remembered an interview I had done with Farocki in London in 1993, where he mentioned his astonishment that IMAGES OF THE WORLD had, as he put it, "returned to him a different film" from the one he thought he had made. It went out as BILDER DER WELT UND INSCHRIFT DES KRIEGES, which would have been Pictures of the World, and it came back as Images of the World. More surprising still, his film was against nuclear energy and about the need to resist, if necessary by direct action, the stationing of atomic weapons on German soil (the controversial NATO-Pershing II missiles); yet IMAGES OF THE WORLD came back—mainly from U.S. university campuses and festivals—as a film about Auschwitz, about smart weapons and war and cinema.[27] This points to another parallel that links (the reception of) IMAGES to (the production of) RESPITE: Breslauer and Gemmeker also thought they were making one kind of film, but their material has come down to us with quite a different kind of meaning. Farocki, in other words, has been subject to appropriation himself, however beneficial this one might have been to his reputation and subsequent career, and it is therefore plausible to see RESPITE advancing (my first impressions to the contrary) quite a profound and personal reflection on repetition-with-a difference as well as on the intended, unintended—indeed, the parapractic—consequences of replay.

This would go some way towards explaining the very particular form that recycling, repetition and replay take in *Respite*, namely that of a *rewind*. Originally a term used to describe the mechanical action of reversing the direction of a roll of magnetic tape or a spool of film, it has (perhaps in direct proportion to its technical obsolescence) taken on metaphoric connotations, meaning the ability to return to an earlier point in time or to a *status quo ante*, in order to proceed, through repetition, on a slightly different path, be it to make something undone, to efface an unwelcome outcome or to start all over again. My argument would be that Farocki, by making a deliberate decision not to edit (nor to editorialize with a voice-over), rewinds the historical footage for us, both metaphorically and literally: we might imagine that we are seeing the scenes as if for the first time (the trope of discovery of something buried in the archive) or we might assume that they finally unwind in the spatio-temporal order that Breslauer shot or scripted them, with Farocki adding a minimum of factual information through the intertitles. But then there is a second, literal rewind: he replays several scenes, now with commentaries that are heavy with the burden of hindsight knowledge: The white coats in the camp's infirmary recall the gruesome experiments of a Mengele, the stripping of the copper wires anticipate the mountains of female hair, and the inmates taking their lunch break in the grass, resting from working the fields, remind us of the sprawled emaciated bodies piled in heaps, before bulldozers tip them into mass graves. The effect is to shock us into a double-take: RESPITE is not (yet another film) about the Holocaust; it is about our knowledge of the images of the Holocaust, and how the memory of this knowledge (and of these images) has forever altered our sense of temporality and causality, and thus how we see an image from the archive. This would be the best reason why Farocki appears to suspend the previous histories of the Westerbork footage.

The dilemma of the Holocaust film, whether fictional or documentary, is that hindsight knowledge inflects our response and all but preprograms our interest. The narrative arcs are pretty well determined in advance: either the storyline is that of a journey into the heart of darkness, meant to discover yet another hidden secret, to pull the mask from ordinary men (or women: THE READER, 2008) and reveal the banality of evil (HOTEL TERMINUS, 1988); or it takes the form of a quest for redemption and atonement (SCHINDLER'S LIST, 1993), even one where self-deception and fantasy are the saving graces of an inescapable fate (LA VITA E BELLA, 1997). Such closures come at a price: not only are the Jews depicted as passive victims, deprived of agency, but the known outcome also makes for passive spectators, shifting their attention to the "how" more than the "why." The typical pathos of melodrama—that recognition always comes too late—is accentuated by the response we normally associate with another genre: in the Holocaust film, we want to warn the protagonists, as in the horror movie, and shout "watch out, you're in imminent danger, turn around, the monster is right behind you." This is especially palpable a feeling one has with the train sequence that has made the Westerbork material famous, but our stifled shouts would never reach them, and our knowledge will forever be of no use to them.

Farocki's counter-strategy, as I see it, is to try and return some of this knowledge (in both its expectations and anticipations) to a point-zero: hence the rewind. Not to erase the knowledge or even to wish it undone (the desperate emotion of melodrama), but to give our train-of-thought another direction. For this he has to take a further step; instead of melodrama (the pathos of "if only they knew"), the thriller (the suspense of superior knowledge) or the horror film (the agony of anticipated, but inevitable disaster) he foregrounds an altogether different genre, that of the industrial film. It is a bold move, fraught with its own kinds of pitfall. First, RESPITE resembles the industrial film in its subject matter: it shows the transit camp organized like a factory, and Farocki makes much of Westerbork's unique camp logo, with its factory chimney and barracks set in a circular frame. As we saw, this is part of the intention of the original footage, one where Breslauer and Gemmeker's objectives converged. The medical, recreational and educational facilities grouped around the production site are furthermore modeled on well-known experiments in planned work/life communities, implemented in such company towns as Eindhoven in the Netherlands (Philips), Zlin in the Czech Republic (Bata) or Wolfsburg in Germany (VW). Second, the industrial film (one of the oldest genres of the cinema) has a clear trajectory: it progresses by separate steps and consecutive processes from raw materials to finished product (progress through process). While Gemmeker's *Westerbork camp* prided itself on processing almost 100.000 internees from West to East (graphically represented with arrows going from left to right on a chart drawn up for Gemmeker and filmed by Breslauer), the *Westerbork* film wanted to demonstrate that it was productively useful, this time not by making finished products, but by recycling redundant products and turning them back into raw materials. In other words, this was an industrial film in reverse, a rewind—reminiscent of one of the earliest rewinds in film history,[28] but also a devastating representation on the part of the camp inmates of themselves as useful waste, and another reflexive self-implication on the part of Farocki's film, whose condition of possibility is the very *mise en abyme* of the different kinds of recycling thus instantiated. Which brings me to the third high-wire moment: the argumentative schema of an industrial film in reverse unsettles the conventional narrative of the Holocaust film, but at the same time reinforces it at another level, confirming our other knowledge about the camps, i.e., that they were deliberately or cynically organized according to industrial principles, whose raw materials were living human beings, either worked to death or treated as organic matter to be processed for profit. Our hindsight (and Farocki's) necessarily "sees" in the metaphoric chimney of the Westerbork logo the all too real chimneys of the crematoria in Auschwitz, Gross-Rosen or Majdanek.

If fraught with pitfalls, the explicit references to the industrial film also yield unexpected possibilities: Farocki's minimal *Verfremdung* (lit: estrangement) of the material, thanks to (in this instance) an especially poignant genre, returns us to another point zero. Because of the particular logics of the rewind just indicated, one is poised on the tip of several reversals, potentially liberated from the passive position of merely being spectators of the inevitable (those arrows pointing left to right). From this new point zero, the Westerbork footage reveals yet another side, another hindsight, that of the genre which most likely was on Breslauer's mind, along with the industrial film, when he set up his scenes. The memory of the *Russenfilme* haunts the Westerbork footage, not in form or technique (we shall never know how Breslauer would have edited the material, nor what Gemmeker would have made of it), but in the idealizing pathos of collective work, communal living and the tilling of the soil. Images from Eisenstein, Pudovkin or Vertov emerge like watermarks into visibility, adding one more to the film's several kinds of optical unconscious, to counter the optical unconscious of the industrial organization of murder, already alluded to. Relativizing not the reality of the camp but *historicizing* its images, Farocki prompts us to a revision and a rethink of what has so far prevented the majority of the footage to be shown: namely that these scenes of everyday life, of sports and recreation either did not fit the conventionalized Holocaust narrative or seemed too unbearably ironic in their innocence and ignorance. The rewind restores ignorance and preserves innocence of another kind in that it suggests that the camp's activities can be seen as *heroic*: through documenting moments of normalcy that the inmates were able to wrest from their fate. In fact, they testify to the determination to live and organize one's life—one's conduct and one's manners—in a dignified way, even in circumstances that are anything but normal, dignified or civilized.

An Epistemology of Forgetting?

Paul Ricoeur—echoing here the historiography of Jules Michelet—once argued that part of the duties of the historian is not only to let the dead render their testimony, but to give back to the past its own future: "*Pris dans une dialectique de l'arché et du télos, le régime d'historicité est tout entier traversé par la tension entre espace d'expérience et horizon d'attente.*"[29] [Caught in the dialectic between arche and telos, the regime of historicity is entirely traversed by the tension between the space of experience and the horizon of expectation.]

To give back to the past its own future may have been the challenge that Farocki faced in RESPITE, and for which he had to find the appropriate aesthetic form. The problem is not so much hindsight knowledge per se (how can we not view the past from the present?), but that in this instance, and after more than three decades of Germany's intense preoccupation with its recent history, we think we know too much about the Holocaust. It forecloses the possibility of new knowledge (other than in the genres of discovery, pathos and irony discussed above), and thus invites the very forgetting that Holocaust memorialization is meant to prevent. The danger is that there seems nothing to learn other than the misleadingly tautologous mantra "never again": tautologous because the past will not repeat itself and misleading because the "concentrationary" mindset is still very much with us.[30] Hence the pedagogic value of repeating the past by way of RESPITE's rewind and replay. Farocki tries to locate the points where the past may have had—within its present—also a future, one that is not necessarily our present. Such efforts of the moral imagination may be dismissed as counterfactual history,[31] but this is precisely where Farocki's politics of minimal interference pays maximum dividends: instead of indulging in the what-if's of alternative universes, his splicing of black leader and spacing of laconic intertitles creates the necessary gaps—*the respites*—into which spectators may insert their own Holocaust memories, be they media images, film narratives, history books or civic lessons.

Farocki's gaps, in other words, engender a kind of forgetting that should not or need not be filled with more evidence or forensic investigation. If the internees' respites are meant to delay and defer the relentless logic of the weekly transports, the filmmaker's respites are meant to forestall the relentless logic of automatically attributed meaning, in the belief that such lapses or gaps of recall may make room for the accidental and the unexpected, in the very midst of such murderous causality and consequentiality. Forgetting, in the sense of *Ausblendung des Vorwissens* (screening out preexisting knowledge) would thus be neither an attempt at becoming innocent nor a slide into denial and disavowal, but might carve out that impossibly possible space between the "known knowns" (of historical scholarship) and the "known unknowns" (of future research), but also intervene between the "unknown knowns (of what we prefer to ignore) and the "unknown unknowns" (of what this past might one day mean for us).

RESPITE thus returns to the Westerbork past not exactly its future (cruelly taken from so many thousands of human beings), but its lacunary present, creating out of Breslauer's images and Gemmeker's narrative a history with holes, so to speak—once more open, without being open-ended. Into the claustrophic world of Holocaust memory, he cuts the breathing room that reinvests the history of Westerbork with the degrees of contingency and necessity, of improbability and unintended consequences, that serve as a counter-music to the relentlessness of the destruction machine that the extracted footage of the transports has so vividly bequeathed to us. No mean feat, if we think about it, not least because achieved with so little intervention, yielding a kind of knowledge that only a certain courage of forgetting can give us.

Notes

1. "There are witnesses who will never encounter an audience able to listen to them and to understand." Paul Ricoeur, *La Memoire, l'histoire, l'oubli* (Paris: Le Seuil, 2000), 208.2. "Noch etwas: kennst Du zufällig jemanden, der über den Film ‚Westerbork' gearbeitet hat? Wahrscheinlich weißt Du das: so wie der Film über Theresienstadt wurde auch dieser von einem Deportierten aufgenommen. Eine recht lange Sequenz kommt in ‚Nuit et bruillard' schon vor. Ich denke, etwas dazu zu machen. In dem Film, der aus ziemlich rohem Material besteht, wird sehr ausführlich die Arbeit gezeigt, die die Häftlinge machen. Es heißt, jeder versuchte, in W. zu bleiben, vielleicht nicht, weil bekannt war, was es bedeutete, von dort ‚zu einem Arbeitseinsatz im Osten' abfahren zu müssen, sondern nur, weil es dort zu essen gab. Die dort arbeiten, versuchen den Eindruck zu erwecken, sie täten etwas wichtiges (‚Kriegswichtig') und der Film selbst ist auch umständlich, um die Gegenwart auszudehnen. Doppelte Arbeit als Aufschub." Harun Farocki, conversation with author, September 10, 2006.
2. "Noch etwas: kennst Du zufällig jemanden, der über den Film "Westerbork" gearbeitet hat? Wahrscheinlich weisst Du das: so wie der Film über Theresienstadt wurde auch dieser von einem Deportierten aufgenommen Harun Farocki, e-mail exchange with author, September 10, 2006.
3. http://www.latrobe.edu.au/screeningthepast/classics/rr0499/terr6b.htm
4. A review, reproduced on Farocki's website, erroneously credits him with the discovery: "The surviving, mostly unedited footage and Farocki's silent intertitle commentary is ambiguous despite the simplicity of content and the surprising specificity of the filmmaker's research — from a barely visible stamp on a suitcase the titles identify not only the person in the image, but the specific date the footage was taken as well as the woman's place and date of death." *Film*, no. 101 (http://www.farocki-film.de/).
5. "Harun Farocki has used found footage in innovative ways throughout his career challenging dominant political perspectives with a simple common sense approach to the world. His films are sometimes almost untouched appropriations and others deeply nuanced assemblages that find incredible connections between disparate source materials. He is a humane, empathetic and serious found footage filmmaker who unlike his colleagues has created uncynical films that speak truth to power without being self-righteous." (http://recycledcinema.blogspot.com/2008/01/harun-farocki-politics-of-found-footage.html)
6. In a later e-mail message, Farocki mentions a brochure he bought at the Westerbork memorial site. This must have been Koert Broersma and Gerard Rossing, *Kamp Westerbork gefilmd — Het verhaal over een unieke film uit 1944* (Herinneringscentrum Kamp Westerbork/Van Gorcum, 1997).
7. Sylvie Lindenperg, "Filmische Verwendungen von Geschichte Historische Verwendungen des Films," in Eva Hohenberger and Judith Keilbach (eds.), *Die Gegenwart der Vergangenheit. Dokumentarfilm, Fernsehen und Geschichte* (Berlin: Verlag Worwerk 8, 2003). Part of her work on NIGHT AND FOG was first published in "*Nuit et Brouillard* , récit d'un tournage," revue *Histoire*, no. 294 (Janvier 2005) and subsequently published in book form *Nuit et Brouillard*: *Un Film dans l'Histoire* (Paris: Odile Jacob, 2007). Lindenperg is able to identify the different interpolations made by Resnais, as well as how he edited the Westerbork footage.
8. See Nora Alter, "The Political Im/perceiptible," in Thomas Elsasser, *Harun Farocki*

Working on the Sight-Lines (Amsterdam: Amsterdam University Press, 2005), 219 and footnote 27. Kaja Silverman, also commenting on this critique, mounts a spirited defense of Farocki's procedure in "What is a Camera," *Discourse,* 15 (Spring 1993), 39–42.

9. Cherry Duyns film was shown at the International Documentary Film Festival in November 1999, in a special program *The Memory of the 20th Century.* "Take *Settela, face the past,* a VPRO documentary by Cherry Duyns 1994. In this film Duyns follows the journalist Aad Wagenaar, who went in search of the identity of the girl with the white scarf in a railway carriage, fixed forever the moment the train left Westerbork. The anonymous girl became the symbol of all the Dutch Jews who from Westerbork were sent to the German death camps. A closer analysis of the film where the image comes from, however, shows that in the train in question, it was Gypsies who were transported. The girl suddenly has a name and Duyns visits survivors who know her from the prewar gypsy community in Limburg. Is it not a shame that the myth is gone, now that the girl has been identified, asks Duyns at the end of his film? A little bit, Wagenaar confirms, but the image remains an indictment. Indeed, thanks to the debunking by Wagenaar and Duyns the image of the girl with the headscarf has been strengthened rather than weakened." Mark Duursma, "Versleten beelden niew leven inblazen," *NRC Handelsblad,* November 18, 1999.
10. On the camp commandant Albert Konrad Gemmeker (Düsseldorf 1907–1982), see http://www.cympm.com/agemmeker.html. On Rudolf Breslauer (Munich 1904–Auschwitz 1944) see http://nl.wikipedia.org/wiki/Rudolf_Breslauer.
11. The literature on the dilemmas of the *Judenräte* and Jewish *Ordnungdienste* is extensive, but—from an ethical point—still inconclusive. See David H. Jones, *Moral responsibility in the Holocaust: A Study in the Ethics of Character* (Lanham. MD: Rowman & Littlefield, 1999). For a summary of the debates about the ownership of the gaze of the photographic records that has come down to us of WW II atrocities and genocide, see Marianne Hirsch, "Surviving Images: Holocaust Photographs and the Work of Postmemory," *The Yale Journal of Criticism,* 14, no. 1 (Spring 2001), 5–37, Susie Linfield, *Boston Review* (September/October, 2005), http://bostonreview.net/BR30.5/linfield.php, and—about a single image—Richard Raskin, *A Child at Gunpoint: A Case Study in the Life of a Photo* (Aarhus, Denmark: Aarhus University Press, 2004).
12. "The Westerbork film is the only realistic depiction of life in the camps from WWII, and that is why it is being used in innumerable documentaries all over the world." Mark Duursma, "Versleten beelden niew leven inblazen." On April 9, 2000, the Dutch television channel VPRO devoted a special programme of *Andere Tijden* to Gemmeker, under the title "De vorige commandant trapte de joden naar Polen, deze lacht ze naar Polen (The previous commandant kicked the Jews to Poland, this one laughs them to Poland)." Besides extracts from the Breslauer film, an extensive website gives further information about the Commandant and his life (http://geschiedenis.vpro.nl/programmas/2899536/afleveringen/2882332/items/2882397/).
13. In addition to *One Train May Be Hiding Another,* I touch on the fate of these Westerbork images in chapter 5 of this volume (first published in German as "Vergebliche Rettung: Geschichte als Palimpsest," in Michael Wedel and Elke Schieber (eds.), *Konrad Wolf— Werk und Wirkung* (Berlin: Vistas Verlag, 2009), 73–92, and "Migration und Motiv: das parapraktische Gedächtnis eines Bildes," in Peter Geimer and Michael Hagner (eds.), *Nachleben und Rekonstruktion: Vergangenheit im Bild* (Munich: Wilhelm Fink, 2012), 159–76.
14. I am here appropriating the much-quoted pronouncement made by U.S. Defense Secretary Donald Rumsfeld at a press briefing on February 12, 2002, but I refrain from adding Slavoj Zizek's "known unknowns"—"the knowledge that doesn't know itself"—although these, too, may have a role to play (http://www.lacan.com/zizek-rumsfeld.htm).

15. Especially if one remembers *Arbeit macht frei* (Work makes you free), the wrought-iron phrase over the gates of Auschwitz and other concentration camps (http://en.wikipedia.org/wiki/Arbeit_macht_frei).
16. H. Farocki, e-mail, cited in note 6.
17. For a detailed account of the background and making of "Theresienstadt —Ein Dokumentarfilm aus dem jüdischen Siedlungsgebiet," see Karel Magny, "Das Konzentrationslager als Idylle," *Cinematographie des Holocaust*, Fritz Bauer Institut, Frankfurt (http://www.cine-holocaust.de/mat/fbw000812dmat.html).
18. "One theory is that Gemmeker commissioned the film in order to impress his superiors and avoid being transferred to the Eastern Front. More generally, it is assumed that Geemmeker tried to persuade his Berlin bosses that Westerbork could make a significant contribution to the German war effort. To that extent, the industrial interest in the camp coincided with the camp commandant's own personal interest. As long as Westerbork maintained the image of being 'Kriegswichtig' for the German war machine, Gemmerker could save his bacon." Han van Bessel, "Onvergetelijke filmbeelden," *de Volkskrant*, April 25, 1997. The first historical research on Gemmeker and Breslauer's film can be found in one of the standard works of Dutch historiography, Jacques Presser, *De Ondergang* (The Hague: Staatsuitgeverij & Nijhoff, 1965), 328–32.
19. See Sylvie Lindenperg, "Respite: vies en sursis, images revenants," *Trafic,* 70 (Summer 2009) and Philippe Despoix, "Travail/sursis — delai sans remission," *Intermédialités*, 11 (Spring 2008), 89–94.
20. I am here alluding to Jacques Lacan's seminar on Edgar Allan Poe's *The Purloined Letter,* translated by Jeffrey Mehlman and published in *French Freud, Yale French Studies*, 48 (1972), 38–72.
21. In the original: "waarom heeft de Duitse kampleiding de film überhaupt laten maken? 'Besefte deze niet dat vooral de scènes van de transporten het gruwelijke beeld van het systeem dat zij dienden, zouden versterken?' De film werd na de oorlog gebruikt als bewijsmateriaal tijdens het proces tegen Gemmeker; 'het was bewijsmateriaal dat de nazi's zélf hadden gecreëerd.'" "Why did the German camp authorities allow the film to be made at all?" Broersma and Rossing, quoted in Han van Bessel, "Onvergetelijke filmbeelden."
22. Farocki repeated the remark in an interview given to Hors Champs: "Harun Farocki: Hier, à la conférence, Philippe Despoix nous a montré cette réclame allemande des années 40-41, qui expliquait que l'appareil photographique pouvait vous protéger sur le front. Achetez une caméra, et vous serez protégé des balles ! Et bien entendu, c'est en grande partie vrai. J'ai connu cette expérience. Nous étions une fois dans un zoo, et nous filmions un tigre, non pas un tigre en cage, mais en liberté. Derrière la caméra, vous n'aviez plus peur!" André Habib and Pavel Pavlov, "D'une image à l'autre: Conversation avec Harun Farocki," *Hors champs*, December 20, 2007 (http://www.horschamp.qc.ca/CONVERSATION-AVEC-HARUN-FAROCKI.html?var_recherche=Harun%20 Farocki)
23. Breslauer's position behind the camera was a tragically illusory invulnerability, as he was to be one of the last deportees, sent to Auschwitz by Gemmeker in September 1944, barely four months after he shot the film. For additional information and an extract from the Westerbork film on the Internet, see http://www.auschwitz.nl/paviljoen/deportatie/westerbork-1942-1944/breslauer.
24. According to Sigmund Freud, "Every finding of an object is in fact a re-finding of it." "Three Essays on the Theory of Sexuality and other Writings (1901–1905)," *Standard Edition vol.7* (London: Hogarth Press, 1953), 222.
25. "Farocki takes up a subject only when it can be presented as a *mise en abyme* of the world, mirrored in his own work: as a feedback system, in other words, but asymmetrical and asynchronous, rather than closed and self-regulating. [...] His films have moral authority and aesthetic credibility only to the extent that their reflexivity cuts

both ways: that it is directed also at the director himself, and that the feedback loop must implicate the artist, [creating] moments that re-instate the eye and the hand as instances of self-implication and solidarity. The true topicality and urgency of Farocki's work may thus be nothing less than that it is an effort to rescue the cinema from its own dialectic of memory and forgetting, of nostalgic evocation of lost reference and modernist self-reflexivity." Thomas Elsaesser "The Future of Art and Work in the Age of Vision Machines: Harun Farocki," in R. Halle and R. Steingröver (eds.), *After the Avantgarde — Contemporary German and Austrian Experimental Film* (Rochester: Camden House, 2008), 47–48.

26. Harun Farocki, "Notwendige Abwechslung und Vielfalt," in *Filmkritik*, no. 224 (August 1975), 360–69. On self-implication and the idea of *Verbund*, see Thomas Elsasser, "HF — Filmmaker, Artist, Media Theorist," in Elsasser, *Harun Farocki*, 32–36.
27. "Making the World Superfluous," in Elsasser, *Harun Farocki*, 185. What had intervened between the making of the film, which took several years, and its reception by a wider public, was the end of the Cold War, and the fall of the Berlin Wall; the atomic threat receded, just as "Auschwitz" returned as an abiding preoccupation of the next decade. The film opened in the United States almost simultaneously with the first Gulf War, which gave the film an additional topical relevance and the conflict a historical depth, neither of which the filmmaker could have anticipated, but which henceforth belong to the film.
28. The Lumiere Brothers *Demolition of a Wall* (1896) was habitually shown twice, first forward and then in reverse, with the wall once more rising from its own rubble. See http://www.docsonline.tv/Archives/description.php?doc=260.
29. Paul Ricoeur, *Du texte à l'action* (Paris: Le Seuil, 1986), 391. Ricoeur is here echoing Rainer Kossellek, and his notion that memory is always constituted by the tension between an *Erlebnisraum* (space of experience) and an *Erwartungshorizont* (horizon of expectations).
30. See, for instance, Zygmunt Baumann, *Wasted Lives: Modernity and its Outcasts* (Cambridge, MA: Polity, 2004).
31. For an argument of the positive uses of counterfactual history, see Niall Ferguson (ed.), *Virtual History — Alternatives and Counterfactuals* (London: Picador, 1977).

PART III

Trauma Theory Reconsidered

10

FROM MASTERING THE PAST TO MANAGING GUILT

Holocaust Memory in the New Century

Identity Politics and Memory: Equal Opportunity Victimhood?

As early as 1993, the historian James E. Young raised the question, whether "without the wall as a punitive reminder, Germany will become a little more like other nations." He went so far as to predict that "Germany's national institutions will recall primarily its own martyrs and triumphs" rather than continue to dwell on the dark side of its history.[1] Young was only partly correct in this assessment, since unified Germany is as much in thrall to the memory of the Nazi period as it was two or three decades ago. But he was right insofar as in the new century Germany has entered into a different "memory regime," even if the reasons go beyond unification, and the changes occurred with a certain time lag. By now sufficient evidence exists for there to be talk of a "paradigm change," pithily summarized in the phrase that a "perpetrator people" had mutated into a "victim nation."[2] The social historian Harald Welzer quotes Günter Grass' first person narrator in *Im Krebsgang* (2002, 32) to hint at one reason for this change: "In all the years," Grass' narrator Paul Pokriefke muses, "when, as a freelancer I wrote longish articles for Nature journals about biodynamic vegetable gardens and the environmental damage done to German forests, not forgetting confessional tracts about "never again Auschwitz," I managed to stay mum about the circumstances of my birth," from which Welzer concludes that Grass is recasting the original trauma of Germany's post-war society from "doing" (perpetrator) to "being done to" (victim), from "agency" to "suffering," from "other" to "self," and thus to "announce a paradigm change in the Federal Republic's memory culture that hitherto was defined, precisely, by "never again Auschwitz."[3] Grass' "circumstances of my birth." in other words, are Young's "Germany, recalling its own martyrs."

Welzer worries about this paradigm change and tries to explain the reversal from victim to perpetrator in several ways, while commentators abroad doubted that the mutations in the memory discourse of post-war Germany could be summed up so neatly.[4] I shall pick out three of the broader symptomatic fields for further comment, and offer the conclusion that rather than constituting a paradigm change, the shifts bring to the fore underlying ambivalences around perpetrators, accomplices and victims, about guilt, accountability and atonement that have been present in *mastering the past* throughout the period since 1945. These ambivalences among Germans regarding the Nazi past ranged from feigned ignorance to piqued resentment and outright denial, besides shock and shame, active remorse and listless regret. They can, however, in the twenty-first century, be seen in a new context: not only, as argued in an earlier chapter, moving from feeling victimized (1945-1960), to accepting their role of perpetrators (1977–1990) before once more ranging themselves alongside the victims (since the mid-1990s), but as persistent attempts at "guilt management" (rather than trauma), which assumes its most appropriate, because "manageable" expression either through melodramatic or what I call parapractic modes of (artistic) representation and (public) discourse. This, at any rate, is the thesis of the present chapter.

The conjunctions affecting the memory discourse of mastering the past as guilt management place the German predicament in a wider context. Especially relevant are first, the perception and self-representation of Jews in Germany "after Auschwitz"; second, the status of the Holocaust not just in German history, but in European memory, and third, a general tendency to consider victimhood a desirable subject position. They form concentric circles, as it were, from Germany to Europe to the Western world, an in this sense, the three circles overlap, compete and interfere with each other. But from a German perspective, they also underline the extent to which both internal events and external circumstances acted as triggers. Few, if any of these events are directly traceable to the cinema. They resonate in literature, in the press, and most often on television, which in matters of memory discourse seems to have taken over from cinema. My argument, however, will be that especially in German cinema—and this throughout the whole post-war period—there are traces and echoes that cast a more nuanced light on the larger contexts, as well as on the different periods of German post-war film history, because of the typical rhetorical and stylistic resources deployed for this guilt management: on one side, the tropes of melodrama and on the other what in previous chapters I have identified as the poetic of parapraxis. This chapter concentrates on the different aspects of excess, some associated with melodrama, and the many ways that guilt feelings find themselves both activated and assuaged by formal structures of balance and equivalence.

Elsewhere I mentioned how it was Fassbinder's play *Der Müll, die Stadt und der Tod* and the protests against its staging in Frankfurt in 1985 that greatly strengthened the self-empowerment of the Jewish minority, which previously had preferred to keep a low profile.[5] A new generation, and the changing politics in the Middle East, where the rise of Palestinian militancy resulted in a divided response from the German left—oscillating between pro-Palestinian sentiment and anti-Zionism bordering on anti-Semitism—had thrust the small Jewish community in West Germany into the limelight, and in the process, had also brought to the fore some potent as well as self-confident voices, speaking on behalf of this constituency, including, for example, Daniel Cohn-Bendit, one of the leaders of May 68 in Paris and a prominent representative of the anti-authoritarian movement in Germany in the 1970s, before becoming a French Euro-MP in the 1990s; Henryk Broder, a publicist and satirist, and Michael Friedmann, the far from uncontroversial lawyer and television personality. As Jews born after the war, they did much, in their very different ways, to make the Jewish voice a recognized element in the German discourse without it being any less German for it.

By the time their presence had established itself, however, the particular past to which they necessarily referred themselves, had also undergone significant changes. Ever since the broadcast of the television series of the same name, and the enormous public response provoked by it, the term *Holocaust* entered the German language. Its path to institutionalization as an integral part of German history that all Germans had to acknowledge and make themselves accountable for was confirmed by a celebrated speech given by the then Federal President Richard von Weizsäcker on May 8, 1985, marking the fortieth anniversary of German capitulation and the end of World War II, in which he asserted that "the forefathers [of today's Germans] have left a grave legacy. All of us, whether guilty or not, whether old or young, must accept the past. We are all affected by its consequences and liable for it. The young and old generations must and can help each other to understand why it is vital to keep alive the memories."[6]

The speech paved the way for "Holocaust memory" to replace the awkward question that had accompanied May 8 for the previous forty years: was it the day of defeat, or the day of liberation? Weizsäcker left no doubt that is was the latter, and so—even preceding unification—the moral compass of Germans mastering the past had been set on a different course. Although this change of course can be summarized and discussed (as it was in a previous chapter) under the general heading of an "institutionalization" of Holocaust memory, it is worth pointing out that it had distinct components: *memorialization* (commemorative dates and occasions, sites of memory in almost every city, *Stolpersteine*, i.e., brass cobble-stones with the names of deported or forcibly evicted Jewish occupants outside houses),[7] *monumentalization* (e.g., the Berlin memorial, the rebuilding of synagogues and restoration of Jewish cemeteries), *nationalization* (each country had to give more detailed account about occupation, collaboration, persecution of Jews and other minorities) and *transnationalization* (to make accountability for and commemoration of the Holocaust a common project among European institutions in their respective task of forging a transnational, European identity).

These developments also raise a question, pertaining to the cinema: why did the *presence* of Jews in the German post-unification imaginary after 1990 raise as many issues as their *absence* did in the 1960s and 1970s, i.e., two or three decades before? One answer is that the political and religious presence of Germans as Jews in the public sphere led to a situation that challenged, explicitly or implicitly, the special status that the fate of the Jews had acquired based on the uniqueness of the Holocaust as a genocide targeting an entire race. The special status, in turn, had repercussions of how Germans saw themselves within a European community whose cultural identity gravitated towards making the Holocaust its foundational event. In this process, Germany took the lead, assuming some kind of exclusivity, of which—paradoxically—the crimes committed against the Jews (and their publicly prescribed acknowledgement) became an integral part.[8] Being a penitent perpetrator almost amounted to a badge of honor.

Even without regarding the special status as an act of appropriation, the convergence of a particularly troubling history with a political agenda, however well intended, has consequences for how one defines or evaluates "cultural memory." One consequence, for instance, is the official nature of such memory; another one is the legal aspect or the juridical consequences, for instance, the laws that deemed Holocaust denial a crime and prohibited the incitement to discrimination and racial hatred. These provisions, which made their way through the parliaments in the 1980s and 1990s not just in Germany, but in several countries of the European Union, indicate the degree to which Holocaust memory extended beyond the Federal Republic to become an essential part of the legal, political and cultural frameworks of the European Union. More generally, since "(re-)visitations of the past are inevitably conditioned by the imperative of national or group cohesion in the present,"[9] such institutionalization of the Holocaust, in other words, also politicized cultural memory.

Having expanded the reach of public memory beyond the individual nation and group can, however, also be considered an achievement, not just in "mastering the past," but in laying out a distinct ethical ground for the new Europe. Two generations of Germans have now been raised with an intense awareness of Europe's troubled legacy with respect to racial discrimination, and what was once a war-torn continent is now often chided for being too pacifist.

The achievement may have its downside for the very group thus put in the forefront of public memory: the Jews. The more taken-for-granted the ethical *normativity* of "remembering the Holocaust" moved to the center of a European transnational identity-in-commemoration, the more it risked turning into formalistic lip service and unthinking ritual. As a catastrophe that all but destroyed one specific ethnic and religious group, namely Europe's Jews, the Holocaust came to stand for the very incarnation of evil. Yet its strength as a universal symbol was also its weakness as the reminder of a specific historical event. On the other hand, the more it became symbolic of extreme suffering per se, the more other groups, who also considered themselves victims of Nazism, felt they, too, deserved consideration, i.e., to be remembered at sites or through acts of commemoration. After all, the Nazi persecuted, incarcerated, exploited, starved and killed many different groups in the course of their twelve-year rule of which six at war with the world: affected were communists and anarchists, Sinti and Roma, homosexuals, lesbians, prisoners of war, slave laborers; Nazi doctors conducted horrible medical experiments not only on inmates of the camps, but also on special hospital patients and they practiced euthanasia on the mentally handicapped. Descendents and representatives of these victims also had a right to mourn their dead and have their sacrifices acknowledged, as well as being entitled to claims for compensation. The question then became whether Holocaust memory can or should contain these different demands for recognition and memory, and what invidious hierarchies of victimhood might be the consequence, if it does not?

"The Germans Will Never Forgive the Jews for Auschwitz": Jews in German Films

As mentioned in previous chapters, up until the 1990s, it is rare to find a German film, where a Jewish character has a central role. Peter Lilienthal's DAVID (1979) is the only example I can think of, along with Alexander Kluge's Anita G. in ABSCHIED VON GESTERN (1966), and, of course, Fassbinder's banned play, *Der Müll, die Stadt und der Tod*, made into the film SCHATTEN DER ENGEL (Daniel Schmid, 1975). An oblique yet plausible reason might be that throughout the 1960s and 1970s, it would have been difficult, if not impossible for a German film to feature a Jewish hero: it would have been an unseemly impersonation, a form of masquerade and appropriation: not only because well into the 1970s, German Jews were all but invisible in the public sphere as Jews, but also because of their problematic status as "the other": the walking reproach, the living question mark addressed to Germany and Germans. As the politically incorrect but acutely observing Henryk Broder noted: "the Germans will never forgive us Jews for Auschwitz," thereby also underlining the degree to which Germans and Jews had become each others' "symbolic people" in what Dan Diner called their "negative symbiosis."

On the other hand, one of the arguments made by Cohn-Bendit was that irrespective of whether Fassbinder's play *Der Müll die Stadt und der Tod* was anti-Semitic or not, the Jewish community should use the occasion to show face, in order to claim this right of being seen and heard, if only to confirm that Germany had become a multi-cultural society, where different nationalities, religions and ethnicities had full rights as citizens, which it was their duty to exercise in the service of free speech and political protest. This also cut both ways, insofar as it did make Jews just one among many minorities in West Germany, rather than its conscience and symbolic "other."

If such dilemmas blocked representation of Jews in the cinema until the 1990s, thereafter, Jewish characters suddenly began to people German screens. An early example was ABRAHAMS GOLD (Jörg Graser 1990), in which "grandfather has a skeleton in the cupboard" (i.e., a chest full of extracted gold teeth), and where deported and murdered Jews of a Bavarian village are a palpably absent presence. Towards the end of the decade, Jewish protagonists took center stage, in quick succession, in COMEDIAN HARMONISTS (Josef Vilsmaier, 1997), AIMÉE AND JAGUAR (Max Färberböck, 1999), VIEHJUD LEVY (Didi Danquart, 1999), GLOOMY SUNDAY — EIN LIED VON LIEBE UND TOD (Rolf Schübel, 1999) and ROSENSTRASSE (Margarethe von Trotta, 2003). Mostly made by non-Jewish directors, the films covered a variety of subjects, including a Lesbian mixed race love affair in war time Berlin, a biopic of an *a-capella* band with Jewish members during the Third Reich, the everyday life of Jewish cattle merchants in the German countryside in the late 1920s, and the story of a group of "Aryan" women successfully protesting against the detention of their Jewish husbands. The reception of the films was mixed, their style entirely within the television drama idiom, and few if any, stirred controversy. Beyond Germany, only AIMÉE AND JAGUAR and ROSENSTRASSE were noticed and had modest international distribution.

Should one see this sudden screen presence as an attempt to portray Jews as Germans, and thus no longer special, or at any rate imagine a Berlin Jew or a Frankfurt Jew to be no more unusual than a New York Jew or a Chicago Jew? Have Jews become hyphenated Germans, much like (but also in competition with) other hyphenated identities within Europe's multicultural societies, such as Turkish-Germans, British-Asians or Franco-Algerians? Or, on the contrary, does the very presence of other hyphenated Germans intensify the need to underline German Jews' status as Germans' favorite "others"? Perhaps an altogether different dynamic is at work, in respect to Jews becoming main characters in German-made feature films? For instead of leading to a sense of multicultural identity also for "ordinary" Germans, it seemed that the privileged, indeed the only *ethnic mirror of the self in the other* that Germans were either able or willing to look into, remained Jews.

In the case of Dani Levy's films, these questions certainly come to mind, as he plays with almost all the possibilities of mirroring and reverse identification. Levy, a self-consciously and self-confidently Jewish director of German-Swiss origin (another, far from unproblematic hyphenation), not only made a film about Jews in contemporary Germany (MESCHUGGE, 1998), but after successfully trying to revive the genre of Jewish comedy, made famous by Ernst Lubitsch, with his film ALLES AUF ZUCKER! (2005), Levi was not afraid to try his hand at a Holocaust comedy, MEIN FÜHRER — DIE WIRKLICH WAHRSTE

WAHRHEIT ÜBER ADOLF HITLER (2007), which was shunned by audiences and left critics embarrassed, not knowing how to react to Levy's slapstick humor when taking on such a tabooed figure.

In MESCHUGGE the trans-generational relations between Germans and Jews after Auschwitz is at the center of a story that cites the thriller atmosphere of the 1950s German melodramas, with their skeletons in the family cupboard and stolen identities. Levy, rather daringly, adds a Treblinka ex-commandant and his innocent-ignorant daughter, who on a trip to New York falls in love with the son of her mother's best friend, who happens to be Jewish. Here, the aftermath of the Holocaust has a transnational Germany-New York's Jewish Upper West Side dimension and denouement (which one also finds in ROSENSTRASSE, and THE READER, 2008), and tries to blend some of the tragic elements of the Romeo & Julia story of star-crossed lovers with the optimism of a new generation not haunted or held back by the sins of their elders: in stark contrast to the films of the New German Cinema, where the family always led into the dark past rather than enabling a more hopeful future.

Once again, whether considered as historical fact or universal symbol, the Holocaust memory in these films cuts both ways. When adducing Germany's multi-cultural society as a reason for making German Jews "visible," one also makes room for other non-Jewish protagonists or groups persecuted by the Nazi to be portrayed as victims of history. COMEDIAN HARMONISTS, AIMEE AND JAGUAR, and ROSENSTRASSE are self-consciously giving other victims (almost) equal space. At the same time, they try to make up for this by encouraging a view of Jews less as victims, than as figures of empowerment or, if the story permits it, as heroic exemplars of resistance. The most notable characteristic, therefore, of these 1990s films is that, despite dealing with this most tragic of subjects, they extract from the Holocaust tales of fortitude, rescue and miraculous survival. Typical examples are HITLERJUNGE SALOMON (Agnieszka Holland, 1990), MUTTERS COURAGE (Michael Verhoeven, 1995) and ROSENSTRASSE. The moral uplift ostensibly justified because their stories are based on actual events, these films rely on genre formulas, where the grim setting becomes the backdrop for a melodrama or morality tale that takes from Nazism or Nazi persecution only the most clichéd of attributes. In GLOOMY SUNDAY, for instance, set in German-occupied Budapest, the SS commandant blackmails a woman he lusts after into having sex, yet rescues not her lover, as promised, but a "rich Jew" from whom he can demand more money. The woman survives, and, many years later, is fortuitously given the opportunity to exact poetic justice by taking revenge for the betrayal: she poisons the perpetrator at her restaurant, where he foolhardily returned to celebrate his eightieth birthday.

In the other films, tropes and themes of stage melodrama are omnipresent, such as torn-apart families, orphans, disguises and false identities, the transmission of guilty knowledge, and the uncovering of disavowed secrets. Von Trotta's

ROSENSTRASSE combines almost all of these motifs: family secrets, generational transfer, heroism, resistance, trauma, and survival. Taking the February-March 1943 protest of two hundred women against the arrest and likely deportation of their Jewish husbands as its premise, the film tells this story by focusing first on a Jewish girl, rescued by a German woman called Lena. Many years later, the Jewish girl, now a recently widowed mother living in New York, is questioned by her daughter, and reluctantly tells of her past in Germany, leading the daughter to Lena, still living in Berlin, across whose reminiscences the story of the women's heroic protest unfolds via flashbacks.

One notes that von Trotta has chosen a story where the heroism celebrated is that of German women, and the narrative turns on the reluctance of a Jewish woman to admit to having been rescued by a German, as well as the grief of a German woman who loses her (adopted Jewish) child to the biological mother. This is a curious reversal, given that the more common historical state of affairs would have been the reluctance of a German to admit to *not* having helped or rescued their German-Jewish neighbors, and it would have been a Jewish mother grieving over a lost child. These oddly allegorical elements are about uneven exchanges, symbolic debts, reversals of expected roles and positions. While historians commented on the factual licenses von Trotta and her screenwriter had to take with the documented Rosenstrasse protest, as well as asking ironically how much credence one can give to the film's depiction of the Holocaust "if a mere seven days of steadfast protest could have prevented it from happening,"[10] the question to ask is also: what is this play with symmetries and reversals in the service of, and what debt is the melodramatic form trying to repay?

As Daniela Berghahn has pointed out, in a sympathetic consideration of both ROSENSTRASSE and AIMÉE AND JAGUAR, "these films construct a memory of the past that is no longer encumbered by guilt, principally because the relationship between Germans and Jews is re-imagined as one of solidarity. As post-memory films, they take liberties with the traumatic memory of the past and, by following the generic conventions of melodrama, family saga and European heritage cinema, even lend it popular appeal."[11]

However, feminist critics considered the spectatorial positions proposed by the films—a solidarity based on notions of "sisterhood"—both naïve and old-fashioned, harking back to the first post-war period in certain Polish films, narrated from a socialist perspective: "The self-reflexive moments of art house cinema [of the 1970s] were largely lost in a new body of Holocaust films emerging in the 1980s that were set among female protagonists. Here the key word of sisterhood would ultimately hamper a feminist consideration of women's complex positionalities during the Holocaust. [... The] most recent example of Margarethe von Trotta's ROSENSTRASSE perpetuates the model of female solidarity inspired by female resisters in socialist films. In this sense, the mainstream 1980s discourse on women during the Holocaust owed much to the socialist paradigm of history from which it ostensibly tried to break by establishing 'the female question' as central rather than secondary."[12]

This solidarity is as necessary for the popular appeal of ROSENSTRASSE as it is troubling from a historical and ethical point of view. Since one of the most egregious facts of the exclusion, expropriation and persecution of German Jews during the Nazi years was the almost complete lack of solidarity of non-Jews towards their Jewish neighbors, colleagues, friends and, often enough, even lovers and spouses, the presumption of solidarity strains not so much credulity as a certain moral honesty. The affirmation that the stories are "based on fact" functions as a fetish in order to protect a wish-fulfilling fantasy. Only by creating a community of victims can such solidarity pretend to the semblance of verisimilitude, and in this respect—in its mode of address to the spectator, who is invited to share this solidarity and enjoy it as complicity—ROSENSTRASSE can be said to revert or return to the subject positions of the 1950s, where Germans saw themselves as victims, and as such, tried to *compete* with Jews, in order to compensate.

AIMÉE AND JAGUAR, possibly aware of the trap, *overcompensates* in that it ostentatiously inverts all the possible binaries, by pairing a German woman of little self-esteem with a Jewish woman full of energy and zest, thus crisscrossing "Aryan" and "Jewish" stereotypes, while also making the Aryan Aimée a convinced member of the Nazi party and a heterosexual mother of four, who has to fight her own anti-Semitism, because she is already too besotted with the sexy and self-confident Jaguar by the time she finds out her lover is Jewish. Also "based on a true story," AIMÉE AND JAGUAR is a torrid tale of Lesbian love, where being Jewish and Aryan are indeed interchangeable attributes of female victimhood, and imminent death and deportation spice up a tragic tale with further elements of *amour fou* transgression. Here, all the positive qualities of a boundless love of life that seizes the moment, regardless of risk, are projected on to the Jewish character, as the embodiment of "freedom," while the German is repressed and confused, her naivety inoculating her against any kind of responsibility or part in the brutality of the regime. Yet this projection, too, is a retrospective act of compensation, much like converting guilt into a debt, in the hope of balancing the books, retrospectively.

Thus, if prior to 1990, the idea of a Jewish character figuring so prominently in a film by one of the directors of the New German Cinema would have had something monstrous (and was seen as such, when figured in a Fassbinder's film, such as the Mendelssohn family in LILI MARLEEN), then the compensating fantasies of ROSENSTRASSE's rescue scenario (and AIMEE AND JAGUAR's passionate Lesbian love affair) serve to protect a self-exonerating solidarity after the fact, and are thus merely the other side of the coin of this monstrosity. In Fassbinder's day, a Jew's appearance was too strongly tabooed, surrounded by too much fear (of committing a faux-pas, of sounding the false note, or of simply not being up to the task). Schloendorff, taking no chances, had found a way around it by making "his" Jew in THE TIN DRUM not only speak with a French accent, but actually be played by Charles Aznavour, putting him on a pedestal, his own myth making him both a sacred and a sacrificial victim. In tiptoeing around these traps, ROSENSTRASSE—valiantly, perhaps, but nonetheless—"fails" as an imaginative exercise in that it cannot find a language either of ambiguity or of reticence, and instead strains painfully after political correctness, constructing an overtly melodramatic scenario, which authenticates itself by historical fact.

The fatal aesthetic flaw (and possible moral failure) is that these films (of the normalized, because institutionalized Holocaust) may have a historically accurate Third Reich setting and be based on "true stories," but they are unable to carry the burden of the retrospective knowledge of what was to be the fate of Jews simply and solely "as Jews," at the hands of Germans. It is this dilemma that determines the representation of the Jew in German films: too uncanny, inscrutable and powerful in Fassbinder, too cold and formidable in von Trotta's melodrama, too passionate and sensuous in Färberböck's love story, too heroic in Verhoeven, too ordinary and normal in Vilsmaier's biopic, and too silly or facetious in Dani Levy's thriller and comedies.[13]

"Remembering the Holocaust" Since 2000

However, by the early 2000s, remembering the Holocaust no longer had the same urgency it had in the early and mid-to late-1980s, at the time of Richard von Weizsäcker's speech and at the end of the Historians' debate. Indeed, countering what has just been said, one could argue that the "dilemma" or "burden" of representation had been freed from anxious soul-searching as the Holocaust in popular culture became a historical backdrop, not unlike other momentous or traumatic periods figured in European heritage films, be it the Edwardian period in Britain, the Resistance in France or the Civil War in Spain.[14] Of course, the Holocaust has remained a subject for professional historians (Saul Friedländer's monumental work, *The Years of Extermination: Nazi Germany and the Jews, 1939–1945*, for instance, appeared in 2007, to wide acclaim),[15] yet the "Europeanization" of the Holocaust (if one follows Daniel Levy and Natan Sznaider),[16] or the way it had "thoroughly entered American life" (in Peter Novick's phrase)[17] also extended to the cinema, even as the sense that each country was using the Holocaust as a mirror to its own historical sensibilities, guilt feelings or repressed traumas began in turn to ignite polemical debates.[18]

While such "nationalizations of the Holocaust" led to yet another round of contested claims to "ownership,"[19] its universalization as absolute evil created a powerful and easily graspable symbol in the struggle for human rights. Levy and Sznaider speak of a "temporal duality" of Holocaust memory: "the Holocaust came to be regarded as unique with reference to the past and universal for the future. That is to say, the Holocaust past is something that happened predominantly to the Jews, while the Holocaust future might happen to anyone."[20] It will be recalled that at the time of NATO forces bombing Serbian positions, in order to end ethnic cleansing in Kosovo, the "never again" of Auschwitz was used to legitimate a military intervention which did not have a valid UN mandate. Not averse to using photographs of dubious authenticity, the Western alliance played the Holocaust card, and, in the case of Germany, it persuaded a reluctant public to allow the *Bundeswehr*, the federal army, to conduct military missions for purposes other than to protect Germany's territorial integrity.

In the case of the United States, the Americanization of the Holocaust has led to a rewriting of the U.S. role and purpose in WWII, making it increasingly appear that the United States had entered the war against Hitler in order to rescue the Jews. James Young, for instance, warned of the dangers "of turning Holocaust memory into a kind of self-congratulatory spectacle" not only because it falsified the historical record, but because it might tempt Americans to be less forceful in taking "real action against contemporary genocide."[21] Similar arguments are often directed at Israel, which tends to defend its policies vis-à-vis the Palestinians by addressing the "never again" to Muslim countries that deny the Jewish state its right to exist. While the Palestinians think of themselves as the Jews of the Middle East, the Israeli think of the Arabs as the Nazi, come back to "finish the job." As Levy and Sznaider also point out, the contradiction between the Holocaust's universality (as a symbol of human rights) and its uniqueness (as a historical event that singled out the Jews) can only be resolved by shifting the referent (Jews/anyone) in the temporal duality between past and future.

However, there is another way that Holocaust memory has been universalized, with quite different implications and intentions. This is associated with Giorgio Agamben, a philosopher who explicitly refuses to talk about "Holocaust memory," and instead speaks of the "Remnants of Auschwitz."[22] For Agamben, there is no sacrificial fire (the literal meaning of Holocaust) and no metaphysics of absolute evil. On the contrary, the most urgent reminder that Auschwitz has for the present is the *Musulman*, a term used by inmates of the death camps to describe fellow prisoners who had given up hope and thus had lapsed into a state of apathy and abjection. Agamben cites Primo Levi's "The Drowned and the Saved," where Levi describes them as: "an anonymous mass, continuously renewed and always identical, of no-men who march and labor in silence, the divine spark dead within them, already too empty really to suffer."[23] Comparing the Musulman to the enigmatic figure and legal fiction of the *homo sacer* of Roman Law, someone who is not part of humanity nor has any rights of citizenship, and thus can be killed, but not sacrificed in either war or a religious ritual,[24] Agamben's argument is that the true lesson of Auschwitz lies in the way that the rules and regime of the camps has become the universal order of the modern world, reflecting both the concentrationary mindset of bureaucratic management and the social engineering of technocratic government. Following Foucault's definition of governmentality and biopower, Agamben sees the "remnants of Auschwitz" in the surveillance apparatus that has been built up, in the wake of terrorism and the state's measures against it, i.e., the fully administered totalitarian society where anyone can find him or herself a Musulman or homo sacer. Paradoxically, therefore, the Holocaust today stands for human rights *and* for the very absence of human rights, the two being the recto and verso of its universalizing and universalized memory.

Paradigm Change: "The Good German"

In view of these broader tendencies that institutionalize Holocaust memory in Europe while also making of it the paradigmatic state of exception, German appropriation of this memory must necessarily remain more ambiguous. This ambiguity, which I associate with guilt management, is also in evidence in ROSENSTRASSE across its moral center. This shows itself to be Lena Fischer, the German woman who in 1943 sheltered the Jewish child, whose daughter then returns to Berlin in the 1990s, to research the story of her mother. Lena, however much she might be a historical figure, is also a trope or cliché, known from German literature since the late 1940s and hotly debated again since SCHINDLER'S LIST: that of the "good German."[25] If Spielberg's good German (once again, in Schindler's case, coming with historical authentication) is someone, whose evident human failings are emphasized (in order to lower the threshold for general audience identification), the same figure when deployed by a German author or filmmaker can easily enough become a wish-fulfilling fantasy. It is how W.G. Sebald saw a protagonist of Günter Grass' *Diary of a Snail* (1972), whose brave defiance of official anti-Semitism Sebald called an "authorial projection" and a way for Germans "to try and heal themselves in the post-war years."[26]

The good German seems to be the opposite of the victim, but in terms of finding a way to "balance the books," of converting guilt into a debt that can be repaid, the good German and the German as victim are two sides of the same strategy. This becomes even more evident when one turns to the historical themes that allowed Germans to see themselves as victims (rather than/as well/ as perpetrators). In particular, there are four events or national traumas that reemerged around 2003, after having been muted, if not altogether kept out of sight since the 1950s: the bombing raids by British and U.S. planes on German cities in the years 1943–45; the expulsion of millions of Germans from the East between 1945–47; the mass rape of German women by Soviet soldiers as well as Allied Forces in 1945–46; and the Prisoners of War held by the Soviet Union in labor camps well into the 1950s.

These long-buried traumas seemed to return mainly due to literary works: a book of lectures and essays (W.G. Sebald's *Luftkrieg und Literatur*, 1999), a novel (Günter Grass, *Im Krebsgang*, 2002), a vivid history of the bombing raids (Jörg Friedrich, *Der Brand: Deutschland im Bombenkrieg, 1940–1945,* 2002) and the reprint of a harrowing autobiographical account of multiple rape (Anonyma, *Eine Frau in Berlin*, 2003).[27] As this purported paradigm change has been so extensively debated in the German press as well as in academia, I can refer the reader to the relevant sources.[28] However, it is of importance to my argument for three reasons: it revises and modifies an earlier point about Holocaust memory and German national identity; it challenges the widespread assumption that "2003 saw the return of 1945,"[29] i.e., that the victim discourse in post-unification Germany was a retread and return to the self-pity and compensatory projection of the early postwar years,[30] and third, it gives ground for a counter-argument about "guilt management" as the impulse that provides the continuity from 1945 to the present, without either negating the breaks or positing a radical paradigm change.

At first glance, it is surprising to note how marginal a role the German cinema seems to have played in this new victimology of the German nation, i.e., the conversion of the *Tätervolk* (a nation of perpetrators) into an *Opfernation* (a victim nation). Bernd Eichinger and Oliver Hirschbiegel's DER UNTERGANG/DOWNFALL (2004), about the final days of Hitler and Berlin, was quickly enlisted, insofar as it was said to "humanize" the monster and show the paralysis at the center of power in the dying days of the Third Reich. Yet apart from depicting in a few flamboyantly staged scenes the devastation of Berlin under the Allied bombs and the Soviet assault, it does not touch on the fate and fears of the "ordinary Germans" who play such a central role in the new memory frame of Germans as victims. Except in one crucial instance: when Traudl Junge, Hitler's secretary, and the real-life person on whose memoir of Hitler's last days the film is based, reacts with shock and surprise when she overhears Hitler coldly discussing the extermination of the Jews. This scene—barely more than a glance and a reaction shot—is the "hook" that allows the spectators to recognize themselves and bring their divided feelings into the film. It is the moment of identification which then carries the viewer through the destruction and self-destruction that follows. But it is identification based on miscognition turned into retroactive recognition. How can Junge not have known? What is her look of shocked surprise actually about? It is the film's necessary parapraxis: necessary, because it belatedly puts into the historical scene both the recognition that "ordinary Germans" did indeed know about Hitler's genocidal policies, and that knowledge's disavowal. Germans could not *not* have known, which is why the film needs a not-innocent Junge to look shocked, rather than a truly ignorant character suddenly learning about the "Final Solution." Junge's shock, in other words, relieves a burden of guilty complicity.

An instructive counter-example to ROSENSTRASSE, in respect of both victimhood and solidarity, is Helke Sander's documentary from 1992, BEFREIER UND BEFREITE/LIBERATORS TAKE LIBERTIES. Investigating the mass rapes of German women by soldiers of the liberating armies, Sander anticipated the perspective correction on victims and perpetrators, from a feminist point of view, to turn the tables on the Allied Victory in 1945. But while politely noted in Germany, it was much more intensively discussed in the United States, as indicated by a special dossier devoted to it in *October*.[31] In Germany, Sander's film must have come too early to break through the taboo against mentioning the subject and its consequences. It suggests that a historical topic, to be topical, needs a specific conjuncture, a "screen memory" or a trigger event.

This event—coming from outside Germany, and capable of breaching the taboos that kept Germany's own traumas hidden from public view—was neither a film nor a debate, such as the "recovered memory debate" about abuse in the United States, but the attack on the Twin Towers on September 11, 2001. The sense of threat and uncertainty, of massive danger and destruction coming from the sky and visited upon thousands of innocent people was a powerfully appropriate trigger for the return of other, in this case, uniquely German traumas. Jörg Friedrich's *The Blaze* probably needed 9/11 (as a "screen memory," in Freudian terminology), in order to find a suitable echo and become the huge publishing success that it was. Yet as critics pointed out, in his descriptions (and images) Friedrich drew on the vocabulary and diction of the Holocaust, even calling the Dresden bombings "a German Holocaust."[32] Sebald, too, borrowed from the *Lager* literature when describing the scenes of devastation after the bombings of Hamburg in *On the Natural History of Destruction* (2003). Sebald's essays, first published in 1999, had a renewed impact after 9/11 (and after his death in December 2001).[33]

In other words, while the turn to victimhood in the new century does have special resonance in German history, it is not a uniquely German phenomenon, and may have been triggered by something apparently quite unrelated. One could even argue that Germans merely joined the general rush to assert their claim to victimhood and take up a place in an increasingly crowded field of damaged individuals, injured communities and traumatized nations. Being a victim was made appealing, on a day-to-day basis, through popular culture, talk shows, soaps and reality television, at the same time as victimhood and trauma became politically appropriated by the United States after 9/11 for the nation as a whole. Trauma, in the twenty-first century, had become a badge of honor, one of the last ways of presenting oneself as authentic and singular in the public sphere.[34] This authenticity in victimhood can be projected backwards into history, as the German cultural critic Diedrich Diederichsen argued in a review of DER UNTERGANG when he pointed out that the core of the film is not the question of how and why the Germans stayed loyal to Hitler for so long, or why those around him did not realize that he was barely rational even when not shaking and raving. Rather, the moral center is closer to that of *Emergency Room* or similar empathy and therapy shows: "Instead of asking pertinent questions, DER UNTERGANG settles for the psychology of television entertainment: [its] morality, however, is structural, and [...] operates with categories like 'bad mother' [Martha Goebbels] or enlists the authority of an SS-doctor [Ludwig Stumpfegger] to summon the energies of humanitarian Germany at the place where German television long ago established its ideological center: the hospital ward."[35] In other words, even historical victimhood requires the generic codes of melodrama, in order to be experienced as authentic.

Evidently, there were quite a few voices in Germany who sharply condemned the paradigm change to victim status as a revisionist, right-wing move. Yet the emergence of trauma as a general cultural trope also revived the older argument that "mastering the past" must also leave room for discussing the scars that the end of the war and defeat had left on millions of civilians' lives in Germany.[36] With the Holocaust now standing for human rights, writers could look once more at the moral and political justification of the bombing raids, especially those ordered by RAF Marshall "Bomber Harris" in the last months of the war; they could question the international legality of the expulsions from the East (the Benes decrees, which led to deportation, for instance), and they could acknowledge the women's suffering caused by the occupying soldiers, not least to do right by the thousands of children born of these rapes. Given that with German unification, other old wounds had to be re-opened, if the two Germanys were to find the terms of a new solidarity out of divided histories and divided memories, these wounds had to include the memories of the first years when families mourned their dead, as well as being divided and estranged by the Iron Curtain and the Berlin Wall. In addition, unrestricted travel after 1990, and indeed the wooing of tourists by Poland, the Czech Republic and the Baltic States allowed Germans to revisit, for the first time in almost fifty years, the sites, the landscapes and the atmosphere of some of the places that their parents or grandparents had called home.

Historians also pointed out that while the official commemoration policy made the Holocaust the central event to reflect upon and remember, there was evidence suggesting that in the families, the "unofficial memory" had never been put aside, and unforgotten were the firestorms or the flight to the West, the sons and brothers fallen in the senseless war, or what had happened to the women "when the Russians came." What Harald Welzer called "family album memory" had always been different from the "public lexicon memory,"[37] and already from the mid-1970s onwards many writers, biographers and historians had begun to collect the oral and visual memorabilia of the post-war period, even before television took over and took charge of it in seemingly endless compilation films, which in turn started a publishing boom in memoirs and coffee table history books. The television programs were often signed by the journalist and historian Guido Knopp, so much so that his name became a verb ("knoppisize"),[38] used whenever "history is given a human face," i.e., when stories told by eyewitnesses are matched with archive material from newsreels or home movies, and stitched together by expert talking heads or voice over commentary.[39]

Possibly the most persuasive reason for the supposed paradigm change, however, is the so-called intergenerational transfer in literature and public life, where it is the "third generation" that now feels the need, and wants to have the right, to learn about their grandparents, not content to take their parents' generally hostile stance towards this first generation (made into a "first generation" by the second who radically disowned it as the *Täter-Väter*, i.e., the perpetrator-parents). Welzer and his collaborators put together the results of a broadly based sociological field study under the suggestive and ironic title *Opa war kein Nazi* (Granddad was no Nazi).[40] There were also several novels that explored the lives of grandfathers or tried to recover the lost emotional terrain of family histories with life stories that had never been told: out of fear, resentment, bitterness or shame, or simply because there did not seem to be the inner necessity or the interest from outside.[41]

While many of these belated oral histories and eyewitness accounts had common themes and shared the emotional need to fill a void in the narrators' biographies, they also gave evidence of the diversity of German lives and circumstances during the Nazi years and after, thereby testifying to the sometimes scarcely believable normalcy under the most abnormal conditions, or the subterfuges and ingenuity human beings were capable of, once they have persuaded themselves that they had better just get on with staying alive.[42] This, of course, has always been the great theme of Alexander Kluge: his hundreds of short stories even more so than his films "bridge" the seeming gap between the 1950s and the 1990s, by doing assiduous memory work. But his is the mode of parapraxis, not melodrama. As my chapter on Kluge sets out, there is a good deal of textual camouflage and narrative subterfuge that has to be deciphered, before the full urgency of his intervention and source of his desperate optimism can be appreciated. Kluge certainly never forgot the German soldiers who died at Stalingrad, or the firebombs that in April 1945 fell on his home town of Halberstadt, and there are remarkably many—often deceptively facetious—incidents of rape in his work that call for context, or rather, whose always present context the "paradigm change" has suddenly made a good deal more visible.

Literature and the feuilleton were the public spheres that registered the turn to what Eric Langenbacher called the "German-themed" memory frame of the early 2000s, but as I show in other chapters, German cinema during this same period responded much more vividly to the afterlife of the Red Army Faction and "terrorism" than it did to the afterlife of Germany's defeat in 1945. Yet similarly, it was the generational change that proved to be one of the major catalysts behind the revival of interest in the RAF. So far, no major film or filmmaker has taken on the topics that heralded the change of memory frame. Or rather, taken on, yes, but perhaps not taken in: Nico Hofmann (who specializes in television adaptations of "memory" literature and German history topics) together with screenwriter Stefan Kolditz and director Roland Suso Richter produced a two-part mini-series DRESDEN for ZDF Television (2006), originally to be called *Der Brand* (*The Blaze*) after the book by Jörg Friedrich. This sixtieth anniversary film of Dresden's destruction settled for the concept of a love story (between a German nurse and a shot-down RAF pilot), put to the test by the firestorm. By focusing on such a love story, involving a British soldier and a German nurse (*Emergency Room* ethics and aesthetics again!), the production was a purely commercial calculation, meant to be sold to Britain and the United States, not least in order to recoup the €10m production budget, one of the highest ever for a German television drama.

Guilt Management, or The Parapractic Memory of German Post-War Cinema

With the Holocaust both a moral "universal" (centered on universal human rights) and a specifically European "memory and identity" issue, the debate about perpetrators and victims necessarily had to change both in definition and direction. Beginning with France, the Netherlands and Austria, many countries formerly occupied by Nazi Germany began revising their own historical accounts of having "resisted" the aggressor. More complex and troubling histories came to the fore, also in Italy, Norway and Hungary, as well as in neutral countries like Switzerland and Sweden. While the official political discourse of the European Union thus sought to spread responsibility for the Holocaust more evenly across its member nations, with other roles—collaborators, accomplices, fellow travelers, bystanders, profiteers—being added to the contrasting pair victim/perpetrator, Germans' claim to their own victims no longer had the same "revanchist" overtones that it had in the early 1980s during the Historians' Debate, or indeed, immediately after the war ended, when the "traumas" that have begun to return were still experienced as the present. Or rather, firestorms, rapes and expulsions were the immediate past, and very much what Germans wanted to (and did) talk about in private, but learned to mention only sotto voce, much to the despair of those who had hoped there would be a genuine change of heart, which would have required more openness on all sides.

From this European perspective, the question of debt (*Schulden*) and guilt (*Schuld*), of moral obligation and material assistance lies at the heart of much of what I have been discussing so far, and, in its different ramifications (including its melodramatic treatments and parapractic supplements), seems to offer another way of understanding the variable relation of Germany to Holocaust memory, both in public and in private, both among politicians and among artists, than the so-called paradigm change, which overlooks, it seems to me, how the questions of Germany's past also feed into Germany's present standing and future role within the European Union. As Germany has to fully assume its strategically and economically crucial responsibilities also in the sphere of politics, a sort of adjustment—within Germany—is taking place, of what had been negotiated, accepted, contested and rejected after 1945. In other words, a paradigm change is under way, but as a redistribution exercise within a much wider context, in which Holocaust memory and guilt management are important, but not the sole elements.

My general focus on the cinema means that, besides highlighting the tropes of melodrama as balancing strategies under conditions of excess and extremes, I am paying particular attention to what I am calling the parapractic supplements of this redistribution exercise, i.e., the political fall-out and its aesthetic surplus value. Parapraxes come about, according to Freud, when contradictory impulses or incompatible desires appear to find a "successful" compromise formation, thanks to verbal compression, puns, tongue twisters and spoonerisms. But as the commonly used term *Freudian slip* connotes, the compromise all too visibly betrays the traces of the contradictions and ambivalences it was meant to hide, which is why "successfully performed failure" is part of the meaning of parapraxis, as I deploy it in this study as a tool for analysis.

In the case of the New German Cinema, I have already pointed out in what ways the contradictions and ambivalences were also of a structural kind. As a self-consciously national cinema, financed by the state to promote the director as author and the author as autonomous artist, the films did not (have to) prove themselves before a public via box office returns, but had to fulfill their representative role as cultural ambassadors of a Germany that was seen to be both critical and self-critical. But this also meant that directors effectively functioned within a double bind, condemned as they were to a form of *dependent independence.*

Their dependence was not only to the state that provided subsidy and finance, and thus expected them to represent the better Germany, especially during the volatile 1970s of a then still fragile democracy and frontline country in the Cold War. They also depended on an international public, one that was mainly interested in Germany thanks to its horrific past, about which it expected the films to give account. Yet as the generation to whom such a demand of accountability and testimony regarding the Nazi years and the Holocaust was addressed, these directors grew up at a time when the destruction of Jewish life and culture in Germany was neither missed nor acknowledged as missing, and where any such "mourning work" or grieving would have been, in a certain sense, hypocritical and dishonest.

Nonetheless, quite a few filmmakers did acknowledge such a mandate of representativeness, on different fronts at home and abroad, assuming accountability for Germany's past in front of an international public while also resisting their films' official character, by insisting on their authorial independence, usually through a highly personal cinematic signature, if one thinks of Syberberg, Kluge, Fassbinder, Herzog and Wenders and their unique, idiosyncratic styles. This balancing act among the contradictions of their objective position is largely the source for the parapractic poetics that so many of them managed to instantiate.

My thesis implies that it is double binds such as these that make a parapractic poetics necessary as well as productive. And, as the preceding case studies have hopefully shown, the films of several directors of the New German Cinema did indeed do memory work (as guilt management) in this oblique but determinately parapractic idiom, traceable in their themes as well as their style. It makes their films neither quite realistic nor melodramatic, neither quite allegorical nor postmodern-deconstructive, though they may share some of the characteristics, and indeed have on occasion been read in this fashion. What is distinctive are the ways either the plot-developments or the protagonists' motives seem to be at odds with each other. Once read within the parapractic logic of "to and fro, both and, neither nor," and with the spectator filling in the gaps of what cannot be shown or is present through its emphatic absence, a persistent set of preoccupations emerges, revolving around trying to undo what has been done, or seeking to create equations or equivalences while fully aware that none can be sustained. The key element, however, is that the attempts to do so persist, in the very knowledge of their absurdity or failure.

I hope to have convinced the reader that the films I discuss in the preceding chapters do indeed show the symptoms that I have identified as pertinent for a parapractic memory, where the palpable violence of the past's unfinished business requires a keen sense of the performative failures this endeavor will always imply. It still remains, however, to give some indication of how this also applies to the films (and literature) of the 1950s, as well as to the works that have emerged in the wake of the supposed paradigm change around 2002–04. In other words, my assumption is that during each of the three main periods of post-war German cinema: the rubble films and retro-comedies of the late 1940s and 1950s, the New German cinema and its outsider perspective of the late 1960s and 1970s, as well as in the post-unification films since 1990, Holocaust memory is variously inscribed. Not only, as has been argued (also alluded to in preceding chapters), in the form of repression and disavowal in the 1950s, as latent anti-Semitism camouflaged as anti-Zionism in the 1970s, followed in the 1990s by an overidentification with the victims of the Holocaust, which since the early 2000s, has mutated into a transfer of victim status retroactively on the Germans of the immediate post-war period, thereby seemingly exonerating what has, from the present temporal perspective, become the "grandparent-generation." Rather, next to the ongoing general rewriting of collective memory in the European context, the various victim discourses are, in one sense, merely filling in the blanks in an effort to either rebalance, or to find new ways of reshaping the overfamiliar narrative of Germany's Nazi past and status as perpetrator nation. In another sense, however, the discourses partake in a much wider reevaluation of the "victim" and the "survivor," two figures of ambiguous agency in the Western imaginary, reflecting the reliance on "trauma" to stabilize individual identity, both retroactively and proactively: the latter justified by referring to the generalized threat of always already imminent catastrophe (terrorism, global warming, environmental disasters). These ongoing processes of Germany's "search for a usable past"[43] used to focus on literature (and professional historians) to provide the master-discourse, but since the 1980s, television and the cinema have had the more significant role in making the Holocaust, and Germans' entanglement in its perpetration and consequences, both contemporary and relevant: on television mainly in the modalities of melodrama, but in the cinema occasionally also by what I call the "poetics of parapraxis," whose formal properties point consistently to the issue of guilt and redress, of the "if only" and "what if," thereby always resonating with regret, but always remaining suspended and unresolved.

Guilt as a Form of Implication and Exchange

It is therefore necessary to regard cultural memory as a way of *remembering and forgetting,* but not as the mutually beneficial division of labor of an individual's psyche, and instead occurring in the exceptionally conflicted context of contemporary Germany. In this context, "guilt" has to be understood more broadly as the ethical consequence of a transgression of binding norms and laws, yet also formally, as a variable and a quantity that can generate movement in a situation of misalignments and asymmetries. Guilt is an ingredient that is malleable and convertible: it can be quantified (when it becomes debt), and it can be temporalized (when it names the length of a sentence). It can be added, in order to balance nonsynchronicities and deferrals, drawing up a ledger of credits and debits. The interface of guilt and shame acts like a mirror reflecting the fragile self-image of the subject back at him/herself or projected towards the other. This other might be the community (to which one wants to belong) or God (whether as organized religion or individual conscience). Yet guilt, in this formalist definition, also represents an exemplary case of deferred action, a temporality important for both melodrama (what if/if only) and trauma (a symptom in search of its cause). Guilt, one can say, is the consequence of an action undertaken in the hope of success, but which turns out in retrospect to have been a failure or a mistake, with the result that the question of intention has to be reexamined in reverse order, so that the causality of guilt runs from the consequences to the causes. Hence my contention that parapraxis is guilt management where the will to undo what has been done (its—impossible—retroactive vector) is as strongly present as the resolve to pay one's debts and square the account.

Of course, guilt also has a vector that points to the future, aiming to establish a new equilibrium, Whether we call this equilibrium punishment, retribution, revenge, forgiveness or reconciliation, in each case we are referring to a new zero-degree or equivalence, or to use a contemporary vocabulary, "closure." However, we also know (and almost every religion knows it and Greek tragedy confirms it), that "an eye for an eye, a tooth for a tooth" does not necessarily reestablish the more encompassing, cosmic (now called "global") equilibrium. On the contrary, such balance-seeking action can just as easily lead to escalation or produce a Moebius strip "infinite loop," because the entities being weighed in the balance may well turn out to be incommensurable. This is usually deemed to be the case with the Holocaust.

There are, evidently, many ways of trying to establish such a balance or neutralization of a given guilt-economy, especially when taking into the equation precisely such an incommensurability. In literature and the cinema, the melodramatic potential of a situation can come to the fore, once we consider not only contradiction, but also substitution, mistaken identities or other errors of comparison and exchange as part of the rhetoric of melodrama. My discussion of ROSENSTRASSE and AIMEE UND JAGUAR has highlighted the advantages (and pitfalls) of melodrama as guilt-neutralizing strategy of seeking balance and negotiating equivalence.

However, to take a specific example, not related to melodrama, but from politics, and relevant for Germany's situation after 1945, consider the compromise that the first Adenauer government decided upon, as the legal successor state to the German Reich: namely to offer to the newly founded state of Israel not an acknowledgement of guilt (*Schuld*), but instead, an acknowledgement of an as yet to be determined debt (*Schulden*), in the form of reparations to compensate the victims, descendant of victims and survivors of the Nazi regime. Or consider the way in which the West German establishment very soon after 1945 seems to have taken the collective decision to convert its erstwhile anti-Semitism into a new philo-Semitism, as if it was just another currency reform, like the one that converted the Reichsmark into the Deutschmark. Or recall the equivalences that Ernst Nolte and Andreas Hillgruber tried to validate during the Historians' Debate around 1986: to count "their" victims against "our" victims, and this in the context of reinterpreting National Socialism as a corrective and defensive counter-move against communism, itself a strategy resurfacing since the 1990s when one totalitarianism (that of the National Socialists) is being measured against another one (Stalinism). The fact that, in almost all these cases, the accounts do not square, just as "the past will not pass" (Nolte) is further proof of how urgently is needed a mechanism or modus that can produce poetic, narrative or dramatic forms of bringing together what cannot be united, of setting as equivalent what cannot be compared, and of creating a happy ending out of a situation or an outcome that only knows losers. If melodrama stands at one end of the spectrum of such mechanisms, parapractic poetics would be its other modus.

Another strategy of guilt management with parapractic potential and consequences may at first glance seem to be the opposite of balance and equivalence, but ultimately follows the same logic: this is the acknowledgement of guilt, but with an afterthought in mind, namely to assure oneself of the higher moral ground vis-à-vis one's creditor. I have cited a surely apocryphal story that made the rounds in West Germany in 1984. The recently elected Chancellor Helmut Kohl paid a State Visit to Israel, accompanied by his foreign minister, Hans Dietrich Genscher. As is customary, the two were taken to Yad Vashem, in order to honor the victims of the Holocaust. In this potentially awkward and embarrassing situation, the joke has Kohl lean over to Genscher and whisper: "die Schuld lassen wir uns nicht nehmen!" (We're not going to let them take away our guilt).[44] Mean and over the top as this may be, it does contain a grain of truth, insofar as official Germany subsequently became proud of the thorough way it tackled the task of "mastering the past," especially when compared to Japan, Italy and even—until relatively recently—France. Now that the Holocaust and "Holocaust Memory" have become integral parts of Germany's national identity, the paradigm change won't change this, on the contrary, it almost seems as if Germany is keen to export its commemorative culture of the nation's crimes to the rest of the world—notably to Poland, Hungary, the Baltic States and other countries in Central and Eastern Europe.[45]

Finally, another strategy of German guilt management should be mentioned: rather more rare but more challenging philosophically and therefore also a special ethical challenge. This concerns the perpetrator—of whom more below—and implies either fully to admit one's deeds or to stand by one's actions (even where they transgress all moral bounds), without showing either guilt or remorse, and without explaining oneself, at least not in public. To mind come Martin Heidegger and Carl Schmitt among German philosophers, Ernst Jünger and Gottfried Benn among German writers, and Leni Riefenstahl among the filmmakers. The potential benefit is once again a certain high ground of personal steadfastness and sovereign superiority. Below, in the section on "perpetrator memory," I discuss one such film, Roland Suso Richter's NICHTS ALS DIE WAHRHEIT (AFTER THE TRUTH, 1999), which, out of a real life biography, constructs counter-factually, such an unrepentant perpetrator, whose intransigence does indeed become a foil of sorts for the historical relativism and opportunism of Germany's successive "memory frames."[46]

In the recent literature, such guilt, defiantly free of all remorse can be found in the character of Max Aue, the main protagonist of Jonathan Littell's novel *Les Bienveillantes* (*The Kindly Ones*, 2006), a meticulously documented fictionalization of many of the key events of the Nazi seizure of power and subsequent political acts that led first to the war and concurrently to the so-called

Final Solution and its implementation. Based on years of historical research and reminiscent in scope and ambition of Thomas Pynchon's *Gravity's Rainbow*, the novel is told from the single point of view of SS-Obersturmbannführer Aue, who—miraculously and improbably, but in terms of the parapractic poetics that underpin the novel, quite logically—is somehow present and therefore an eye-witness to all the events we now remember as "inevitably" having "led to" the Holocaust. Aue is thus a construct, much the way Zelig is in the film of this title by Woody Allen and Forrest Gump in the eponymous film by Robert Zemeckis, in order to make us face up to truths we may not even realize as either truths or as situations we need to confront. As Klaus Theweleit put it: "From the moment I heard the announcements for this book—a Jewish author in the body of an SS killer—I knew: this was going to be awful. And I also knew: I'm going to have to read it."[47] Theweleit here responds to the parapractic posture that motivated the book's author, by performatively instantiating a similar self-contradiction as reader.

Guilt Management in the 1940s and 1950s

By 2006 it was clear that assuming the position of the perpetrator after decades of Holocaust memory from the point of view of the victims can only be done by deploying the full register of post-modern literary devices and deconstructivist tactics. But into what body did the perpetrator have to slip in the 1950s and 1960s? If one goes back to some of the strategies of guilt management in literature and film during the immediate post-war period, one notes the structural reliance on melodrama or comedy, although in each case, with an uncanny supplement. Typical for the attempt to join both perpetrator and victim to guilt management in the mode of melodrama, for instance, is one of the very first stories in West German literature to thematize the reality of the death camps—while bringing it into direct relation with the areal bombing raids and firestorms. Albrecht Goes' *Das Brandopfer* (1954), made into a film in 1962 as Der Schlaf der Gerechten (Rolf Hädrich) is remarkable already by its title, since the original German "Brandopfer" would be the exact translation of the Hebrew word "Holocaust"—and this more than a decade before the term was first used in its present-day meaning as referring to the persecution and destruction of Europe's Jews. It is a striking example of the right word appearing in the wrong place, as well as a superimposition of temporalities, the narrative being set in Hamburg in 1944. But if the action is to be historically credible, the location should be Auschwitz or Sobibor, and, if happening in Hamburg, the time frame would have to have been between 1936 and 1938.

As so many narratives will do subsequently, *Das Brandopfer* sets up a rescue scenario, whose central conceit is that a Jewish man saves a German woman from her burning home, after she had unsuccessfully tried to save a Jewish family from deportation. In an attempt to atone for her failure, she offers herself as a burning sacrifice, accepting death by fire, rained down from the sky by Allied bombers, as just retribution. But she is rescued, not least in order to be able to tell the tale in a framing narrative as a "survivor." The twofold improbability of the situation constitutes its melodramatic core, because the idea that a Jewish man rescues a German woman, who does not want to be rescued, preserves, as if in mirror-fashion, its own reversal: a German woman (in 1938-39) fails to rescue a Jewish man (or family) from deportation or worse, namely leaving them to the flames of the Holocaust (in 1943–44), causing her pangs of conscience, but which she does not have to act on, because she herself will be rescued, i.e., absolved. by the victim himself. In addition, the fire is not that of the German crematoria, but British bombers (of 1944–45), thus insuring her own guilt-feeling with a kind of double indemnity: "rescue" for "failure to rescue," and the exchange of "crematoria" for "bombing raids."

Read like this, *Das Brandopfer* becomes legible as a parable of German guilt, trying to find an appropriate form of equivocation as equivalence. As if to underline the didactic side of the story with a touch of the uncanny and even the grotesque, the author gives a broad hint of how he wants it to be read: the woman is the wife of the local butcher, who is licensed by the Nazi to sell kosher meat to the remaining Jews, among whom he is known as the *Juden-Metzig*, the butcher *for* Jews (presumably as opposed to being a butcher *of* Jews).[48]

What Mihal Bodemann, in discussing this story, calls "memory negatives," using an analogy from photography ("derived conceptually from the negative of a photography or a cast, [the reversals make] objects recognizable only in their negative forms"), coincides with what I call parapraxes, with the difference, perhaps, that in parapraxes, the positive and the negative are simultaneously, if not visible, then palpably present.

If it was thanks to the films of Alexander Kluge that these parapraxes became the starting point for the hermeneutic project elaborated in this study, then the Goes story retrospectively contextualizes Kluge, whose oddities and idiosyncrasies are hard to overlook, but even harder to make sense of. Goes still calls guilt by its name and crafts a parable that tries to balance the books not by any quick equivalence or tit for tat, but by going to an inordinate length of convolutions and involutions, in order to square a circle he must know cannot be squared. In this respect, Goes' only successor in German cinema would be Kluge. He too, calls guilt guilt, but which guilt? Instead of using the rhetoric of melodrama for his guilt-management balancing acts, Kluge presents his double takes and inversions in the mode of slapstick and comedy (though opera is also a preferred reference point). The closest parallel to Goes' novella is the scene in Kluge's Powers of Feeling (a title aptly blending melodrama and opera) already analyzed in a previous chapter and called "rescue through someone else's fault" (*Rettung durch fremde Schuld*). A young woman, it will be recalled, about to commit suicide after having been abandoned by her lover, parks her car close to some trees, is rescued because a travelling salesman, who happens to park next to her, notices the unconscious woman and decides to take advantage of her sexually. Jostled and jolted, the woman throws up and thereby inadvertently gets rid of the overdose of sleeping pills she had ingested. Mixing opera motifs with sinister farce, Kluge, too, then, has to twist the rescue motif such that only by its reversal and substitution does it yield a pertinent meaning: to rescue someone = to let someone perish; it is someone else's fault = it is my guilt (feelings). The implicit referent is once more the deportation of German Jews and the lack of help or assistance they received from their neighbors (the ones parked next to them), along with the exploitation of the helpless victims through sham sales and outright theft, which can be fairly described as "rape." At the same time—and Kluge is well aware of it—rape, like the fire bombs dropped by the Allies in Goes' novella, belongs to the victim's discourse that post-war Germans appropriated for themselves, so that Kluge's parapraxes neatly manage to compress and superimpose Jewish and German victims in a single, but multiply layered figuration, without naming either.[49]

The motif of a woman's attempted suicide in both Goes and Kluge is furthermore reminiscent of three of the best-known melodramas of the year 1947, where it is the Jewish characters (in one case, of a mixed marriage) who commit suicide, as if to relieve the non-Jewish Germans (in the film and those watching the film) from not preventing their imminent death: EHE IM SCHATTEN (Kurt Maetzig), ZWISCHEN GESTERN UND MORGEN (Harald Braun), and IN JENEN TAGEN (Helmut Käutner).[50]

Moving to West German Cinema of the 1950s, the parapractic mode found perhaps its most unlikely manifestation in comedies and thrillers. More work would have to be done on this, but some preliminary proof is provided by the research project of Drehli Robnik, who has analyzed a number of films—in this case a thriller—as to Freudian slips and double takes, deployed both on the verbal surface and as structural plot principles: "The way a film can misspeak and trip itself up sometimes starts already with the title: the story may be about policemen and their police-work, but how wrong would one be if one assumed that the title *Bandits of the Autobahn* (1955, Geza von Cziffra) conjures up and makes reference to the criminal gang that had it built? The fact that the film alludes to something it does not wish to define too directly is announced in the disclaimer: 'this film does not pretend to documentary veracity. It merely shines a light on general problems of human nature, which—following similar incidents that took place in our recent past—could well recur and repeat themselves. Names and persons are freely invented'." The action has traits of a parable: a policeman, chasing a gang of black marketeers on the motorway, kills an innocent motorist, but soothes his conscience and pacifies his superior by redoubling his effort and finally catching the gangsters. Guilt and innocence, redemption through substitution seem to be the narrative elements that work towards cancelling out whatever moral unease the story generates. But the uncanny remainder returns in the jocular banter between the agents. To quote Robnik once more: "the film is littered with allusions, explicit and implicit, secret code words, verbal malapropisms and innuendo. They suggest that each image contains a lot more than is manifest in its forced normality. For instance, the dialogue, without being required by the plot, keeps returning to phrases like 'the thousand-year war,' which it is as impossible to 'eradicate' as are 'weeds,' not even after 'ten years of peace.' Military locutions pop up like 'MG-Schütze' (machine gunner) and 'Grubenältester im Massengrab' (pit-senior of the mass-grave); an exchange of fire on the motorway is compared to executing deserters in Poland. Army euphemisms like 'an order is an order,' 'we're covered,' 'esprit de corps,' 'special leave' are used in such a jocular way that it makes them sound even more sinister, because out of context, while the (police) uniform is a 'skin you can neither take off nor wear with pride'."[51]

Guilt Management in the 1990s: Remaking as Revoking

If one fast-forwards to the 1990s, a further variant of parapraxis in German cinema can be noted at the metalevel, which links up with the trope of taking back and undoing, mentioned earlier in connection with the New German Cinema. It, too, seems both symptomatic and structural, insofar as it tries to reestablish an equilibrium or a counterweight in relation to a previous imbalance or distortion, now perceived as affecting German film history itself. I am referring to the tendency—beginning in the late 1990s, but especially noticeable in the new century, to make "remakes" of key films of the New German Cinema from the 1970s and early 1980s. These remakes, however, are not intended as homage or as ways of exploiting a known source and proven property, but they are remakes that take back or revoke core statements of the films they refer themselves to. "Repeal through repetition" might be the way to describe it, and in an earlier chapter, recapitulating my argument from the essay "Antigone Agonistes," I summarize how and why the two-part television docu-drama *Death Games* (Heinrich Breloer, 1997) should be considered a mirror-image remake of GERMANY IN AUTUMN (Alexander Kluge et al., 1978). DIE INNERE SICHERHEIT (THE STATE I AM IN, Christian Petzold 1999) is an avowed remake of Sidney Lumet's RUNNING ON EMPTY (1988) but it also strongly references Margarethe von Trotta's THE GERMAN SISTERS (1981), notably in that both films feature as film-within-the-film a scene from Alain Resnais' NIGHT AND FOG (1955), but contextualized quite differently and thereby giving it almost the opposite meaning, just as Petzold turns Lumet's film gesture of parental self-sacrifice inside out. Bernd Eichingers DER UNTERGANG (2004) is, in this perspective, a remake of HITLER A FILM FROM GERMANY (H.J. Syberberg, 1977), a film that to an international audience became iconic for the way German film directors were "mastering the past" (as my case study on the film tries to show), but also one that happens to have been produced for Syberberg by the very same Bernd Eichinger. If in Syberberg's film, Hitler is barely more than a projection screen, a hand puppet and empty shell—for Germans and Germany to project or act out collective fears, resentments and fantasies of power—Eichinger's film categorically revokes such a reading. He and director Edel concentrate instead on Hitler, the all-too-human monster, whose body language and verbal violence speak of inner demons, prescription drugs, permanent hypochondria and irrational phobias: in other words, a thoroughly psychologizing portrait of an individual pathology, which once more tends to abstract, but also exonerate the German people from responsibility in their "downfall."

Among the remakes revoking a previous film, special mention should be made of Sönke Wortmann's DAS WUNDER VON BERN (THE MIRACLE OF BERN, 2003). It tells the story of Germany's unexpected, but fervently desired victory against Hungary in the finals of the 1954 World Cup in Bern, Switzerland, seen through the eyes of a football-crazy boy from the Ruhr region, and his coming of age in an all-but dysfunctional family. What turns out to be traumatic for the single-parent household is the return from Russian captivity of the father, whom the boy—and his brother and sister—scarcely know and who in turn finds it impossible to accept the authority of his wife, running the family her way and with evident success. Dismissed by critics as sentimental and maudlin, the film must have struck an immediate chord, because it proved to be hugely successful in Germany. For its portrayal of a late-returning prisoner of war, it should probably be counted among the harbingers of the paradigm change, symptomatic for the terms by which Germans portrayed themselves as victims. But DAS WUNDER VON BERN has found a topic and a narrative in which strong, but hitherto tabooed emotions are allowed to come to the fore, treating the World Cup victory as compensation for the lost war (and thus considering Germany as a country that lost a war, rather than one liberated from an criminally odious political regime). As Diedrich Diederichsen wrote: "[THE MIRACLE OF BERN] is less about football and more concerned with that German feeling of having suffered World War II rather than initiated it, and after a terrible defeat having found a different playing field to finally see justice done. [...] The film puts at its centre a so-called late-returning PoW. Ten years as a Russian prisoner serve as the guarantee that the person concerned must have suffered more than he could have sinned. This fate, however, is not being presented as an individual one; it becomes paradigmatic when the depth of suffering is juxtaposed with the euphoria of winning the final. [...] Only the humiliated 'you-are-nobody' of the PoW-camp can balance and justify the 'you-are-once-more-somebody' of the world champion. The trouble is, before 1945, it was the Germans who tortured and murdered in the camps, not the other way round. If one decides to tell such a national-allegorical tale as Wortmann does, one cannot hide behind the individual case, especially when used as such a neatly fitting parable of post-war German history."[52]

In other words, the terms by which this oedipal drama is eventually sorted out—rather than worked through—seem like a fudge: instead of having to choose between the "good" father (the captain of the local football team) and the "bad" (i.e., the bitter ex-PoW biological) father, the boy becomes the lucky "mascot" of the first, while the second woos him as his "best buddy." What made it more melodramatic-nostalgic rather than a fully parapractic contribution to the memory discourse is the lack of pressure this feel-good treatment of the momentous occasion of post-war Germany's identity formation put on the present (except as a warm-up for the 2006 World Cup staged in Germany), compared to say, the same World Cup's aural appearance off-frame at the end of R.W. Fassbinder's THE MARRIAGE OF MARIA BRAUN (1980). Wortmann's film endorses the notion that out of all the horrible things that the war did to people—in this instance, to both parents and children—the Germans could justifiably use a football tournament to reward themselves with and come together as a family, and by extension, a nation.

And this is what makes DAS WUNDER VON BERN a remake-revoke of THE MARRIAGE OF MARIA BRAUN.[53] Not only is the setting in both films the Rhein-Ruhr area between Cologne and Essen: Fassbinder's film, too, culminates with the 3:2 victory of Germany over Hungary in Bern. But the meaning of this climax is entirely different from the tenor of triumph in Wortmann's film. With Fassbinder, it will be recalled, Germany's football victory coincides with Maria Braun's death in an explosion caused by a parapraxis par excellence, when—distressed by learning about the secret contract made by her husband and her lover—she lights her cigarette in a kitchen filled with gas from a burner she had distractedly opened a minute or so before. To once more cite Diederichsen: "With the words 'Game over, over, over, Germany is world champion' really everything is over and finished in Fassbinder's MARRIAGE OF MARIA BRAUN: the film, her life, the hope for a different Germany. Tired, he looks at Germany, the world champion, lets his characters die, and turns the other way."[54] Here, Germany's new-found identity as a nation-of-winners is countered by the price to be paid, the bargains entered and the losses this entails, all concentrated in the final scene, imparting ironic, but productive meaning to both parts of parapraxis: to the "performance" and to "failure."

Maria Braun, of course, would never have thought of herself as a victim, which is another reason to believe that the more interesting aspects of the change in Germany's memory frame around 2003 are inadequately understood under the victim discourse. Earlier, I mentioned that I thought it an achievement if Holocaust memory had indeed become an integral part of Germany's post-unification identity and a confirmation of the civic self-understanding of its citizen. In light of the above, one may want to modify this assertion by also indicating one of its more problematic aspects, whose "working through"—namely the relation between identity and identification—seems an eminently cinematic topic, but one which, to my knowledge, few German film focusing on the Holocaust or the Nazi period have broached, but which nevertheless has found challenging expression in novels and films intended for an international audience, and explicitly starting from the perspective of the perpetrators, before exploring the repercussions of memory, guilt and trauma. It is to this complex that the last part of the chapter turns.

"Perpetrator Memory": Parapraxis in an Inter- and Post-National Context

As Holocaust memory goes through its different phases and cycles, as it changes "frames" and oscillates between Germans seeing themselves as victims and acknowledging their direct and indirect roles as perpetrators, "perpetrator memory" has only recently become part of Holocaust memory studies. But if the term was taboo for so long, because it seemed to dignify the murderers and war criminals with (undeserved) subjectivity and humanity, thus insulting the memory of the victims and survivors, then the reason for the appearance of "perpetrator memory" must first be sought in the present. Because the "never again" of Auschwitz has been disproved in genocides (Cambodia, Rwanda), brutally repressive regimes (Argentina and Chile under the generals), apartheid (South Africa) and civil wars, the subsequent war crime trials and "truth and reconciliation" tribunals were premised on giving voice to victims and perpetrators alike. In the cases before the Courts in The Hague (ex-Yugoslavia, Rwanda, Liberia), for instance, alleged perpetrators (or their defense counsels) were given a platform. With respect to Nazism and the Holocaust, too, it was not always that the perpetrators' past caught up with them; sometimes, those who had preferred to keep silent and a low profile about their actions, sensing the end of their lives, felt compelled to speak out, or were enticed to commit their memories to print or voice them in interviews. In the 1970s and 1980s, filmmakers like Claude Lanzmann and Marcel Ophuls developed special interviewing skills and even resorted to disguise and deception to get the perpetrators to speak and reminisce. Belated trials, such as those of Klaus Barbie (1987), Paul Touvier (1994), and Maurice Papon (1998) in France, or the protracted extradition case and eventual trial of John Demjanjuk in Munich (2009–11) have furthermore given a face, as well as media attention, to perpetrators for a public mostly too young to have first-hand memories of the crimes the accused were said to have committed.[55] In the case of the French trials, they exposed collusion, complicity and collaboration in high places, and thus helped relativize national mythologies of France's brave resistance to German occupation. The vehemence of Lanzmann's stance (in his debates with Spielberg or Didi-Huberman, for instance) may have something to do with this belatedness of justice, with Lanzmann feeling entitled, as filmmaker, to be prosecutor, judge and jury all in one, in order to fill the justice gap.

However, there has also been a different kind of interest in perpetrator memory among writers and filmmakers, which prompts the question, whether here, too, one can speak of parapractic (and melodramatic) modes of representation. I already briefly discussed DER UNTERGANG, based on the memoir of Traudl Junge, Hitler's secretary during the last days in the Berlin Führer-Bunker. While Junge's perspective is that of an ambiguously innocent/ignorant bystander, the film's focus (and that of its critics) was on Hitler, and his human all too human foibles, failings and weaknesses. I also pointed out one crucial parapractic moment, when Junge's face expresses shock at Hitler's mention of the Final Solution.

Likewise, I have alluded to Jonathan Littell's *The Kindly Ones* as an example of guilt management through an insistence on the perpetrator's proud amorality. Not only does the main protagonist show neither regret nor remorse, but he also seems to possess perfect recall and a quasi-photographic memory. These are aspects of his personality that the author stresses, possibly in order to draw as sharp a contrast with those Nazi war criminals brought to trial, who profess to not remember anything, or blame old age for their lack of recall.

In other respects, too, Littell depsychologizes his protagonist to have a clear witness to the machinery of Nazism, including its origins and process, and all of it in minute and lacerating detail. Yet his hero is a witness neither in trial mode, nor in atonement mode, but seemingly fully cognizant of what he has done and also fully cognizant that these are crimes. This full knowledge, in the absence of remorse, but also in the absence of any ideology that might provide a superstructure, however mad or misguided, has puzzled many readers and on occasion outraged critics. After all, the Nazis did have ideologies, however hateful, and they justified their actions in the light of what these ideologies appeared to demand of them: whether it was their anti-Semitism or their conviction of the Germans as the master-race, whether it was their belief in the historic mission of liberating Europe from Bolshevism, or their obsession with Germany requiring *Lebensraum* (space to live) and therefore had the right and duty to invade its Eastern neighbors. Yet Aue's amorality is a powerful narrative and literary device in that it acts as a lens for drastically shifting the reader's perspective to one of extremely uncomfortable intimacy and participation, divided between illicit empathy and dreaded fascination.

Littell's novel followed another controversial literary bestseller crucially involving a perpetrator, Bernhard Schlink's *Der Vorleser/The Reader* (1995, English translation 1997), which was made into an Oscar winning film of the same title (2008). Before turning to the debates that both book and film provoked, I want first to examine some of the other reasons for the contemporary turn to perpetrator memory. As argued in the early part of this chapter, the universalization of the victim in Holocaust memory also opened up a potential for identification and even overidentification. It risked taking from the individual fates of the victims much of their individual identity and so deprive them of the respectful distance due to the singularity of their suffering.[56] Paradoxically, depicting the perpetrator restores distance and singularity, but now the singularity of motives, the unique historical context, and the external contingencies that make an often ordinary human being capable of committing the most unspeakable atrocities.[57] In other words, access to the perpetrator always involves both the question of a shared humanity ("could it have been me?") and the recognition of a distance (of time, of place, of circumstances: "thank God, it wasn't me").

That there is a certain thrill in slipping into the body of a "monster" probably counts for something, too; the kind of camouflage that attracted and repelled Theweleit when he first encountered Littell's novel. And as there are different kinds of victimhood, as we saw with respect to Primo Levy's Musulman, and the "grey zone" he identified when prisoners in the camps were drafted by the SS guards to police other prisoners, when kapos were even more brutal than the SS in order to curry favor or simply to survive, or when Jews assisted Germans in rounding up Jews in occupied territories or ghettos, so there must also be degrees of culpability and collusion on the side of the perpetrators. For instance, in several Italian films from the 1970s that had Nazism as their subject or the camps as setting, such as Luchino Visconti's THE DAMNED (1969), Bernardo Bertolucci's THE CONFORMIST (1970), Liliana Cavani's THE NIGHT-PORTER (1974), Lina Wertmüller's PASQUALINO SETTEBELLEZE (1975), or Pier Paolo Pasolini's SALO (1975), the categories of victim and perpetrator were blurred and complicated by being embedded in gendered power-relations of sexual dependency, homosexuality and the pleasures of submission.[58]

In more recent literature and films focusing on perpetrators, such (gendered, racialized) master-slave dialectics are still in evidence, but tend to have superimposed on them additional layers of complicity and antagonism, where the varying degrees of culpability are played off against each other, for instance, by differentiating between guilt and shame. This is a key strategy in the novels and stories of Bernhard Schlink, thematizing the relation between Germans and Jews, and between Germans and Germans of different generations. However, it is also to be found in recent U.S. literature about slavery, such as Valery Martin's *Property* (2003), Edward P. Jones' *The Known World* (2003), as well as Kathryn Stockett's *The Help* (2009), made into a film in 2011.[59] This layering can be a sign of the added reflexivity required of post-modern artists when tackling such historical traumas and national disasters as slavery, the Holocaust or colonialism. However much these topics of cultural theory now imply the deconstruction of any fixed subject position, including those of "victims" and "perpetrators," it does not preclude the texts from partaking in a less conscious or indeed less self-conscious "guilt management" on behalf of particular constituencies of readers and audiences, especially if one remembers that it is most likely some unresolved dilemma in the present, rather than the past for its own sake, that their memory narratives want to bring to light.

In German films, outside documentary, one finds few, but symptomatic films dealing with a single perpetrator or detailing the life of a known Nazi criminal. An early (but little seen) feature film to focus on the perpetrator was Theodor Kotulla's AUS EINEM DEUTSCHEN LEBEN (A GERMAN LIFE, 1977). Based on the story of Auschwitz-Commandant Rudolf Höss (called Franz Lang in the film and played by Götz George, one of Germany's best-known actors and television stars), it charts another "career," not that of Hitler, as in the documentary of that title, made the same year (HITLER, EINE KARRIERE, Joachim Fest, 1977). Kotulla reconstructs Höss' rise from the ranks of the right-wing Free Corps to member first of the SA, then of the SS, his pride in being promoted to Commandant of this important camp, to his trial in Nuremberg and the eventual death sentence. In a style that eschews all spectacle and instead owes much to the distanced observational manner of Jean Marie Straub, Kotulla focuses on the small, logical steps that lead an ordinary man to dedicate himself with all his formidable intellectual powers to implementing the diabolically efficient machinery required to kill so many thousands of human beings and disposing of their remains.

Götz George, whose biography and family history as the son of the famous (Nazi) actor Heinrich George adds to such roles a further retrospective-reflexive layer, has bravely taken on other parts of perpetrators of unfathomable crimes. In 1995 he played the serial murderer Fritz Haarmann in Romuald Karmakar's *Der Totmacher*, the same historical case from 1924 that had served Fritz Lang for M, a part that Peter Lorre made immortal. Set in a single, sparsely furnished interrogation room, *Der Totmacher* is intent to record the monster "in his own words," a trope familiar from the Eichmann trial and Hannah Arendt's "banality of evil." The emotional weight is in the rapport between Haarmann and the investigating forensic psychiatrist, who acts as a stand-in for the spectator's ambiguous feeling of what it means to "understand" the motivation behind horrific deeds. Reviving the case of Haarmann, in a part-forensic, part-therapeutic context, makes sense as the "archaeology" of a mentality that extends beyond the Weimar years, while not transgressing the taboo that such an "understanding" must not include Nazi criminals.[60]

Four years later, George took on the role of another, even more notorious Nazi perpetrator than Rudolf Höss, namely Joseph Mengele, the death dispensing doctor of the most inhumane medical experiments conducted at Auschwitz. NICHTS ALS DIE WAHRHEIT (*After The Truth*, Roland Suso Richter, 1999) also revives the forensic mode of the courtroom drama, discussed in a previous chapter, but adds several twists, aware that it is citing a genre whose value now is its belatedness, or as in this case, its hypothetical, counter-factual status of "what if." A young lawyer and obsessive student of the unresolved case of Mengele, finds himself kidnapped and taken to Mengele's secret hideout in Brazil. Ready to face, at the end of his life (after having faked his death by drowning in 1979), a court in Germany, Mengele wants to admit to everything, while still pleading not guilty, and therefore needs an able lawyer.[61] Mengele's case, as imagined in the film, raises not only the usual questions of the Hippocratic oath and whether "following orders" can ever exonerate someone for committing what he knows to be inhuman acts, but also *the* historical question par excellence: whether those who come after can judge the circumstances, the scale and a mindset so alien and monstrous that all moral standards and possibly even legal provisions must fail. Mengele's barbaric actions *then*, are matched by his brutal candor *now*, in the light of which some of the pious lies and self-deceptions of contemporary society seems shabby. "I was never a Nazi. I arranged myself with the system, so that I could do my scientific work" is the kind of statement that is meant to reverberate well beyond the Nazi period and his Auschwitz laboratory of death. Mengele's interest in the trial is to have a sufficiently prominent platform on which to demonstrate that the biologism, to which he dedicated his life's work, including his work at Auschwitz, has long since become the dogma and doxa of genetics, the neuro-sciences and evolutionary biology.

Mengele, appearing in the dock in a black suit, roll neck sweater and white, bloodless features, looks—as one critic put it—more like the Nosferatu of German history than the "banality of evil" of Eichmann in Jerusalem,[62] suggesting that the director's thought-experiment of bringing the (as far as we know) unrepentant and unforthcoming Mengele back from the dead, intends to outline a different relation to the perpetrators. They are here allowed to become the phantasmatic mirror into which the present generation is invited to look, and recognize their own failings and shortcomings (underscored in the way Mengele's deeds eventually lead to the lawyer's own family, and thus binds the children's affective memory to their parents' guilty secrets). It is almost as if the film not only wished that Mengele could have been brought to justice, but as if this film could have been made in the 1970s, rather then, belatedly, having to be made in the late-1990s. This sense of belatedness and the hypothetical premise of the film, combining the "what if" with the "if only," as well as the family history that Götz George brings to the part, add yet another version of parapraxis to Holocaust memory, while inviting the (German) viewer to reflect on perpetrator memory in a more radical, and thus more troubling and ambiguous form.

Perhaps the best-known of all these perpetrators' narratives in recent years, which pushes the boundary beyond the usual binary oppositions of *Schuld* and *Schulden*, of remembering and forgetting, of showing remorse or being unrepentant was Bernhard Schlink's already mentioned novel *Der Vorleser*, made into a successful film, The Reader (2008), directed by Stephen Daldry, starring Kate Winslet and with a script by the renowned British playwright David Hare.

Ostensibly the retrospective memoir of a brief, but intense love affair between a fifteen-year-old boy and a thirty-year-old woman in Germany in the 1960s, *The Reader* proceeds by uncovering layers upon layers of guilty and pleasurable entanglements. For Michael Berg, the boy, from whose point of view the story is told, the affair ends mysteriously and bafflingly, when one day Hanna simply disappears. She reenters his life when—now a student of jurisprudence—he recognizes her as the chief defendant at the trial of former female concentration camp guards. Sentenced to prison, he visits her regularly, eventually discovering another secret: she is illiterate and that her choices in life—including her time as a Nazi guard—were determined by this stigma.

The Reader seems to suggest that there are things worse than being suspected of having helped burn down a church full of Jewish women, whom you were to guard. The illicit affair with a teenager may have caused Hanna guilt feelings which hide another guilty secret—her career as a camp guard—which in turn becomes a way of hiding the further secret: her inability to read and write. A trivial fault or transgression becomes the envelope for a major fault, which is reversed by another fault, having sex with a minor. Such a layering of guilt, with one guilt hiding another, as it were, may be more of a "thought-experiment" than it is a credible historical story, but precisely because of these elements straining credibility, *The Reader* is able to draw from this unlikely material some powerful and surprising subject effects. This is because both the book and the film suggest a hierarchy of guilt, insofar as Hanna's shame about not being able to write (even her name) in some sense trumps the guilt she might have incurred by abandoning the prisoners in her charge, which seems a problematic proposition to say the least, but which would constitute a novel way of guilt management, in which the mutual misunderstanding between the lovers Michael and Hanna function as the necessary parapraxes: asymmetric (underlining the incommensurability of the different secrets), but also regulatory (insofar as some sort of possible redemption is suggested).

While both book and film became commercial and critical successes, there were many dissenting voices, and especially Jewish commentators denounced the novel (and film) as a fake.[63] They charged Schlink with not actually confronting the issue of the perpetrator's moral stance, making her form of atonement (suicide, with her savings going to a Jewish institution for combating illiteracy, as if such an institution existed) not only maudlin and morally hollow. Schlink also assigns to the only Jewish figure in the film the remote, uncanny power of superior knowledge one recognizes from the 1970s: "The film finally maneuvers the daughter of a concentration camp survivor into the position of becoming the instance of the super-ego, whose icy cold demeanor constitutes surplus-enjoyment as the forbidden, and thus especially sophisticated form of enjoyment: the exaggeratedly dignified, highly cultivated old lady refuses absolution to both the ageing reader and to his now dead lover, thereby indirectly allowing their affair to assume near-tragic dimensions.[64]

Others read the novel more self-reflexively, as a parable (or even satire) of Germany's never-ending need to "master the past." Each "turn" of the novel's narrative seems to spell out a version and variant of the German-Jewish relationship after Auschwitz, clearly marking the story as addressed to and intended for the second post-war generation: "With this remarkable parable Schlink retraces with astonishing accuracy the arc of official post-war dealings with guilt: an accepted but finally never fully assumed feeling of guilt, as if one had been, during the Nazi years, illiterate; followed by a dutifully exemplary working off of the past, and finally, paying compensation and reparation. The irony, of course, is that the money is supposed to go to a 'Jewish Association Against Illiteracy,' as if of all people, it was up to the Jews to provide the necessary remedial education and enlightenment that persuades others not to kill them."[65]

However, such a multiplication of different kinds of guilt is rare in German cinema, and the THE READER can stand as an example of a layering of guilt which effectively blurs the lines between victim and perpetrator. Shifting the levels allows the latter to become the former, in a balancing act of seemingly incompatible (and certainly improbable) values, without one mitigating the other or one cancelling the other.

Whereas in AFTER THE TRUTH, Mengele's monstrous guilt is such that it grants him a certain freedom to be able to accuse others, and thereby—as absolute evil—attaining a perverse moral high ground, not least because he speaks from beyond the grave, the woman in THE READER is an allegory of the perpetrator generation, as seen from the moral perspective of their (grand-)children. For this to work, the central figure has to be a woman to make plausible not only that shame might trump guilt, but that shame might be an adequate substitute for the admission of guilt, in the guilt management where remaining silent was both a self-indictment and a sign of self-possession and proud steadfastness: "never apologize, never explain…."

THE READER and the controversy it engendered is of interest to my argument because its layering of incommensurable kinds of transgression in the form of shame covering for guilt would be another version of my parapraxis argument, another way that one thing stands for another, but where the fundamental incompatibility or incommensurability creates the corresponding performed failures. Hanna "performs failure" (of morality, of ordinary humanity) in order to hide (but also draw attention to) another truth. Indeed, one could read her suicide as another way of "performing failure," namely the failure of her rehabilitation, in which case the improbably "Jewish Association against Illiteracy" more than the rejection of the gift by the Jewish survivor in New York, would be the signifier of that failure, drawing attention to itself.

Conclusion: From Guilt Management to the Debt Crisis?

To call "guilt management" the overall strategy that binds together the various memory discourses and memory frames present in German public life and in the arts since 1945, with respect to the Nazi period and the Holocaust, evidently does not imply a consciously planned strategy. But neither is it unconscious in the psychoanalytic sense. Rather, it points to the way the conflicted awareness of the ethical consequences of the Nazi period have shaped the shifting relations between cultural memory and national identity in post-war Germany. Management thus designates both purposiveness *and* self-divided defensiveness, both pragmatic moves and unconscious motives, both intended effects and unintended consequences. Guilt, on the other hand, is also used in a more special sense, insofar as it is normally understood to imply its complement: that there should be atonement—and closure. What melodrama and parapraxis as guilt management offer is an alternative within the same constellation, namely deferral of closure in the form of both excess and absence, answering in the German case to the impossible hope of finding a modality of exchange, a means of equivalence, compensation, redress, forgiveness or justice, which does not leave a residue, a remainder, an unresolved "remnant" (to use Agamben's term). But as we saw, intransigence, obdurate silence, or brutally frank admissions of horrible deeds can also be an attempt to establish or impose a framework of equivalence and exchange, even if at the self-aggrandizing scale of "world history" or the progress of "science."

The choice of melodrama and parapraxis as forms of guilt management focuses on actions, discourses (in the public sphere) and symbolic actions (including novels, poems and films) that seem to address—in an effort to redress or redeem—this surplus. In German cinema (and literature) certain excessive incidents, stories and situations can be identified, which—by default and by design—acknowledge the past's presence in the present (which is, after all, what memory is), and it does so in its persistently conflicted manifestations. But melodrama and the parapractic mode are only among several forms or genres that seek to extract balance from excess (another notable one being opera)[66]: complement but also antidote or counter-strategy to realism, the melodramatic and parapractic modes are inherently unstable and volatile. Only the latter, however, is liable to being overlooked or misunderstood, by the very fact of performing the failure of that which it seeks to be the redress.

Yet there may also be a different gain from Holocaust memory having become institutionalized and victimhood universalized both in Germany and Europe: it has reignited the debate about the legacy of the Enlightenment. The renewed faith in human rights as the only "universal" still credible is based on facing up to this faith's most severe test, symbolized by the Holocaust. If it was a test that the Enlightenment failed, then the project "Europe" once more pledged its commitment to these Enlightenment values, out of the very acknowledgement of that failure. With the end of the classical political ideologies of the twentieth century and the end of the social utopias originating in the nineteenth century, Holocaust memory remains the negative symbol of a deeper knowledge about human beings which any belief in a more rational and more sustainable future must now take into account.

Such knowledge, however obliquely encoded, is—so my argument goes—anticipated and preserved especially in the manifestations of parapractic memory that runs through post-war German literature, cinema and public life, rich in failed performances as well as in performances of failure. That such guilt management can also be observed elsewhere, as I suggest, with a look to Hollywood, is a feature that deserves more attention than I can give it here.[67] Guilt management through melodrama and parapraxis, in other words, is not confined to Germany, if one thinks of the many legacies of colonialism, whose political consequences are arguably more pressing today than those of the Holocaust. Perhaps even more importantly, guilt management is not confined to events that are situated in the past, which in any event, is often the "screen memory" for the urgent concerns of the present.

One of these urgent concerns of the present that affects the whole of Europe but once more centers on Germany now has a different name: the Debt Crisis. Without going into its history or offering an economic analysis, Europe's debt crisis has created a situation of asymmetry and uneven exchange which puts my discussion of *Schuld* and *Schulden* into yet another context, while making it no less melodramatic and parapractic in the public sphere. For instance, that it should pit Germany against Greece adds a special poignancy, when one considers how the Germany of Weimar classicism has sought in Greece *edle Einfalt, stille Grösse*, i.e., the sources of beauty and harmony, of enlightenment and democracy. The new imbalance and disharmony looks like a cruel parody of the German yearning for Greece, when poets and thinkers "sought the land of the Greeks with their souls," as Goethe put it in his play *Iphigenie*. Today, the Greeks would argue that Germans seize rather than seek their land, voicing resentment and feelings of grievance and injustice over a situation where Germany appears to have a triple hold over them, given that it was German banks that lent Greece the cheap money, with which to buy German goods in the first place, only to make the Greeks feel guilty about their profligacy, while still collecting a good part of the interest on the loans that bankrupted Greece in the first place. While this is clearly not the whole story, it illustrates an asymmetric antagonistic mutuality, which mirrors the situation of "symbolic peoples" and their mutual entanglements as I have tried to analyze them in this chapter. And insofar as it puts guilt and debt and thus guilt management into a new context, the crisis may well be a good thing for Europe; not because it brings the collapse of capitalism closer to hand, or because Europe needs the cleansing force of fire and brimstone, but because it obliges a more fundamental rethinking about the relation between money and debt, between debt and guilt, between guilt and accountability, between accountability and the community. If this is the lesson that will be drawn from the memory debate around the Holocaust, it would indeed point to the future rather than the past, while indicating that guilt management no less than debt management is ultimately a question of rights and obligations, but even more so of justice and equality beyond equivalence and mere symmetry.

Notes

1. James E. Young, *The Texture of Memory: Holocaust Memorials and Meaning* (New Haven: Yale University Press, 1993), 26.
2. Andreas F. Kelletat, "Von der Täter- zur Opfernation?" *Triangulum. Germanistisches Jahrbuch für Estland, Lettland und Litauen 2003/2004* (Riga, 2006), 132–47; journalist Peter Reichel used the same phrase to characterize Japan after the dropping of the atom bomb on Hiroshima: "aus einem Tätervolk wurde buchstäblich mit einem Schlag eine Opfernation," Peter Reichel, Das "Geschenk des Himmels," *Süddeutsche Zeitung* (May 8, 2005), 13. See also: "The recent surge in representations of German suffering amounts to the greatest shift in German memory discourse since 1979, when the screening of the U.S. TV series Holocaust again brought the theme of Nazi extermination policies to the fore of German public memory. This shift is all the more astonishing as it appears to revert and contest the institutionalisation of the memory of the Holocaust in the memory culture of the Berlin Republic in the 1990s." Helmut Schmitz (ed.), *A Nation of Victims? Representations of German Wartime Suffering from 1945 to the Present* (Amsterdam: Rodopi, 2007), 2.
3. Harald Welzer, "Schön unscharf," *Literatur,* no. 1 (2004), 53 (www.his-online.de/fileadmin/verlag/leseproben/9783936096125.pdf).
4. The more skeptical note can be found in the introduction to Stuart Taberner and Karina Berger (eds.), *Germans as Victims in the Literary Fiction of the Berlin Republic* (Woodbridge, UK: Camden House, 2009), 1–8.
5. For a fuller discussion, see Thomas Elsaesser, *Fassbinder's Germany: History Identity Subject* (Amsterdam: Amsterdam University Press, 1996), 175-96 (chapter 7: "Frankfurt, Germans and Jews")
6. http://www.mediaculture-online.de/fileadmin/bibliothek/weizsaecker_speech_may85/weizsaecker_speech_may85.pdf
7. "Stolpersteine" is a Europe-wide commemorative project begun by the Cologne artist Gunter Demnig. It consists of small, cobblestone-sized memorials for individual victims of Nazism placed on the pavement outside their last known residence prior to being deported (http://www.stolpersteine.com/).
8. Henryk M. Broder puts it most sarcastically: "Is there a German identity in Germany? And if there is, why does it express itself mainly in the search for a Jewish identity?" (Henryk Broder, homepage: *Selber schuld wenn Sie mir schreiben,* http://henryk-broder.com/hmb.php/blog/article/1061).
9. Jonathan Dunnage, "Perpetrator memory and memories about perpetrators," *Memory Studies,* 3 no. 2 (2010), 91.
10. Beate Meyer, "Geschichte im Film: Judenverfolgung, Mischehen und der Protest in der Rosenstraße 1943," *Zeitschrift für Geschichtsforschung,* 52 (2004), 36. For more historical background, see Nathan Stoltzfus, *Resistance of the Heart: Intermarriage and the Rosenstrasse Protest in Nazi Germany* (New York: W.W. Norton, 1996).
11. Daniela Berghahn, "Post-1990 Screen Memories of the Third Reich," *German Life and Letters.* 59, no. 2 (April 2006), 294.

12. Cathy S. Gelbin, "Double Visions Queer Femininity," *Women in German Yearbook: Feminist Studies in German Literature & Culture,* 23 (2007), 190.
13. "Almost every German film that addresses the Shoah has to renegotiate the relationships between self and other, German and Jew, perpetrator/bystander and victim; respect the rules of historical authenticity; and yet tell a new story that differs from the already known history. It is at this potential gap between individual story and collective history that the strategy of historical displacement enters narrative films." Stephan K. Schindler, "Displaced Images: The Holocaust in German Film," in Stephan K. Schindler and Lutz Koepnick (eds.), *The Cosmopolitan Screen: German Cinema and the Global Imaginary, 1945 to the Present* (Ann Arbor: University of Michigan Press, 2007), 198.
14. Holocaust films have been explicitly referred to as heritage cinema in Lutz Koepnick, "Reframing the Past: Heritage Cinema and Holocaust in the 1990s," *New German Critique,* 87 (2002), 47–82.
15. Saul Friedländer, *The Years of Extermination: Nazi Germany and the Jews, 1939–1945* (New York: HarperCollins, 2007) was awarded the 2008 Pulitzer Prize for General Non-Fiction and the Leipzig Book Fair Prize for Non-Fiction.
16. Daniel Levy and Natan Sznaider, *The Holocaust and Memory in the Global Age* (Philadelphia: Temple University Press, 2005).
17. Peter Novick, *Holocaust in American Life* (New York: Houghton Mifflin, 1999).
18. For a highly polemical response to what the Americanization of the Holocaust means for other minorities and genocides, see Lilian Friedberg, "Dare to Compare Americanizing the Holocaust," *The American Indian Quarterly,* 24, no. 3 (Summer 2000), 353–80.
19. Henryk M. Broder published an essay entitled "Die Germanisierung des Holocaust," in *Volk und Wahn* (Munich: Goldman Verlag, 1996), and, after another round of disparaging remarks by Claude Lanzmann, Jorge Semprun sarcastically remarked that Lanzmann didn't have the copyright on the Shoah (quoted in Klaus Theweleit, *New German Critique* (Winter 2009), 29. As to the uses made of Holocaust memory in Israel, see Tom Segev, *The Seventh Million: The Israelis and the Holocaust* (New York: Hill & Wang, 1993).
20. Daniel Levy and Natan Sznaider, "Memory Unbound — The Holocaust and the Formation of Cosmopolitan Memory," (http://www.sunysb.edu/sociology/faculty/Levy/EJSTFIN.pdf).
21. J. Young, "America's Holocaust: Memory and the Politics of Identity," in Hilene Flanzbaum (ed.), *The Americanization of the Holocaust* (Baltimore: Johns Hopkins University Press, 1999), 82.
22. Giorgio Agamben, *Remnants of Auschwitz: The Witness and the Archive* (Cambridge, MA: Zone Books, 2002).
23. Primo Levi, "The Drowned and the Saved," in Primo Levi, *If This is a Man* (London: Abacus, 1991), 97.
24. Giorgio Agamben, *Homo Sacer: Sovereign Power and Bare Life* (Stanford, CA: Stanford University Press, 1998).
25. *Der Spiegel* famously carried a photograph of Liam Neeson with the caption "Der gute Deutsche" (http://www.spiegel.de/spiegel/print/d-13684768.html). See also Christoph Weiss (ed.), *"Der gute Deutsche": Dokumente zur Diskussion um Steven Spielbergs "Schindlers Liste" in Deutschland* (St. Ingbert: Röhrig Universitätsverlag, 1995).
26. I take the discussion of the "good German" in the context of W. G. Sebald from Brad Prager, "The Good German as Narrator: On W. G. Sebald and the Risks of Holocaust Writing," *New German Critique,* 96 (Fall 2005), 75–102. The reference to Grass is on p. 86.
27. *"Anonyma: Eine Frau in Berlin."* Tagebuchaufzeichnungen vom 20. April bis 22. Juni 1945 (Frankfurt: Eichborn Verlag, 2003).

28. Besides Harald Welzer's review essay mentioned above, see special issues of *Der Spiegel* (2/2002) "Die Deutschen als Opfer" (http://www.spiegel.de/spiegel/spiegelspecial/d-22937237.html). Among the English-language academic literature see Bill Niven (ed.), *Germans as Victims: Remembering the Past in Contemporary Germany* (Houndsmills, UK: Palgrave, 2006), and Schmitz, *A Nation of Victims?,* Taberner and Berger, *Germans as Victims* and Robert G. Moeller, "Germans as Victims?: Thoughts on a Post-Cold War History of World War II Legacies," *History & Memory*, 17, no. 1/2 (Spring/Summer 2005), 147–94.
29. Ulrich Raulff, "1945: Ein Jahr kehrt zurück — Tausche Geschichte gegen Gefühl," *Süddeutsche Zeitung* (October 30, 2003), 11.
30. This view is taken, among others, by Robert Moeller "The Politics of the Past in the 1950s: Rhetorics of Victimisation in East and West Germany," in *Germans as Victims*, 26–42, and is also present in several chapters of Schmitz, *A Nation of Victims?*
31. "Berlin 1945: War and Rape: Liberators Take Liberties, *October,* 72 (Cambridge, MA: MIT Press, 1995) with contributions by Stuart Liebman, Helke Sander, Andreas Huyssen and others.
32. Heinz-Peter Preusser argues that coffee table books on the bombing raids, including the one that was published to go with Jörg Friedrich's *Der Brand,* tended to select shocking photos of bombing victims that were reminiscent of Holocaust images, leaving it to the reader to draw the analogies between German trauma and Jewish suffering. H-P Preusser, "Regarding and imagining: contrived immediacy of the Allied bombing campaign in photography, novel, and historiography" in Schmitz, *A Nation of Victims?*, 141–60. Intriguingly enough, the same comparison of the Dresden bombings with Nazi atrocities was made by Red Army Faction member Ulrike Meinhof almost thirty years earlier, possibly after reading David Irving's (pro-Hitler and anti-Churchill) book on the bombing of Dresden (1965). See Alois Prinz, *Lieber wütend als traurig. Die Lebensgeschichte von Ulrike Meinhof* (Weinheim: Beltz, 2003), 251.
33. See Annette Seidel-Arpaci, in Schmitz, *A Nation of Victims?*
34. Television, for instance, seems to know only three kinds of human beings: experts (which includes politicians), talents (which includes performers) and victims (which includes everybody else). See also Eva Illouz, *Oprah Winfrey and the Glamour of Misery: An Essay on Popular Culture* (New York: Columbia University Press, 2003).
35. Diedrich Diederichsen, "Der Chef brüllt schon wieder so (*Der Untergang*)" *Die Tageszeitung* (Berlin), September 15, 2004 (http://www.taz.de/1/archiv/archiv/?dig=2004/09/15/a0202).
36. "[T]he institutionalized recognition of Jews as victims [… has] given breathing room to private, family disseminated memories [and] has also led many Germans to feel free to break taboos and claim victimhood in public discourse through film and literature." Jason Crouthamel, reviewing Schmitz, *A Nation of Victims?* (http://www.h-net.org/reviews/showrev.php?id=14219). A further complaint was that in the new century it was left-wing authors who took up the revanchist causes formerly championed by the right, such as the expulsion of the German population in what became Poland and the Czech Republic. Günter Grass' *Im Krebsgang* was mostly cited as evidence.
37. Harald Welzer in H.Welzer et al, *"Opa war kein Nazi." Nationalsozialismus und Holocaust im Familiengedächtnis* (Frankfurt am Main: Fischer Verlag, 2002).
38. "The trick […] known as 'knoppisize' after its inventor Guido Knopp, [is to] re-enact 'smoking gun' history, whenever moving images are unavailable." (http://www.tagesspiegel.de/medien/der-kaiser-und-der-krieg/532494.html). See also http://www.uni-protokolle.de/buecher/isbn/3423307943/ and, for a comparison of Knopp's method with"steampunk" literature, see http://www.zeit.de/2004/10/Steam_Punk
39. For a more scholarly discussion of Guido Knopp's method, see Judith Keilbach, *Geschichtsbilder und Zeitzeugen: Zur Darstellung des Nationalsozialismus im bundesdeutschen Fernsehen* (Münster: LIT Verlag, 2008).

40. Harald Welzer, Sabine Möller, and Karoline Tschuggnall, *"Opa war kein Nazi." Nationalsozialismus und Holocaust im Familiengedächtnis* (Frankfurt am Main: Fischer Verlag, 2002).
41. See three novels, all published in 2003: Stephan Wackwitz, *Ein unsichtbares Land* (2003), Ulla Hahn, *Unscharfe Bilder* (2003), Reinhard Jirgl, *Die Unvollendeten* (2003).
42. "The question is not whether Germans can remember the war, but how they remember it and the implications of their memories. What were the Germans fighting for? How much of it remained relevant after 1945? How was the war experience reinterpreted by the FRG? To what extent was this interpretation influenced by post-war circumstances and beliefs, disillusionments and denials? Can we now perceive a new cycle of interpretations and reinterpretations in the wake of reunification? What may be the political consequences of such revisions?" Omer Bartov, "Germany's Unforgettable War: The Twisted Road from Berlin to Moscow and back," *Diplomatic History*, 25, no. 3 (Summer 2001), 410.
43. See Robert G. Moeller, "War Stories: The Search for a Usable Past in the Federal Republic of Germany," *American Historical Review* (October 1996), 1008–48.
44. Helmut Kohl's 1984 Israel visit is officially remembered thanks to a different, but perhaps no less telling phrase, spoken when he addressed the Knesset: "I stand before you as someone who could not have burdened himself with guilt during the Nazi years; I benefit from the grace of a late birth." As *Der Spiegel* wrote: "Chancellor Kohl carries his good conscience before him like a flag." (http://www.dradio.de/dlr/sendungen/kalender/227514/)
45. The memory-regimes of the formerly communist countries differ significantly from those of Western Europe, and the question of who is victim, collaborator or perpetrator becomes even more complicated. The consequences of first Nazi then Soviet occupation, as well as the different strains of nationalism tends to give Holocaust memory a lower priority in the competing claims for commemoration, group-recognition and (post-national) identity-formation. See the "Memory at War" transnational research projects at the Universities of Tartu, Helsinki, Cambridge, Groningen and Bergen (http://www.memoryatwar.org/projects-tartu-overview) and Richard Esbenshade, "Remembering to Forget: Memory, History, National Identity in Postwar East-Central Europe," *Representations*, 49 (Winter 1995), 72–96. The emphasis on the "plurality" of victimhood also brings Central and Eastern European countries closer to the "paradigm change" in Germany discussed in this chapter. See Eric Langenbacher, "Twenty-first century memory regimes in Poland and Germany," *German Politics and Society*, 26, no. 4 (Winter 2008), 50–81.
46. It would be interesting, but goes beyond the scope of this chapter, to consider Quentin Tarantino's INGLOURIOUS BASTERDS (2009) as such a film that maintains its high ground by allowing both sides to be at their amoral worst, and out of this "level playing field" to explore the full potential of "parapractic" situations. Mostly, but not always, they are accommodated under the general, counter-factual premise of Hitler having been defeated by a team of bad-ass Jews. This possibility sustains each of the intertwined narratives and their twists.
47. Klaus Theweleit, "On the German Reaction to Jonathan Littell *Les bienveillantes," New German Critique*, 106, 36, no. 1 (Winter 2009), 23.
48. See Y. Michal Bodemann, "Eclipse of Memory: German Representations of Auschwitz in the Early Postwar Period," *New German Critique*, no. 75 (Autumn, 1998), 69.
49. See also "Die Gefühle haben ihre eigene Zeit, sie arbeiten zeitversetzt (feelings have their own temporality, they work with delays and displacements)." Alexander Kluge, *Chronik der Gefühle*, 1 & 2 (Frankfurt/M: Suhrkamp, 2000), 4.
50. In a perceptive discussion of another highly commented upon, overtly symbolic film about guilt management from the immediate post-war period, Wolfgang Staudte's DIE MÖRDER SIND UNTER UNS/THE MURDERERS ARE AMONG US (1946), Stephan Schindler

makes a similar point: "The film's intended antifascist and anticapitalistic message shatters [...] because the 'good German' forced to do evil is an accomplice who failed to prevent atrocities and symbolically re-enacts them by crushing the star. When the film ultimately 'offers redemption to its troubled male subject, the potential of domestic happiness to the long-suffering woman, and a promise of ... moral order restored to a confused community,' then a historic reversal of victim and perpetrator has occurred. [...] The fate of the (Jewish) victims in Poland serves only one purpose: to address the different degrees of guilt among the Germans themselves as they renegotiate their postwar relationships with each other." Stephan K. Schindler, "Displaced Images," 199.

51. Drehli Robnik, "NS-Verbrechen vor Gericht. Der Nürnberger Prozess in der visuellen Erinnerungskultur" (Wien: Österreichische Gesellschaft für Zeitgeschichte, 2007).
52. Diedrich Diederichsen, Wunder von Bern (http://www.filmzentrale.com/rezis/wundervonberndd.htm).
53. Diederichsen also refers to WUNDER VON BERN as a remake, but names a different film: "Der filmische Bezugspunkt von das *Wunder von Bern* durch den Titel, ist das *Wunder von Mailand*: ein Film von Vittorio De Sica aus den fünfziger Jahren, in dem die Unterdrückten und Beleidigten der italienischen Stadtrand-Slums plötzlich fliegen können und durch das Wunder ihrer Flucht der Realität die Quittung für ihre Unerträglichkeit ausstellen. *Das Wunder von Bern* ist das Gegenteil eines solchen Wunders, das materielle Zwangsläufigkeiten einmal unterbricht, nämlich kein Wunder, sondern das ganz normale Nachkarten der Bürger eines ehemaligen Schurkenstaates, auch über das Recht auf Triumphe verfügen zu wollen." Ibid.
54. Ibid.
55. See the extensive Wikipedia entries on both the Klaus Barbie and Demjanjuk trials.
56. In a polemical formulation: "'Auschwitz' as a self-service shop for protestations of empathy ('Betroffenheitsdiskurse') and occasions for identification ('Idenfikationsangebote')." Jan Ceuppens, "Im zerschundenen Papier herumgeisternde Gesichter: Fragen der Repräsentation" in W.G. Sebalds Die Ausgewanderten, *Germanistische Mitteilungen*, 55 (2002), 79.
57. See Hannah Arendt, *Eichmann in Jerusalem: A Report on the Banality of Evil* (New York: The Viking Press, 1963) and Christopher Browning, *Ordinary Men: Reserve Police Battalion 101 and the Final Solution in Poland* (New York: Aaron Asher/HarperCollins, 1992).
58. "Holocaust film has traditionally used the disruptive implications of the queer figure to undermine historical narratives of power, although to very different ends. Here, the queer figure mediates the visual invocation of pleasure and displeasure to align viewer identification with particular positionalities and constellations of agency during the Holocaust. Where early socialist films, such as Wanda Jakubovska's OSTATNI ETAP and Andrzej Munk`s PASAZERKA contrast feminised political initiates with the masculinised Kapo figures and the harsher contours and dark uniforms of the female guards to catalyse sympathy and identification with the socialist cause, art house cinema during the 1960s and 1970s developed a postmodern style of Holocaust signification employing sexual and particularly queer imagery as a historical and cultural agent. The strength of this latter body of films, which is exemplified by works such as Luchino Visconti`s THE DAMNED, Liliana Cavani's IL PORTIERE DI NOTTE and Pier Paolo Pasolini`s SALO lies in their self-reflexive style to convey the deep disturbance of all moral and aesthetic values after Auschwitz. These strategies, however, fail to full account for the intersections and discordances produced by the racialised, sexualised and gendered dimensions of the Holocaust." Cathy S Gelbin, "Double Visions Queer Femininity," *Women in German Yearbook: Feminist Studies in German Literature & Culture,* 23 (2007) 186.
59. See Richard Crownshaw, "Perpetrator Fictions and Transcultural Memory," *Parallax,* 17, no. 4 (2011), 75–89.
60. Karmakar went on to make THE HIMMLER PROJECT (2000), where in a similar min-

imalist setting the actor Manfred Zapatka reads one of Heinrich Himmler's Posen speeches from October 1943, commending his SS colleagues for having remained "decent" and "steady" in the face of killing tens of thousands of human beings.

61. Admitting to horrendous crimes while pleading "not guilty" has also been the strategy of Anders Behring Breivik, the Norwegian who shot and killed over seventy people in July 2011 (http://www.independent.co.uk/news/world/europe/anders-breivik-admits-massacre-but-pleads-not-guilty-claiming-it-was-self-defence-7647009.html).
62. Jan Distelmeyer, "Nichts als die Wahrheit," epd-film, 10/99 (http://www.filmzentrale.com/rezis/nichtsalsdiewahrheit.htm).
63. For a negative review of the book, see Ruth Franklin, "Immorality Play," *New Republic* (October 15, 2001), 54–60 expanded in *A Thousand Darknesses: Lies and Truth in Holocaust Fiction* (New York: Oxford University Press, 2010), 199–214, and of the film, notably David Hare's script, see Peter Bradshaw's review of *The Reader* in *The Guardian*, January 2, 2009.
64. Drehli Robnik, "Schuld-Buben: Die Wende ins Ethische (und heraus)," in "*The Reader, Revanche* und *Jerichow*," *Diagonale-Webnotizen* (June 2009) (my translation). (http://2011.diagonale.at/fetcharticle.php@puzzle&page=5899.htm)
65. Harald Welzer, "Schön Unscharf," 55.
66. Opera is an important reference point for Alexander Kluge, as well as for Hans Jürgen Sybergberg, Werner Schroeter, Werner Herzog and—from a subsequent generation—Christoph Schlingensief.
67. See my forthcoming book *Melodrama, Trauma, Mindgames: Affective Memory in American Cinema* (New York: Routledge, 2014).

11

POSTSCRIPT TO TRAUMA THEORY

A Parapractic Supplement

In an essay published early in 2001, called "Postmodernism as Mourning Work: Trauma Theory," I tried to give a preliminary assessment of trauma theory and the possible significance of its intervention in the humanities, after Cathy Caruth had introduced the term in her book Unclaimed Experience *in 1996.*[1] *I outlined several symptomatic perspectives: first, to point to the emergence of trauma in the different memory discourses; second, to note the paradoxical role it played in identity politics, in that it gave victimhood an aura of positive agency, enabling new kinds of subject-positions; third, to speculate on the strategic role of trauma within the crisis of 'theory' itself: especially how it reinterpreted the status of history, reference and the event, after postmodernism's "end of grand narratives" and deconstruction's* il n'y pas de hors-texte *("there is no outside to the text," but also "there is nothing but context," i.e., text and context cannot be played off against each other). Finally, there was the question whether trauma theory proposed itself as a new hermeneutics that could bridge the gap between literary theory and cultural studies (including film studies), by promoting a more embodied form of reading, emphasizing not only active but also affective spectatorship, without however giving "the body" an essentialist definition, and preserving instead its signifying properties: including the possibility of signifying through absence or silence.*

The following remarks try to evaluate whether trauma theory has retained its intellectual momentum and strategic usefulness, even after 9/11 made "trauma" into a cliché, or worse, into a tool that lent itself to be appropriated for acts of revenge and a politics of retaliation. Did trauma theory become a counter category to this appropriation, meant to acknowledge the sudden re-emergence of history (so soon after the end of history had been declared), while maintaining that geopolitics and religious fundamentalism could not by themselves account for the violence of history's spectacular return? Or had trauma theory anticipated some of the tremors, but became itself caught up in the ideological polarization and intellectual paralysis that followed the fall of Western complacency? In an earlier chapter I argued the shift in the semantics of "terror" and "terrorism" from 1977 to 2007, brought about by the "war on terror." In this postscript I turn to some of the critiques of trauma theory that have been voiced, and try to clarify the stakes and implications. I conclude with a more speculative outlook on my own preferred alternative to trauma theory, while keeping in mind its strategic uses as stand-in and placeholder, in the debate over how an ethics of accountability and implication can be aligned with a politics of justice and equality, and how traumatic forgetting might be the optimal way of remembering, in the era of moving images and electronic media.

Trauma Theory in the Humanities

Most of the relevant debates regarding the strategic role of "trauma" in the humanities took place before the attack on the Twin Towers in September 2001.[2] This is important to stress, because as indicated, there is a break between trauma theory before and after 9/11. Before, the absence of an immediate historical or topical referent, and the relative remoteness of the Holocaust as living memory, compared to its ubiquity as memory discourse, greatly aided the metaphoric transfer of "trauma" from the clinical and therapeutic terrain to that of culture, art works and texts, which is one of the reasons why it offered (literary) theory an opportunity to develop around the term "trauma" a unique kind of hermeneutics, touched on in the preceding chapter and to which I shall return.

After 9/11, of course, trauma took on an entirely different degree of urgency as an explanatory tool in the United States and elsewhere, making it appear—not unlike Hollywood disaster movies—that the catastrophe had already been anticipated in virtual form, as trauma theory, before it occurred in actuality, reversing the usual belatedness of trauma into a special kind of predictive prescience. Trauma theory was then enlisted to cope with the aftermath of this national disaster, and, not surprisingly, it was found wanting. Once a specific, highly emotional—and heavily politicized—referent had been re-introduced, much of what had seemed strategically useful in the humanities about trauma theory no longer applied: absence, latency, unrepresentability, the invisible trace, deferral or belatedness were terms that seemed entirely misplaced in the face of the thousands of victims, the smoking ruins of ground zero, the endless flow of images, not to mention that ensuing "war on terror." Likewise, 9/11 also put an end to the empowering role that trauma theory had played for identity politics around the various sources of keenly felt victimization among individual as well as minorities and discriminated groups. Without specific referent, but with a claim to referentiality as such, trauma theory prior to 9/11 had filled a pre-existing need, namely that of claiming victimhood or survivor status, as the preferred subject-positions in the public sphere, even or especially in the absence of a locatable origin of the pain, or the precise source of the sense of loss.

On the other hand, some of the strategic uses of trauma theory in the academy, both before and after 9/11, clearly outweighed or even thrived on the term's perceived shortcomings and "category mistakes."[3] When deployed as a counter theory to cultural studies in the humanities, trauma also filled a gap, answering to some of the aporias or deadlocks that had arisen from social constructivism, postmodernism and deconstruction. This is why I argued that trauma theory was "not so much about recovered memory, as it was about recovered referentiality," insofar as trauma—as the traceless trace of an event, or as the symptom with a palpable but absent or inferred cause—allowed one to speak about history without relying on linear causalities, determinism or teleology. But one could also use the term *deferred action* without invoking latency or the "return of the repressed"; one could endorse constructivism without denying material constraints, as well as mention index and trace without remaining within a linguistic straightjacket, and one could insist on truth and reference without becoming an empiricist or realist. As Kerwin Lee Klein somewhat sarcastically, but perhaps appropriately, remarked of trauma theory: "it promises to let us have our essentialism and deconstruct it, too."[4] This sentence—the put-down turned compliment—neatly sums up what is meant by trauma theory's strategic uses.

Critiques of Trauma Theory

Klein was not the first or only scholar to question trauma theory; it had been introduced by Shoshana Felman and Dori Laub in *Testimony: Crises in Witnessing* (1992), before being popularized and made widely accessible in the two books that Cathy Caruth authored (*Unclaimed Experience*, 1996) and edited (*Trauma: Explorations in Memory*, 1995). The critiques ranged from demanding more precise definitions, suggesting modification through wider and more diverse examples, basic methodological challenges, warnings about too monolithic an application, all the way to polemical engagements and outright rejection, on the grounds of tautology and circular reasoning. The disciplinary spectrum of these voices also ranged widely from Freudian psychoanalysts to clinical psychologists, from anthropologists to neuroscientists, from literary scholars to film scholars, from feminists philosophers to law professors, from historians to sociologists.

In this respect, Caruth was the victim of her own success, since her books, and especially the edited volume, set out to address a very wide spectrum of disciplines and critical practices. Especially as editor, Caruth took the then unusual step for a literary scholar to open the debate about trauma once more to clinical psychology and also neuroscience, first by noting the importance of the decision by the American Psychiatric Association in 1980, to recognize posttraumatic stress disorder (PTSD) as a distinct and classified mental disorder, and second, by including in her edited collection a chapter by Bessel van der Kolk and Onno van der Hart, two leading experts on PTSD, and equally at home in clinical psychiatry, psychoanalysis and neuroscience.[5] *Trauma: Explorations in Memory* was conceived to be both transhistorical and interdisciplinary. It also wanted to give new impetus to scholarly work on a whole range of historical, social and political experiences of injustice, such as slavery and AIDS, Hiroshima, the Holocaust, Vietnam and sexual abuse. Besides contemporary scholars, it also featured writers such as Georges Bataille, the filmmaker Claude Lanzmann and the medical doctor and historian Robert Jay Lifton.

Despite this broadly conceived inquiry, and the open spirit in which it invited dialogue, the criticisms of Caruth's model were both sustained and specific, though usually acknowledging how crucial Caruth's intervention had been in putting trauma on the intellectual map and fashioning it into a hermeneutic tool.[6]

Susannah Radstone, in several books and articles, has made the case for following Freud's original formulations, especially in allocating more scope to psychic fantasy in the etiology of trauma, instead of aligning it with the deconstructivists' tendency to give priority to absence, undecidability and deferral, while also complaining about Caruth's rather too literal view of trauma's psychic imprint as an embodied effect[7]—a charge originally formulated by Ruth Leys, another major critic of Caruth's trauma theory.[8] E. Ann Kaplan argued that trauma in film and literature should be analyzed as a social phenomenon, and not only grounded in the individual psyche.[9] Elsewhere, Kaplan stresses the interpersonal, communicative aspect of trauma, as well as the *therapeutic* value of survivors' and victims' narratives, which seem to be precluded by Caruth's insistence on the unspeakable and the unrepresentable in trauma.[10] Kaplan's stance reflects two phenomena that bring it closer to post-9/11 trauma theory: the emphasis on therapy envisages actual victims of trauma rather than its discursive effects, an acknowledgement of the human anguish caused by suicide bombings as well as the "war on terror" on the population of Iraq and Afghanistan. But the stress on the communicative aspects also highlights the extent to which trauma had become a password for confession and revelation in talk shows on television and in the popular media.

The accent on therapy can also be found in Dominick LaCapra, who detected in Caruth's trauma theory the symptoms of Freud's melancholia and the arrested stage of "acting-out," while neglecting to consider the "working-through" of trauma (and mourning), on the way to recovery, with decathecting and closure as the natural phases of the mourning process.[11] In addition, LaCapra warned against "sacralizing" trauma, in the way that some, according to him, had sacaralized the Holocaust.[12] As an intellectual historian, LaCapra's own theory of trauma wanted to bring psychoanalytic topics to bear on how the work of writers, critics as well as historians is embedded in unconscious processes, notably the return of the repressed, acting out versus working through, and the dynamics of transference. He especially stressed how historical events can be regarded as traumatic, if their impact is at first ignored or does not register ("repressed"), but when it unexpectedly returns, it is in form of symptoms of compulsive repetition. For instance, the German *Historikerstreit*, the de Man affair over the renowned deconstructivist scholar's anti-Semitic writings in Belgium before the war, as well as the continuing controversies over Martin Heidegger's (possibly life-long) support of the Nazi takeover of power are for LaCapra symptomatic returns of the repressed. In this respect, his classical Freudian vocabulary for analyzing repetition differs from the one proposed in the preceding chapters, where "parapraxis" is introduced specifically to point to another functioning of these periodic and symptomatic returns, since their compulsiveness is accompanied by mis-speaking and gaffes that lets one see not only the countervailing forces in play, but also the simultaneous need to speak a particular truth *and* to disguise its consequences.

On the other hand, LaCapra's concern with transference, and in particular, with the failure to recognize it, is similar to my understanding of parapraxis, namely as an ambiguous acknowledgement of one's own emotional or ideological investment in the event or situation. However, while Kaplan and LaCapra in their different ways put the stress on therapy and closure, where the temptation is to construct a redemptive narrative, the parapractic paradigm is closer to Caruth's insistence on deferral along with repetition. In Kaplan's case, the affinity is with melodrama, as the genre that tries to extract closure from excess (as discussed in chapter 10), which in my scheme is the alternative to a poetics of parapraxis as the mode for managing traumatic returns. LaCapra, again, may be closer to parapraxis when, in response to Shoshona Felman's characterization of Claude Lanzmann's filmic practice as a "working through," but one that considers "life itself as [...] a learning that in fact can never end" (55), he concedes that every "working through" also implies or is preceded by a phase of "acting out."[13]

Each of these critics (myself included) tends to promote a preferred version of trauma, which is to be expected. The very ability to have so many versions is, of course, the consequence of the initial move of trauma theory to shift the term's primary meaning as a psychic disorder subsequent to a violent event and a life-threatening experience, to a cultural theory of trauma that justifies its (metaphoric) use in all manner of circumstances where an individual or collective response to shocking and unexpected events is at issue, or where the current preference for affect and embodiment in aesthetics, in film and media studies has found in "trauma" one of its more suggestive labels. Caruth, as indicated, tries to keep both the clinical and cultural aspects in play, and her own version stresses the embodiment and materiality of trauma, at the same time as she asserts its presence as ungraspable and its persistence as inassimilable. In this, she remains faithful to the deconstructivist aporias and paradoxes of Derrida and DeMan.[14]

Ruth Leys on Trauma Theory: Mimetic versus Anti-Mimetic Trauma

The most sustained critique on historical and theoretical grounds of trauma theory has come from Ruth Leys, whose study *Trauma: A Genealogy* (2000) meticulously retraces the history of the concept of trauma since the late nineteenth century. From the emergence of multiple personality disorders to Freud's own approaches to trauma, both before WW I, and in response to shell shock after the war, from Pierre Janet to Sándor Ferenczi, and from contemporary neurobiology to postmodern theory, Leys is able to show that trauma is an inherently unstable concept, where two competing models—she calls them the mimetic and anti-mimetic theories of trauma—tend to get confused, collapsed into or combined with each other.

An important aspect of the mimetic theory of trauma is "hypnotic imitation." It reminds us that Freud's original insights into trauma stem from his experiments with hypnotized patients. Their susceptibility to repeating and bodily mimicking what they are told to say or to do becomes the model for the traumatic experience. The crux here is the extent to which hypnosis is accepted as a legitimate way of interfering with a person's integrity as an autonomous agent. Trauma would be, on the side of the subject, a shattered state of dissociation, passivity and self-absence, answering to a force or figure like the hypnotist, who exerts power over the subject as an external agent, indeed as an "aggressor [whom] the victim unconsciously imitated or identified with,"[15] but thereby can also embody the otherwise ungraspable force and unrepresentable presence of the traumatic event.

The mimetic model, thus, is very much in evidence, when trauma is imagined as visiting the subject involuntarily, or when compulsive repetition suggest a hidden power that either incapacitates the victim or forces it into a kind of remote-controlled behavior. As Leys points out, this raises not only the question of the autonomous individual, dear to bourgeois ideology, but also whether trauma is something internal to the subject, i.e., an experience that has become an unpredictable and alien thing within, or is seen as external, more like a ghost, a monster or revenant. Mimetic trauma presupposes a compliant subject, one who identifies with the exigencies of trauma, and hands over the controls.

The anti-mimetic theory of trauma, on the other hand, wants to retain the autonomy of the subject, and opts for seeing trauma "as if it were a purely external event coming to a sovereign if passive victim."[16] This puts more emphasis on the inassimilable nature of the traumatic experience or event, locked away and out of reach for either consciousness or memory, and to the extent that

Caruth subscribe to the fundamentally inassimilable material nature of trauma, hers would be an anti-mimetic theory.

What is at stake here is not only the ideology of the autonomous individual versus the always already deconstructed subject, but a different concept of the psyche, and with it, a different relation to the Freudian legacy. Thanks to Leys distinction, one can see why LaCapra's therapeutic strategy of "acting out" and "working through" cannot simply be added to Caruth's model of trauma, since the former, mimetic theory regards trauma as internal, whereas the latter conceives it as external. Furthermore, in one case, trauma is close to repression (and its returns, as in "return of the repressed"), in the other case, trauma has nothing to do with repression, because it is inaccessible in an altogether different way. Ultimately, the anti-mimetic theory of trauma does not need the concept of the Freudian unconscious, and can explain the gap between trauma and its conscious representation in a number of different ways, for instance, by espousing a neurobiological theory of the mind (as proposed by van der Kolk, in Caruth's collection), or it can follow a psycho-semiotic path of analysis and speak of the gap itself as the material manifestation of the signifier. It is this deconstructive turn that Leys finds problematic in Caruth's theory, since it puts nonrepresentability above all else; in which case, trauma theory is not so much a theory of trauma, but a way of suggestively designating a (literary-philosophical) trope familiar from writers such as Georges Bataille and Maurice Blanchot, and taken up in Levinas and Derrida. As Leys comments, hinting at a "sacralizing" of trauma: "We might put it that the entire theory of trauma proposed by van der Kolk and Caruth is designed to preserve the truth of the trauma as the failure of representation—thereby permitting it to be passed on to others who can not only imaginatively identify with it but literally share in the communion of suffering."[17]

Radstone, who chooses to remain within more orthodox psychoanalytic categories, sides with Leys, but for slightly different reasons, when she prefers the Freudian "depth" model of the psyche to what she sees as a flatter, horizontal view, implied in the anti-mimetic conception of trauma. "The model of subjectivity inscribed in theories of testimony [such as Caruth's] conforms to Leys' description: the knowledge this subject lacks is not that of its own unconscious process, but of an event that cannot be remembered. In trauma theory, then, it is almost as though the topographical flattening out of the psyche that substitutes dissociation for repression displaces previously intrapsychical processes of displacement into the space of the inter-subjective."[18]

In all fairness, Caruth's rigorously theoretical model is meant to accomplish several tasks at once. Thus, the literal in Caruth is there to give trauma, at the intersection of history and memory, an experiential dimension, but without sliding into phenomenology. Also, it should not be tied to (the problematics of) representation, i.e., the usual forms of symbolization, but neither is it presymbolic or prelinguistic (hence the literal, along with the materiality of the signifier). This preserves for trauma the possibility of promoting a new theory of subjectivity (at least in Lacanian terms), where the subject is always already displaced in relation to self-presence. In the mimetic theory (which deems the subject to be whole and autonomous), trauma would "shatter" the subject, and must be put together by some therapeutic process (such as those variously implied by LaCapra, Kaplan, Radstone). By contrast, in terms of the anti-mimetic theory, trauma can be the "new normal" of subjectivity, present not to itself, but persistently exposed to the materiality of history and of language.

While the debate on trauma often seems yet another version of the turn to embodiment and to (unmediated) affect, which is to say, a turn away from symbolization and a return to some form of the immediate and the instantaneous, Caruth's theory is considerably more sophisticated, deftly navigating many of these dangers of oversimplification. For instance, at no point is she committed to making her notion of materiality and the literal seem "foundational," in ways that "embodiment" or "affect" (usually by default) are presupposed as foundational.

In almost all these respects, my notion of parapraxis is on the side of the anti-mimetic and the nontherapeutic. It is dispensing with the "return of the repressed" and the "depth" model of the psyche, while still retaining a Freudian terminology, and it has a notion of embodiment that is non-foundational, insofar it conceives of the body and its performativity under the sign of "failure," as its apriori condition, which also means that parapraxis is on the side of the semiotic and not of symbolization.

Historians Against Memory Studies and Trauma Theory

If so far I have looked at critics of Caruth's trauma theory who are at least, in principle, sympathetic to the enterprise, because they recognize some of the epistemological and hermeneutic problems to which trauma theory wanted to provide an answer, the critique of trauma theory on the part of the historians has been more severe and even scathing. One such highly critical voice in the memory studies and trauma theory debate has been that of the social historian Wulf Kansteiner, who, like many professional historians, distrusts the turn from history to memory studies. He objects even more strongly to any suggestion that psychoanalysis might help to illuminate our relation to the past, notably when this is claimed to be a collective response. In a much-quoted article, Kansteiner set out his doubts: "Reservations about the use of psychoanalytical methods in collective memory studies extend to the concept of trauma, which has particular relevance for our understanding of the legacy of collective catastrophes. However, unlike the concepts of the unconscious and repression that inappropriately individualize and psychologize collective memory processes, the use of the concept of trauma has had an opposite yet equally misleading effect. Some recent works in trauma theory invoke the example of the Holocaust as illustration of a more general post-modern claim about the undecidability of the nature of our historical experience and our representations of it. The very specific and unusual experiences and memory challenges of survivors—who find that their memories of the 'Final Solution' form a volatile, independent realm of memory that remains painfully irreconcilable with subsequent experiences—are offered as proof of the general traumatic characteristics of the postmodern condition. In this vein Cathy Caruth has argued with regard to the Holocaust that such 'a crisis of truth extends beyond the question of individual cure and asks how we in this era can have access to our own historical experience, to a history that is in its immediacy a crisis to whose truth there is no simple access'."[19]

After citing some of the dissenting voices within the trauma theory camp, such as LaCapra, discussed above, Kansteiner continues: "I would go even further in my criticism to suggest that though specific visions of the past might originate in traumatic experiences they do not retain that quality if they become successful collective memories. [...] Even in cases of so-called delayed collective memory (as in the case of the Holocaust or Vietnam), the delayed onset of public debates about the meaning of negative pasts has more to do with political interest and opportunities than the persistence of trauma or with any 'leakage' in the collective unconscious.

"Small groups whose members have directly experienced such traumatic events (veterans' or survivors' groups) only have a chance to shape the national memory if they command the means to express their visions, and if their vision meets with compatible social or political objectives and inclinations among other important social groups, for instance, political elites or parties. Past events can only be recalled in a collective setting 'if they fit within a framework of contemporary interests'."[20]

Kansteiner is surely right to recall the power structures operating in all aspects of society, including those pertaining to collectively endorsed versions of (national) history. But this is precisely why the concept of trauma can be transferred from the clinical and individual sphere to the cultural and collective realm, where it becomes the emotively charged register through which non-negotiated claims and unresolved conflicts can find their voice and place in the public sphere.

Similar positions have been emphatically set out by the historians Eric Hobsbawm and Terence Ranger, with their notion of "the worlds of the invention of tradition," which they distinguish from the "worlds of custom." As Jeffrey Olick explains the Hobsbawm/Ranger reasoning: Since the late nineteenth century, not only have nation-states sought to shore up declining legitimacy by propagating fictional pasts and a sense of their institutions' ancientness, people have invented the very category of tradition (as opposed to custom): the idea of self-conscious adherence to past ways of acting (whether genuine or spurious) is itself a product of our distance from the past, which has come to be seen as "a foreign country."[21]

The film scholar Nancy Wood (also quoted by Kansteiner) has made a similar point about the asymmetrical power-relations underpinning what have sometimes been called not "memory studies" but the "memory wars," to indicate the contentious and embattled nature of collective memories. She is, however, more sympathetic to the confluence of collective memory, the unconscious, and agency than Kansteiner, but points out that "while the emanation of individual memory is primarily subject to the laws of the unconscious, public memory—whatever its unconscious vicissitudes—testifies to a will or desire on the part of some social group or disposition of power to select and organize representations of the past so that these will be embraced by individuals as their own. If particular representations of the past have permeated the public domain, it is because they embody an intentionality—social, political, institutional and so on—that promotes or authorizes their entry."[22]

Wood's position reflects one of my main contentions in this study, namely that the promotion of collective memory and the centrality of the Holocaust, respond, in Europe at least, to a felt need to shape from a common catastrophic past a culture of commemoration that can serve as the basis for a common vision of the future: a risky undertaking, as indicated, and so far not blessed with demonstrable success,[23] but one that acknowledges the presence of external forces and a political agenda, pressing on the memory and trauma debates: something that my concept of the politics of parapraxis (failed performance versus performed failure) explicitly draws attention to.[24]

However, both Kansteiner and Wood do not pay sufficient attention to what seems to me the crucial element that allows subject-effects such as those implied by a psychoanalytically inflected trauma theory as part of collective memory to be thought together in the first place, namely the shaping power of modern media. For the common ground on which political agendas articulate themselves in the public sphere are the technical and electronic media, notably television, the press and (in Germany) radio, but to a considerable extent—and here the poetics of parapraxis makes its entry—also the cinema. The visualization techniques of television, as well as the skills and effects invested in Hollywood blockbuster movies are such that they deliver both the mediated impact of traumatic singular events and the lasting versions of the past—precisely, in the interest of "important social groups." These, however, go beyond "elites and politicians" of a single country or nation, not only because of their popular reach and mass appeal, but also because such media products are often addressed also to transnational global audiences.

Is Trauma a Media Effect?

The historical basis for a cultural as opposed to a clinical theory of trauma is the disruptive experience of modernity. Trauma and shock became important new conceptions of memory and subjectivity in the writings of Sigmund Freud and Walter Benjamin, two of the most astute analysts of how human physiology and the senses responded to industrialization and urban living. In the case of Freud, who had initially begun to write about trauma in connection with female hysteria, World War I became a defining moment for thinking about trauma as a collective experience, in light of shell shock produced by the impact of modern warfare and the extremity of experience that the new technologies of mass killing had subjected individuals and groups to, such as troops serving in the front lines at Ypres or Verdun. The notion of parapraxis, by contrast, was related to new kinds of transport (train travel) and the urbanist upheavals in his native city at the time he was writing *The Psychopathology of Everyday Life*.[25]

Benjamin's well-known theories of shock and trauma, on the other hand, are intimately related to the modern city, the mass media, and overstimulation. Taking his cue from Freud, namely that the need of an organism to protect itself against too many sensory stimuli from the outside world is almost more important than the processing of these stimuli, Benjamin develops, notably around the poetry of Baudelaire, a theory of shock as the disruptive-creative principle of the modern artist in the urban scene. A duelist who engages in thrust and parry, the creative mind enters into a dialectical exchange with the shock experience. Yet when Benjamin reflects on the impact of the cinema, he hesitates between regarding it as a phenomenon of modernity that overstimulates the spectator, and thus weakens the protective shield that is consciousness, or conversely, welcomes it as a machine that simulates and rehearses overstimulation, the better to prepare consciousness and the senses for their encounter with the shock-experiences of everyday living. In the first case, cinema could be considered an extension of the trauma-inducing impulses, while in the second, it would be a kind of culturally sanctioned collective therapy, or perhaps, to stay within the mechanical vocabulary of media and automotive technologies, a sound-and-image-stimuli "shock-absorber."

Transferring some of this thinking to contemporary media, much the same options are still being discussed around the impact of television or computer games, insofar as they are either judged as deadening our sensibilities ("amusing ourselves to death") or on the contrary, sharpening our reflexes and responses in order to cope with overstimulation, intermittence and variable attention ("everything that's bad for you is good for you"),[26] which would make a typically contemporary phenomenon such as attention deficit disorder merely the negative description of a new adaptive skill—"a rapid-reaction-first-responder"—in much the same way that "shock" and "trauma" are in

Benjamin the recto to the verso of adapting to the motor-sensory demands of metropolitan modernity.

It is in this sense that live transmission and real time coverage of the news are inherently "traumatic": one might speak of a low-level trauma-by-attrition, and consequently argue that trauma theory is so problematic and contradictory because it is the placeholder for a media theory that has not yet quite worked out or formulated the core problem it seeks to answer. The placeholder function might explain why the historical referent of trauma theory often seems to be so exchangeable—Holocaust, Vietnam, childhood abuse, 9/11—or altogether expendable, as in the more context-free, linguistic-philosophical versions of deconstructivist trauma theory discussed above.[27] Parapraxis could be seen to accommodate such a view, since it is evident that contemporary politicians are so gaffe-prone because of the pressures of the twenty-four-hour news cycle. Indeed, the very notion of the gaffe, which usually means letting slip an unpalatable truth, is that of a failure to perform the protective shield. Television and the Internet act as electronic amplifiers and magnifying zoom lenses, to the point where the only newsworthy items are the gaffes themselves. In other words, the media outlets, talk shows and news broadcasts now triumphantly harvest the missteps and capture the telltale giveaways they are themselves responsible for producing in the first place. A "positive" feedback system is in place, which is nonetheless a closed and self-perpetuating loop which it would not be wrong to diagnose as the symptoms of "trauma," except that no one would dare to call it that.

In my 2001 essay I argued that it is the groundless, placeless media image[28] that imparts to contemporary experience a traumatic "turn," leading to a repetition of the same image sequences on television, or to YouTube clips gone viral, whose compulsiveness and pathological behavior not only comes from the anxiety of having to fill "empty" time, but from the intuited awareness that these images, however "authentic," "real" and "live," can no longer be accommodated in the viewer's personal experience, nor are they located within livable life-narratives. Instead, the viewer encounters the world in the form of trauma, insofar as self-representation as presented in the media is experienced in disjointed images and looped narratives. The (fantasized) assumption of a personal—or national—trauma can fill the gap and thus can substitute for other, more traditionally located forms of identity. But it also means that the repetition regime of contemporary media culture is, to this extent, mimicking trauma, so that the relation between historical traumas and their cinematic, audio-visual representation becomes one of mutual implication and over-determination.

By suggesting for these media-induced trauma-effects the term *parapraxes*—in the sense of an intertwining of failed performance and performance of failure—I hope at least to point in the general direction of the contemporary problems and political agendas that trauma theory might be a placeholder for, without presuming to have formulated it adequately. At the same time, I accept that E. Ann Kaplan and Susannah Radstone, with their elaboration of cinema-specific trauma theories, envisaged within their therapeutic-redemptive memory frame (not unlike Alison Landsberg's prosthetic memory, discussed in chapter 2) also align themselves with the possibility that the variable historical traumatic referents might perform as substitutes. However, as laid out in the previous chapters, I do not see the cinema as having the power to produce closure other than within the generic constraints and redemptive possibilities of melodrama. It, too, has at various points in its history, served as a placeholder for a politics either no longer or not yet possible.[29]

Trauma, Politics and Ethics

It raises, inevitably, the question of what might be the relation between trauma theory and politics. A clear, if somewhat polemical take is offered by John Mowitt, in an essay titled "Trauma Envy," in which he explicitly associate trauma theory with the "ethical turn" in the humanities. Like other commentators on the ethical turn, speaking from a Marxist perspective, such as Jacques Ranciere and Alain Badiou, Mowitt first notes that a displacement has occurred, whereby the ethical is made to substitute for the political, of which it becomes the neoliberal surrogate. The moral high ground presupposed by trauma theory and Holocaust memory, so his argument goes, can be enlisted on the side of a critical stance, without however having to seriously engage either with the blind spots of (academic) identity politics or with neo-liberalism. Referring himself to Wendy Brown's critique of victim culture (which she typified as a moralizing reproach to power that purposefully maintains a posture of impotence), and addressing mainly the chronic weakness of the left in American politics and public discourse, Mowitt argues that like the left, which has consistently allowed the conservative right to set the terms of the debate on social issues, values and morality, trauma theory and the ethical turn try to outflank the right with a more radical ethics, but they do so without reflecting their own position, as one which is itself confined within the two-party consensus politics: "When the political is conceived as a matter of taking sides, specifically sides separated along the fault between good and evil (whether banal or not), its link to the labour of 'making' sides, of producing and advancing positions, is obscured. What is risked in this obscurity is not just the elaboration of the ethical as such (its production as 'that which matters most'), but the importance of the political as the field within which groups struggle in and for power. Here, I would submit, the vital question is not 'whose trauma provides one with greater moral capital' ... but 'what kind of institutions, relations, practices need to be forged so that the trauma of capital accumulation can be abated?'"[30]

In other words, Mowitt takes issue (as do I in my 2001 essay) with this vying for victim position in the *world-as-is*: interpreting the need to struggle for core political issues such as social justice and equal rights, first of all as a competition for entitlements and empowerments, without at the same time challenging that under the name of liberal democracy (and free trade), old inequalities are being cemented, and new ones created. However, Mowitt prefaced this critique of trauma theory as victim culture by a very robust defense of feminism. This takes its cue from Adorno's critique of Nietzsche's essentialist notion of femininity (deconstructed by Adorno as the displacement of male dominance into a projection of female duplicity), and is in dialogue with Wendy Brown's essay "Injury, Identity, Politics," where she points out how it is a Nietzschean "resentment" or "envy" that characterizes contemporary U.S. "identity politics," and by extension, liberal thinking generally. What bothers Brown is that identity politics seems to have settled for a concept of injury that accepts the definitions of inclusion and exclusion as defined by classical liberalism, which means that the struggle against exclusion or discrimination wholly accepts liberalism's notion of inclusiveness, based as it is on tolerance, rather than on equality and justice.[31]

Mowitt and Brown's political critique of trauma theory could be complemented by a brief consideration of Slavoj Žižek's difference with Derrida about the political significance of the "trauma" of 9/11. What for Žižek amounts to the traumatic kernel of recent events (and the missed encounters with Islam) is the way globalization has displaced and rendered opaque what Marxism used to call the class struggle: that is, the fundamental antagonisms that underwrite historical change. For Žižek, 9/11 was a reminder and a wake-up call, the intrusion of the perverted "reality" of Jihadist Islam into the "virtual" reality of Western finance capitalism. Derrida, as discussed in chapter 1, has cautioned against reading 9/11 as a readily decipherable symbol or political allegory. Allen Meek has rightly pointed out that for Derrida, the event—and 9/11 is such an "event"—must be considered "as the always-initially incomprehensible arrival of the unknown. In these terms any attempt to immediately interpret or label the event is rendered impossible by its traumatic incomprehensibility."[32]

Here, trauma does indeed have a double function: it is both a de-accelerator in any "rush to judgment," a deferral-device putting the brakes on allegorizing "the event" and it functions as the fetish of a political taboo, i.e., a more fundamental questioning of neo-liberal globalization. As a Marxist, Žižek must therefore take issue with the implied reluctance of Derrida to draw direct political consequences from his ethical position, while Derrida would see in the latency signaled by trauma the only possible political stance in relation to equality and justice.

From these positions, it would seem that trauma theory, where it claims to represent a constituency and pursue a particular politics, such as fighting injustices and discrimination—in Cathy Caruth's *Trauma: Explorations in Memory* it will be remembered, the traumas of slavery and AIDS, of sexual abuse and Vietnam are given equal treatment next to the Holocaust and the atom bomb—remains broadly within a liberal consensus politics that inconveniences few established interests and unsettles almost no-one in positions of power. On the contrary, as indicated in the beginning, it can hand a welcome tool to those intent to use moments of crisis and disarray, in order to preemptively implement anticipated social or political change.[33]

Another problem with trauma theory may be in the name itself, if one subscribes to Christopher Fynsk's harsh words about the acquisitive, imperial gesture of theory, which he contrasts to "fundamental research": "research is impelled by its own neediness and its sense of being answerable, whereas theory, governed by the concept, proceeds with ever-expanding appropriations; fundamental research proceeds from encounter (always from a sense that something has happened to which it must answer), and it seeks encounter. In theory, there are no encounters."[34] The paradox—or even tragic irony—would be that trauma theory entered the humanities precisely with the "sense that something has happened to which it must answer," and as a way of enabling the impossible but necessary encounter: (en)countering the unsayable with words, the unrepresentable with representations. Trauma theory may yet have endured and even thrived by this very ambiguity and paradox of making ambitious claims to being the master trope that can unite the best in the humanities, building bridges to the social sciences and neurosciences, enjoying an unassailable ethical authority that also tried to ensure its social relevance, while politically enjoying the neutrality of being a stand-in and a placeholder.

These difficulties, political and institutional, have persuaded me—in the limited form that it is present in this study at all—to favor trauma theory primarily as a hermeneutic move, which keeps in play the various relations that a text or performance must engage with its audience and the world: mimetic and semiotic, embodied but also palpable through absence, making its mark through latency and belatedness, and allowing for its effects to invent their causes retroactively.

The same relations can also be instantiated and accommodated within the term whose viability I have opted to explore in this study. Parapraxis, in the way I understand it, also allows me to think in political categories; furthermore, it is a term that, happily, has no institutional standing whatsoever, and therefore is not burdened with the scars of trench-warfare identity politics. Nonetheless, insofar as I have been using "trauma" it implies a media-theory-by-default, and has—and here I do rely on Derrida—a vector towards the future, rather than the past, and belongs as much to anticipation as it does to memory. I might even go so far as to claim that a critical approach to new media can work with trauma as an explanatory term better than film studies. In the end, the very instability of "trauma" can do double duty: it substitutes for a direct experience of events that are "real" only in retrospect and in discourse (their referentiality answers to the question "where were you when...")— this would be the condition of the digital that retroactively now applies to all media.[13] Second, trauma is a way of coping with the exposure to media representations that, irrespective of their ostensible subject, speak of violence and terror, because presented without context or the necessary means of narrativization other than the ones that stresses the ubiquity of a threat and the precariousness of existence, i.e., that reinforce the notion that life is only lived under the shadow of death. The politics of fear with which I began, can now be understood as the only politics the media are able to pursue, and thus, once more, the media represent as "reality" the matrix of traumatic affects its own mode of being necessarily projects and generates, in a self-fulfilling prophecy and a self-sustaining loop. The argument from trauma in other words, establishes a different relationship between remembering and forgetting, between rewriting and transposing, between displacement and reversal, between homeopathic and prosthetic, so that *forgetting*—including the traumatic forgetting I call parapraxis—becomes not the opposite of remembering, but the very form of remembering required in the era of the electronic media.

Notes

1. Thomas Elsaesser, "Postmodernism as mourning work," *Screen*, 4, no. 2 (2001), 193–201; Cathy Caruth, *Unclaimed Experience* (Baltimore: Johns Hopkins University Press, 1996).
2. Besides Dori Laub and Shoshona Felman's *Testimony: Crises of Witnessing in Literature, Psychoanalysis, and History* (New York: Taylor & Francis, 1992), Cathy Caruth's books from 1995 and 1996, and Ruth Leys *Trauma: A Genealogy* (2000), there was an important essay by Hal Foster, "Obscene, Abject, Traumatic," *October*, 78 (Autumn 1996), 106–24, which opens with the sentence: "In contemporary art and theory, let alone in contemporary fiction and film, there is a general shift in conceptions of the real: from the real understood as an effect of representation to the real understood as an event of trauma." The "*Screen* Dossier on Trauma," *Screen*, 42, no. 2 (2001), too, had been commissioned and published prior to 9/11.
3. Wulf Kansteiner, "Genealogy of a category mistake: a critical intellectual history of the cultural trauma metaphor," *Rethinking History*, 8, no. 2 (2004), 193–221.
4. Klein speaks of memory studies in general, but might be referring to trauma theory as well. Kerwin Lee Klein, "On the Emergence of Memory in Historical Discourse," *Representations*, 69 (Winter 2000), 144.
5. Ruth Leys claims that Caruth's theory of trauma cunningly but perhaps too ingeniously interprets Van der Kolk's account of trauma, where he mentions a gap between consciousness and representation, as the neurobiological version of Lacan's "materiality of the signifier." Ruth Leys, *Trauma: A Genealogy* (Chicago: University of Chicago Press, 2000), 266.
6. I shall focus on four representative critiques and reformulations of trauma theory, reliant on or arguing with Caruth: Susannah Radstone, "Introduction," and "Screening Trauma: Forrest Gump, Film and Memory" both in Susannah Radstone (ed.), *Memory and Methodology* (Oxford: Berg, 2000), 1–22 and 79–107, as well as her introduction to the "*Screen* Dossier on Trauma," 188–93; Leys, *Trauma*; E. Ann Kaplan, *Trauma Culture* (Piscataway, NJ: Rutgers University Press, 2005) and Dominick LaCapra, *Writing History, Writing Trauma* (Baltimore: Johns Hopkins University Press, 2001).

7. Radstone, "*Screen* Dossier" (2001), 191.
8. Leys, *Trauma*, 229–32 and 266–97.
9. See E. Ann Kaplan and Ban Wang (eds.), *Trauma and Cinema: Cross-Cultural Explorations* (Hong Kong: Hong Kong University Press 2004), 5. Kaplan prefers to cite a whole variety of responses to traumatic experiences in film, including traumatic contagion, trauma transfer and empathetic identification, rather than commit herself to a single (medical or cultural) definition of trauma.
10. Kaplan, *Trauma Culture*, 37.
11. LaCapra, Writing History, Writing Trauma, 43–85.
12. Elsewhere, LaCapra criticizes Shoshona Felman for an "absolutization of trauma" that converts it into a "universal hole in Being or an unnamable Thing" without a historical context, and thus "sacralizes" it. Instead, he argues for an ongoing process of working-through that assigns to traumatic experience the possibility of meaning within a symbolic or narrative context. Dominick LaCapra, *History in Transit: Experience, Identity, Critical Theory* (Ithaca: Cornell University Press, 2004), 119–21.
13. Dominick LaCapra, "*Shoah*: "Here there is no Why." *Critical Inquiry,* 23/2 (1997), 55.
14. Caruth argues that trauma's unassimilation and return carries both "the truth of an event and the truth of its incomprehensibility." *Unclaimed Experience*, 153.
15. Leys, *Trauma,* 8–9.
16. Ibid., 10.
17. Ibid., 253.
18. Susannah Radstone, "Trauma Theory: Contexts, Politics, Ethics," *Paragraph*, 30, no. 1 (2007), 20.
19. Wulf Kansteiner, "Finding Meaning in Memory: A Methodological Critique of Collective Memory Studies," *History and Theory*, 41, no. 2 (May, 2002), 186.
20. Ibid., 187. Kansteiner quotes Yael Zerubavel, who argues: "Collective memory continuously negotiates between available historical records and current social and political agendas." Yael Zerubavel, *Recovered Roots: Collective Memory and the Making of Israeli National Tradition* (Chicago: University of Chicago Press, 1995), 5.
21. I am here quoting Jeffrey K. Olick from the entry on "Collective Memory" in the *International Encyclopedia of the Social Sciences*, 2nd edition, 7–8, who in turn quotes Eric Hobsbawm, and Terence Ranger (eds.), *The Invention of Tradition* (Cambridge: Cambridge University Press, 1992) and David Lowenthal, *The Past is a Foreign Country* (Cambridge: Cambridge University Press, 1985).
22. Nancy Wood, *Vectors of Memory* (Oxford: Berg, 1999), 2.
23. Except, perhaps, if one counts the award of the Nobel Prize for Peace to the European Union in 2012, a gesture of encouragement that was immediately criticized and even ridiculed.
24. See also Marita Sturken: "In the field of cultural negotiation through which different stories vie for a place in history, failure is the rule." Marita Sturken, *Tangled Memories* (Berkeley: University of California Press, 1997), 1.
25. On Freud's disruptive experience of travel and urbanism, see John Mowitt, "Stumbling on Analysis: Psychoanalysis and Everyday Life," *Cultural Critique*, no. 52 (Autumn, 2002), 61–85.
26. I am referring, respectively, to Neil Postman, *Amusing Ourselves to Death: Public Discourse in the Age of Show Business* (New York: Viking, 1985) and Steven Johnson, *Everything Bad Is Good for You: How Today's Popular Culture Is Actually Making Us Smarter* (New York: Riverhead, 2006).
27. A deconstructivist version of parapraxis can be found in a critique of Slavoj Žižek's reading of trauma in Ridley Scott's ALIEN in terms of a material Thing. Contra Žižek, Matt Tierney (paraphrasing Jean Francois Lyotard) argues: "the signifier is all we have, and that repetition, retroactivity, and meaninglessness are what make up that signifier's affective matrix. [...] The utterance of John Hurt ["Oh no, not again!"] demands that

we see the only mark of trauma to be one that speaks of itself as such—not as an event of failed representation, but as an affect of failure that is both constitutive and thoroughgoing—and that can speak of nothing else." Matt Tierney, "'Oh no, not again': Representability and a Repetitive Remark," *Image & Narrative*, 11, no. 2 (2010), 154.

28. This groundlessness and placelessness clearly precedes the digital turn, but can now be conveniently and retroactively given a technological "cause"—hence the heated but wrong-headed debate about the "loss of the index" in the digital image, traumatizing our photographic heritage.
29. See Thomas Elsaesser, *Melodrama Trauma Mind-Games: Affect and Memory in Contemporary American Cinema* (New York: Routledge, 2013).
30. John Mowitt, "Trauma Envy," *Cultural Critique*, 46, "Trauma and Its Cultural Aftereffects" (Autumn, 2000), 272-97.
31. Wendy Brown, "Injury, Identity, Politics," in Avery Gordon and Christopher. Newfield (eds.), *Mapping Multiculturalism* (Minnesota: University of Minnesota Press, 1996), 149-65. Tolerance is also the bête noire in Slavoj Žižek's attack on multi-culturalism. See Slavoj Žižek, "Tolerance as an Ideological Category," *Critical Inquiry*, 34, no. 4 (Summer 2008), 660–82.
32. Allen Meek, *Trauma and Media* (New York: Routledge, 2009), 16.
33. This preemptive obedience to a presumed and anticipated historical necessity was one of the most powerfully coercive strategies of Stalinism. Noami Klein, for one, finds it in what she calls "disaster capitalism." Klein explicitly links theories of shock and trauma to the violent imposition of neo-liberal economics in Latin America in the 1970s and 80s and in the Middle East since the 1990s. Drawing direct historical parallels between psychiatric shock therapy and the covert experiments conducted by the Central Intelligence Agency to improve torture techniques, she argues that tabula rasa tactics via individual shock by torture and collective shock following natural or man-made disasters have been essential tools of U.S. foreign policy and their client regimes in implementing aggressive "free market" reforms. See Naomi Klein, *The Shock Doctrine: The Rise of Disaster Capitalism* (London: Picador, 2008), 27–86.
34. Christopher Fynsk, *The Claim of Language: A Case for the Humanities* (Minneapolis: University of Minnesota Press, 2004), xi.
35. On this specific conjunction of displacement and deferral, in order to be located without having to be grounded, see Thomas Elsaesser, "Where Were You When...?"; Or, "I Phone, Therefore I Am," *PMLA*, 118, no. 1 (January, 2003), 120–22.

SELECTED BIBLIOGRAPHY

The literature on terror, trauma, the Holocaust and the Red Army Faction (RAF) is so voluminous that any bibliography must remain selective. The following includes books cited and books consulted, but neither category is exhaustive. Not all essays and articles cited in the footnotes are listed. Those included have proven most useful or provocative.

Theodor W. Adorno. "What Does Coming to Terms with the Past Mean?" in G. Hartman (ed.), *Bitburg in Moral and Historical Perspective* (Bloomington: Indiana University Press, 1985), 114–29.

Giorgio Agamben. *Homo Sacer: Sovereign Power and Bare Life* (Stanford, CA: Stanford University Press, 1998).

Giorgio Agamben. *Remnants of Auschwitz: The Witness and the Archive* (New York: Zone Books, 2002).

Jon G. Allen. *Coping with Trauma: A Guide to Self-Understanding* (Washington, DC: American Psychiatric Press, 1995).

Nora M. Alter. *Projecting History: German Nonfiction Cinema, 1967–2000* (Ann Arbor: University of Michigan Press, 2002).

Paul Antze, and Michael Lambek (eds.). *Tense Past: Cultural Essays in Trauma and Memory* (New York: Routledge, 1996).

Nerea Arruti, with Bob Plant (eds.). "Trauma Therapy and Representation." Special issue. *Paragraph* 30, no. 1 (2007).

Aleida Assmann. *Erinnerungsräume. Formen und Wandlungen des kulturellen Gedächtnisses* (Munich: C. H. Beck, 1999).

Aleida Assmann. "Four Formats of Memory: From Individual to Collective Constructions of the Past," in C. Emden, and D. Midgley (eds.), *Cultural Memory and Historical Consciousness in the German Speaking World Since 1500* (Bern: Peter Lang, 2004), 19–37.

Aleida Assmann. *Der lange Schatten der Vergangenheit. Erinnerungskultur und Geschichtspolitik* (Munich: C. H. Beck, 2006).

Aleida Assmann, and Ute Frevert. *Geschichtsvergessenheit, Geschichtsversessenheit: Vom Umgang mit deutschen Vergangenheiten nach 1945* (Stuttgart: Deutsche Verlags-Anstalt, 1999).

Ilan Avisar. *Screening the Holocaust* (Bloomington: Indiana University Press, 1988).

Karyn Ball (ed.). *Traumatizing Theory: The Cultural Politics of Affect in and Beyond Psychoanalysis* (New York: The Other Press, 2007).

Omer Bartov. *Germany's War and the Holocaust: Disputed Histories* (Ithaca, NY: Cornell University Press, 2003).

Omer Bartov. *The "Jew" in Cinema* (Bloomington: Indiana University Press, 2005).

Jean Baudrillard. *Power Inferno. Requiem pour les Twin Towers. Hypothèses sur le terrorisme. La violence du mondial* (Paris: Galilée, 2003).

David Bathrick, Brad Prager, and Michael D. Richardson (eds.). *Visualizing the Holocaust: Documents, Aesthetics, Memory* (Rochester, NY: Camden House, 2008).

Zygmunt Baumann. *Wasted Lives: Modernity and its Outcasts* (Cambridge: Polity, 2004).

Ulrich Beck, Anthony Giddens, and Scott Lash. *Reflexive Modernization: Politics, Tradition and Aesthetics in the Modern Social Order* (Stanford, CA: Stanford University Press, 1994).

Torsten Beermann. *Der Begriff "Terrorismus" in deutschen Printmedien* (Münster: LIT, 2004).

Daniela Berghahn. *Hollywood Behind the Wall: The Cinema of East Germany* (Manchester: Manchester University Press, 2005).

Klaus L. Berghahn, Jürgen Fohrmann, and Helmut J. Schneider (eds.). *Kulturelle Repräsentationen des Holocaust in Deutschland und den Vereinigten Staaten* (New York: Peter Lang, 2002).

Donald Bloxham, and Tony Kushner. *The Holocaust: Critical Historical Approaches* (Manchester: Manchester University Press, 2005).

John Bodnar. *Remaking America: Public Memory, Commemoration and Patriotism in the Twentieth Century* (Princeton, NJ: Princeton University Press, 1992).

W. James Booth. "The Unforgotten: Memories of Justice," *American Political Science Review*, 95, no. 4 (2001), 777–92.

Giovanna Borradori (ed.). *Philosophy in a Time of Terror. Dialogues with Jürgen Habermas and Jacques Derrida* (Chicago: University of Chicago Press, 2003).

Bodo von Borries. *Das Geschichtsbewußtsein Jugendlicher: Eine repräsentative Untersuchung über Vergangenheitsdeutungen, Gegenwartswahrnehmungen und Zukunftserwartungen von Schülerinnen und Schülern in Ost- und Westdeutschland* (Weinheim: Juventa Verlag, 1995).

Svetlana Boym. *The Future of Nostalgia* (New York: Basic Books, 2001).

John S. Brady, Beverly Crawford, and Sarah Elise Wiliarty (eds.). *The Postwar Transformation of Germany: Democracy, Prosperity and Nationhood* (Ann Arbor: University of Michigan Press, 1999).

Henryk M. Broder. *Der ewige Antisemit. Über Sinn und Funktion eines beständigen Gefühls* (Frankfurt/M: S. Fischer Verlag, 1986).

Wendy Brown. *States of Injury: Power and Freedom in Late Modernity* (Princeton, NJ: Princeton University Press, 1995).

Heinz Bude. *Das Altern einer Generation* (Frankfurt am Main: Suhrkamp, 1995).

Jan Bulig, *Von der Provokation zur "Propaganda der Tat": Die "antiautoritäre Bewegung" und die Rote Armee Fraktion RAF* (Bonn: Bouvier, 2007).

Judith Butler. *Bodies that Matter* (New York: Routledge, 1993).

Judith Butler. *The Psychic Life of Power* (Stanford, CA: Stanford University Press, 1997).

Cathy Caruth. *Trauma: Explorations in Memory* (Baltimore: Johns Hopkins University Press, 1995).

Cathy Caruth. *Unclaimed Experience: Trauma, Narrative and History* (Baltimore: Johns Hopkins University Press, 1996).

Paul Cooke, and Marc Silberman (eds.). *Screening War: Perspectives on German Suffering* (Rochester, NY: Camden House, 2010).

Paul Cooke. *Representing East Germany since Unification: From Colonization to Nostalgia* (Oxford: Berg, 2005).

Paul Connerton. *How Societies Remember* (Cambridge: Cambridge University Press, 1989).

Jill Ker Conway. *When Memory Speaks* (New York: Knopf, 1998).

Richard Crownshaw. "Perpetrator Fictions and Transcultural Memory" *Parallax,* 17, no. 4 (2011), 75–89.

Gilles Deleuze. *Cinema 1: The Movement Image* (Minneapolis: University of Minnesota Press, 1986).

Gilles Deleuze. *Cinema 2: The Time Image* (Minneapolis: University of Minnesota Press, 1989).

Gilles Deleuze. "Postscript on the Societies of Control," *October,* 59 (Winter, 1992), 3–7.

Jacques Derrida. *Specters of Marx. The State of the Debt, the Work of Mourning & the New International* (London: Routledge, 1994).

Claudia Dillmann, and Ronny Loewy (eds.). *Die Vergangenheit in der Gegenwart. Konfrontationen mit dem Holocaust in den Filmen der deutschen Nachkriegsgesellschaften* (Frankfurt/Main: Deutsches Filminstitut - DIF, 2001).

Dan Diner. "Negative Symbiose — Deutsche und Juden nach Auschwitz," *Babylon,* 1 (1986), 9–20.

Don deLillo. *White Noise* (New York: Penguin, 1985).

Judith E. Doneson. *The Holocaust in American Film* (Ithaca, NY: Syracuse University Press, 2002).

Tobias Ebbrecht. *Geschichtsbilder im medialen Gedächtnis: Filmische Narrationen des Holocaust* (Bielefeld: transcript, 2011).

Friederike Eigler. *Gedächtnis und Geschichte in Generationenromanen seit der Wende* (Berlin: Erich Schmidt, 2005).

Andreas Elter. *Propaganda der Tat. Die RAF und die Medien* (Frankfurt am Main: Suhrkamp, 2008).

Kirby Farrell. *Post-traumatic Culture: Injury and Interpretation in the Nineties* (Baltimore: Johns Hopkins University Press, 1998).

Shoshana Felman, and Dori Laub. *Testimony: Crises of Witnessing in Literature, Psychoanalysis, and History* (London: Routledge, 1992).

James Fentress, and Chris Wickham. *Social Memory* (Oxford: Blackwell, 1992).

Hilene Flanzbaum (ed.), *The Americanization of the Holocaust* (Baltimore: Johns Hopkins University Press, 1999),

Eva Fogelman. "Stages in the Mourning Process," in R. Braham (ed.), *The Psychological Perspectives of the Holocaust and its Aftermath* (Boulder, CO: Social Science Monographs, 1988).

Hal Foster. "Obscene, Abject, Traumatic," *October,* 78 (Autumn 1996), 106–24.

Anne-Marie Fortier. *Migrant Belongings: Memory, Space and Identity* (Oxford: Berg, 2000).

Michel Foucault. "Film and Popular Memory," in Sylvère Lotringer (ed.), *Foucault Live: Interviews, 1961–1984* (New York: Semoitext(e), 1996), 122–32.

Thomas C. Fox. *Stated Memory: East Germany and the Holocaust* (Rochester, NY: Camden House, 1999).

Ronald Fraser. *In Search of a Past* (London: Verso, 1984).

Mark Freeman. *Rewriting the Self: History, Memory, Narrative* (London: Routledge, 1993).

Saul Friedlander (ed.). *Probing the Limits of Representation: Nazism and the Final Solution* (Cambridge, MA: Harvard University Press, 1992).

Jörg Friedrich. *Der Brand: Deutschland im Bombenkrieg, 1940–1945* (München: Propyläen, 2002).

Margrit Frölich, Hanno Loewy, and Heinz Steinert (eds.). *Lachen über Hitler — Auschwitz-gelächter?* (Munich: text + kritik, 2003).

Sigmund Freud. *The Psychopathology of Everyday Life*, 2nd edition (1913, first published in 1904).

Sigmund Freud. *Introductory Lectures on Psychoanalysis* (1916/17), Lecture IV (Parapraxis Concluded).

Christian Fuchs, and John Goetz. *Die Zelle. Rechter Terror in Deutschland* (Reinbeck: Rowohlt, 2012).

Christopher Fynsk. *The Claim of Language: A Case for the Humanities* (Minneapolis, University of Minnesota Press, 2004).

Matteo Galli, and Heinz-Peter Preusser (eds.). *Mythos Terrorismus: Vom Deutschen Herbst zum 11. September* (Heidelberg: Universitätsverlag Winter 2005).

Ralf Giordano. *Die zweite Schuld oder Von der Last Deutscher zu sein* (Hamburg: Junius Verlag, 1987).

Günter Grass. *Im Krebsgang* (Göttingen: Steidl, 2002).

Sabine Hake. *Screen Nazis: Cinema, History, and Democracy* (Madison: University of Wisconsin Press, 2012).

Maurice Halbwachs. *On Collective Memory* (Chicago: University of Chicago Press, 1992).

Geoffrey Hartmann. *The Longest Shadow* (Basingstoke: Palgrave Macmillan, 2002).

Elizabeth Heineman. "The Hour of the Woman: Memories of Germany's "Crisis Years" and West German National Identity" in H. Schissler (ed.), *The Miracle Years: A Cultural History of West Germany, 1949–1968* (Princeton, NJ: Princeton University Press, 2001), 21–56.

Jeffrey Herf. *Divided Memory: The Nazi Past in the Two Germanys* (Cambridge, MA: Harvard University Press, 1997).

Herbert Hirsch. *Genocide and the Politics of Memory: Studying Death to Preserve Life* (Chapel Hill: University of North Carolina Press, 1995).

Marianne Hirsch. *Family Frames: Photography, Narrative and Postmemory* (Cambridge: Cambridge University Press, 1997).

Eric Hobsbawm, and Terence Ranger (eds.). *The Invention of Tradition* (Cambridge: Cambridge University Press, 1992).

Katherine Hodgkin, and Susannah Radstone (eds.). *Regimes of Memory* (London: Routledge, 2003).

Bruce Hoffmann. *Terrorismus — der unerklärte Krieg. Neue Gefahren politischer Gewalt* (Frankfurt/Main: Fischer, 2006).

Martin Hoffmann (ed.). *Rote Armee Fraktion, Texte und Materialien zur Geschichte der RAF* (Berlin: ID Verlag, 1997).

Jeffrey Hou. (ed.). *Insurgent Public Space: Guerrilla Urbanism and the Remaking of Contemporary Cities* (New York: Routledge, 2010).

Andreas Huyssen. *Twilight Memories: Marking Time in a Culture of Amnesia* (New York: Routledge, 1995).

Andreas Huyssen. *Present Pasts: Urban Palimpsests and the Politics of Memory* (Stanford, CA: Stanford University Press, 2003).

Michael Ignatieff. "The Terrorist as Auteur," *New York Times*, November, 4, 2004.

Annette Insdorf. *Indelible Shadows. Film and the Holocaust* (New York: Cambridge University Press 1983).

Iwona Irwin-Zarecka. *Frames of Remembrance: The Dynamics of Collective Memory* (New Brunswick, NJ: Transaction Publishers, 1994).

Steven Johnson. *Everything Bad is Good for You: How Today's Popular Culture Is Actually Making Us Smarter* (New York: Riverhead, 2006).

Richard Joos, Isolde Mozer, and Richard Stang (eds.). *Deutsche Geschichte ab 1945: Zwischen Vergangenheitsbewältigung und utopischen Entwürfen, Filmanalytische Materialien* (Frankfurt/M: Gemeinschaftswerk Evangelische Publizistik, 1990).

Wulf Kansteiner. "Finding Meaning in Memory: A Methodological Critique of Collective Memory Studies," *History and Theory,* 41, no. 2 (2002), 179–97.

Wulf Kansteiner. "Genealogy of a category mistake: a critical intellectual history of the cultural trauma metaphor," *Rethinking History,* 8, no. 2 (2004), 193–221.

Wulf Kansteiner. *In Pursuit of German Memory: History, Television and Politics after Auschwitz* (Athens: University of Ohio Press, 2006).

Wulf Kansteiner. "Sold Globally — Remembered Locally: Holocaust Cinema and the Construction of Collective Identities" in Stefan Berger, Linas Eriksonas, and Andrew Mycock (eds.), *Narrating the Nation* (Oxford: Berghahn Books, 2008), 153–80.

Ann E. Kaplan. *Trauma Culture* (Piscataway, NJ: Rutgers University Press, 2005).

Ann E. Kaplan, and Ban Wang (eds.). *Trauma and Cinema: Cross-Cultural Explorations* (Hong Kong: Hong Kong University Press, 2004).

Peter Katzenstein. *Tamed Power: Germany in Europe* (Ithaca, NY: Cornell University Press, 1997).

Judith Keilbach. *Geschichtsbilder und Zeitzeugen: zur Darstellung des Nationalsozialismus im Bundesdeutschen Fernsehen* (Münster: LIT Verlag, 2010).

Jane Kilby. "The writing of trauma: trauma theory and the liberty of reading," *New Formations: A Journal of Culture/Theory/Politics,* 47 (2002), 217–30.

Jan-Holger Kirsch. *Wir haben aus der Geschichte gelernt: Der 8. Mai als politischer Gedenktag in Deutschland* (Köln: Böhlau, 1999).

Kerwin Lee Klein. "On the Emergence of *Memory* in Historical Discourse," *Representations,* 69 (2000), 127–50.

Naomi Klein. *The Shock Doctrine: The Rise of Disaster Capitalism* (London: Picador, 2008).

Alexander Kluge (with Oskar Negt). *Geschichte und Eigensinn,* volumes 1–3 (Frankfurt am Main: Suhrkamp, 1981).

Alexander Kluge. *Die Macht der Gefühle* (Frankfurt/M: Zweitausendeins, 1984).

Ewout van der Knaap. "The New Executioners' Arrival: German Left-Wing Terrorism and the Memory of the Holocaust," in Gerrit-Jan Berendse, and Ingo Cornils (eds.), *Baader-Meinhof Returns: History and Cultural Memory of German Left-Wing Terrorism* (Amsterdam: Rodopi, 2008), 285–99.

Friedrich Knilli, and Siegfried Zielinski (eds.). *Holocaust zur Unterhaltung. Anatomie eines internationalen Bestsellers* (Berlin: Elefanten Press, 1982).

Gertrud Koch. *Die Einstellung ist die Einstellung: Visuelle Konstruktionen des Holocaust* (Frankfurt am Main: Suhrkamp, 1992).

Wolfgang Kraushaar. *Die Bombe im jüdischen Gemeindehaus* (Hamburg: Hamburger Edition, 2005).

Wolfgang Kraushaar (ed.). *Die RAF und der linke Terrorismus*, 2 vols. (Hamburg: Hamburg Institute for Social Research, 2006).

Wolfgang Kraushaar. "Zwischen Popkultur, Politik und Zeitgeschichte." http://www.zeithistorische-forschungen.de/site/40208214/default.aspx

Neil J. Kritz (ed.). *Transitional Justice: How Emerging Democracies Reckon with Former Regimes* (3 vols.), Vol. I: General Considerations (Washington, DC: United States Institute of Peace Press, 1995).

Annette Kuhn. *Family Secrets: Acts of Memory and Imagination* (London: Verso, 1995).

Annette Kuhn. *An Everyday Magic: Cinema and Cultural Memory* (London: I.B. Tauris, 2002).

Dominick La Capra. "Revisiting the Historians' Debate: Mourning and Genocide," *History and Memory*, 9, no. 1–2 (Fall 1997), 80–112.

Dominick LaCapra. *History and Memory after Auschwitz* (Ithaca, NY: Cornell University Press, 1998).

Dominick LaCapra. *Writing History, Writing Trauma* (Baltimore: Johns Hopkins University Press, 2001).

Alison Landsberg. *Prosthetic Memory: The Transformation of American Remembrance in the Age of Mass Culture* (New York: Columbia University Press, 2004).

Eric Langenbacher. "Memory Regimes in Contemporary Germany." Paper presented at the European Consortium for Political Research (ECPR), Edinburgh, Scotland, September 18, 2003.

Eric Langenbacher, Eric Shain, and Yossi Shain (eds.). *Power and the Past: Collective Memory and International Relations* (Washington, DC: Georgetown University Press, 2010).

Walter Laqueur. *No End to War: Terrorism in the Twenty-First Century* (New York: Continuum, 2003).

Christopher Lasch. *The Culture of Narcissism* (New York: Norton, 1979).

Daniel Levy, and Natan Sznaider. *The Holocaust and Memory in the Global Age* (Philadelphia: Temple University Press, 2005).

Daniel Levy, and Natan Sznaider, "Memory Unbound — The Holocaust and the Formation of Cosmopolitan Memory," http://www.sunysb.edu/sociology/faculty/Levy/EJSTFIN.pdf

Ruth Leys. *Trauma: A Genealogy* (Chicago: University of Chicago Press, 2000).

Sylvie Lindenperg. *Nuit et Brouillard: Un Film dans l'Histoire* (Paris: Odile Jacob, 2007).

David Lowenthal. *The Past is a Foreign Country* (Cambridge: Cambridge University Press, 1985).

Roger Luckhurst. "Traumaculture," *New Formations*, 50 (2003), 28–47.

Felix Philipp Lutz. *Das Geschichtsbewußtsein der Deutschen: Grundlagen der Politischen Kultur in Ost und West* (Köln: Böhlau, 2000).

Andreas Maislinger. "Vergangenheitsbewältigung in der BRD, der DDR und Österreich," in U. Backes (ed.), *Die Schatten der Vergangenheit: Impulse zur Historisierung des Nationalsozialismus* (Frankfurt: Ullstein, 1990).

Peter Märthesheimer, and Ivo Frenzel (eds.), *Im Kreuzfeuer: Der Fernsehfilm Holocaust. Eine Nation ist betroffen* (Frankfurt/M: Fischer, 1979).

Avashai Margalit. *The Ethics of Memory* (Cambridge, MA: Harvard University Press, 2002).

Andrei S. Markovits, and Beth Simone Noveck. "West Germany," in D. S. Wyman (ed.), *The World Reacts to the Holocaust* (Baltimore: Johns Hopkins University Press, 1986).

Andrei S. Markovits, and Simon Reich. *The German Predicament: Memory and Power in the New Europe* (Ithaca, NY: Cornell University Press, 1997).

Matt K. Matsuda. *The Memory of the Modern* (New York: Oxford University Press, 1996).

Allen Meek. *Trauma and Media* (New York: Routledge, 2009).

Peter Merkl (ed.). *The Federal Republic of Germany at Fifty* (New York: New York University Press, 1999).

Joseph Metz. "'Truth Is a Woman': Post-Holocaust Narrative, Postmodernism and the Gender of Fascism in Bernhard Schlink's 'Der Vorleser'," *The German Quarterly*, 77, no. 3 (2004), 300–23.

Peter Middleton, and Tim Woods. *Literatures of Memory: History, Time and Space in Postwar Writing* (Manchester: Manchester University Press, 2000).

Alexander Mitscherlich, and Margarete Mitscherlich. *The Inability to Mourn: Principles of Collective Behaviour*, (trans.) Beverley R. Placzec (New York: Grove Press, 1975).

Robert Moeller. *War Stories: The Search for a Usable Past in the Federal Republic of Germany* (Berkeley: University of California Press, 2001).

Robert Moeller. "The Politics of the Past in the 1950s: Rhetorics of Victimisation in East and West Germany," in Bill Niven (ed.), *Germans as Victims* (Houndmills: Palgrave Macmillan, 2006), 26–42.

Tillmann Moser. "Die Unfähigkeit zu trauern: Hält die Diagnose einer Überprüfung stand? Zur psychischen Verarbeitung des Holocausts in der Bundesrepublik," *Psyche*, 46, no. 5 (1992), 389–405.

John Mowitt. "Trauma Envy," *Cultural Critique*, no. 46 (Autumn 2000), 272–97.

John Mowitt. "Stumbling on Analysis: Psychoanalysis and Everyday Life," *Cultural Critique*, no. 52 (Autumn 2002), 61–85.

Joyce Marie Mushaben. *From Post-War to Post-Wall Generations: Changing Attitudes toward the National Question and NATO in the Federal Republic of Germany* (Boulder, CO: Westview Press, 1998).

Klaus Naumann. *Der Krieg als Text: Das Jahr 1945 im kulturellen Gedächtnis der Presse* (Hamburg: Hamburger Edition, 1998).

Heinz Nawratil. *Schwarzbuch der Vertreibung 1945 bis 1948: Das letzte Kapitel unbewältigter Vergangenheit* (München: Universitas, 1999).

Klaus Neumann. *Shifting Memories: The Nazi Past in the New Germany* (Ann Arbor: University of Michigan Press, 2000).

Bill Niven (ed.). *Germans as Victims: Remembering the Past in Contemporary Germany* (Houndsmills: Palgrave, 2006).

Pierre Nora. "Between Memory and History: Les Lieux de Memoire," *Representations*, 26 (1989), 7–25.

Pierre Nora. *Realms of Memory: Rethinking the French Past*, (ed. and foreword) Lawrence D. Kritzman, (trans.) Arthur Goldhammer (3 vols.) (New York: Columbia University Press, 1996–98).

Pierre Nora. "Reasons for the Current Upsurge in Memory," *Eurozine*, April 19, 2002. Available at http://www.eurozine.com/articles/2002-04-19-nora-en.html

Peter Novick. *Holocaust in American Life* (New York: Houghton Mifflin, 1999).

Jeffrey K. Olick, and Daniel Levy, "Collective Memory and Cultural Constraint: Holocaust Myth and Rationality in German Politics," *American Sociological Review*, 62 (1997), 921–26.

Leith Passmore. "The Art of Hunger: Self-Starvation in the Red Army Faction," *German History Review*, 27 (January 2009), 32–59.

Luisa Passerini. "Memory," *History Workshop Journal*, 15 (Spring 1983), 195–96.

Helmut Peitsch. *Deutschlands Gedächtnis an seine dunkelste Zeit* (Berlin: Sigma, 1990).

Anke Pinker. *Film and Memory in East Germany* (Bloomington: Indiana University Press, 2008).

Neil Postman. *Amusing ourselves to Death: Public Discourse in the Age of Show Business* (New York: Viking, 1985).

Kristin Platt, Kristin Daba, and Mihran Dabag (eds.). *Generation und Gedächtnis: Erinnerungen und kollektive Identitäten* (Opladen: Leske und Budrich, 1995).

Brad Prager. "The Good German as Narrator: On W. G. Sebald and the Risks of Holocaust Writing," *New German Critique*, 96 (Fall 2005), 75–102.

Bernhard Rabert. *Links- und Rechtsterrorismus in der Bundesrepublik Deutschland von 1970 bis heute* (Bonn: Bernard & Graefe, 1995).

Susannah Radstone (ed.). *Memory and Methodology* (Oxford: Berg, 2000).

Susannah Radstone. "Trauma and Screen Studies: opening the debate," *Screen*, 42, no. 2 (Summer 2001), 188–93.

Susannah Radstone. "Trauma theory: Contexts, Politics, Ethics," *Paragraph*, 30, no. 1 (2007), 9–29.

Susannah Radstone. "Memory Studies: For *and* Against," *Journal of Memory Studies*, 1/1 (January 2008), 31–9.

Susannah Radstone, and Bill Schwarz (eds.). *Mapping Memory* (New York: Fordham University Press, 2011).

Peter Reichel. *Erfundene Erinnerung: Weltkrieg und Judenmord in Film und Theater* (München: Carl Hanser Verlag, 2004).

Paul Ricoeur. *La mémoire, l'histoire, l'oubli* (Paris: Seuil, 2000). In German: *Gedächtnis, Geschichte, Vergessen* (Munich: Wilhelm Fink Verlag, 2004).

Thomas R. Rochon. *Culture Moves: Ideas, Activism and Changing Values* (Princeton, NY: Princeton University Press, 1998).

Michael Rossington, and Anne Whitehead (eds.). *Between the Psyche and the Polis: Refiguring History in Literature and Theory* (Aldershot, UK: Ashgate, 2001).

Michael Rossington, and Anne Whitehead (eds.). *Theories of Memory: A Reader* (Edinburgh: Edinburgh University Press, 2007).

Eric Santner. *Stranded Objects* (Chicago: Chicago University Press, 1993).

Stephan K. Schindler. "Displaced Images: The Holocaust in German Film," in Stephan K. Schindler, and Lutz Koepnick (eds.). *The Cosmopolitan Screen: German Cinema and the Global Imaginary, 1945 to the Present* (Ann Arbor: University of Michigan Press, 2007), 192–205.

Helmut Schmitz (ed.). *A Nation of Victims? Representations of German Wartime Suffering from 1945 to the Present* (Amsterdam: Rodopi, 2007).

Karl Schorske. *Thinking with History* (Princeton, NY: Princeton University Press, 1998).

Howard Schuman, and Jacqueline Scott. "Generations and Collective Memories," *American Sociological Review,* 54 (1989), 359–81.

Barry Schwartz. "The Social Context of Commemoration: A Study in Collective Memory," *Social Forces,* 61, no. 2 (1982), 374–402.

James C. Scott. *Domination and the Arts of Resistance: Hidden Transcripts* (New Haven: Yale University Press, 1990).

W.G. Sebald. *On the Natural History of Destruction* (Toronto: Knopf, 2003).

Christian Semler. "Is the Tide of German Memory Turning?" *Eurozine,* June 23, 2005. Available at: http://www.eurozine.com/articles/2005-06-23-semler-en.html

Mark Seltzer. "Wound Culture: Trauma in the Pathological Public Sphere," *October,* 80 (1997), 3–26.

Mark Seltzer. *Serial Killers: Death and Life in America's Wound Culture* (London: Routledge, 1998).

Robert R. Shandley. *Rubble Films: German Cinema in the Shadow of the Third Reich* (Philadelphia: Temple University Press, 2001).

Efraim Sicher. "The Future of the Past: Countermemory and Postmemory in Contemporary American Post-Holocaust Narratives," *History and Memory,* 12, no. 2 (2000), 56–91.

Vivian Sobchack (ed.). *The Persistence of History: Cinema, Television, and the Modern Event* (New York: Routledge, 1995).

Susan Sontag. *Regarding the Pain of Others* (New York: Farrar, Straus and Giroux, 2002).

Marita Sturken. *Tangled Memories* (Berkeley: University of California Press, 1997).

Susan Rubin Suleiman. *Crises of Memory and the Second World War* (Cambridge, MA: Harvard University Press, 2006).

Stuart Taberner, and Karina Berger (eds.). *Germans as victims in the literary fiction of the Berlin Republic* (Woodbridge: Camden House, 2009).

Petra Terhoeven, "Opferbilder — Täterbilder. Die Fotografie als Medium linksterroristischer Selbstermächtigung in Deutschland und Italien während der 70er Jahre," in *Geschichte in Wissenschaft und Unterricht,* 58 (2007), 380–99.

Klaus Theweleit. "Playstation Cordoba," *Cultural Critique,* nos. 54 & 55 (2003), 1–24 and 1–28.

Klaus Theweleit. "On the German Reaction to Jonathan Littell *Les bienveillantes," New German Critique,* 106, 36, no. 1 (Winter 2009), 21–34.

Martina Thiele. *Publizistische Kontroversen über den Holocaust im Film* (Münster: LIT Verlag, 2001).

Karen E. Till. *The New Berlin. Memory, Politics, Place* (Minneapolis: University of Minnesota Press, 2005).

Sebastiano Timpanaro. *The Freudian Slip* (London: New Left Books, 1976).

Matt Tierney. "'Oh No, Not Again': Representability and a Repetitive Remark," *Image & Narrative,* 11, no 2 (2010), 150-64.

Jamie Trnka. "'The Struggle Is Over, the Wounds Are Open': Cinematic Tropes, History, and the RAF in Recent German Film," *New German Critique,* 101, 34, no. 2 (Summer 2007), 1–26.

Charles Turner. "Holocaust Memories and History," *History of the Human Sciences,* 9, no. 4 (1996), 45–63.

Peter Waldmann. *Terrorismus. Provokation der Macht* (Hamburg: Murmann, 2005).

Sigrid Weigel. "Generation as a Symbolic Form: On the Genealogical Discourse of Memory since 1945," *The Germanic Review,* 77 (2002), 264–77.

Gabriel Weimann, and Conrad Winn (eds.). *The Theater of Terror. Mass Media and International Terrorism* (New York: Longman, 1994).

Klaus Weinhauer, Jörg Requate, and Heinz-Gerhard Haupt (eds.). *Terrorismus in der Bundesrepublik: Medien, Staat und Subkulturen in den 1970er Jahren* (Frankfurt/Main: Campus, 2006).

Harald Welzer. "Schön unscharf: Über die Konjunktur der Familien- und Generationsromane," *Literatur* Nr 1 (Beilange zum *Mittelweg 36,* Hamburg) (January/February 2004), 53–64.

Harald Welzer, Sabine Moller, and Karoline Tschuggnall. *"Opa war kein Nazi". Nationalsozialismus und Holocaust im Familiengedächtnis* (Frankfurt/Main: Fischer, 2002).

Caroline Wiedmer. *The Claims of Memory: Representations of the Holocaust in Contemporary Germany and France* (Ithaca, NY: Cornell University Press, 1999).

Michael Wieviorka. *The Making of Terrorism* (Chicago: University of Chicago Press, 2004).

Joan B. Wolf. *Harnessing the Holocaust: The Politics of Memory in France* (Stanford, CA: Stanford University Press, 2004).

Edgar Wolfrum. *Geschichtspolitik in der Bundesrepublik Deutschland: Der Weg zur bundesrepublikanischen Erinnerung, 1948–1990* (Darmstadt: Wissenschaftliche Buchgesellschaft, 1999).

Nancy Wood. *Vectors of Memory* (Oxford: Berg, 1999).

James E. Young. *The Texture of Memory: Holocaust Memorials and Meaning* (New Haven: Yale University Press, 1993).

James E. Young. *At Memory's Edge: After-Images of the Holocaust in Contemporary Art and Architecture* (New Haven: Yale University Press, 2000).

John Zaller. *The Nature and Origins of Mass Opinion* (New York: Cambridge University Press, 1992).

Slavoj Žižek. "Tolerance as an Ideological Category," *Critical Inquiry,* 34, no. 4 (Summer 2008), 660–82.

ACKNOWLEDGMENTS

The germ of this book was a slim volume published in Germany in 2007 to mark the thirtieth anniversary of the period of political violence and civil unrest in 1977 that culminated in the events known variously as the Hot Autumn (*Heisse Herbst*) or German Autumn (*Deutsche Herbst*).[1] I was intrigued by the media afterlife of this relatively brief episode, wondering what compensatory logic might bind especially the cinematic reenactments of political terrorism to the apparently quite different media afterlife of the Nazi crimes and the Holocaust. It seemed the insistent presence of the Red Army Faction indirectly communicated with the insistent absence of the Holocaust from German screens, the former acting as the parapractic supplement of the latter. In the years since 2007, the historical and affective contours of this double "violence of the past" (the subtitle of the German publication) in and for the present have become clearer to me, which is why *German Cinema — Terror and Trauma* has retained only three of the original chapters[2] and now contains fresh theoretical and historical material, written with a wider Anglo-American readership in mind. To account for the turns in the memory discourses, but also to document their diversity and specificity, a number of case studies have been added, some of which have been presented at conferences, notably in Tel Aviv, where the idea of *parapraxis* found its most attentive audience.

As is often the case with books that take their time, chapters found their way into conference volumes, collections and catalogues. "Rescued in Vain" was included as digital sleeve notes in the DVD edition of Konrad Wolf's STARS (DEFA Film Library, University of Massachusetts, 2011).[3] Parts of the chapter "The Persistent Resistance of Alexander Kluge" were published in *Alexander Kluge: Raw Materials for the Imagination*, edited by Tara Forrest (Amsterdam: Amsterdam University Press, 20012), 22–29. A shorter version of "Retroactive

Causality and the Present: Fassbinder's THE THIRD GENERATION" is featured in the catalogue for the exhibition "Fassbinder-JETZT," organized by the Deutsche Filminstitut-Filmmuseum Frankfurt in January 2014, and "Rewind after Replay" was included in the Harun Farocki exhibition catalogue, edited by Antje Ehman and Kodwo Eshun, *Against Whom Against What* (London: Craven Walk, 2010), 57–68. I thank these editors and publishers for their permission to use the essays in the present volume.

Thanks are especially due to many of my friends, colleagues and companions, not forgetting translators, editors and conference organizers and to Nurith Gertz, for recognizing the heuristic value of *parapraxis*; Warren Buckland for patiently reading chapters on films he had not seen, and nonetheless commenting perceptively; Barton Byg and Sky Arndt Briggs for including me in their editorial work on STERNE; Matteo Galli and his team for hosting me so generously in Ferrara; Catherine Smale, for undertaking a tricky translation; Drehli Robnik, for frequently quoting from the German volume; Ria Thanouli, for graciously suspending her scepticism regarding the memory discourse; Randall Halle for his reader's report, as well as Geoffrey Nowell-Smith and Jack Zipes for their willingness to read chapters at short notice. Special thanks must go to Erica Wetter at Routledge, whose energy, support, and good cheer immensely helped the book in its final stages.

Notes

1. Thomas Elsaesser, *Terror und Trauma: Zur Gewalt des Vergangenen in der BRD* (Berlin: Kadmos, 2007).
2. "Terror and Trauma: Siamese Twins of the Political Discourse"; "Mourning as Mimicry and Masquerade: Herbert Achternbusch's THE LAST HOLE," and portions of the chapter on "The Politics and Poetics of Parapraxis."
3. The essay was also published in German as "Vergebliche Rettung: Geschichte als Palimpsest," in Michael Wedel/Elke Schieber (eds.), *Konrad Wolf — Werk und Wirkung* (Berlin: Vistas Verlag, 2009), 73–92, and in French as "Histoire palimpseste, mémoires obliques. À propos de *Sterne* de Konrad Wolf" in 1895 — *Revue d'Histoire du cinema*, no. 58 (2009), 10–29. My thanks to Michael Wedel and François Albera.

INDEX